Feminism and Motherhood in Germany, 1800–1914

Feminism and Motherhood in Germany, 1800–1914

Ann Taylor Allen

Rutgers University Press

New Brunswick, New Jersey

Library of Congress Cataloging-in-Publication Data

Allen, Ann Taylor, 1944–
    Feminism and motherhood in Germany, 1800–1914 / Ann Taylor Allen.
    p. cm.
    Includes bibliographical references and index.
    ISBN 0-8135-1686-2
    1. Motherhood—Germany—History—19th century. 2. Motherhood—Germany—History—20th century. 3. Feminism—Germany—History—19th century. 4. Feminism—Germany—History—20th century. 5. Maternal and infant welfare—Germany—History—19th century. 6. Maternal and infant welfare—Germany—History—20th century. 7. Child welfare—Germany—History—19th century. 8. Child welfare—Germany—History—20th century. I. Title.
HQ759.A42   1991   90-21164
305.42′0943—dc20   CIP

British Cataloging-in-Publication information available.

Copyright © 1991 by Ann Taylor Allen
All Rights Reserved
Manufactured in the United States of America

For my mother

Contents

Acknowledgments ix

Introduction 1

1 Spiritual Motherhood

1 From Authority to Nurture: Theoretical Origins
of Maternal Feminism, 1780–1840   17

2 The Personal and the Political: Social Origins
of Maternal Feminism, 1800–1848   41

3 Spiritual Motherhood and Revolution: The Beginnings
of Organized Feminism, 1848–1852   58

4 The Great Social Household: The Kindergarten
and Women's Mission, 1850–1864   79

5 Mothers of the Nation: Spiritual Motherhood
and Organized Feminism, 1865–1877   95

6 Mothers of the City: The Pestalozzi-Froebel House
and the Creation of an Urban Role for Women, 1873–1900   111

2 Motherhood, Social Reform, and the State

7 Mothers, Children, and the Law, 1888–1902   135

8 Motherhood, Culture, and Evolution: Some New
Perspectives, 1890–1914   149

9 Motherhood as Right and Duty: The Campaign against Infant
Mortality, 1904–1914   173

10 Motherhood as Choice: The Campaign for Reproductive
Rights, 1908–1914   188

11 Motherhood and Social Reform: The Careers of Alice
   Salomon, Anna von Gierke, and Frieda Duensing, 1890–1914   206

Conclusion   229

Notes   245

Archival Sources   287

Index   289

Acknowledgments

During ten years of research and writing, I have received help from many individuals and institutions. The staffs of the Bundesarchiv in Koblenz, the Zentrales Staatsarchiv der deutschen Demokratischen Republik in Merseburg and in Potsdam, the Niedersächsisches Staatsarchiv in Wolfenbüttel, the Staatsarchiv Hamburg, the Pestalozzi-Froebel Haus, the Deutsches Zentralinstitut für soziale Fragen, the Helene-Lange-Stiftung, and the Staatsbürgerinnen-Verband in West Berlin, the Stadtarchiv Frankfurt am Main, and the Internationaal Instituut vor Socialgeschiedenis in Amsterdam have helped me to gain access to archival materials and provided many helpful suggestions for further research. I have also received valuable assistance from the staffs of the Staatsbibliothek Preussischer Kulturbesitz in West Berlin, the Widener and Schlesinger Libraries of Harvard University, the Indiana University Library, the M. I. King Library at the University of Kentucky, the Library of Congress, the Welch Medical Library at Johns Hopkins University, the National Library of Medicine, and, last but certainly not least, the Interlibrary Loan Department at the Ekstrom Library of the University of Louisville, which has shown great patience and ingenuity in tracking down source material.

Funding for this project has been provided by several research grants from the College of Arts and Sciences and the Graduate School at the University of Louisville and by the German Academic Exchange Service. This funding has enabled me to make many research trips, to Europe and to libraries in the United States. My parents, Ann Updegraff Allen and Franklin Gordon Allen, have also provided much generous support, both financial and emotional, for all of my endeavors.

The encouragement and assistance that I have received from colleagues has been so important that no mere list can adequately express my appreciation. For comments on work presented at conventions, I thank Roderick Stackelberg, John N. Fout, Catherine N. Prelinger, Amy Hackett, and Molly Ladd-Taylor. Karen Offen has provided insightful comments on the articles in which preliminary results of this work were published and on the present manuscript. She has been a patient, perceptive, and encouraging reader. Jürgen Zinnecker and Imbke Behnken of the Universität-Gesamthochschule Siegen have provided hospitality, access to their extensive library, and suggestions for research. Ilse

Brehmer and Juliane Jacobi of the Zentrum für Interdiziplinäre Frauenforschung at the Universität Bielefeld have also extended a collegial welcome and helpful suggestions. Annette Kuhn and Karin Hausen have provided useful information on source material and current research. My research trips to Germany have also been made much more pleasant by the hospitality and friendship of Heidrun and Bruno Buss of Bonn and Mira Böhm of Berlin. Marlie Wassermann, associate director and editor-in-chief of Rutgers University Press, has offered valuable advice. Brian Butler has helped diligently with the preparation of the manuscript.

Several colleagues at the University of Louisville, including John Cumbler, Susan Broadhead, and Lee Shai Weissbach of the department of history, have offered comments at various stages of the research and writing. Julia Dietrich, M. Nawal Lutfiyya, and Nancy M. Theriot, all members of the Feminist Theory Discussion Group at the University of Louisville, have helped me to identify and clarify the central theoretical issues of this book. I thank them for many challenging, convivial, and exhilarating evenings of discussion.

Throughout the process of research and writing, I have been fortunate to receive the professional and personal support of two colleagues. Nancy M. Theriot, my colleague in the department of history at the University of Louisville, has patiently read several versions of the manuscript. Her understanding of theoretical issues in women's history has had a formative influence on my own work. Her friendship has helped me through many moments of discouragement and perplexity. James C. Albisetti of the University of Kentucky has worked with me on all stages of this project, from the preliminary outline to the final proofreading. He has generously shared with me the results of his own research, and provided invaluable bibliographical assistance. My work has been immeasurably enriched by his deep knowledge of German and women's history, his incisive, demanding, but sympathetic criticism, and his wide knowledge of source material.

Feminism and Motherhood
in Germany, 1800–1914

Introduction

In 1921, Helene Lange looked back on her response to J. S. Mill's *The Subjection of Women*, which she had read in 1870. "Equality," she stated, "should not be demanded because of the similarity but because of the difference of the genders, so that a one-sidedly masculine culture can be completed by a feminine culture. . . . Under male dominance, the world has been a motherless family." The world as mother-centered household, centered on an egalitarian male-female couple and pervaded by maternal values of nurture, compassion, and individualized concern became the dominant metaphor expressing the goals of German feminists in the nineteenth century. Not confined to the moderate feminism of which Lange was for a time the leading representative, this maternal metaphor also shaped the rhetoric of radical and of some socialist feminists.[1]

The importance of maternal ideology has, of course, been noted by all historians of German feminism. But most of these historians have seen this ideology chiefly as it served the political or organizational strategies of feminist movements at specific points in their development. Few such accounts take maternalism seriously as an evolving intellectual tradition that shaped as well as reflected practice. This study will analyze ideas of public and private motherhood as part of an evolving intellectual tradition within German feminist movements from the early nineteenth century until the First World War. The primary focus of the analysis will be on issues concerning children, such as familial nurture, pedagogy, and the broader question of social and collective responsibility for the welfare of the younger generation. The main characters will be the women who, in both their theoretical and practical work, explored the relationship between the status of women and that of children, or more generally of the next generation. This group includes some comparatively well-known figures, such as Helene Stöcker and Lily Braun, and some who have received much less attention from historians, such as Bertha von Marenholtz-Bülow, Adele Schreiber, Henriette Fürth, Anna von Gierke, and Frieda Duensing. Though concentrating on these historical actors, the analysis will not be limited to them, but will explore the interaction of their ideas and practical activities with the developing agenda of feminist movements as a whole.[2]

Motherhood—private, public, biological, and social—was the center of a feminist discourse that, although constantly developing, was also continuous from the first feminist writings in the late eighteenth and early nineteenth centuries until the twentieth century. It developed in the context of a larger, public discourse, also constantly evolving, on child-rearing, family, and the state. The historical narrative will begin with the rise of two ideas that proved central to feminist ideas of public and private motherhood: the secularization of concepts of child-rearing and maternal duty and the incorporation of these functions into public policy. This dominant discourse both imposed limitations on and opened possibilities to female speakers. Maternal roles in the family, though in one sense limiting women's possibilities, in another sense provided a model of empowerment and ethical autonomy.

Part One will show how women extrapolated from their experience of private motherhood a claim to public participation, through speech, organization, institution-building, and social reform. The idea of public motherhood will be traced as it contributed to the first forms of organized feminism in 1848, to the survival strategies developed by feminists during the postrevolutionary period, to concepts of female professionalism, and to the development of the first national feminist organizations after unification. The creation of an urban role for middle-class women and the responses of many feminists to the beginning of the welfare state in the 1880s will also be examined in relation to the evolving idea of public motherhood.

Part Two will describe a decisive shift of focus that began in the 1890s—a recasting of the discourse on motherhood in predominantly biological and medical rather than moral and spiritual terms. This shift, manifested in the culture as a whole as well as in feminist movements, led to changes, but not to total innovation, in feminists' ideas of motherhood. It was during this period that issues concerning private life—family structure, child health and welfare, and reproductive rights—briefly became central to feminist theory and practice. Such issues, although causing division and controversy within the feminist movement, were also integrally related to mainstream feminist concerns, such as the roles of women in social reform and the development of a new relationship between the private world of the family and the public world of the state.

Throughout this evolutionary process, the feminist discourse on motherhood continued to be centered on a few basic themes, already present in the earliest feminist texts, that recurred in changing but nonetheless recognizable forms. Chief among these was the idea of motherhood as a basis for a specifically female ethic—what a modern psychologist, Carol Gilligan, has called an "ethic of care"—which provided a standpoint for understanding, criticizing, and ultimately changing the world. This standpoint was often expressed symbolically through biological metaphors, by far the most important of which was the mother-child bond. However, this female standpoint was by no means identified with a biological function; on the contrary, it was asserted to be equally, if not more available to women who were not biological mothers. The individual mother-child bond became the basis of a concept of social morality that linked the self to the other and the individual to the community.[3]

Thus the maternal ethic, developed into a concept of public motherhood, called into question the antithesis between public and private worlds that was fundamental to nineteenth-century culture. This connection between home and world provided the basis of a claim to female power, which at first was conceived as primarly cultural and pedagogical and later as political. Feminists thus often questioned conventional (that is, male-identified) structures of political discourse that placed the family outside politics. They asserted the underlying connections between private and public concerns—the personal dimension of political life and the political nature of the family. A central metaphor, recurring throughout the writings of feminists throughout this period, was that of society as family, or "great social household."

I chose to concentrate on issues specifically related to children and child-rearing partly in order to focus my approach to the extraordinarily diffuse and widespread use of maternal arguments. Of course, maternal arguments were applied to innumerable other issues, from the admission of women to nursing and medicine to woman suffrage. All of these could not be described in the framework of one book. The study is thus focused on the intersection of women's and children's issues. Its main figures are women who were specifically identified with feminist ideas or movements (though, in a few cases, identifying themselves more as advocates of children than of women). Like most works of intellectual history, this one centers upon an elite rather than a cross-section of society. Its central figures, though coming from diverse social backgrounds and regions, were predominantly from the middle and upper classes, and were Protestant or Jewish—Catholics were underrepresented in this group, as in feminist movements as a whole. Likewise, especially during the early period, they were chiefly from northern Germany rather than from predominantly Catholic regions such as Bavaria or Austria.

However, in another way this, like any other study of women's ideas, must challenge the elitist assumptions behind many histories of ideas or of high culture. Unlike the members of the male pantheon on which traditional history of ideas is focused, these women often lacked formal education and access to academic positions or other forms of support for lives of contemplation and intellectual creativity. Their ideas were thus closely linked to practice, often to the female-identified practices of child-rearing, pedagogy, and domestic reform. The analysis of their ideas must also take into account their work as activists, educators, and builders of institutions.

These activities and ideas are placed in the broad and diverse context of feminist movements, where ideas of social motherhood interacted with many others, including most crucially the liberal ideas of individualism and equal rights. This interaction often caused conflicts, within movements and within individuals. However, without underestimating these elements of disunity and conflict, I contend that feminists of this era usually perceived no basic contradiction between arguments based on social motherhood and on equal-rights doctrine. Their conception of citizenship linked rights to duties, and defined individual self-fulfillment in the context of community.

The central theoretical question involved in this work is the understanding of women's ideas in relation to the two overlapping contexts of German political and cultural history and of feminism as an international movement. One approach to this very complex problem is through issues that have recently been raised in the fields of both German and women's history. Historians in both of these fields have weighed the advantages of two approaches to historical interpretation—contextualism versus presentism, or "present-mindedness." A related question is that of continuity in historical narrative—should the historian's dialogue with the past emphasize its relationship with the present, or its distance and "otherness"? Both of these questions have been raised in previous treatments of German feminism. Historians of Germany have sometimes tended to see the pervasively maternal (as opposed to equal rights) emphasis of German feminist movements as a symptom of a specifically German tendency to illiberalism, often identified as a long-term cause of the rise of National Socialism. Historians of women have often judged the figures to be discussed here according to a present-day feminist ideology based on equal-rights theory and the questioning of all gender differences. According to this standard, maternalism appears as at best a conservative and at worst an outright "reactionary" approach to feminism. Both of these groups of historians, though focusing on different issues, share a common tendency to present-mindedness. Both are far more concerned with contexts of which women active before 1914 could have known nothing, such as the rise of National Socialism or modern feminist movements, than with the historical situation of those protagonists themselves.[4]

The more contextual approach that I intend to adopt is not based on the naive belief in the possibility of a view of the past uncontaminated by the historian's own concerns. Indeed, my own involvement in the feminist controversies of the present day often informs my view of the past. Nor do I propose a historicist approach that will absolve historical actors of responsibility for their mistakes, limitations, and prejudices. Like many recent writers on intellectual history, however, I regard history as a dialogue between past and present, in which the historian is called upon to play the role of listener as well as judge. A central purpose of feminist scholarship is to recover a historical record that has often been submerged or trivialized, and to reconstruct it in all of its sometimes puzzling diversity. The present-minded approaches mentioned previously have not achieved this objective, but have tended to marginalize important aspects of women's work and experience.[5]

The tendency to judge the history of feminism according to criteria derived from the present is exemplified by the work of a pioneering historian of German feminism, Richard J. Evans. Evans's approach remains influential because he was one of the first historians to explore the connection between the history of German feminist movements and German national history as a whole. Evans, who bases his definition of feminism on the equal-rights traditions of the present-day, English-speaking world, defines maternal feminism as a contradiction in terms. "Equal rights and separate spheres are mutually contradictory doctrines," Evans states. "The only position upon which it is possible to base an argument for equal rights or for the elimination of gender-based injustice is the principle of the equal rights of women, as individuals." The prevalence of arguments based on gender difference within German bourgeois feminist movements appears to Evans as a symptom at once of feminist false consciousness and German political backwardness.

He dismisses all German feminist movements before 1880 as "timid and conservative," dates the rise of "true" feminism only to the rise of radical organizations in the 1880s, and proclaims its demise in 1908 with what he terms the catastropic decline of liberalism in feminist organizations.[6]

Another approach that similarly rests on a present-minded equation of "true" feminism with individualism is summed up in the title of a recent book, *Listen der Ohnmacht* ("Ruses of Powerless People"). In its introduction, German historians Claudia Honegger and Bettina Heinz assert that because middle-class women had no choice but to accept the domestic roles, including maternity, imposed on them by male-dominated culture, their use of these ideas can be understood as chiefly a strategy. "Middle-class women did not accept the male stereotype passively," write Honegger and Heinz, "but used it as an instrument of their resistance. . . . While domestic feminists tried to change familial working and living conditions, social feminists carried the maternal myth into the public realm and struggled in its name for an expansion of their rightful share of responsibility." This approach is similar to that of American historian Aileen Kraditor, who describes the emphasis of American suffragists on "organized motherhood" as arising from considerations of political expediency rather than from genuine convictions. The "true" intention hidden behind the nineteenth-century texts is assumed to be individualist.[7]

Other historians have questioned these judgments and have recognized the validity of diverse forms of feminist ideology and practice. Our study of nineteenth-century movements, writes Amy Hackett, must be based on a definition of feminism that is not limited to the individualist or "equal rights" positions. Barbara Greven-Aschoff explains that ideological positions based on gender difference legitimated women's protest against "asymmetrical relationships and social discrimination" and their aspirations to improved economic and social status. Catharine N. Prelinger, who has studied the relationship of women's religious ideas to their charitable activities in nineteenth-century Hamburg, stresses the importance of maternal and familial experience in shaping progressive movements. In a study of women's social work in Bremen, Elisabeth Meyer-Renschhausen has traced the roots of feminist approaches to social problems to a specifically female culture that cannot be described through conventional (that is, male-created) political theory. Bärbel Clemens, focusing on the history of suffrage movements during the Imperial period, sees ideologies based on both gender difference and similarity, or gender-neutral "equality," as valid, though problematic, bases for feminist movements.⁸

However, interpretations that link maternalist feminism to specifically German authoritarian and illiberal tendencies have not lost their appeal. Herrad-Ulrike Bussemer, who studies feminist movements in the 1860s, identifies equal-rights ideology as progressive and maternalism as reactionary. The editors of an anthology dealing with women's history in the Weimar period identify a tendency to argue for "women's rights on the basis of innate female characteristics, even if this argument is used to support pacifism and international understanding" as among the factors leading to the rise of National Socialism. And the widely read book of Claudia Koonz, *Mothers in the Fatherland*, similarly burdens German feminist movements, because of their preference for maternalist over equal-rights ideology, with some of the responsibility for the development of Nazi ideology and practice; the Nazi state, writes Koonz, was the "nineteenth-century feminists' view of the future in nightmare form."⁹

The interpretation of this problematic history clearly requires a more thorough investigation of the development and implications of the many ideas that informed feminist ideology and practice in the nineteenth and early twentieth centuries. Although the idea of motherhood is routinely identified as a central component of feminist ideology, German feminists' specific experience and views of motherhood, the mother-child relationship, and society's responsibility for child welfare have never been systematically examined. Perhaps because of the influence of the liberal, or equal-rights, model of feminism, many women who were regarded by their own contemporaries as important advocates of women's interests and values have been given little or predominantly negative treatment. Though the practical activities of women such as Henriette Goldschmidt and Henriette Schrader-Breymann are sometimes described, their ideas, which centered chiefly on child-rearing and pedagogy, are seldom taken seriously. Other women who were important in their own time, such as Frieda Duensing, Henriette Fürth, Adele Schreiber, and Anna von Gierke, are almost never mentioned. Accounts of better-known figures, such as Louise Otto-Peters, Helene Lange, and Helene Stöcker, give more attention to ideas and activities that conform to historians' own paradigms than to those that deviate from it; for example, Stöcker is often portrayed as a pioneer of sexual liberation and

Lily Braun as an advocate of woman suffrage, but their ideas on the rights and duties of mothers have received less attention. Therefore, not only have the contributions of these women themselves been undervalued, but the importance of the mother-child relationship, as experience and metaphor, to the development of ideology among both moderate and radical feminists has never been recognized.[10]

Even more important to our exploration of this topic are new theoretical perspectives on the conventional antithesis, often crudely expressed as "equality versus difference," between feminist ideologies based on equal-rights doctrine and those based on ideas and goals identified as specifically female, or woman-centered. Koonz, like Evans, Bussemer, and many others, has classified these two types of ideology as "antithetical concepts of emancipation." Clemens, though regarding them as equally valuable, nonetheless treats them as alternatives. Other historians, however, notably Joan Scott and Gisela Bock, have called for the deconstruction of this and other dichotomies, which in their opinion reflect categories created by male theorists more than the actual experience of women. Indeed, the liberal idea of "equality" was invented by elite men of a specific period, the seventeenth and eighteenth centuries, and culture, that of England and western Europe, to describe their own status as free and competitive individuals. Women were, of course, excluded in fact and theory from such a position—their status continued to be defined by their role as members of an interdependent group, the family. Feminists thus often asserted that liberal ideas of equality were not gender-neutral, but rather privileged male modes of existence and behavior. Familial values of cooperation, interdependence, and community continued to be important to women's everyday life and political thought. Likewise, a gender-neutral concept of individual rights, even if one could be developed, would be a problematic basis for feminist movements. The basis of these movements is a group known as "women," with distinct grievances, interests, and cultural characteristics. The dissolution of the category "woman" undermines the basis of feminist movements. Therefore, as Joan Scott has pointed out, women have often claimed the right to be both different and equal. They have often defined equality as the legitimation of gender difference, demanding the right to equal legal, social, and cultural recognition for cultural patterns identified as distinctively female. Indeed, the transformative and utopian energy of feminist movements has usually been derived from such concepts of female cultural difference.[11]

Introduction

Like the conventional "equality versus difference" antithesis, paradigms of feminist orthodoxy derived from present-day feminist movements provide an inadequate basis for the understanding and evaluation of past generations. We must not make the past "usable" by ignoring its difference or "otherness." Nor should we regard the history of feminism as an unbroken, evolutionary process culminating in the present. As Michel Foucault and others have pointed out, the history of ideas is not such a unitary process, but is characterized as much by breaks and ruptures as by continuity. Thus any definition of feminism must be historically situated, linked to period, national culture, class and material conditions.[12]

The attempt to formulate a contextual and historically situated definition of feminism has recently been made by a historian of French feminism, Karen Offen. A feminist, Offen proposes, is "a person who recognizes the validity of women's own interpretation of their lived experiences and needs, protests against the institutionalized injustice perpetrated by men as a group against women as a group, and advocates the elimination of that injustice by challenging various forms of coercive power that uphold male prerogatives in a given society." According to this definition of feminism, all of the figures to be described here were in some sense feminists, except for some very early ones such as Johann Heinrich Pestalozzi and Caroline Rudolphi, who nonetheless created empowering images of women that influenced the later development of feminism. To be sure, most of them did not use that term to describe themselves. The term "feminism," in fact, was not in general use in Germany until the 1890s. Until that time, German women had used the term "women's movement" as an inclusive term for a great variety of endeavors aimed at both gaining women's rights and advancing a broader agenda of cultural change through women's agency. Even after 1890, most women whom we would now describe as feminists preferred this term for their movement. Most of the women discussed here—including some, like Bertha von Marenholtz-Bülow, who did not identify themselves primarily as feminists—were included in accounts of the "women's movement" written during their own time or shortly after it. In such accounts, moreover, the endeavors in which these women were involved were classified as central, rather than marginal, to this movement. Some historians, notably Nancy Cott, have differentiated between the general "women's movement" of the nineteenth century and the specific "feminism" that developed in the twentieth century. My use of the term "feminist" is not intended to deny the differences, but to emphasize the continuity.[13]

Such a historically situated understanding of feminism must provide the basis for our understanding of the relationship of women's language, ideas, and forms of self-expression to their cultural context. Elisabeth Meyer-Renschhausen has proposed one possible view of this relationship. Women, she speculates, simply inhabited a separate culture from that of men, and their ideas thus expressed an entirely separate reality. However, as long as women shared a common language with men, they could not understand their experience as entirely separate and distinct. Recent theoretical discussions of intellectual history have emphasized that experience and the resulting subjective attitudes, beliefs, and worldviews are constituted by socially constructed discourses—defined as collections of statements on any given subject that possess their own rules, parameters, limits, and structure. The rules of discourse are set chiefly by authority-structures, which control access to knowledge in order to consolidate and organize their power. Women, as oppressed and muted members of society, are seldom in a position to create discourse and set its terms. Their ideas are thus always subject to the constraints of a dominant (that is, male-oriented) discourse. The perception of this dimension of women's oppression has led some historians to a highly pessimistic assessment of women's capacity for intellectual creativity, and sometimes even to the conclusion that women's position in the history of western thought has been only absence or silence. Historian Carroll Smith-Rosenberg, in her discussion of early women contributors to the male-dominated field of the social sciences, remarks that "the act of adopting another's language can be tricky and costly. . . . As long as gender remained a major factor in the inequitable distibution of power—a major determinant of women's life experiences—women's assumption of men's symbolic constructs constituted a fundamental act of alienation."[14]

Although women's ideas, like others, must be seen in the context of prevailing discourses, discourse itself cannot be regarded as rigid and immutable. If it were, no resistance or change would be possible. But, as Foucault points out, discourses are not unified and monolithic, but varied, permitting many different strategies, including those of resistance and reversal. New theories of language also emphasize its fluidity; the meaning of words and concepts is not entirely fixed, but can be modified, and even sometimes created, by the speaking subject. Language and conceptual frameworks therefore are not the fixed property of any power structure, but become the focus of struggle. In the nineteenth century, the concept of motherhood was constantly developed and reconstituted in different contexts and by different speakers. Though never free of constraint, women can thus create alternative views of the world by exposing the contradictions and exploiting the unexplored possibilities of dominant discourse.[15]

The German feminists' idea of motherhood developed in the context of a specifically German national culture and German conceptions of citizenship. These ideas did not rest on liberal doctrines of natural rights; as Amy Hackett has observed, German political thought has no concept equivalent to the American phrase "born free." Rather, German ideas of citizenship were derived from organic theories of society that stressed the relationship of the indivdal to the community and linked rights to duties. As Karen Offen has remarked, "relational" forms of feminism, stressing social contributions rather than individual rights, predominated over individualist forms in nineteenth-century Europe as a whole. In Germany, the connection between rights and duties became particularly clear when military service in the wars of unification was widely proclaimed to be the basis of the universal male suffrage in elections to the national representative body, the Reichstag, granted by the North German Confederation in 1866 and the unified German Empire in 1871. In women's political discourse, "motherhood" became a metaphorical term for a distinctively female claim to rights based on women's service to society.[16]

However, the relationship of women's ideas to the dominant discourses of their national culture was marked by tension and dissent as well as complicity. As a basis for resistance to male-dominated cultural values, feminists used another body of theory—that of international feminism. Feminist ideologies were the products of women's status and experience, which, although obviously differing somewhat according to national culture, also showed many common elements throughout the western world. In the nineteenth century, the English-speaking world, and especially the United States, was widely regarded as the home of individualist feminism based on natural-rights doctrine and emphasizing political equality. Cross-cultural comparisons are obviously indispensable to our understanding of the relationship of feminist movements and other aspects of women's work and status to national cultures. Thus, throughout this study, I shall compare the ideas and activities of the German women described to those of their contemporaries in the United States. Comparisons to many other nations would be possible, but a thorough exploration of all these comparisons would require another book.[17]

My definition of feminism as a "politics of experience," positing a relationship between ideas and material conditions, does not rest on any form of determinism. In this study, the relationship between material conditions, or experience, and ideas is explored as a dialectical process that continued thoughout the life of the individual. During the nineteenth century, motherhood and more generally nurturing roles were a major aspect of most women's experience. Some feminist thinkers have characterized the experience of biological motherhood as in itself the basis of women's ideas. "If material life structures existence," writes Marxist philosopher Nancy Hartsock, "women's relationally defined existence, bodily experience of boundary challenges, and activity of transforming both physical objects and human beings must be expected to result in a world view to which dichotomies are foreign. . . . The child carried for nine months can be defined as neither me nor not-me. . . . Inner and outer are not polar opposites but a continuum." The social construction of gender was indeed connected to the bodily realities of sex and reproduction. The idea of motherhood as a source of ethical authority, however, was not merely a product of biology; in fact, it was adopted by many women who were not biological mothers, sometimes in order to avoid biological motherhood. The ideology that made motherhood a basis for empowerment was chosen, not determined, in response to a specific historical situation, among a specific group of women. For them, it provided a way to shape their experience by devising a symbolic framework in which to understand it.[18]

Another aspect of the material world that shaped feminists' ideas on this as on other subjects was economic class. Feminist ideas of motherhood were based on a familial culture that originated with the upper and middle classes. The ascendancy of this ideology resulted from the ascendancy of middle class women within the feminist movement. Moreover, the practice of "social motherhood" through education and philanthropy supported the wider claim of the middle class to cultural hegemony over the lower classes. Women's use of motherhood as a basis for authority was not determined by their class, however. On the contrary, this form of ideology could also legitimate criticism of the class system. It expressed the complex and ambiguous subjective position of women who, while sharing the culture and the interests of their class, were also marginalized and oppressed within it. Motherhood was a useful metaphor for this standpoint; it could be used to legitimate authority over, or solidarity with, women of other classes, and cooperative or critical attitudes toward men of the speakers' own class.[19]

The starting point for this study is the late eighteenth century, when the first official discourses on child-rearing, family, and state connected the private welfare of families to the public welfare of society. The intersection of private and public motherhood as a central idea within feminist movements will be examined in subsequent chapters. These chapters will show that the mother-child relationship was not only an important theme in itself, but provided a metaphorical framework for speech on a wide variety of topics, including the major political issues of each period. Feminist scholars, remarks Joan Kelly, must reject the myth of "separate spheres" in order to examine "how the social relations arising from each sphere influence each other." In the feminist discourse on private and public motherhood we can see an early example of such an inquiry into the connection between personal and political aspects of life.[20]

Part 1
Spiritual Motherhood

Chapter 1
From Authority to Nurture: Theoretical Origins of Maternal Feminism, 1780–1840

"Truly, the saying that 'Your child will become whatever you are' is of such immeasurable importance," wrote schoolteacher Betty Gleim in 1810, "that, if she really feels it and lives by it, every mother ought to tremble before the responsibility that she takes on as teacher and educator of the coming generation." The belief in the importance of maternal nurture was central to the intellectual and social origins of nineteenth-century feminism. This new ideology of motherhood arose out of a transformation in maternal practice, caused by the change in family structure that allotted major responsibility over the rearing of children to mothers rather than fathers. Some historians have seen this new maternal ideal chiefly as a rationalization for the privatization of the female role, and thus for restrictions on women's independence. Maternity and child-nurture were by no means solely private functions, however. Child-rearing, on the contrary, was often regarded as an important public issue, vital to the well-being of the state. Therefore, the maternal role, whether conceived as biological or social, provided a basis for the entrance of women themselves into public life as speakers and actors.[1]

The intellectual origins of maternal feminism must thus be seen in the context of a wider debate, beginning in the eighteenth century, on the relationship of motherhood, child-rearing, and family life to the welfare of the state. This debate was shaped by changing ideas of the state, of citizenship, and of public-private boundaries. The most striking change, centrally illustrated by the works of Pestalozzi, was the shift from father-centered to mother-centered theories of child-rearing. This shift was linked to an intellectual transformation—the search for new forms of social bonding as the social upheaval caused by the French Revolution undermined confidence in traditional social relationships based on deference. The new importance given by many political theorists and pedagogues to the mother-child bond as the source of social morality went along with the development of organic theories of society that identified emotional commitment rather than mere authority and obedience as the basis of citizenship. By stressing the importance of good mothering to political and social order, prestigious pedagogical theories such as those of Pestalozzi and Froebel legitimated the efforts of women to enter, and thus ultimately to shape, their period's discourse on the public sphere of politics, society, and the state. This chapter will explore the earliest theoretical orgins of maternal feminism in the German-speaking world, as they appear in the writings of both male philosophers, such as Johann Heinrich Pestalozzi, Theodor Gottlieb von Hippel, and Friedrich Froebel, and the period's most prominent writers on female education—Amalie Holst, Caroline Rudolphi, and Betty Gleim.[2]

Family and State in the Late Eighteenth Century

The wide-ranging changes in child-rearing theory and practice that occurred in the late eighteenth century are often linked to the development of a sentimental and domesticated ideal of motherhood. Edward Shorter, one of the most prominent historians to attribute changes in child-rearing practice to a "maternal revolution," sees women as chiefly the passive recipients of cultural change, overcome by what he vaguely characterizes as "a wave of maternal sentiment."[3]

However, public concern for child care in the German-speaking world antedated the development of a mother-centered domestic ideology. In the eighteenth century, the first major child welfare measures were designed to enhance not the sentiment of mothers but the power of fathers and such authority figures as pedagogues, physicians, and rulers. The writings of such men provide ample evidence of an increased concern, at least among educated segments of society, for the survival and welfare of infants. As historian Mary Lindemann points out, the first political rationale for governmental involvement in child welfare was provided by the populationist concerns of the eighteenth-century state. In all of the advanced European nations, the heightened concern of government for population growth resulted in the first state-sponsored efforts to improve maternal and child health; by the end of the eighteenth century, almost every major European city had established some kind of publicly financed maternal and infant care. The theory and practice of "biopolitics" was developed to its greatest extent by Frederick the Great of Prussia and the Prussian Legal Code (*Allgemeines Landrecht*) which, though published in 1794 after Frederick's death, clearly reflected his influence. The Code supported the major priority of the Prussian state—military strength. As the source of military manpower, the family assumed a public function, vital to the welfare of the state. Although only one of the many legal codes that existed in the German states before unification, the Prussian Legal Code was widely admired and influential.[4]

The Code's laws on parent-child relationships showed an important transition from traditional ethical and religious norms to pragmatic considerations, or *raison d'état*. The clearest example of this change was the new status of the unmarried mother and her child. Infanticide, a major cause of child mortality, was portrayed by contemporary moralists as a crime of desperation, motivated by the social ostracism, religious condemnation, and economic insecurity of the unmarried mother. The Code discounted conventional religious strictures by giving the unmarried mother, if she had been engaged to the father, the rights of an innocently divorced wife, and in almost all circumstances the right to some support. Her child, though declared by law to be unrelated to the father, was entitled to paternal support and even to a share of the father's inheritance if he had no legitimate issue. Paternity could be established simply by the mother's sworn testimony, and if several men came into question, all were held financially responsible. This early legal precedent, which linked the survival of infants and the welfare of the state to the status of women and children, was probably an important influence on the strongly maternalist emphasis of German feminist movements.[5]

The Prussian lawgivers' concern for the survival of children did much more to uphold and expand the power of fathers than to improve the status of the majority of mothers, however. The Legal Code carried the practice of bio-politics to an unprecedented length by making the most intimate family relationships the object of public and political concern. The law on parent-child relationships began by defining the chief end of marriage as the enhancement of the state through "the bearing and rearing of children." The authority of the father, as "head of the marital society," was derived from, and analogous to, that of the enlightened ruler. Paternal authority was conceived as absolute; daughters, regardless of age, remained under it until marriage and sons until they were self-supporting. Although responsible for the physical care of children, mothers had no decision-making power over their persons or rearing. Fathers controlled the children's education, vocational choices, and financial affairs and could remove them from the mothers' care without their consent. Even as a widow, the Prussian mother could not control the rearing of her children, but was forced by law to accept the authority of a court-appointed guardian. By contrast to French and some other German legal codes, which at least in theory recognized both maternal and paternal rights over children, Prussian law set up the family as a realm of nearly absolute paternal despotism.[6]

Thus, although eighteenth-century governments did indeed take a new interest in maternal behavior, their view of motherhood was largely limited to basic physical and custodial functions, by far the most important of which was breast-feeding. Despite the fact that the custom of consigning infants to wet nurses seems to have been less widespread in the German-speaking than in the French-speaking world, the encouragement of maternal breast-feeding was a major preoccupation of physicians and lawgivers, who also often set up agencies to regulate the selection and licensing of wet nurses. Like the Prussian Legal Code, this biological conception of motherhood shows the tendency of eighteenth-century authority figures to separate maternal duty from its traditional religious and ethical basis, and to justify it through secular concepts of natural or political order. "Why did the creator give women breasts?" wrote physician G.F.C. Wendelstädt. "Because every mortal must submit to the laws of nature, and no one can rebel against nature, without later being punished by nature." This view of motherhood as ineluctable instinct, however, prompted no increased confidence in women's dedication to maternal responsibility but rather harsh criticism of women who refused it and chose instead to entrust their infants to "the breast of a filthy slut . . . where they gradually starve." The Prussian Code expressed this mistrust of women through a law requiring all healthy women to breast-feed their children and assigning to fathers the responsibility for determining when their children should be weaned.[7]

The secularized pedagogy that developed alongside these legal measures in the German-speaking world showed the same conflation of private and public, paternal and governmental authority. Eighteenth-century pedagogues, though beginning to stress mothers' responsibility for children's psychological development, usually assigned leading roles in the education of children past infancy, even of toddlers, to fathers or other male authority figures. The popularity in the German-speaking world of Rousseau's treatise, *Emile*, was reflected in the prestige of a male-centered science of pedagogy, represented most prominently by a group of writers known as the Philanthropists (*Philanthropen*). This secularized approach to child-rearing at first affected only a narrow group within the population—chiefly educated Protestants and Jews of the upper and middle classes—and did not displace more traditional religious approaches, which competed for influence well into the nineteenth century. However, the sales records of bookstores patronized by educated upper- and middle-class readers testify to the popularity of child-rearing "à la Jean-Jacques" among this progressive segment of the population.[8]

The Philanthropists called on fathers to act as agents of a modernizing state that now, at least among its elite, prized energy and initiative as well as obedience. The fictional narrator of Christian Gotthilf Salzmann's popular treatise on the raising of a toddler questioned concepts of original sin and urged respect for the child's natural development. "People often used to ask me, 'Herr Kiefer, where did you learn to raise children so well?'" remarked Salzmann's narrator, "and I always answered, 'from my children.'" The Philanthropists encouraged fathers to abandon rote memorization as a pedagogical technique, and to encourage children to learn from practical activities and observation. But, like many pedagogues of the period, they took a cautious and ambivalent view of such natural energy (*Tätigkeitstrieb*). If allowed to develop spontaneously, they feared that it could easily lead to the dangerous self-indulgence and sensuality that they considered the major threats to social order. They insisted that play, though no longer forbidden, must nonetheless be supervised, and assigned this task chiefly to fathers, who were often portrayed as present in the home and active participants in child-rearing. Far from regarding play as a sinful waste of time, wrote Salzmann, fathers and teachers now "join the circle of players, suggest games, and help to supervise them."[9]

This advice on child-rearing reflected the transition that began during this period from traditional forms of the household as center of economic as well as personal life to the newer form, limited to private life, that developed first among educated elites. The Philanthropists' concept of motherhood was also transitional. Though often acknowledging the importance of the maternal role, they did not regard it as a potential source of moral or practical autonomy. Moral authority over child-rearing was still held by fathers, whose influence in rural communities extended beyond the family. In Joachim Heinrich Campe's *Book of*

Good Behavior for Children (1788), the central figure was a respected older man who sat on the village green and acted as teacher to the children of the community.[10]

Thus the emergence of child-rearing into public discourse in the eighteenth century was not immediately linked to the development of bourgeois family life, doctrines of separate spheres, or the sentimentalization of the maternal role. Clearly, the state's intervention in child-rearing and household management benefited women only incidentally, if at all. The central purpose of these measures was not the empowerment of mothers, but their exploitation as docile servants of family and state. Similarly, new pedagogical theories, although assigning important functions to mothers, often also devalued them by defining motherhood chiefly as a "natural" and biological activity, and fatherhood as a culture-producing one. Nonetheless, this discourse on child-rearing, family, and state was important to the later development of feminist positions on these issues. The separation of ideas of maternal duty from religious prescriptions and the reconstitution of these ideas in the secularized context of "nature" and the state provided important opportunities for discussion and dissent. Ideas about nature and the state were clearly not eternal or God-given truths, but human constructs, subject to change, revision, and historical evolution. The next decades, in fact, were to witness a wide-ranging debate on the structure and meaning of both the natural world and the state, in the context of which the first feminist arguments developed.

Motherhood and Culture: The Contributions of Pestalozzi and Hippel

The work of Johann Heinrich Pestalozzi provides the clearest and most influential example of the relationship of ideas of motherhood to changing conceptions of state, nature, and society. Though Pestalozzi, as moralist, pedagogue, and children's advocate, worked in the tradition of the Philanthropists, he also modified this tradition by transferring much of the moral and cultural as well as physical responsibility of child-rearing from father to mother.

Like that of the Philanthropists, Pestalozzi's pedagogy predated major changes in familial structure and evolved in the context of a peasant society that, though already affected by incipient industrialization, was still largely intact. Born in Zürich in 1746, Pestalozzi was influenced in childhood by a peasant nurse whom he later described as a model of good sense and integrity. His later career as a school proprietor and teacher was dedicated to the development of new methods for the education of peasant children. His enthusiasm for the "natural" existence of the countryside obviously showed the influence of his compatriot Rousseau, of whom Pestalozzi, like many other Swiss intellectuals of his generation, was an ardent disciple. His approach to pedagogy, which advocated learning through direct sensory stimulation and experience rather than through books, was based on *Emile*. But unlike Rousseau himself and many of Rousseau's German disciples, Pestalozzi showed great respect for the energy and abilities of women. Moreover, unlike his contemporaries who dismissed traditional child-rearing practices as merely unscientific, Pestalozzi claimed that his entire approach to early-childhood education was based on the observation of peasant mothers. "We are not yet so advanced," he wrote in his enormously influential book, *Wie Gertrud ihre Kinder lehrt* ("How Gertrude Teaches her Children"), "as the Appenzell woman who, in the first week of her child's life, hangs a painted paper bird over the cradle, and so begins the process through which human skill creates the child's firm and clear awareness of natural objects."[11]

The image of the peasant mother and the paper bird served as a metaphor for Pestalozzi's view of human connectedness as the beginning of intellectual and moral consciousness. Pestalozzi shared the central concern of his German contemporary, Johann Gottlieb Fichte: How can we understand the relationship of the self to the not self? His view of motherhood was integrally related to his evolving conception of the relationship of the individual to the larger social and political environment. Despite his republican Swiss background, Pestalozzi began in the 1780s as an admirer of enlightened monarchy. One of his earliest works, *Uber Gesezgebung und Kindermord* ("On Legislation and Infanticide"), advocated reforms of the criminal laws penalizing infanticide. The book, which called upon the enlightened monarchs of the period to encourage marriage and to care for illegitimate children, appealed to much the same combination of humanitarianism and *raison d'état* as had prompted the reforms of Frederick the Great. Like Frederick, Pestalozzi saw family life as a public issue, and called upon the ruler, as father of his people, to support it. The earliest editions of his most famous novel,

Lienhard und Gertrud ("Leonard and Gertrude"), assigned a very important role to a fatherly ruler who encourages the heroine, Gertrude, in her establishment of an exemplary domestic regime.[12]

But the experience of the French Revolution and the Napoleonic occupation undermined Pestalozzi's faith in any traditional form of authority and thus prompted the search for a new basis for human community that runs through all his later work. For Pestalozzi, the revolutionary period revealed the fundamental problem of human history: the failure to create a social order that integrated the values of individual freedom with those of community. The Old Regime, an order without freedom, had been overturned by the revolutionaries, who in his opinion had descended into an anarchic freedom without order or social responsibility. Pestalozzi, who had witnessed Napoleon's invasion of Switzerland and had set up a school for children orphaned by the Napoleonic wars, regarded the French dictator as the embodiment of individualism run amok. For him, the mother-child relationship often served as a metaphor for the resolution of tensions between self and other and between freedom and order through a new social bond. Pestalozzi's idea of motherhood reflects the transition from individualist to organic views of social relationships that was a major theme in the intellectual life of this period. Rousseau had portrayed society as a collection of independently contracting individuals; Pestalozzi imagined it as a community united by the bonds of love and trust most perfectly learned from the mother.[13]

In the works of Pestalozzi, the emotional relationship to the mother displaced the more formal and deferential relationship to the father as the basis for community. He depicted the mother's gratification of the child's physical needs as not a menial but a profoundly significant task that inspired the sense of mutual and reciprocal trust on which social morality was based. "The seeds of love, of trust, and of gratitude soon burgeon and grow. The child knows its mother's footstep and smiles at her shadow; the child loves anyone who resembles her . . . the child smiles at its mother and smiles at other human beings, whatever she loves, the child loves, whomever she kisses, the child kisses. . . . The seeds of the love of humanity, and of human fraternity have begun to grow." Pestalozzi based the highest expression of this social morality, religious faith on the mother-child bond: "Mother, Mother, if I love you I love God, and my duty is my highest satisfaction." He attributed the corruption of society to the disruption of affiliative bonds rather than (as

Rousseau had asserted) individual autonomy, identifying the primal tragedy as separation from the mother. "Mother, if I forget you I forget God . . . and I live like a wild beast for myself alone, trusting only myself and using my powers only for my individual well-being and against my own kind."[14]

Pestalozzi advocated the elevation of the sense of affiliation that occurred naturally in the mother-child relationship to a consciously adopted principle guiding behavior in both private and public life. His first and most influential work on this theme was the popular novel *Leonard and Gertrude*, which was published in 1781 and frequently revised thereafter to reflect the author's changing political and pedagogical outlook. Set in the fictional peasant village of Bonnal, where home and community, family life and work were integrated, Pestalozzi's novel started from the same basic conception of the household as was held by the Philanthropists. However, Pestalozzi departed from the morality tales of his contemporaries by assigning the chief authority over child-rearing, like most other activities, to the mother, Gertrude. Gertrude was utterly unlike Rousseau's passive and compliant heroine, Sophie, whose sole aim was to please her husband. Gertrude functioned as mother, housewife, craftsperson, teacher, and counselor to her husband (portrayed as weak, alcoholic, and docile) and the neighbors. In a rural setting where public and private spheres were not yet firmly divided, her activities and ideas could be shown as quite naturally flowing outward from the household to the community. Moreover, Pestalozzi showed maternity as a primarily moral and social rather than biological function. Gertrude's role in the care even of newborn infants was portrayed as pedagogical rather than purely custodial. "From the moment a mother takes a child on her lap, she teaches it. . . . She brings nearer to its senses what Nature has scattered afar . . . and makes the action of receiving sense-impressions and the knowledge derived from them easy and delightful." In an important departure from the prevailing picture of the father as moral head of the household, Pestalozzi also showed Gertrude presiding over her children's religious education and leading them in family prayers.[15]

The children for whom Gertrude acted as mother, teacher, and employer included both her own children and the apprentices in her home workshop. Later, *How Gertrude Teaches her Children*, first published in 1802, Pestalozzi made Gertrude's workshop the model for the ideal school environment. Pestalozzi, who rejected abstract book learning and advocated the integration of practical and intellectual training, regarded pedagogical talent as essentially female. By contrast to the masculine intellect, which he regarded as artificial, abstract, and "monkish," he portrayed the female intellect as contextual, practical, and sensitive to human relationships. In accordance with the usual practice, Pestalozzi depicted a reformed village school headed by a male schoolmaster. But the schoolmaster, the retired soldier Lieutenant Glülphi, visited Gertrude's workshop, where the children learned reading and arithmetic in the process of performing manual work. Gertrude's motherly regimen provided the model for his school's curriculum and discipline and the schoolmaster hired a female assistant to supervise the practical training.[16]

The voluminous works of Pestalozzi, and especially the Gertrude story, provided a valuable source of intellectual legitimation to female writers, teachers, and pedagogues throughout the nineteenth century, in Germany and elsewhere. Quotations from Pestalozzi appeared frequently in the works of German feminists of several generations and of widely differing political persuasions, from the liberal bourgeoise Henriette Schrader-Breymann to the socialist Klara Zetkin. Pestalozzi's importance lay chiefly in his revision of the eighteenth-century discourse on women, children, motherhood, and the state. Whereas contemporary lawgivers and pedagogues had degraded the value of the mother's work by portraying it as almost entirely limited to merely "natural" or instinctive activities, Pestalozzi gave it a central culture-producing significance. Pestalozzi himself, although a strong advocate of humanitarian treatment for both women and children, was certainly not consciously a feminist; indeed, his exaltation of rural simplicity had strong conservative implications. However, precisely because of his admiration for traditional, preindustrial culture, Pestalozzi portrayed a village world in which women's roles in family, economy, and community were integrally linked. As in relation to all such prestigious male authorities, women acted as critical, sometimes resisting readers, transforming Pestalozzian theory in the process of adapting it to radically changed social conditions. As we shall see from the following chapters, Gertrude's role in her village ultimately served as a metaphor for an expanded role for women in the modern state—a role that Pestalozzi himself could, of course, never have envisaged.

By contrast to Pestalozzi's immense influence on the development of nineteenth-century feminism, that of Theodor Gottlieb von Hippel, the leading feminist author in the German-speaking world in the late eighteenth century, who was much less often quoted, seems to have been limited. Hippel's contribution to the discourse on women, family, and state was nonetheless important, for he was among the first authors to develop an argument for women's rights based on an analysis of their historical role in the development of culture. Hippel, a civil servant and philosopher who published his pioneering work, *Über die bürgerliche Verbesserung der Weiber* ("On Improving the Status of Women"), in 1792, echoed the rhetoric of the French Revolution by stating that women were "called by nature" to the same rights as men.[17]

Unlike other contemporary proponents of that position, such as the British Mary Wollstonecraft, Hippel showed an interest in cultural evolution. Influential German thinkers such as Herder had been the first to depart from the ahistorical and abstract models of society developed by French Enlightenment theorists and to depict societies as analogous to physical organisms, produced by a distinctive and continuous historical development. Hippel started with a picture of the "state of nature," based not on an abstract model of unspoiled human nature but on the actual evidence provided by existing primitive societies. This state, he insisted, was not one of solitude but of society. For Hippel as for Pestalozzi, the impulse toward community-building appeared as the central and universal condition of human cultural development. Hippel identified women, specifically mothers, as the earliest community-builders and thus as the founders of human culture. Because of the forced inactivity imposed by pregnancy and childbirth, he speculated, women must have been the first to plan for the future, to create a stable food supply, and to accumulate and store food—practices that led to the first forms of household, community, and social order. Maternity was again depicted as a rational and culture-bearing function; "wherever it was a question of using reason," Hippel remarked, "the woman seems always to have led the way." Male dominance was thus not due to any God-given or natural order but only to physical force, oppression, and usurpation. Men, he asserted, love to "gloss over the manner in which we came to this superiority. . . . Above all else we would like to convince the other half of the human race that it was not we, but nature who pushed them into the background and subjected their will to ours." Hippel insisted that the improvement of women's social and political status would affirm, rather than overturn, the true order of nature, and concluded his treatise by detailing the benefits to the state that the public exercise of female, community-building virtues would bring.[18]

Despite their marked differences, Pestalozzi and Hippel agreed on certain fundamental premises that would remain central to German feminist thought. Hippel, showing a tendency that would be characteristic of later feminist thinkers in the German-speaking world, made no firm distinction between equal rights and maternal feminism, seeing the individual rights of women entirely within the context of their contribution to culture and the state. For him as for Pestalozzi, motherhood as a cultural and biological function provided an important basis of that contribution.[19]

The Home: Shadow or Substance

In the early nineteenth century, ideals of maternal behavior were further influenced by the development of new definitions of the family as a private sphere, separated from economically productive activity and serving as a center only of unpaid housework, child-rearing, and emotional intimacy. This type of household, which in England is often linked to industrialization, predated the industrialization of the German-speaking world and showed the rising influence of a bourgeoisie composed chiefly of civil servants and professionals. By 1800, this class had developed ideals of family life that redefined women's work as private rather than public, and as exclusively domestic and nurturing rather than economically productive. This redefinition is often linked to a decline in women's status. In their examinations of the privatization of women's sphere, historians Barbara Duden and Ute Frevert both concentrate on the subservient wifely role prescribed by the new domestic ideology. But the redefined child-rearing role, by contrast, seemed to many contemporary women to offer new opportunities for moral and practical autonomy.[20]

Certainly the new discourse on public/private boundaries had many antifemale implications. Whereas Pestalozzi and his contemporaries had regarded the order of the household as continuous with the order of the state, their early-nineteenth-century successors denied that simple continuity and instead defined distinct forms of order for public and private realms. The order of the household was commonly associated with subjectivity, partiality, and emotional intimacy, and that of the state with objectivity and impartial justice. This public/private distinction served as a justification for the assignment of personal characteristics and social roles to males and females.[21]

Three examples illustrate this changed discourse. Philosopher Johann Gottlieb Fichte, the best-known supporter of Pestalozzian pedagogy, nonetheless denied that mothers could be its agents. Defining the home as a center of female—that is partial, emotional, and private—virtues, Fichte recommended the removal of male children to male-run institutions that taught the public virtues of objectivity, justice, and altruism. G.W.F. Hegel, who created the most comprehensive synthesis of the intellectual achievements of his period, subordinated the merely "natural" and personal bonds of the family to the more "universal" and thus ethically higher obligation to the state. "Because it is only as a citizen that he is real and substantial," Hegel wrote, "the individual, when not a citizen and belonging to the family, is merely unreal insubstantial shadow."[22]

The most prestigious and widely quoted writer on child-rearing of the Romantic era in the German-speaking world was Jean Paul Richter, whose treatise, *Levana* (published in 1811), was widely quoted by both male and female writers. Like other Romantic writers, Jean Paul denied original sin and portrayed children as naturally innocent, good, and in touch with divine truth (or, in the words of his British contemporary William Wordsworth, "trailing clouds of glory"). He assigned child-rearing tasks to women not only because of fathers' increasing absence from the home—only pastors and country gentlemen, he complained, could still be fathers in the old sense—but because of their innate nurturing abilities and distinctively female ethical values. But he assigned these female virtues solely to the private sphere. Women, he asserted, were well qualified to raise children because, in their characteristic emotionality and sensitivity, they resembled children. Thus many mainstream thinkers portrayed the public rather than the private sphere as the source of the highest morality, consigning the inhabitants of the private sphere, women and children, to a secondary and inferior role in the creation of ethical values, to which they could have access only through the male head of household.[23]

Women writers on family and child-rearing and state were forced to accept the basic premises of a discourse that was clearly intended to exclude them, from the rights of citizenship and from public life. A challenge to conventional conceptions of public and private would be a fundamental theme of nineteenth-century feminism. In order to influence or change the prevailing discourse, however, feminist writers had to find a point of entry by taking advantage of its unexplored possibilities and areas of ambiguity. One possibility was offered by the change in conceptions of the household, from a public and paternal to a private and female sphere. The conception of the household as a separate (though inferior) realm with its own distinct ethos implied that women did have the capacity, within their own sphere, for creating their own distinctive ethical values. And conventional definitions of these private virtues contained some ambiguities and unresolved contradictions, for the hierarchical ranking of the rational and public over the emotional and private sphere conflicted with the prevailing recognition of emotional unity as the basis for a revitalized public as well as private life. Hegel, for example, although he separated family and state, nonetheless defined familial ties as the basis for a sense of community on which the ideal state of the future should be based. Moreover, child-rearing, although now increasingly confined to the nuclear family, was never defined as simply a private matter but was always accorded a vital public significance. Indeed, Pestalozzi's idea that the new social order must depend on the moral training of childhood, although often detached from Pestalozzi's mother-centered pedagogy, gained widespread acceptance during this period.[24]

The first response of many women writers of the early nineteenth century to prevailing evaluations of public and private spheres was simply to try to reverse them. The domestic realm could be seen not as the shadow of the public world but as a world complete in itself. Moreover, this familial sphere could be depicted as the vital center of personal relationships and values of which public morality was only the cold and abstract extension. Among the earliest writers who can be identified as feminists, three—Amalie Holst, Caroline Rudolphi, and Betty Gleim—established a clear link between motherhood, the status of women, and pedagogical theory, and are thus of special interest to this study.[25]

The first feminist cause that was supported by arguments derived from this view of the maternal role was women's right to education and the development of their intellectual faculties. One of the earliest female advocates of improved education for women was Amalie Holst, the proprietor of a girls' school near Hamburg who published her only well-known work, *Über die Bestimmung des Weibes zur Höhern Geistesbildung* ("On the Capacity of Women for Higher Education"), in 1802. Although Holst herself cited few contemporary authors as sources, she was probably strongly influenced by both Wollstonecraft and Pestalozzi. Holst began her argument with the angry question, "Are we here only for the sake of men?" For Holst, women's independent function as mothers provided an essential basis for a defense of women's right to create their own values. Motherhood, she emphasized, was not simply a menial function but among the most important of social tasks, requiring training, education, and a high sense of responsibility. She cited Pestalozzi's popular theory that the child's bond to the mother was the source of its moral and social development. Furthermore, she observed, in the middle-class families of her own time, the mother was a far more important source of moral and intellectual training than the father. Thus, by implication at least, Holst reversed Hegel's public/private dichotomy; for the child, the mother's love was "real and substantial," and the authority of the absent father was insubstantial. "In early childhood, children are much more in the company of their mothers than of their fathers. . . . Even though the father is the breadwinner and head of the family, the child is not in a position to recognize this, but acknowledges the help only of the companion of its joys and sorrows."[26]

An increasing measure of control implied an increasing measure of responsibility; the development of individual children showed "how much a skillful hand can achieve, and how much harm an unskilled hand can do." Therefore Holst asserted that the task of skilled motherhood required extensive education, not just in the necessary practical techniques of child-rearing but in many other academic disciplines. By taking the work of child nurture seriously as equal in importance to male vocations, Holst was able to argue against the many contemporary authors who warned that a broad and liberal education would estrange women from their proper role, or *Bestimmung*. Like Wollstonecraft, who also emphasized responsible motherhood as a central aim of women's education, Holst insisted that intellectual self-development and maternal duty were complementary rather than conflicting goals. Holst emphasized the inseparable connection between rights and duties. "Our duties will only become meaningful to us when we are in a position to see them in all their implications," she wrote, "when we perform them from the only truly pure motive, for the sake of humanity, as the goal of our existence."[27]

An important formative stage in the development of feminist movements was the emerging view of the domestic realm as a center of a distinctively female culture that encouraged ties of solidarity among women. Such a conception, characterized by Americanist Carroll Smith-Rosenberg as a "female world of love and ritual," was developed in great detail by teacher Caroline Rudolphi (1754–1811), who founded girls' schools in Trettow, near Hamburg, and in Heidelberg and was one of the few well-known female writers on education during this period. In *Gemälde Weiblicher Erziehung* ("Pictures of Female Education"), which first appeared in 1807, Rudolphi revealed herself clearly as a disciple of both Rousseau and Pestalozzi; in fact, the book itself, a narrative of child-rearing in the countryside, might be called a female-centered version of *Emile*. Through the sentimental style of the book, Rudolphi, like many other female writers of the nineteenth century, emphasized the importance of emotional issues that were often downgraded by the male-dominated literary mainstream. The central character, Selma, was a single, educated woman living in a small country town, who first wrote letters advising her married sister on child care and then, when the sister and her husband left for a diplomatic post in Turkey, took over the care of the sister's two daughters and reported through an extensive correspondence on their educational progress. Although the sister also had a son, Selma quickly found a male tutor for him and sent them both on a tour of Europe. Through this plot device, Rudolphi paid pious tribute to prevailing notions of the unfitness of women to educate boys. However, she also subverted such notions of male superiority by creating a world where men were absent and where women were thus largely free to create a community life according to their own values.[28]

The female culture of this fictional community was centered on a nurturing or maternal ethic that was now entirely separated from its biological base and portrayed as a freely chosen vocation. The heroine, Selma, had no children of her own and cared eventually not only for her own nieces but for several other girls who had lost their parents. The rituals of this extended household, including academic education according to Pestalozzi's methods, extensive outdoor activities, training in sewing and other female crafts, and visits to neighboring families, were tailored not only to current pedagogical theories but also to the individual needs of the pupils. Rudolphi's central principle, asserted against the theoretical rigidity of many male educators, was that both child-rearing and education should be adapted to individual personality. Selma expressed her interest in individual personality through long, intense, intimately emotional conversations with her pupils. In such an atmosphere, she asserted, coercive discipline or harsh punishment became unnecessary. The threat of withdrawal of love or temporary exclusion from the intimate circle was sufficient to control behavior. "Kathinka doesn't want to wash her face this morning," Selma advised her sister. "What should you do? Perhaps not allowing her to give you a good-morning kiss would be enough." Rudolphi's picture of a maternal discipline resting on psychological pressure rather than on force reflected the growing emphasis on emotional intimacy and individuality that characterized the middle-class family of this era. In this sphere governed by the bonds of personal relationships, maternal nurture was a source of power.[29]

Like other domestic literature of the period, Rudolphi's narrative presented a picture of the domestic sphere as a center of female-centered cultural as well as pedagogical values. But she was still strongly aware of the limitations of the private sphere. Women, although powerful within their own sphere, were powerless outside it. This realization clearly informed Rudolphi's pedagogical approach, which along with nurture stressed training to obedience, self-control, and self-sacrifice. Rudolphi viewed feminine submissiveness chiefly as an adaptation to a social environment not created or controlled by women. The individuality of the female child must be controlled, Selma explained to her sister, not only in order to avoid spoiling but because "under our (feminine) circumstances, in which not only our own consciences but so many external pressures determine our behavior, our own statements 'I want this, I don't want that' will meet with a very harsh resistance. . . . These spoiled little creatures are doomed to a life of struggle and bitterness." Whatever its rationale, Rudolphi's support of conventional ideals of feminine nature won her wide influence and approval among her female and male contemporaries. In a preface to her book, the well-known clergyman and pedagogue C.F.H. Schwarz praised her "beautiful soul" and her exemplary piety, criticizing only her idealized view of childhood, which denied original sin and portrayed children "as if they had just come from Paradise."[30]

Betty Gleim, the proprietor of a girls' school in Bremen who in 1810 published her chief work, *Erziehung und Unterricht des weiblichen Geschlechts* ("Education and Instruction of the Female Sex"), had a more ambitious vision of women as creators of community. Gleim, who visited Rudolphi's school in Heidelberg, criticized her older colleague's sentimentality, lack of intellectual rigor, and limited conception of women's potential. As a reader of Pestalozzi, Fichte, and Schleiermacher, Gleim placed the issue of women's status in the context of the dominant philosophical ideas of her time. The fundamental problem of the age, she insisted, was selfish, individual "egotism"; "political upheavals and model constitutions" had failed to reform society because such external events had not changed the human heart. A new order to replace the old one could only be brought about through a new system of education that would teach "that all individuals form a great organic whole, in which each part is at the same time means and end. The whole represents perfection, holiness and the realization of the divine will." Gleim insisted on this as a human, not just a feminine, ideal. Education for both sexes, she wrote, should aim not at narrow vocational or purely practical training but at the development of all the creative faculties, for only the harmonious personality could appreciate and realize the ideal of a harmonious society.[31]

But Gleim, although asserting the equal right of both genders to intellectual development, did not believe that their intellectual abilities were the same. She ascribed to women not only a distinctive set of personal characteristics but a distinctive role in the evolution of social harmony. Women, she asserted, were characterized by the affiliative and cooperative virtues: sensitivity, tact, aesthetic responsiveness, and "warm participation in the troubles and joys of others, the strength of patience, love, hope and faith." Influenced by Romantic theories that identified the will to perfection as a force guiding biological evolution, Gleim obviously saw these characteristics as the outcome of both innate tendencies and willed commitment. She responded to her contemporaries' fears that education for women would undermine family cohesion by asserting that, on the contrary, the development of the feminine personality promoted harmony; "cultivation, which directs the individual's attention and interest to the universal realm of ideas, weakens self-love, kills base desires, and diverts concern from self-interest to the welfare of others." A great portion of Gleim's book discussed the crucial role of mothers in bringing about the change in individual attitudes that alone would regenerate society. Mothers, she wrote, must cultivate individual potential while discouraging antisocial expressions of individualism such as "sensuality, egoism, and passion." Such social virtue could not be externally imposed but must be internalized in a female-centered nurturing atmosphere: "In a happy family where the mother is the central figure, around whom everything good and beautiful gathers, . . . [she is] the sun, which gives warmth and light to everything."[32]

Gleim, however, admitted that not all women would marry and create such a family. She was among the earliest advocates of a cause that would become the central practical goal of nineteenth-century feminists, the provision of career opportunities for unmarried women. She thus specifically rejected any conception of motherhood and child-rearing as purely or chiefly biological functions and insisted on the importance of motherhood as a social task, in the performance of which single women, too, could gain a sense of human worth. In addition to a serious academic education, she advocated professional training for women, modeled on a school for female teachers that Pestalozzi had founded at Yverdon. Such institutions, she stipulated, should offer training in teaching on the elementary level and in child care in institutional and private settings. Gleim's book, one of the first and most important feminist documents of the German-speaking world, was widely cited in later feminist arguments for vocational opportunities for unmarried women.[33]

Thus the emergence of early feminist positions was linked to the development of organic theories of society. Holst, Rudolphi, and Gleim defined women's individual status as inseparable from their roles as builders of families and communities. They urged the cultivation of specifically female qualities, based largely on a uniquely female experience—the mother-child bond—but applicable to both private and public realms. The assertion of the culture-building function of the home, and especially of the maternal role, challenged rather than affirmed conventional domestic ideology that associated motherhood with subservience, intellectual inferiority, and childlike dependence. By criticizing conventional views of the private as the mere "shadow" of the public sphere, and making it the source of important ethical values, writers such as Holst, Rudolphi, and Gleim created the foundation for a public role for women.[34]

Friedrich Froebel and the Kindergarten

Friedrich Froebel, founder of an educational institution for small children known as the kindergarten, also made a major contribution to the evolution of German feminism. In his life as in his work, Froebel shared the preoccupation of his intellectual contemporaries with the relationship of the part to the whole, of diversity to wholeness, and of the human individual to the social organism. By integrating women and children into this philosophical inquiry, he contributed to the formation of a public nurturing role for women to which he himself gave the subsequently widely used name "spiritual motherhood."

Friedrich Froebel's narrative of his own childhood, later told and retold by his female disciples, served as a morality tale demonstrating the failure of traditional paternal and religious authority to create order in the absence of maternal love. He was born in 1782 into the family of a country pastor in the tiny Thuringian village of Oberweissbach and lost his mother shortly after his birth. Froebel recollected his hardworking father's inability to provide emotional support and his bitter disappointment when his stepmother neglected him in favor of her own children. The loneliness and disorder that the young Froebel felt in his own life were also reflected in the lives he saw around him. From observation of his father's pastoral counseling sessions he learned that his own experience of familial disharmony was far from unique. Froebel's more positive recollections involved the discovery of new forms of order, often associated with female or maternal influence. He appreciated the quiet, orderly atmosphere of a girls' primary school where he was the only male pupil. When sent to live with a benevolent uncle at the age of ten, he enjoyed outdoor activities and discovered another form of harmony, the harmony of nature, which he often described figuratively as a nurturing and all-encompassing mother.[35]

Before finally choosing teaching as a profession, Froebel pursued a strong interest in natural science, first as a forester's apprentice, then for two years as a student in Jena, and subsequently for brief periods as a land surveyor and head of a mineralogical museum. As a naturalist with a contemplative and philosophical bent, he was deeply influenced by the Romantic philosophy of nature, and especially by philosopher Friedrich Schelling, who taught at Jena. Schelling argued that, despite their great variety, the phenomena of Nature functioned as parts of a whole, metaphorically pictured as a great organism endowed with purpose by a central consciousness, or divine spirit. The striving to overcome diversity through unity, latent in all creation, became fully conscious only in human beings; Schelling regarded the social as analogous to the natural organism.[36]

In 1807, Froebel decided to work "for the culture and ennobling of man" by becoming a teacher. Because "Pestalozzi was the the watchword" in progressive educational circles, he immediately traveled to Yverdon. In 1814, he served briefly as a volunteer soldier in the German states' war of liberation against Napoleonic domination. This experience added a new, political dimension to his philosophical conception of unity; he imagined a future united German "motherland" as an alternative to Prussia, the land of authority and tradition. In 1817, along with two former military comrades, Froebel founded a school for boys at Keilhau; he also founded schools in Switzerland and in Berlin. Convinced since his association with Pestalozzi of the importance of early childhood education, he developed a pedagogical approach to young children, which he first designed to be used by mothers in homes but later adapted for use in an institutional setting. When he opened the first such school in the Thuringian town of Blankenburg in 1839, Froebel gave it the name "kindergarten."[37]

Like Pestalozzi, Froebel saw the origin of all moral and social consciousness in the child's first relationship with the mother. Froebel's best-known book, which was popular throughout the nineteenth century and translated into countless languages, was his *Mother and Nursery Songs*, a collection of songs and games that promoted both sensory and motor skills and emotional bonding between mother and child from the first days of the child's life. Froebel based these songs on the traditional culture of peasant mothers, whom he portrayed much more sentimentally than had the down-to-earth Pestalozzi. In these verses, the idea that all of nature was endowed with moral consciousness—and especially with that greatest of all virtues, mother love—was made understandable to small children:

> In the bushes, see the nest,
> Little eggs within it rest.
> When the babies break the shell,
> Mother feeds them very well.
> Little birdies sing together,
> "How we love you, dearest mother."[38]

Froebel's nostalgic picture of rural families, animal and human, served partly as a critique of the contemporary middle class, which by separating family life from its traditional basis in craft work and agriculture had created an environment that Froebel considered too narrow for children's optimal development. "Instead of being stimulated, children are inhibited and stifled," he complained; "instead of alertness we see listlessness, instead of health, sickness." Kindergarten theory synthesized the institutional approach to education advocated by Fichte with the mother-centered pedagogy of Pestalozzi. The kindergarten was an institution designed to introduce children to the wider world outside the family. But it also brought private, or maternal, values into this public realm. Froebel proposed not only that women should teach in this new institution, but that its discipline should rest on the familial practice of maternal love.[39]

Froebel, though by no means the first to advocate the involvement of women in early childhood education, greatly elevated the status of this occupation by associating it with high ethical ideals. The aim of all education, he asserted, was "the training of the human race" to create new form of order based not, as previously in history, on force and authority, but on the free commitment of the individual to the community. Froebel believed that the mother-child bond, which reconciled freedom and order through the force of love, could become the basis of such new social norms. Froebelian pedagogy affirmed the belief of Romantic theorists such as Jean Paul Richter in the child's original goodness, but tried to compensate for their one-sided individualism. One aim of the kindergarten pedagogy, which was based on play, was to develop the independence and self-reliance of each individual child; "from the day of their birth," Froebel wrote, children must be given the "free, many-sided use of all their powers." But Froebel insisted that the individual will must be directed toward cooperation with others. He banished conventional toys from the kindergarten and himself created a series of playthings (or "gifts") designed to demonstrate the relationship of the whole and its parts: balls of different colors, indicating unity and universality; blocks in the shapes of sphere, cylinder, and cube demonstrating the relationship of different forms; and building blocks showing "the whole and its parts, outside and inside, relations of size and number, arrangement and direction." The group games designed by Froebel taught order through human interaction. Each game involved the individual child in cooperation with others. The role of the teacher was to supervise these games gently, encouraging shy children and restraining unruly ones, but never suppressing natural energy with rules or punishments.[40]

Froebel asserted that child-culture required a specialized training that would develop both the practical and the intellectual abilities of women. "It is the characterisic of our time," he declared solemnly, "to rescue the female sex from its hitherto passive and instinctive situation and through its nurturing mission to raise it to the same level as the male sex." With the acknowledgment of the "destination and dignity" of the female sex, he insisted, would come "the reciprocal relation between the life of the family and that of the community." Though certainly no advocate of political rights for women, Froebel gave women's educational mission a certain political significance; "for we know that the state in the totality of that which it gives or demands . . . is in great measure an educational institution, whether good or bad we may not here inquire."[41]

Froebel at first attempted to sell the idea of the kindergarten to fathers and to the male-dominated elementary school teaching profession— indeed, in 1845 he called on fathers to join a General Educational Union to develop kindergarten associations. However, in 1840, on the four hundredth anniversary of the invention of printing, or Gutenbergfest, he also addressed a "sketch of a plan . . . for founding and developing a German kindergarten" to "German wives and maidens." The date was significant, for the widespread participation of young women in the festivities of the Gutenberg anniversary had testified to middle-class women's rising patriotic and civic consciousness, and to their interest in contributing to the public welfare. Froebel appealed to their patriotic concern "for the welfare of the German but ultimately of all people, for the benefit of their own but ultimately of all children, as a blessing to this nation and ultimately to all nations." The somewhat fanciful proposal, which solicited the investment of women in a new joint stock company promoting the kindergarten but offered as dividends only such intangibles as "family welfare . . . the happiness of the children . . . joy of heart and peace of mind" does not seem to have attracted much support, but it was the beginning of Froebel's campaign to promote kindergarten education, which produced its first major results in 1848.[42]

In considering the origins of maternal feminism in the German-speaking world, we have seen that it formed part of a broader discourse on motherhood, child-rearing, the family, and the state. During the period 1780–1840, this discourse was transformed in two major ways. In the late eighteenth century, maternal and child-rearing practices were for the first time defined as public concerns, important to the welfare of the state. At the turn of the century, the increasing recognition of emotional commitment, unity of feeling, and organic bonding as bases for citizenship prompted a new emphasis on the emotional and psychological as well as biological significance of the mother-child bond. When women entered the public realm as speakers and advocates, they derived much of their intellectual legitimation from prestigious male writers such as Pestalozzi and Froebel.

These developments were not limited to Germany, but were part of an international response to the eighteenth-century revolutions. American historian Linda Kerber has described how American women of the early national era found a niche in political discourse through the idea of "republican motherhood." But although the American ideas were in some ways similar to the German, their position on the political spectrum was somewhat different. Kerber sees the idea of republican motherhood, although important to women's political development, as basically conservative—a ladylike alternative to the more radical forms of emancipation that had surfaced during the revolutionary period, and a "deferential" model of citizenship that she contrasts to men's more egalitarian conception. In the United States, "deference was adopted and displayed by women," remarks Kerber, "at a time when men were gradually abandoning that attitude." In the German-speaking world, individualist models of female emancipation were much less immediately available, and the deferential model of citizenship was still normative. Thus arguments based on equal-rights theory and on maternal responsibility do not appear as antitheses, but as complementary aspects of ethical systems linking the part to the whole and the individual to the community.[43]

The writings of early female authors such as Holst, Rudolphi, and Gleim show how women can attempt to enter and change a male-dominated discourse by taking advantage of its ambiguities, unresolved contradictions, and unexplored possibilities. A prerequisite for entry into public discourse was the creation of a standpoint, identified as specifically female, that would provide a basis for the recognition of male bias and the validation of female experience. The development of such a standpoint among a younger generation of female intellectuals will be the subject of the next chapter.

Chapter 2
The Personal and the Political: Social Origins of Maternal Feminism, 1800–1848

The earliest feminist positions developed in the framework of the nineteenth-century discourse on motherhood, family, and state. Women's intellectual standpoints, based on their interpretations of their own lives and experiences, evolved within the dominant theoretical framework, sharing many of its assumptions. This dominant discourse imposed limitations on female speakers, but it also opened a field of possibilities. Among the generation of feminists who first emerged in the 1840s, an important group made the concept of widened, or social, motherhood (to which I have given the name "maternal feminism") the center of their theoretical and practical work. For these women, Pestalozzian and Froebelian pedagogy provided the basis for a new definition of "woman" and for a female standpoint from which to criticize both the private world of the family and the public world of the state. This chapter will evaluate their ideas in the context not of any ideal conception of feminist ideology but of a specific historical situation, shared by a specific group of women and reflecting their developing sense of self, their response to the events of their time, and their ethical and religious aspirations.[1]

The private and public lives of six important figures—Emilie Wüstenfeld, Charlotte Paulsen, Bertha von Marenholtz-Bülow, Malwida von Meysenbug, Henriette Breymann (later Schrader), and Henriette Benas (later Goldschmidt)—from childhood until 1848 will illustrate the relationship of ideas to their historical situation. These women were chosen because they were prominent early proponents of "spiritual motherhood" in general and of Pestalozzian and Froebelian pedagogy in particular. Their careers as reformers and intellectuals, which will be examined in later chapters, were shaped by their early lives, in which each had used her experience of private nurturing or maternal roles as the foundation for a conception of a widened public role for women.

Both the private and the public lives of these women were affected by some broader trends in German history. The defeat of Napoleon in 1815 had resulted in the creation of the German Confederation, a loose organization of German states. The 1820s were a time of political quiescence and conservatism, reflected in the still very traditional familial mores experienced by the women who grew up or married during this period. But the 1830s saw a revival of political activism and intellectual life, which coincided with the incipient stages of industrialization. Both of these trends contributed to the crisis of the 1840s, precipitated by social unrest, intellectual ferment, and renewed demands for social change and national unification. This crisis culminated in 1848, when revolutions occurred in most of the German states. All of these women, at very different stages of their lives, responded to the intellectual and political ferment of the 1840s by developing new conceptions of both personal self-determination and social involvement.

For these new conceptions, the experience of child-rearing and nurturing roles formed an important basis. These women tended to see the values of individual self-realization and of familial nurture as complementary. Their sense of individuality was formed, in part, through familial roles, and their visions of self-fulfillment included new forms of familial harmony. The theory and practice of "spiritual motherhood" could provide a means of reconciling individual and social commitments; it could be understood as a basis for the transformation of both self and world.[2]

The Joys and Sorrows of Motherhood

Sources of biographical information on the six women I have focused on here, and on others to be discussed later, reflect the complex relationship between narrative and discourse. Written by the protagonists themselves or by relatives, close friends, or associates, they are clearly biased and partial; yet other biographical accounts from different perspectives are usually not available. These biographical and autobiographical writings will therefore be used as sources not of "objective" information but of the individual's own understanding of her life: How did she, or the people who shared her values and objectives, use her life experience as the basis of her (or their) theory and practice?

Certainly the evidence provided by these accounts does not suggest any deterministic relationship between ideas and such material realities as class, economic situation, religious background, or marital status, for these women differed in all of these respects. The only material condition that they shared, in fact, was membership in an upper- and middle-class culture in which familial intimacy, and especially the mother-child bond, took on increasing importance during this period. The evaluation of motherly experience in these accounts reflects important aspects of ideology. Critic Ruth-Ellen Joeres warns us in her discussion of women's biographies that tributes to the subject's strong motherly or family affections may well reflect the biographer's stereotype of conventional "feminine" behavior. These biographies and autobiographies are not conventionally "feminine," however; they frankly record the subjects' dissatisfaction with many, if not most, aspects of women's status, including the obligation to obey fathers and husbands, the tedious duties of the household, the vapidity of conventional education, and many others. Motherhood and the care of children, however, was not mentioned as one of these burdens—indeed, all of these women viewed the maternal or nurturing role as an enhancement of individual self-esteem. Moreover, all derived their first understanding of women's general situation from their confrontation with the continuing power of fathers and male-dominated institutions over their own rearing or that of their children, and all eventually used maternal nurture as a model of power in the public sphere.[3]

The narrators' desire to reinterpret the mother-child relationship to emphasize emotional intimacy and pedagogical involvement was expressed in their acccounts of their own mothers, whether positive or negative. The most cheerful childhood reminiscences were of households where fathers were absent or remote. Emilie Wüstenfeld was born as Emilie Capelle to a prosperous merchant family in Hannover in 1817. She was the third of four surviving children. Frau Capelle, who became a widow shortly after Emilie's birth, greatly impressed her daughter through her competence and independence in managing her family and household alone. The well-read Emilie, although generally disapproving of Goethe, admired his definition of a truly capable mother as one who could replace a father. Malwida von Meysenbug, who was born in 1817 to an aristocratic family in Cassel, adored her father, but as a busy civil servant he "had little time for his children," and she was raised chiefly by her mother. She described her mother as a capable woman and talented hostess. Malwida and her sister were encouraged to develop physical fitness as well as intellectual skills. Despite their positive tone, these accounts are also, at least by implication, critical of the traditional emphasis of the upper-class household on public display of status rather than private intimacy.[4]

Other narrators were far more bitterly critical of upper-class family life. The oldest of the six women, Charlotte Paulsen, was born as Charlotte Thornton to a prosperous merchant family in Othmarschen (near Hamburg) in 1798 as one of eighteen children of her father's two marriages. Paulsen criticized her mother for emphasizing the accomplishments considered essential to the family's elite status—"chattering in English and French, curtseying and dancing"—more than the formation of character. Bertha von Bülow was born in 1810 into the aristocratic Bülow-Wendhausen family, who were landowners in the Braunschweig region. She, like Paulsen, remembered a superficial training in female accomplishments and social graces that left her intellectually and emotionally unsatisfied. A bookish child who withdrew from social pressures into religious contemplation, she learned chiefly "to find pain in everything, and to understand pain thoroughly." As a marriageable girl, she found her obligation to enhance her family's prestige by making her own person an object of display an unbearable burden. Although in her late teens she was a celebrated beauty and favorite dancing partner of the Prussian princes (including the future Emperor William I), she was deeply depressed, like her British contemporary Florence Nightingale, by a life devoid of moral purpose.[5]

Still stronger affirmation of the value of maternal nurture came from the two youngest of the six women, both of whom grew up in entirely father-dominated homes where mothers played a subservient and subordinate role. Henriette Goldschmidt (born Henriette Benas), whose mother died shortly after her birth in the Prussian town of Krotoschin in 1825, recounted with considerable bitterness how her father, although himself highly educated, married an illiterate woman because he believed that a mind not "distracted by useless reading" could devote itself more thoroughly to the rearing of five motherless children. Goldschmidt traced her future decision to become an educator to her resentment of her father's devaluation of child-rearing.[6]

A more differentiated and ambivalent picture was given by Henriette Breymann, born in 1827 into a large family headed by Pastor Ferdinand Breymann in Mahlum. Ferdinand Breymann's working conditions enabled him to run a traditionally patriarchal household. Every aspect of Henriette's rearing, including academic and religious education and even domestic skills, was closely supervised by her father. In sharp contrast to this stern authority was the unconditional love bestowed by Henriette's mother, who sometimes intervened to protect her daughter from her father's discipline. Henriette passionately loved her mother in return. But her reluctance to learn her mother's domestic skills—a cause of conflict with her father—was in part motivated by resentment not of the work itself but of her lack of control over the aims and conditions of such work in her father-dominated household. Her anger at her father, which she could not voice directly, was expressed indirectly through retreat into a fantasy world of more egalitarian families. "I took up my lazy life again," she recalled. "I wrote novels at night and spent my mornings lying on the sofa." In one of these stories, a fictional heroine confronted a father who warned her that, if she did not learn her mother's household skills, she would never find a man. "But father," responded the fantasy-heroine, who was more daring than her creator, "maybe there are some men who want a woman just like me."[7]

Whatever their memories of their own parents, the three women who became mothers or stepmothers themselves affirmed the value of the mother-child bond by attempting to establish a more intimate relationship with their own children than they themselves had known. For the three oldest—Wüstenfeld, Paulsen, and Bülow (later Marenholtz-Bülow)—intimacy with their children probably compensated for the lack of intimacy in their marriages. These three women entered arranged marriages at young ages. Charlotte Paulsen was married at the age of sixteen to a friend of her father's, twenty years older than herself; her father's financial misfortunes at this time lead one to suspect that the marriage was prompted by economic considerations. The young woman, who took only a limited interest in social life, found greater fulfillment in motherhood. The birth of her first child motivated her to make up for the deficiencies of her own education by reading current literature, including especially Jean-Paul's *Levana* and works of progressive theology. Paulsen also nurtured other children. She nursed a younger sister whom her own mother could not feed, along with her own daughter. Her relationship to her daughter in adulthood remained so close that she found the absence of the younger woman, who married and moved to a nearby town, hard to endure, and she was very attached to her granddaughter Johanna. "You can't imagine how hard everyone tries to cheer me up," she wrote to her daughter in 1836. ". . . Don't be angry at me because I love Johanna so much. . . . I have to admit that I miss her terribly . . . and that, in short, she is a sweet angel." At the age of forty-one, Paulsen took in a foster daughter, the illegitimate child of a friend.[8]

Like Paulsen, Bertha von Bülow was married to a man twenty years older than herself, the Baron von Marenholtz. At the age of twenty, she took charge of his estate at Schwülper, near Braunschweig, and of his five children from earlier marriages. Out of concern for his children and for the reputation of this prominent family, she never revealed the causes of her later separation from Marenholtz (her niece tells us that she burned all of her private papers and correspondence), but it is plain even from the published portions of her diary that she was deeply miserable and perhaps a victim of marital rape. "That the thought of attaining their ends through mere force should not cause noble men to blush with shame would be incredible," she wrote in 1836, "were it not that habit and ancient prejudice had blunted their perceptions. By a woman conscious of her own honor, love will be freely given and due submission freely yielded." Like her aristocratic contemporary the Countess Hahn-Hahn, a novelist who later became a close friend, Marenholtz knew from her own experience the terrible indignity of a loveless marriage of convenience. "Is there in the whole world a disgrace equal to this: to belong to a man without loving him?" declared one of Hahn-Hahn's heroines. Marenholtz's fantasies, recorded in her diaries, centered not on escape into individual freedom, but on new forms of family life based on love and mutual respect. "Then man, if he had become what he ought to be," she speculated, "would really find in marriage the happiness of which he dreamed."[9]

Her only experience of such familial harmony came through her relationship to her children—to five stepchildren, whom she raised and educated, and later to her own son. She conscientiously took over the education of the stepchildren, which had been seriously neglected, and thus discovered her interest in pedagogy. Her effectiveness in raising children who were not related to her by blood caused her to reflect, perhaps for the first time, on the importance of motherhood as a social rather than merely as a biological function." The motherly instinct," she wrote, "that is not trained, not brought fully into consciousness, will never rise much above animal nature." Her relationship to her own son, Alfred, was her only experience of love. As Alfred grew up, however, she discovered that the spiritual empowerment that she derived from motherhood could not compensate for her legal powerlessness. She was indignant at the education prescribed for Alfred by his father, who insisted that the boy prepare for the military academy in order to follow the family's tradition. The mother sensed that the rigorous and unimaginative curriculum required by tutors who had been hired by her husband was ill suited to the boy's personality. "His lively and wandering imagination," she recollected later, "could not be fettered by the dry mode of the instruction that his teachers handed out to him." In 1846, much against her will, Marenholtz saw her son leave for military academy. Her friend Henriette Goldschmidt speculated that the postponement of her decision to leave her husband until her son and stepchildren were independent showed her commitment to them.[10]

Not only the joys but the sorrows of motherhood could provide the basis for personal growth and social commitment. High rates of child mortality affected even the prosperous circles to which these women belonged. According to one set of statistics based on fourteen villages, about one-third of all children born to middle-class families between 1800 and 1829 died before the age of five. High rates of child mortality, which in earlier periods perhaps encouraged indifference to the lives of small children, caused immense personal grief to women of the early nineteenth century—a sign of the increasing importance given to each child's individual development. One measure of increasingly intimate relationships between mothers and children was the popularity among middle-class women of poetic and fictional laments for the death of children. Caroline Rudolphi prefaced her book with pious words of comfort for grieving mothers. But Charlotte Paulsen responded to the death of her beloved granddaughter Johanna more with indignation than with pious resignation. She criticized the various forms of neglect and artificial restraint to which children were subject and advocated a more natural approach. "In a century, we'll do it better, we'll leave it more to nature."[11]

Emilie Wüstenfeld's experience of bereavement was also an essential stage in the development of her religious and social awareness. Married at the age of twenty-four, she devoted all of her time and energy to the care of her three children, who were often sick, and was devastated by the loss of two of them. From this personal tragedy arose her increasing alienation from the bustling social life of her prosperous circle, her critical attitude toward organized religion, and her resolution to put the Christian commandment to "love thy neighbor" into active practice.[12]

Although neither Henriette Benas, Henriette Breymann, nor Malwida von Meysenbug became mothers during the pre-1848 period, they all played nurturing roles, Goldschmidt to the children of a sister who died prematurely, Breymann to her many younger brothers and sisters, and Meysenbug to her nieces. Breymann's biographer and coworker Mary Lyschinska, whose account of her subject's early years was probably based on the reminiscences of Breymann herself and members of her family, wrote that the "selfish" girl developed a sense of responsibility "far beyond her years" when entrusted with the care of her many younger siblings. This anecdote implies that the young girl whose restricted life offered her few other opportunities for independence found in the care and nurture of children some of the autonomy and sense of purpose for which she longed.[13]

Private and Public Worlds

Thus, nurturing roles did not conflict with but rather reinforced the development of these women as individuals. Their belief in the importance of child-nurture, gained in large part from personal experience, eventually led all six to protest against the conventionally narrow and private definition of motherhood and to argue for a broader application of the ethical values based on nurture. For some of them, this protest first took the form of an adolescent crisis in religious belief. The highly personal and individual concept of salvation taught by orthodox Lutheranism could not fulfill the desire of these young women (all of whom were Protestants, except for Benas, who was Jewish) for a more socially oriented code of ethics and behavior. Henriette Breymann, who had looked forward to confirmation by her pastor father with devout ecstasy, failed to find the expected sense of personal salvation. In part, her increasing rejection of her father's unworldly and inward-turning piety was also a revolt against her own confinement to the private sphere of the home: "the deepest reason," she later recollected, "lay in my impulses . . . toward a freer religious outlook and a new position for women in the home and in human society."[14]

Meysenbug also failed to experience religious bliss at her confirmation—"No God appeared to invite me into the ranks of the saved and the wonders of heaven," she recalled. She, too, justified her rejection of traditional piety by an appeal to a more public and social form of ethical commitment. It was difficult, she wrote, to give up the belief in individual salvation: "This phase of personal egoism . . . this poetic pretension of the I that would like to live on forever." The solution to Meysenbug's religious crisis came through her relationship to the radical theologian Theodor Althaus, who converted her to a social, this-worldly, and secular concept of salvation; children, he asserted, were our only valid form of immortality. When Meysenbug later reread Fichte, she was led by his advocacy of a Pestalozzian system of national education to a new awareness of the importance of educating women: "How could a woman, in whose hands lies the education of the future citizen, form his heart and mind to the realization of his duties if she herself did not know them?" For Meysenbug as for the other women discussed here, the commitment to "spiritual motherhood" affirmed personal autonomy—in her case, the freedom to maintain the relationship to Althaus, of whom her family disapproved, rather than enter a marriage of convenience.[15]

Bertha von Marenholtz-Bülow, whose fervent piety helped her endure her private anguish, likewise protested against her burdensome domestic confinement in the name of a more socially oriented code of Christian ethics. This code, she argued, should extend the female capacity for love and caring, gained through the private experience of motherhood, to public activities. Marenholtz's conception of social motherhood was at the same time a strong protest against her individual oppression. She attributed the callousness and insensitivity of men to their excessive individualism, the "false self-dependence" maintained "at the expense of feeling." Women, she argued, must not pursue this false and destructive ideal of freedom and power; their fulfillment must come not through the denial, but through the affirmation of love. In the 1830s, long before she met Froebel, Marenholtz urged the creation of professional opportunities for women that would enable them both to support themselves and thus avoid marriages of convenience and to put their maternal talents to use in the public sphere. She declared that "all such offices as Superintendant of Public Charities, Poor Houses, Hospitals, female Houses of Correction" and positions in many other "institutions for the benefit of humanity" should be open to women—a radical demand in a period when all municipal poor-relief and law-enforcement agencies were staffed exclusively by men.[16]

For women dissatisfied with traditional piety and searching for a new basis for personal ethics and social behavior, the intellectual culture of the 1840s offered many options. Marenholtz was probably influenced by utopian socialism, especially of the Saint-Simonian variety, which had originated in France in the 1820s and became immensely popular in intellectual circles in Germany in the 1830s and 1840s. Most utopian socialists, although advocating radical changes such as the abolition of inherited wealth and private ownership of business, believed that these changes should be realized through evolution toward social harmony rather than class conflict. By far the best-known and most sensational aspect of Saint-Simonianism was the demand for a new sexual ethic that allowed for nonmarital relationships and for free divorce—in a famous phrase, "the emancipation of the flesh." Marenholtz was exposed to these ideas during a visit to Dresden in 1840. There she met two of the foremost female literary figures of the time, the Jewish intellectual Rahel Varnhagen and the aristocratic novelist Ida Hahn-Hahn. Both these women, who were famous as examples of female emancipation, were ardent admirers of Saint-Simon, as well as of some of his French female disciples such as George Sand. The influence of women such as these was probably important in Marenholtz's personal decision, which she reached during this period of her life, to live separately from her husband after her children and stepchildren were grown. Though she herself decided not to seek a formal divorce, she defended her divorced friend, Ida Hahn-Hahn, against the scandalized disapproval of her aristocratic circle.[17]

Despite her admiration for these formidably self-determining and unconventional women, however, Marenholtz was clearly dissatisfied with their very private and elitist definition of emancipation. The Saint-Simonian enthusiasm for sexual liberation—the "emancipation of the flesh"—could only be pursued as an individual and personal solution by the few women, such as Hahn-Hahn herself, whose economic and social status permitted them to defy convention with impunity. Marenholtz, though also a member of this privileged group, nevertheless saw the need for a more socially involved role for women. Like many intellectuals of the 1840s, she believed that imagination should be used to change the world rather than to create escapist fantasies of personal fulfillment. Imagination, she wrote, "should never degenerate into sentimentality, which poisons all pure feeling. All thought, all reveries, all dreams should make the spirit clearer, the feelings purer. They should not unfit but capacitate for practical work. . . . Poetry without practical work is a useless dreaming away of life without fulfillment of the serious destiny of man and can never lead us to our ideal goal—the goal of true and total humanity."[18]

Paulsen, Wüstenfeld, and Meysenbug eventually expressed their own disillusionment with "egotistical" personal piety and their longing for a sense of community by their support of the "German Catholic" sect, which was founded in Stuttgart in 1844 by former members of both Protestant and Catholic churches and soon spread to other urban areas, including Hamburg. This radical sect was deeply influenced by the secularized ethic of love and community developed the the utopian socialists, and expressed by theologian Ludwig Feuerbach (of whom Meysenbug and her lover Althaus were also disciples). An important aspect of German Catholic theology, which has been extensively explored by Catherine N. Prelinger, was its rejection of traditional personal piety and its advocacy of a social ethic, a "practice of love," which was expressly linked to progressive political goals. The practice of Christian love, declared ex-Catholic priest Johannes Ronge, was the special domain of women, to whom the German Catholic congregations allotted a far higher status than the traditional Catholic and Protestant churches. The German Catholics appealed to progressive women particularly through their advocacy of an egalitarian form of marriage based on mutual love rather than on economic convenience. This love, argued Ronge in 1845, should not be limited to the private sphere. "The love expressed through marriage and the family," said Ronge, "should be broadened . . . and must be revealed through the education of state and people." The German Catholics explicitly identified the emancipation of women, not with individual fulillment, but with a familial ideal of service that would "free the nations from egotism . . . the sinfulness of privilege and of despotism in Church and State."[19]

The first opportunities for the practice of this ideal of public motherhood came through charitable work. During the three decades preceding the 1848 revolution, the growing commitment of women to practical activity outside the home had been expressed through their participation in the charitable organizations that had been founded in all the German cities. Among the insititutions founded by charitable organizations in many cities were infant schools, or *Bewahranstalten*, and visiting societies that sent volunteers to help individual families in crisis. In 1847, for example, Charlotte Paulsen joined an organization called the Pestalozzi Society, which was set up to help poor children. Most such institutions, though making use of the volunteer labor of women, had all-male boards of directors and thus excluded women from leadership roles. An important exception to this general pattern was the Female Association for the Care of the Poor and the Sick, founded by Amalie Sieveking of Hamburg in 1832 and subsequently imitated in other cities. The Association was led by women and encouraged women to venture outside the home in order to help less fortunate members of their own sex. But the scope of such work was limited by an attitude toward poverty, often based on conservative Protestant religious belief, which regarded it esentially as an individual problem that could be remedied by short-term aid and moral instruction. Such charitable work, which lacked any vision of social change, could not satisfy women who were searching for new forms of family and community life. When Charlotte Paulsen applied for memberhip in this organization, Sieveking rejected her for her dissenting religious beliefs.[20]

Thus Paulsen, Wüstenfeld, and many Hamburg women of similar beliefs were forced to create their own organizations. In 1846 they joined a prominent Jewish woman, Johanna Goldschmidt, to found an organization they called the Association for the Support of the German Catholics. Goldschmidt, who was born Johanna Schwabe in 1806 and was married to Jewish businessman Moritz Goldschmidt, published a book (which first appeared anonymously) entitled *Rebekka and Amalie* in 1847. This novel, which consisted of a correspondence between a Jewish and a Christian woman, was a passionate plea for religious tolerance.[21]

In Goldschmidt's novel, the basis for new understanding between the two communities was a female friendship based on many kinds of common experience, including that of motherhood. "Heaven has sent us children, gifted with inward and outward charm," wrote the Jewish Rebekka to her Christian confidante, Amalie, "and you know best, my dear sister, how deeply involved I am in the care of these precious beings." The practice of careful motherhood, moreover, was presented as the indispensable prerequisite for reform of church and community. Mothers, Goldschmidt insisted, must develop new approaches to child-rearing that emphasized religious tolerance rather than confessional narrowness. Rebekka appealed to Amalie's motherly sympathy for the suffering of Jewish children among a hostile peer group. "Oh, I wish I could tell you how the poor Jewish girl—for I will only speak of her—suffers under the cold, mistrustful glances that she encounters from all sides. . . .

That's why we place so much emphasis on intellectual achievement. We realize very early that we will have to show exceptional achievement to get even the smallest recognition." In 1848 Goldschmidt expanded her advice on child-rearing in a second book, *The Joys and Sorrows of Motherhood*. As Catherine Prelinger has pointed out, the Hamburg women thus established a strong connection between reformed child-rearing and a reformed public life before 1848.[22]

Revolution and Personal Transformation: The Response to 1848

The revolutionary events of 1848 brought the social, religious, and educational concerns of activist women into the political mainstream. As the sudden collapse of governments and the repeal of press censorship precipitated a ferment of political discussion, these and other women attempted to integrate their interest in new forms of authority, education, and social bonding, previously explored in the context of the family or of charitable pursuits, into the broader public issues of the era.

The connection between personal emancipation and new ideals of community at the beginning of organized feminism in 1848 may be seen in the reactions of the women who later became Froebel disciples to the events of 1848. In a tract written for her German Catholic congregation, Emilie Wüstenfeld deplored the "position of women in Hamburg," which failed "to meet the needs of those to whom the raising of the new generation is entrusted." Challenging the widespread prejudice that confined all the "thoughts and feelings" of women to the home, Wüstenfeld called for new forms of education and "the elevation of social life to a nobler level." Charlotte Paulsen intensified the commitment to charitable work that would result in the creation of a new organization, the Association for the Support of Poor Relief, in the next year.[23]

Bertha von Marenholtz-Bülow, who had recently separated from her husband, sought a new focus for her life. "My life had to make a new turn," she wrote in 1847. "I dared not hold what was yet so hard to lose. I knew I must relinquish the old life for a new one, though the new one should be full of fresh tortures. That to which moral dignity impels us must be right no matter what it may cost." She professed a "burning desire" for "some satisfying kind of work" and dedicated herself to some new, though as yet undefined, social mission. "I have been much used in life," she wrote, "used indeed for bitter work. But I have not been used in all the ways in which I could be serviceable. Therefore God must have destined me for something that is yet to come." The events of 1848 inspired her for the first time to establish a theoretical connection between her own personal situation and that of her class. Probably influenced by Saint-Simon's assertion that the archaic system of hereditary aristocracy must give way to the more dynamic and energetic rule of the new economic and scientific elites, she hailed the growth of the middle class as "one of the mightiest of revolutions" and the "mainspring of progress." She called on the nobility to forsake its "obsolete prejudices," which she condemned as "sins against the spirit of the age."[24]

Henriette Benas also responded to the liberating atmosphere of 1848 by taking major steps toward both personal autonomy and political awareness. As has already been mentioned, she had discovered her talent for pedagogy by taking care of the three children of her sister, who had died. Her widowed brother-in-law, impressed with her maternal skills, offered a marriage that her family considered very suitable. Unlike many of her older contemporaries, Benas, who had concluded that her affection for the children was not simply transferable to their father, was able to refuse a marriage of convenience. At the same time she protested another form of "obsolete prejudice," the social discrimination against Jews expressed through the exclusion of herself and her sister from a ball given by officers stationed in her area. Five years later, in 1853, she entered a freely chosen marriage to a liberal rabbi, Abraham Goldschmidt, and the couple's move to Warsaw prevented her from active involvement in public concerns until their move to Leipzig in 1859.[25]

Malwida von Meysenbug went to Frankfurt and followed the discussions of the Frankfurt Assembly eagerly, interpreting them as the realization of a new, secular ideal of salvation. Her interpretation of the revolutionary events was informed by her reading of materialist philosopher Ludwig Feuerbach (to whose thought she was first exposed by Theodor Althaus), who debunked supernatural beliefs as mere projections of earthly hopes and developed a secular morality based on the principles of love and human solidarity. Feuerbach's writings, which she had previously been forbidden to read, confirmed her already developed religious and political beliefs. "But these are the thoughts that I have had for a long time, only I never dared admit them." Unlike the church, which promised paradise, she wrote, democracy had undertaken a more difficult task: "It wanted to give people the earth, make it possible for them to lead a more worthwhile life down here." For Meysenbug, political and personal emancipation were linked. Her decision to take up a pedagogical career, reached during this period, was motivated by individualist strivings for self-fulfillment through economic independence and personal self-determination and by visions of new forms of community permitting a wider sphere of usefulness.[26]

The first of the six women actually to experience a new form of communal life was Henriette Breymann. That experience came as a result of her personal contact with Friedrich Froebel, her great-uncle on her mother's side. Breymann, like Meysenbug and Goldschmidt, faced the urgent problem of finding some alternative to a marriage of convenience. Her mother, perceiving the dissatisfaction of the restless girl who had watched her friends get married without herself receiving a suitable offer, for once asserted decision-making power in the patriarchal household. She gave her daughter permission to attend Froebel's institute for kindergarten training in the Thuringian town of Keilhau. In the institute, which was organized as an extended family of teachers, their spouses, students, and children, Breymann discovered values that were extremely different from those of her traditional family. Confessional differences were merged in a common acknowledgment of a God manifested through nature. The sexes associated with a degree of freedom and equality that was very unusual for the time; in fact, she soon began an intellectually and emotionally intense romantic relationship with a young instructor (culminating in an engagement that was later broken) without the supervision of her parents. In this community, Breymann found a profession, which gave her the intellectual and social independence—"the right to think and to use my mind"—that had been denied her in her father-dominated home. She conceived of her emancipation, however, not as a liberation from but as a reintegration into her family as a self-determining adult; her new profession, she wrote to her mother, gave her for the first time the opportunity to be "a good daughter and sister." By assigning a high status to the maternal role, Breymann had found a way to remain close to her mother while rejecting her mother's powerlessness. A resolve to endow the maternal ethic of nurture with transformative power, to "bring to the broader community a quality which until now has been entirely lacking—the spirit of motherhood in its deepest meaning and in its most varied forms," became the guiding principle of her life.[27]

Breymann reacted with mixed feelings to the revolutionary uprisings that occurred in the rural area of Thuringia where she was living. Her response to these events, though as yet immature, already showed the complex combination of feelings—sympathy, fear, cultural superiority, and pedagogical interest—that would shape her attitudes toward working-class people in later years. Lacking the intellectual sophistication of Marenholtz and Meysenbug, she was not fully acquainted with the utopian socialist ideas that were current among the French revolutionaries, but she approved of their striving for something which she vaguely designated as "communism," and wondered if they might, after all, be "the instruments of God." The rebellious peasants and artisans in her own area did not live up to this naively idealistic image, however; she criticized them (as Pestalozzi had condemned an earlier generation of revolutionaries) for what she considered their individualist "egotism" and lack of responsibility. She did not, however, deny the necessity for social change, but instead affirmed her own new profession, pedagogy, as a means toward peaceful evolutionary development. "Instead of all this empty talk about freedom," she wrote, "they should work to tear out the roots of evil—only then can the tree of freedom grow."[28]

The early lives of these six German women illustrate much the same process that has also been described in historical analyses of middle- and upper-class women in other countries. One such analysis is Barbara Berg's account of charitable organization among urban women in the United States, *The Remembered Gate: Origins of American Feminism*. Berg identifies charitable work as a crucial opportunity to escape from the household, to engage in public work, and ultimately to establish the roots of a feminist ideology and an organized feminist movement. Perhaps imposing assumptions derived from late twentieth-century feminism upon her material, Berg strongly implies that these women regarded private and public worlds as antithetical, and aspired chiefly to escape the one and enter the other. Once embarked on public work, she tells us, women renounced traditional ideals of female behavior and professed an ideology affirming that "woman, a complete and independent person . . . possessed a nature identical to man's." Linda Kerber's description of the ideology of "republican motherhood" as a basis for women's participation in civic culture challenges this simple antithesis and emphasizes the integral connection between women's private and public roles.[29]

The life stories and ideas of the German women described here show that in Germany, as in America, charitable work outide the home provided relief from the limitations of family life and the opportunity to forge the bonds of female solidarity upon which organized feminist movements were based. They also, however, suggest that many nineteenth-century women did not perceive the antitheses of home and world and of private and public spheres as these antitheses are often perceived by twentieth-century historians. They aspired not to leave the private sphere for the public sphere but to break down some of the public/private boundaries established by male-dominated society. Domestic roles, and especially child care, were not regarded in themselves as a form of oppression; oppression was attributed not to the work itself but to the power relations of the father-dominated household. Nor were maternal forms of behavior left behind by women entering the public sphere. On the contrary, the commitment to public work arose directly from the experience of private work and was inspired by the same ethical values. The next chapter will show how female reformers attempted to create new forms of community and civic culture that linked the reform of the family to the reform of society.

Chapter 3
Spiritual Motherhood and Revolution: The Beginnings of Organized Feminism, 1848–1852

The revolutionary period 1848–1849 witnessed a struggle for control of both private and public worlds. The challenge to the traditional power structure of church and state was accompanied by a challenge to the power structure of the family. The sudden emergence of this revolutionary discourse gave women such as the ones discussed in the preceding chapter the opportunity for which they had been searching—a legitimate context for the application of theoretical insights gained from private experience to public speech and action. "Reform, reform, everyone cries reform!" proclaimed an editorial in the best-known feminist periodical of this period, the *Frauen-Zeitung*. "'Reform the Church!' say the *Lichtfreunde* [a popular term for dissenting Protestants]. 'Reform the Constitution,' say the democrats. 'Reform society,' cry the socialists. We women should also raise our voices and demand, 'Reform the family.' For only the reform of the family will make the basic change possible, on which the reform of religion, society, and politics must depend."[1]

The search for new forms of authority and community was a central theme of mainstream political discourse in 1848. The liberals, the predominant political group among the revolutionaries, called for new political institutions that would limit monarchical authority through the guarantee of civil rights and liberty and through representative government. The creation of a new, national community through the reconciliation of regional, religious, and class differences was another goal of liberal reformers. The Frankfurt Assembly, a body composed of representatives of all the German states, was convened in May 1848, with unification and the creation of a liberal constitution at the center of its agenda. But liberals, most of whom belonged to the upper and middle classes, feared the results of class conflict that had erupted in popular uprisings in all parts of Germany. Liberals of this era, though they claimed to speak for "the people" and not for a specific class, were well aware that most working people did not support many of their goals. The working class, still composed chiefly of artisans, was especially hostile to liberals' advocacy of free enterprise, economic competition, and the removal of traditional constraints on industry. Class relations—the fear of conflict, the hope for reconciliation—was thus a central theme of political discourse.

During these years, the subject of child-rearing—one of the very few on which women could speak with any authority—provided a philosophical and metaphorical basis for women's discussion of most of these topics, including politics, class relations, and social and religious issues. The traditional form of the family had rested on the same basic idea of authority as the traditional state—the authority of the fatherly, enlightened ruler. Theorists such as Pestalozzi and Froebel had developed a conceptual link between a new form of the family, centered on maternal love rather than paternal discipline, and new forms of the state based on unity of feeling rather than authority. Women's status as mothers, whether biological or "spiritual," often legitimated their entry into public speech and activity. Female activists of this period sometimes differentiated between two ideals of "emancipation," one centered on individual rights, the other on maternal service. The great majority of German feminists of this period, however, did not see these two forms of ideology as antithetical, but linked individualist and communitarian ideals. As their life stories have shown, individual self-determination, whether in intellectual, religious, or personal choices, was immensely important to these women. But from the beginning they envisaged their individual self-fulfillment in the context of new forms of community, for which the utopian theories of the period had provided some models. As a basis of their social vision, most feminists used an ideal model of the family, now governed not by paternal authority but by maternal love. The statement of Louise Otto that "emancipation is not just a right but a duty" can only be understood in the context of these utopian aspirations toward new forms of social harmony. A major theme of this chapter will be the efforts of these female reformers to build institutions that exemplified these new ideals of community life.[2]

The Revolution and the Kindergarten Movement

The first attempt to create institutions that linked innovations in child-rearing to the creation of new forms of social and political life was the kindergarten movement. Transplanted from the village society of Thuringia to several cities, including Berlin, Hamburg, and Breslau, the movement provided a new model of female activism that aimed at social reform rather than works of individual charity. The kindergarten founders responded to the class conflict caused by the decline and impoverishment of the small-town artisan class, the growth of an urban proletariat, and the economic crises of the 1840s. Earlier forms of institutional child care, which originated in the German-speaking world in the 1820s and 1830s, had been straightforward attempts to contain the threat of working-class violence by the maintenance of traditional forms of child-rearing. Female kindergarten founders were haunted by some of the same fears and shared some of the same prejudices as other early childhood educators. But a comparison of the kindergarten to its conservative rival, the infant school, will show that the new institution was not just another effort toward social control, but in some ways also a challenge to traditional ideas of class hierarchy and political authority. Some kindergarten founders aimed to prevent and remedy, rather than reinforce, class polarization, and used kindergarten theory as a utopian ideology of class reconciliation.[3]

The concern of social reformers with early childhood education was a response to the perceived breakdown of traditional forms of child-rearing, especially among working-class families uprooted from rural communities and newly settled in growing cities. Many of the new child care initiatives were prompted by middle-class disapproval of working-class parents' approach to child-rearing. The urban working class had not yet adopted the protective, home-centered, and pedagogically involved child-rearing methods that had become popular in the homes of the upper and middle classes. Urban working-class children grew up on the streets, receiving a considerable portion of their socialization from informal contacts with age mates and with adults other than parents. Middle-class reformers of all persuasions agreed on a central problem—working-class *Strassenkindheit* ("street childhood"). They also shared a central aim—to compensate for what they perceived as a breakdown of family control through institutional forms of child care.[4]

In the period from 1820 to 1848, infant schools, or *Bewahranstalten*, had been founded in many German cities. Most of these were controlled by religious authorities or by groups of citizens with an explicitly religious orientation. Although often founded through the initiative of philanthropic groups of women, these institutions were usually administered by all-male boards of directors, who assigned chiefly menial tasks to women volunteers. The explicit intention of the infant-school societies was to restore the values of the father-headed family and the spirit of deference, obedience, and inward-turning piety that it had reinforced. Admissions policies affirmed the legitimacy of this private, family-centered form of child-rearing by limiting services to children of the very poor, whose parents were unable to care for them. Head teachers were usually male, and their role was described by one of the larger infant-school societies, the Berlin Society for the Support of Day-Care Centers, as that of a "Christian foster-father." Many of the religious day care centers based their pedagogy firmly on the traditional doctrine of original sin. Children who, because of overcrowding and inadequate supervision, were forced to sit still for long periods of time were kept busy memorizing Bible verses and singing hymns that stressed obedience, humility, and the fear of God. The moving deathbed scenes that filled the yearly reports of the infant-school societies suggested that the pious deaths, rather than the energetic lives, of pupils were the chief testimony to the schools' pedagogical effectiveness. Protestant pastor Theodor Fliedner substituted more appealing songs and games for this severe routine and used women rather than men as teachers; he set up an institution to train deaconesses as nursery school teachers in 1836. But he retained the conventional belief in original sin and emphasis on religious training.[5]

The Froebelian kindergarten departed from this pattern. The very selection of a new name, "kindergarten," had signaled a break with traditional early childhood education. Many kindergartens were intended for children of all classes, not just of the poor, and their pedagogical approach emphasized constructive play, self-development, and training in the values of citizenship. Perhaps the most controversial aspect of this new instititution was its approach to religious training, which emphasized interdenominational tolerance rather than confessional orthodoxy. Chiefly because of this challenge to the control of churches over early childhood education, Froebel's pedagogy had found few adherents since the opening of the first kindergarten in 1839. But in 1848, when the seeming collapse of political authority structures had suddenly opened the way for reform in many areas, including education, the kindergarten experiment attracted a great deal of interest among progressive educators. Froebel, encouraged by this newfound support, summoned a meeting of teachers to the town of Rudolstadt, near Keilhau, where they witnessed demonstrations of kindergarten methods by the young women who were students at his kindergarten-training institute.[6]

At this meeting, both the role of women and class relations became controversial issues. In the German-speaking world of this period, unlike the United States and England, the teaching profession, even at the elementary level, was almost entirely male. Some of the teachers expressed approval of the new method but objected to the involvement of women as professional teachers. "Froebel expects that his kindergartens will be led by women—that his philosophical ideas will be carried out by women. I have a horror of philosophical women," declared one delegate. This remark aroused protest among the women present. Johanna Küstner, a teacher who later married Friedrich Froebel's nephew Carl Froebel, responded that women should be treated as "complete persons, who were also capable of philosophical education." Henriette Breymann, then a student at the institute, expostulated to her diary, "We should do nothing but serve men, they should dominate us, and without them we are nothing? . . . I was happy from the bottom of my heart . . . that Froebel and Middendorff think so very differently about women . . . that they believe in our worth."[7]

A majority of the teachers agreed to send a petition to the Frankfurt Assembly, which was then in session, recommending the incorporation of kindergarten education into public school systems. The petition advocated neither the participation of female teachers nor the mixing of classes in the kindergarten. Instead, it praised the benefits of the kindergarten to the children of the urban working class who entered school "neglected in body and mind, already little beggars, liars, and thieves." Breymann, who objected to the teachers' class as well as gender prejudices, complained in a letter to her parents that they were attempting to distort Froebel's ideas "and to make the kindergarten into a kind of infant school."[8]

Because this petition was not successful—neither in 1848 nor later in the nineteenth century were kindergartens incorporated into most German public school systems—the kindergarten developed as a private institution. Such a structure, though obviously limiting possibilities for growth, nonetheless gave more scope to female leadership than would have been possible in the male-dominated school hierarchies. Although kindergartens, like other preschool insititutions, sometimes had male boards of directors, the actual day-to-day classroom activities were supervised by professionally trained female teachers. Whereas the infant school had reflected the values of the father-headed household, the kindergarten offered to its female teachers a zone of autonomy similar to the mother-centered home. The practical application of Froebel's theories by women teachers required the interpretation, criticism, and revision of Froebel's methods, which the young Henriette Breymann declared were too abstract and mathematical to be of much use in the classroom.[9]

The pedagogical approach of the first female kindergarten teachers (at least according to their own accounts) was based on the Pestalozzian idea of the mother-child bond as the source of learning, morality, and social relationships. Advice literature written by women who were sympathetic to the kindergarten movement advocated an approach to discipline that was attuned to the child's individual character. Doris Lütkens, who later set up the first kindergarten in Hamburg, published an advice column for mothers in a publication entitled *Unsere Kinder* ("Our Children"). To a mother who was concerned about her child's imitation of the bad habits of his schoolmates, Lütkens replied that a child could not be restrained by "external rules, but only by the ennoblement of his inner life," and advised the mother to shape the child's character through undersanding and sympathy rather than through coercive discipline. A familial culture that stressed intense involvement in the child's individual development was transferred to the classroom. Alwine, the daughter of Froebel's close collaborator, Wilhelm Middendorff, was invited by Lütkens to lead a kindergarten in Hamburg. Her description of a typical teaching day was composed of accounts of individual children whose restlessness, even in its most troublesome forms, she understood as the expression of potentially healthy energy rather than of sinful energy. "Karl is the embodiment of restlessness, he never finds it possible to be still and attentive. . . . The child has so much life, but it is so constrained by exterior circumstances. I don't yet know how to release and channel it." The right approach to such disiplinary problems, she reflected, could only arise from an understanding of each individual; when children follow "the desires of their hearts, we can follow them too . . . and understand them with the clear consciousness of an awakened one."[10]

Women's discussions of the purpose and methods of the kindergarten often used this miniature world as a metaphor for their more general ideas about citizenship, social responsibility, and new forms of community. Kindergarten pedagogy was designed to raise a new generation of Germans as citizens, not as subjects. The Froebel games directed the child's natural energy into contributions to the common good. Unlike that of the infant school, the kindergarten's discipline stressed not obedience to authority but the active participation of the individual child in what Lütkens termed a "community of play" (*Spielgemeinschaft*). The kindergarten, said Lütkens, was a social organism in microcosm, "in which they [the children] can satisfy their drive for activity, under expert leadership, without falling into anti-social behavior." In this miniature utopia, individual and social interests were ideally in perfect harmony. The child, wrote Lütkens, "feels free, the child acts and creates, the child gives and receives, the child feels stimulated and supported, the child feels discipline only as a beneficial force . . . and that is what pure, innocent and uncorrupted childish nature requires for growth."[11]

This picture of the kindergarten as preparation for a new form of national community, or *Gemeinschaft*, was made more explicitly political by Alwine Middendorff's father, Wilhelm Middendorff, who submitted to the Frankfurt Assembly a petition probably based in part on observation of his daughter's kindergarten. Middendorff cited his liberal contemporaries' criticism of the private and unpolitical values of a people accustomed to authoritarian government. "We often complain that we Germans have a tendency to keep to ourselves, to cut ourselves off from other people, and should we not nip this problem in the bud by bringing up children in a community?" He praised the kindergarten as an environment where "children of rich and poor, of upper and lower classes, of Jews and Christians play together." Middendorff praised the Froebel games, many of which were designed to introduce the child to adult work skills, for overcoming the "egotistical" isolation of the middle-class home and encouraging social responsibility. "A girl has built a model of the Town Hall," wrote Middendorff in a description of his daughter's classroom. "Her father goes there every day and has told her about how other men also go there to discuss political matters. So she is glad to hear the song.

> Here the city councilmen
> Represent the citizen.
> They watch out for you and me,
> Also for our property.[12]

By urging governmental sponsorship of kindergarten education, Middendorff expressed a theory of the state which was central to the development of German liberalism in 1848. Since the early nineteenth century, liberal theorists had developed a model of the liberal state, known as the *Rechtsstaat*, which required an active role for government not just in protecting individual freedoms but in positively encouraging a sense of community. According to Middendorff, the kindergarten promoted this ideal of freedom within community by working against selfish "laziness, pleasure-seeking, lack of understanding and willpower" and by stimulating the child's "early instinct for self-activity . . . to vigorous exercise."[13]

The establishment of kindergartens open to children of all classes was a conspicuous expression of the revolutionary spirit among women in several communities. Prelinger estimates that thirty-one Froebel kindergartens were set up in German towns and cities, many if not all of which were open to children of all social backgrounds. The women of the German Catholic congregation of Breslau announced in 1850 that they had set up "the first kindergarten where the children of middle-class and proletarian parents are accepted. We lay a lot of stress on this, and expect that in all the kindergartens, that we hope will develop here, we can follow this democratic principle." Likewise in Hamburg, in addition to the two original kindergartens founded in 1849, which charged tuition and were thus accessible only to middle-class children, several "Citizens' Kindergartens" (*Bürgerkindergärten*) were founded in 1850 which charged lower fees and thus made possible "for less wealthy children what originally had been available only to the rich." Because kindergartens, dependent upon private subsidies, were forced to charge at least some tuition and kept children for only four hours per day, one can imagine (no figures are available) that they served few really poor children. But this was only a beginning—the development of child-care services for urban families, begun during this period, would continue to be an important area of activity for female social reformers.[14]

Thus the women who became active in the kindergarten movement expressed in this still very limited field of activity a wider vision of social change that included the reform of both family and society. Their belief in "spiritual motherhood" as a principle of class reconciliation, though certainly idealistic, cannot be dismissed as a sentimental fantasy; it was, in fact, very much in tune with the political climate of this era. As historian Jürgen Reulecke has pointed out in his history of the first general organization devoted to social reform, the Centralverein für das Wohl der arbeitenden Klassen (Central Association for the Welfare of the Working Classes), founded in 1844, bourgeois social reformers of the 1840s did not see class division and conflict as inevitable. Instead, they often believed that the process of proletarianization could be arrested through measures promoting education, self-help, and improved material conditions among workers. Although this idea clearly contained elements of class prejudice, it also found some support among workers themselves. The elite of the working class, still composed of artisans, who themselves feared the loss of skills, independence, and social status, sometimes shared such hopes.[15]

Education and Utopia

The kindergarten movement had translated the theory of "spiritual motherhood" as a force for social change into practice. It had created an ideology encouraging social activism and justifying educational roles for women outside the family. The most famous insitution that promoted these ideals during this period was the Hamburg Academy for Women (Hochschule für das weibliche Geschlecht), founded in 1850 by a group of Hamburg women including Emilie Wüstenfeld and Johanna Goldschmidt. This educational institution initially based its curriculum largely on the ideas of Friedrich Froebel and of his nephew, Carl, both of whom taught at the school for a brief period. The story of the Hamburg Academy, like that of the kindergarten, shows the blending of individualist and communitarian ideas of emancipation among feminists of this era. Many of the women who supported this educational experiment saw the institution as a means to both pursue their own personal and professional goals and create a new and utopian form of community.

One of the most enthusiastic proponents of the kindergarten in Hamburg was Emilie Wüstenfeld. Gravely disappointed by the narrowly confessional orientation of existing charitable organizations, she was receptive to a cause that seemed to promote an active role for women in social reform. Wüstenfeld and Charlotte Paulsen, both of whom were members of the dissenting religious sect known as the German Catholics, had formed an organization, the Soziale Verein (Social Association), designed to bring Christian and Jewish women together. A prominent member of this organization was Johanna Goldschmidt, already well known for her reform activities and for her publications on child care and on religious questions. In 1849, the association met at Wüstenfeld's house to celebrate the political emancipation of the Jews in Hamburg. The women decided to devote themselves to a common philanthropic undertaking, the encouragement of kindergarten education.[16]

To this end, they decided to invite Friedrich Froebel, whose acquaintance Johanna Goldschmidt had made through her writings on motherhood, to lead a kindergarten-training course in Hamburg. Shortly thereafter, Wüstenfeld and her friend Bertha Meyer Traun, who were already convinced of the need for improved higher education for women, received a proposal from Froebel's nephew, Carl Froebel, and his wife, Johanna Küstner Froebel, for the founding of a *Hochschule*, or academy, for the higher education of women, based partly on Friedrich Froebel's teachings. In 1849 the Frauenbildungsverein (Society for the Education of Women), an organization created from a merger of the Social Union and the Society for the Support of the German-Catholic congregations, sent Wüstenfeld and Traun to Zurich to meet Carl and Johanna Froebel and decided subsequently to invite them to Hamburg. This led to complications—Friedrich Froebel did not wish to work with his nephew, of whose principles he disapproved—but nonetheless the Hamburg Academy for Women was opened in January 1850.[17]

The founding of the Academy shows the increasingly active role of women in shaping intellectual discourse as well as in building institutions. Intellectual life, of course, was still male-dominated, and even feminists such as the Hamburg women looked to men such as Friedrich and Carl Froebel for leadership. However, the women also used and promoted these men to advance their own agenda. Johanna Goldschmidt had persuaded her friend Adolph Diesterweg, a prominent and influential figure in the male educational establishment, to make Friedrich Froebel's acquaintance. When Friedrich Froebel was invited to Hamburg, Diesterweg, who had become a strong supporter of the kindergarten, predicted that women would save Froebel's ideas from oblivion. "I am worried about him," Diesterweg wrote to Goldschmidt. "Most men will not understand him or support his ideas. Women must save him." Likewise, Carl Froebel was an obscure figure until the Hamburg women decided to adopt his ideas. Diesterweg, who himself had been enlisted into the cause of kindergarten education through his friendship with Goldschmidt, wrote of the Society for the Education of Women, "The fact that the organization was founded by women, and that only women (in some rare cases assisted by men) belong to it is remarkable. . . . If one remembers our German housewives, one immediately sees signs of our changing times."[18]

The news of this experiment in women's education, which soon spread throughout the German-speaking world, was greeted with delight by Malwida von Meysenbug. Meysenbug, who had briefly observed the Frankfurt Assembly, found that her political views made return to her family impossible and saw this as an opportunity to gain the independence she so profoundly craved. "One must free oneself from the authority of one's family," she wrote, "painful as the process may be. . . . Freedom of individual convictions and a life in conformity with them—this is the first right and duty of a human being." Like Henriette Breymann, Meysenbug received some support from her mother in her bid for independence. Meysenbug immediately found herself warmly welcomed by a community of like-minded women, including Wüstenfeld, the head of the Academy. "She received me most heartily and, as she explained her plans, I saw that my dreams would take shape here," Meysenbug recollected. "The college was founded on the principle of making possible the economic independence of woman through her development as a being complete in herself and capable of growing in her own way."[19]

The story of the Hamburg Academy for Women has been well told by Catherine N. Prelinger; thus, no detailed description of its curriculum and faculty politics is necessary here. But it is important to see this educational experiment not only in the religious context of German Catholic theology as outlined by Prelinger but in the broader and more secular context of the utopian socialist ideas of this period. The pamphlet submitted to the Hamburg Society for Women's Education by Johanna and Carl Froebel, which served as the basis for the institution's curriculum, was based on a synthesis of ideas taken from the Pestalozzian educational tradition and from the French utopians, especially Saint-Simon and his German disciples. Saint-Simon and his followers searched for a new principle of social harmony to supersede the chaos and violence of the 1789 revolution. Claiming that the history of the human race was structured in alternating critical and organic periods, they saw the present age as marking a transition from revolutionary violence to new forms of association based on love and cooperation. Carl Froebel identified the family as the source of this new spirit, describing it as a form of association that transcended the coercive law of the state and created a higher law of freely accepted and loving community.[20]

Like Pestalozzi and Friedrich Froebel, however, Carl Froebel declared existing forms of the family inadequate to inspire the regeneration of society. To the German-speaking educators' ideas about the ideal function of the family, he added a new awareness of the effects of urbanization and industrialization on family structure, particularly among the working classes. "For whole classes of society family life has been destroyed," he stated, "and this is especially true of our proletarians, who are only exploited to enable others to develop, while they themselves are condemned to physical and intellectual starvation." Existing educational institutions, he claimed, merely contributed to social fragmentation by separating children from families, and upper from lower classes. The task of creating a new harmonious social order he thus assigned to a reconstituted educational system, which would operate through loving communities of students and teachers. For Carl Froebel the proposed institution for women's higher education represented an example of this new approach to education.[21]

This approach was based on a view of woman's nature that reflected the Saint-Simonian ideal of gender equality as the cooperation of opposing but complemetary male and female principles, symbolized by a religious cult centered on a divine couple. Carl and Johanna Froebel, although insisting that the sexes were "completely equal," assigned them very different intellectual characteristics. They identified the creation of abstract knowledge as masculine and its practical application and transmission to others as feminine. However, this distinction between male and female aptitudes implied no derogation of female intelligence. As disciples of Pestalozzi, the Froebels criticized traditional, or "masculine," academic learning and exalted practical, motherly wisdom and the female communicative skills that transmitted this cultural heritage to the younger generation.[22]

These female skills found their outlet in the kindergarten, portrayed by Johanna Froebel as a miniature utopian community where the child was treated "not simply as an individual, but as a member of society" and where "every activity, every thought and every feeling that the child experiences as an individual in the family, he/she shares with many companions." For Johanna Küstner Froebel, as for many other kindergarten advocates of this period, the association among children of different classes in the kindergarten was a means of overcoming class conflict through the spirit of love. When conservative Hamburg philanthropist Amalie Sieveking objected that the new form of early childhood education would lead to social disruption by removing poor children from their proper spheres, Johanna Froebel responded, "What exactly is the sphere of the poor child? And are there, in fact, different spheres for rich and poor children? We have now touched on what is called the social question. . . . If it is not to be solved through bloody revolution, then we must resolve it through education." Though commonly carried out within the family, she specified, this nurturing function must also be placed on a professional basis and given a public application in educational institutions. This was an important addition to Froebel's theory, which while affirming women's pedagogical abilities had not advocated their use in paid work. Because of the control of public schools, even at the elementary level, by a male-dominated teaching profession, the opening of kindergarten teaching, and the teaching of kindergarten training courses, to women served an important practical purpose.[23]

The Hamburg experiment in higher education for women thus sought to realize all of these ideas through a curriculum offering academic training in subjects such as philosophy, literature, mathematics, and kindergarten pedagogy, combined with practical work in a kindergarten supervised by Friedrich Froebel. The brief history of the school suggests that the students found the experience of living in a female community as stimulating as the curriculum itself. Meysenbug, who has left us the fullest account, found the lectures exciting and her practice teaching in the kindergarten delightful. Students who, like Meysenbug herself, came from areas outside Hamburg, were lodged in a boarding house supervised by Johanna Froebel. When Meysenbug was promoted by Wüstenfeld to the position of codirector of the school, she temporarily took over the management of the boarding home from Johanna Froebel. She insisted that the boarders spare expenses by participating in household tasks, including laundry. Like the utopian socialists, she assigned both practical and moral importance to physical labor. "Once a week, we stood in the garden around a washtub, and while our hands were rubbing clothes, we discussed subjects from the lectures or some other important questions. . . . We did the rough work because it was for the good of the college . . . and we did not feel humiliated by it because even the most menial work, when it is a duty, is ennobling." Meysenbug also committed herself to such communal values as religious tolerance and social solidarity by joining a German Catholic congregation and making contact with workers' organizations.[24]

In fact, this exhilarating experience seems to have stimulated the students to dissatisfaction with their teachers' rather limited view of female education. Johanna Froebel, who had expected to supervise young girls, was apparently uncomfortable as head of a community including mature women. After their initial enthusiasm, students expressed dissatisfaction with both Friedrich and Carl Froebel, complaining that the former gave disorganized and incomprehensible lectures and that the latter often went to sleep during classes. Moreover, the enthusiasm of the women students for "abstract" subjects such as mathematics appears to have alienated some of the eminent male observers and participants, including Friedrich Froebel, who departed in evident disapproval, and Diesterweg, who complained that "a know-it-all, critical, argumentative woman is a specter to frighten all healthy souls." By 1850, the revolutionary goals of 1848, including the unification of Germany and the creation of a liberal constitution, had clearly been defeated. In the atmosphere of reaction and counterrevolution that pervaded Hamburg, the nonconfessional and diverse religious climate of the school and the outspoken democratic sympathies of some of the faculty and students provoked increasing criticism. Responding to the decrease in financial support and the threat of official action, the founders of the school decided to close it voluntarily in 1852; it had lasted less than two years.[25]

Though the hopes of the revolutionary period were soon dashed, the Hamburg experiment exerted an important influence on later feminists. It is thus important that the radicalism of this institution was derived from a utopian and communitarian ideology, which aimed not to assimilate women to male roles but, on the contrary, to use distinctively female skills and capacities in the service of a broadly conceived social mission. The utopian ideology of the Hamburg Academy shows that the feminist theory of this period, like many other currents of thought, had as its central theme the dialectical relationship of antitheses—paternal authority and maternal love. Though aspiring to freedom from patriarchal authority, the women of the Academy did not aim at the dissolution of family into separate individuals. Rather, they envisioned the breakdown of paternal authority as the liberation of its antithesis, maternal love, which would then become the basis for a new form of harmony and wholeness.

In nineteenth-century Germany, although women's teacher-training institutions did develop, there were no women's liberal arts colleges, and German women had to wait until the 1890s or even, in Prussia, until 1908 to gain admission to male-dominated universities. The Hamburg Academy professed goals that were comparable to those of some early American women's colleges, such as Mount Holyoke, which were set up to train women as teachers. However, the access of American women even during this early period to teaching careers in the public school system gave them distinct educational and professional advantages over their German counterparts, who were largely limited to careers in private early childhood institutions and girls' private schools.[26]

Maternal and Individualist Feminism during the Revolutionary Period

The development of both the kindergarten and the Hamburg Academy must, of course, be seen in the context of a much broader debate about the content, meaning, and purpose of feminist ideology. In histories of feminism in the German-speaking world, 1848 is often given as the date of the first emergence of equal-rights feminism. The most cogent expression of this form of feminism was the best-known feminist periodical of the era, the *Frauen-Zeitung*, founded by Leipzig journalist and author Louise Otto in 1849. The editors of a collection of excerpts from this periodical hail Otto and her coworkers as pioneers of modern feminism but find it strange and even "irritating" that, in addition to their advocacy of rights in the public sphere, these feminists also praised the maternal role as an important basis for women's ethical values and social mission. Louise Otto and other feminists of the period, however, did not perceive the relationship between individualistic and maternal arguments as contradictory. On the contrary, they usually regarded the communitarian ideal of "spiritual motherhood" as the fulfillment rather than the denial of women's striving for autonomy. A comparison between the ideas of the kindergarten advocates and those of the contributors to the *Frauen-Zeitung* during its brief existence from 1849 to 1852 will show how feminists of many different shades of opinion intertwined these two kinds of argument.[27]

Many writers for the *Frauen-Zeitung*, while attacking the oppression of women within the family, did not see the maternal role in itself as an aspect of such oppression, but on the contrary as a basis for claims to improved educational opportunities and social status for women. In her autobiographical writing, Otto presented a picture of her childhood and her relationship to her own mother that justified this high estimation of the maternal role. Otto, who was born in Meissen in 1819, grew up in a household that was still a self-contained economic unit. As the supervisor of such a household, she recalled, a woman needed many forms of knowledge and skill. "A woman was, in fact, one of the most useful members of society. . . . The good housewife and manager gained a legitimate honor, and the incompetent one was justly scorned." Otto later used this vanishing form of the household as a symbol of community; women, she recalled nostalgically, had been united in common tasks, and families had enjoyed evenings at home more than expeditions to places of public entertainment. Otto's positive regard for the domestic role was expressed through her decision to publish many essays, some of which she had written herself, demanding increased respect for motherhood. Nothing could be more misguided, wrote a regular correspondent identified only as "Georgine," than the belief that "a woman needs only training in household skills in order to fulfill her domestic duties"; the pedagogical demands of motherhood required "intellectual elevation" that "teaches her [the mother] to recognize her most exalted duties and to counteract the prejudices that bind us." The reform of the private sphere was linked to the reform of society. "Unity gives strength," wrote a contributor to the journal, "the family must become strong . . . for the reform of the entire nation depends on the reform of the family."[28]

Otto admired the Froebel kindergarten movement and publicized it actively in the *Frauen-Zeitung*. As Prelinger has explained, Otto had strong German Catholic sympathies and ties to the Hamburg congregation. Her support of the kindergarten movement was also related to the most important and constantly repeated theme of her feminist campaign—the demand for work opportunities for unmarried women. Otto's conception of female employment opportunities, which included industrial and craft work, was not limited to kindergarten teaching. But she stressed the importance of education as a professional opportunity as well as a social mission for women. Many essays in the journal praised the Froebel kindergarten-training system and advocated the establishment of institutes for the training of children's nurses, governesses, and teachers. This service-oriented ideal of female professionalism, of which the kindergarten movement provided one of the earliest examples, could be understood as an adaptation to limited opportunities in a society where more lucrative professions were restricted to men. However, Otto and her colleagues emphasized not the limitations but the potential power of women's role in "the reform of education by the female sex."[29]

The search for professional opportunities was linked to another important individualist argument—the opposition to marriages of convenience and the advocacy of free matrimonial choice. As we have seen, feminists of this period regarded the right to choose a marital partner or to remain unmarried as absolutely essential. What was often termed the "freedom of the heart," however, was advocated not just as an individual right, but as a basis for a wider sphere of usefulness than was provided by the household. Henriette Breymann, who had avoided a marriage of convenience, reflected that Froebel's course had enabled her "even outside of marriage . . . to work with understanding and conscious purpose, for the ennoblement of the human race." Bertha von Marenholtz-Bülow's decision to live apart from her husband, although certainly motivated by an individualistic resistance to the painful indignities of a loveless marriage, was also part of a search for a broader form of social commitment.[30]

Still more controversial was the association of the Froebel movement with radical views of divorce, for the two most active founders of the Hamburg Academy, Emilie Wüstenfeld and Bertha Meyer Traun, showed their new sense of religious and ethical autonomy by dissolving unhappy marriages. They viewed this personal liberation not simply as an end in itself but as a means toward the development of their social mission. When her divorced friend Bertha Traun married German Catholic leader Johannes Ronge and departed for England, Wüstenfeld cautioned the couple not to retreat into private happiness but to continue their involvement in the community. Bertha Ronge, in fact, introduced the Froebel kindergarten system into her new country, and her sister Margarethe, who married German exile Carl Schurz, introduced the system to the United States.[31]

The relationship of individual desire to familial responsibility was a cause of controversy. The scandal resulting from the Wüstenfeld and Traun divorces, which had offended some contributors, had been a major cause of the closing of the Hamburg Academy. Kindergarten advocates, who exalted the "holy trinity" of mother, father, and child, did not usually support their radical contemporaries' demand for the abolition of all laws regulating marriage and divorce. In a response to feminist author Luise Dittmar's advocacy of free divorce, Johanna Froebel raised both theoretical and practical objections. Women, she argued, should work for private and public harmony rather than discord, and the welfare of children required some legal protection of the marital bond. She insisted, however, that young women should train for professions in order to attain the economic independence that would allow them to wait for the partner with whom they could experience marital and parental love in its highest form. Thus, in her view, the integrity of the individual was not at odds with that of the family, but a prerequisite for it. All of these views of marriage, despite their differences, linked individual freedom of choice to a wider conception of a purified social ethic promoting private and public harmony.[32]

Opposed to this maternal ethic of love and service was the image of the "emancipated woman," negatively portrayed by Otto as the "caricature of a man." The model for this picture of a woman who aspired to imitate male behavior was clearly George Sand, the French novelist who had become famous in Germany even more for her masculine dress and romantic adventures than for her novels. The rejection of Sand's example, often mingled with sympathy for the woman herself, was sometimes justified by the practical argument that, under existing conditions, such individualistic and self-realizing behavior must lead to disaster. Bertha von Marenholtz-Bülow, while admiring Sand as embodying "a vision of a new world which is ready to be born," commented that the French writer's expectations exceeded "the limits of what is at present attainable." But another reason for this skeptical attitude toward "emancipation" was that Sand's freedom seemed purely individualistic, extending only to the private forms of behavior such as sexuality and dress, without wider social applications. Otto criticized her female contemporaries who affected male manners and dress for preferring a show of political radicalism that could only be superficial and inauthentic. She urged a more substantial show of commitment though service.[33]

Henriette Breymann, although wrestling with her envy of male freedom, likewise championed a distinctively female ethic. Her aim, she wrote to her pastor father, was not to imitate men, but to resurrect images of female and motherly power that the Protestant tradition had suppressed. "We have lost our good Mother Nature," she explained, "and her daughter Mary, the mother of Jesus. In Protestantism we have only the Father and the Son, and that is why women have been given a status that is wrong for them. . . . Froebel doesn't want to make women like men, but to make them into real women and good mothers, and if he succeeds, men will benefit, too." Although some historians have regarded maternal ideologies as male-identified, and individualistic ones as truly feminist, many women of this period seem to have made the reverse judgment, identifying individualism as an imitative, and "spiritual motherhood" as an autonomously female and thus feminist ideal.[34]

The chief difference between Otto's ideas and those of most of the kindergarten advocates was in their attitudes toward political rights. While Otto demanded full equality with men in the rights of citizenship (although she did not mention suffrage in the *Frauen-Zeitung*), most kindergarten founders, although critical of many aspects of women's legal and social status, did not make such political claims. They justified their hesitation to demand full rights of citizenship by arguing that citizenship required responsibilities that women, so long trapped in menial tasks and deprived of education, were not equipped to perform. Mere "external" rights without the "moral strength" derived from a sense of social responsibility, stated Johanna Froebel, could have little effect on women's status. Otto's seeming retreat from her political demands was certainly due in part to the reimposition of press censorship in 1850, which made the advocacy of radical political views dangerous. But even before the reimposition of censorship, Otto had reflected sadly that attempts to win full rights of citizenship for both men and women had been premature. "We have learned," she wrote in 1849, "how we should really make a revolution, not by building barricades and through a few days of fighting in the streets—not through a fit of enthusiasm which can last only a few hours, but through the peaceful conversion of the entire population to democratic values." Thus, by arguing that citizenship could not simply be conferred by legal fiat but must be cultivated through the education of a new generation, Otto established an important link between the ideology of equal rights and that of "spiritual motherhood."[35]

In the revolutionary period, German women used the maternal role as a legitimation for their first major entry into public life, through social reform, institution-building, and political activism. As in earlier periods, women thought and acted within the constraints of a dominant discourse on motherhood, family, and state that they could adapt, but not wholly reject. Their activity during this period must therefore be understood as both an adaptation to the limitations of this discourse and an exploration of its possibilities. The limitations were clear—the public sphere of action permitted to women was exceedingly narrow. Even in the field of pedagogy, in which they claimed a legitimate authority, their activities were limited by a male-dominated educational establishment to early childhood education and to the private education of women. By accepting these limits, women adopted what Linda Kerber has described as a "deferential" approach to politics. However, women also played an increasingly active role in shaping discourse on domestic life, society, and politics. Although paying formal tribute to the ideas of men such as Pestalozzi and the Froebels, women freely made use of the ideas, and sometimes of the men themselves, to advance their own agendas. The topic of child-rearing, one of the few on which women's authority was recognized, often provided a metaphorical framework for a broader discussion of political and social issues. A fundamental metaphor was the mother-child bond, in which the origin of the child's individuality was in a human relationship. Such institutions as the kindergartens and the Hamburg Academy may be seen as attempts to create forms of community in which self and other, individual freedom and social harmony, were reconciled.[36]

A comparison of events in Germany and America during this period seems at first glance to show a sharp contrast between the American and German feminist movements, but there were also many underlying similarities. The women of the Seneca Falls Convention, in their adaptation of the American Declaration of Independence, used the rhetoric of "inalienable rights," and one of their demands was for suffrage, an issue even the *Frauen-Zeitung* had not raised. In part, this difference reflects the differing political structures of the two societies. As historian Ellen Carol DuBois has shown, the fact that all white American men already possessed the franchise encouraged their female fellow-citizens to demand it. Universal male suffrage in the German states was still no more than a controversial idea which, although incorporated in the constitution drawn up by the Frankfurt Assembly, was not supported even by the majority of liberals. Even in the democratic American context, women's claim to suffrage was widely regarded as an unacceptably radical demand. American feminists shared with their German counterparts a history of developing political consciousness through involvement in community and philanthropic work, culminating for the Americans in the Abolitionist movement, which aimed at the abolition of slavery. Many of the grievances expressed in the Seneca Falls Declaration—at the disadvantaged position of women in the churches, at their lack of educational and employment opportunities, at their oppression by laws regulating marriage, divorce, and guardianship, and at other constraints on their personal liberty—closely resembled similar issues raised by the German feminists. Moreover, like the Germans, the Americans emphasized both rights and duties. The Resolutions passed by the Seneca Falls Convention asserted not only the right to the franchise but "the right and duty of woman, equally with men, to promote every righteous cause by every righteous means."[37]

Chapter 4
The Great Social Household: The Kindergarten and Women's Mission, 1850–1864

The utopian ideals of 1848 were soon deflated by the failure of the revolution and the imposition of new restrictions on women's political activities and on educational institutions. As the work of Charlotte Paulsen, Bertha von Marenholtz-Bülow, and Henriette Breymann during this period will show, however, female reformers persisted in their work amid adverse circumstances. When forced to give up the prospect of immediate and wide-ranging change, they formulated more practical plans that, although accepting some existing limitations, did not lose sight of long-term objectives. In this process, the female kindergarten advocates made an important contribution to the creation of a public and professional role for women based on "spiritual motherhood." In the liberalized climate of the early 1860s, this conception of women's public mission was a central influence on the further evolution of feminist movements.

In the area of politics, the period from 1850 to 1858 was dominated by reactionary regimes that attempted to restore traditional forms of authority in church, state, and civil society. Attempts at reform were met with hostility and police repression. Rapidly changing economic and social conditions, however, defied these attempts to restore the stability of an earlier period. German society during these years experienced the transformative effects of early industrialization. The conditions of an industrializing society, including urbanization and heightened class conflict, led to changes in liberal ideology. Liberals, who during the revolutionary period had presented themselves as leaders of a progressive coalition that transcended class, now developed a view of society based on specifically middle-class hegemony. But for many political activists of both the middle and working classes, cooperation within a broad democratic and national movement was still the chief goal. When workers' organizations, which were prohibited during the 1850s, were reorganized in the early 1860s, they were at first allied with liberal reform organizations and shared many of their political and social objectives. A central tenet shared by both liberal and working-class reform movements was the importance of improved education to the integration of workers into a new national community.[1]

The female reformers' conception of "spiritual motherhood" as a force for social change developed within this liberal discourse and made use of its possibilities. The defeat of the revolution, although a blow to female reformers' short-term hopes, had confirmed one of their most important arguments. A new political order, they continued to insist, could not be created by violence or by mere changes in the public sphere that did not change the human heart. Enduring change, they asserted, would come only through a transformation of culture, brought about through child-rearing in both family and educational institutions. The child-rearing process provided an effective metaphor for an approach to social change through organic and evolutionary growth rather than through revolutionary upheaval. The metaphorical image of woman's social mission as the maternal role within the "great social household" provided a basis for a critique of some aspects of male liberal ideology and for the creation of woman-centered approaches to social reform.

From Revolution to Reaction

Among the institutions that survived the revolutionary period and provided new models of female social involvement were the school and nursery founded by Charlotte Paulsen in Hamburg in 1849. Paulsen had founded her own organization, known as the Women's Society for the Support of Poor Relief, in 1849. The society distinguished itself from more conventional charitable enterprises through its emphasis on providing work rather than financial handouts and its special focus on the problems of mothers and children. The Society created an infant school, headed by Paulsen herself, and a school for older children under the leadership of Johanna Goldschmidt and and another prominent member of the Society, Amalie Westendarp.[2]

Paulsen's justification for these efforts reflects attitudes toward class that were common among progressive reformers of both sexes during this era. Although increasingly aware of class conflict, they did not think of it as hardened and permanent. Rather, they still believed that the process of proletarianization might be reversed by the revival of the manual skills and the sense of independence and self-respect that they associated with the traditional artisan class. Paulsen was dismayed at the breakdown of traditional community life among workers and described their children as physically deprived and morally neglected. Her intention, she said, was to rescue the "helpless children" from their "damp and unhealthy dwellings, where they are ruined by inadequate care and malnutrition." Paulsen ran her institution as a Froebel kindergarten promoting health, creativity, and manual skills. "The children are encouraged to be creative and to trace and draw figures. . . . They run around and play games, outdoors if possible . . . and they strengthen their limbs. Thus the life of these little people is fresh, free and happy." She attempted to introduce these methods into the local infant schools and also addressed an unsuccessful request to the Hamburg Senate to be allowed to participate in the supervision of children in foster families—a job not opened to women until 1900. Her activities linked private and public spheres, and social and familial responsibilities. Known to the children as "Grandmother Paulsen," she took up residence in the institution after her husband's death in order to devote herself fully to the children.[3]

The survival of the kindergarten as an institution after the revolution and its spread beyond North Germany, and indeed beyond the German-speaking world itself to other European peoples and to North America, was largely the work of the single-minded and energetic Bertha von Marenholtz-Bülow. In 1849 Marenholtz went to take the waters at Liebenstein, a resort town where Friedrich Froebel was in charge of a kindergarten and a training program. She heard from the villagers about a strange old man who danced and played with the ragged children of the local peasants and craftsmen. "Some days after," she later recollected, "I met on my walk this so-called 'old fool.' A tall, spare man, with long gray hair, was leading a troop of village children between the ages of three and eight, most of them barefooted and but scantily clothed. . . . Having marshalled them for play, he practised with them a song belonging to it. The loving patience and abandon with which he did this, the whole bearing of the man . . . were so moving that tears came into my companion's eyes as well as my own." Marenholtz did not hesitate to address the stranger. "You are occupied, I see, with the education of the people," she remarked.[4]

Froebel invited his new acquaintance to visit his kindergarten. For Marenholtz, as for many of her female contemporaries, the appropriately female topic of child-rearing immediately provided a context for the discussion of broader issues. Her conversation with Froebel turned to politics. Both lamented the failure, already apparent, of the 1848 revolution, and both agreed that the causes of the failure were cultural; the population as a whole had not understood, or responded to, the ideas of the reformers. When Froebel declared that broad cultural change could come only with a new form of education, Marenholtz was at first skeptical. Traditional education, she objected, had served chiefly to confine "poor human nature in the strait-jacket of conventional prejudice and unnatural laws." Froebel persuaded her that his own method encouraged natural growth rather than artificial constraint. Nature held the secret of evolutionary, constructive, and peaceful development. "We cannot tear the present from the past or the past from the future. . . . In *children* lies the seed-corn of the future."[5]

Froebel's idea of motherhood as a force for cultural evolution changed the life of his new disciple by both legitimating the skills that she had gained through motherhood and providing her with a new opportunity to use them. Marenholtz, who had now found the "satisfying work" for which she had longed, abhorred the label of "emancipated" woman and insisted that the rights of children, rather than those of women, were the center of her work. As we have seen, however, she had already made highly unconventional choices in her private life. Her work for the kindergarten cause required still more conspicuously unfeminine, even "emancipated," behavior, including public speaking and the vigorous advocacy of controversial ideas. Her behavior was sometimes perceived as uncomfortably strident and aggressive. "If her *heart* had not been broken . . . I would like her better," wrote Diesterweg to Johanna Goldschmidt. "She now emphasizes only her intellect, as is typical of talented women who have failed in affairs of the heart."[6]

When Froebel departed to participate in the short-lived Hamburg experiment, Marenholtz left for Berlin, where she used her family's prestige and her wide contacts to win converts to the kindergarten movement. Her friends of this period included some notable figures in the elite intellectual and artistic circles of the time—Bettina von Arnim, Karl August Varnhagen von Ense, Franz Liszt—as well as many politicians and civil servants. Among this sophisticated set, she emphasized political rather than narrowly pedagogical issues. She announced her crusade in the rhetoric of utopian socialism. Revolution, that "child of hatred," could destroy, but only love could build. "A revolution of love," she passionately declaimed at an outdoor social occasion, standing dramatically on a rock in the midst of a stream, "must come over the world." Some of her acquaintances were invited to come to Liebenstein, where they engaged in long discussions with Marenholtz and Froebel about the wide-ranging political implications of the new pedagogy. These political discussions combined conservative and progressive themes. The kindergarten was presented as a bulwark of social order, but of a new form of order, resting on education and voluntary assent rather than coercion. The "rough masses," she argued to a visiting politician, must be made to see that "only the self-restraint of individuals and their voluntary subjection to law makes greater freedom possible."[7]

Certainly the progressive rather than the conservative implications of the kindergarten movement were most apparent to the reactionary regime that was imposed in Prussia in 1850. Marenholtz's campaign was abruptly interrupted by the prohibition of the Froebel kindergarten by Prussian Minister of Education Karl von Raumer in 1851, a prelude to the Stiehl Regulations of 1854, a set of governmental decrees that suppressed progressive educational trends and imposed religious control on schools. The Prussian decree that forbade the kindergarten, characterizing it as part of a conspiracy "to convert the youth of the nation to atheism," was also directed against dissenting religious sects and political movements. Influenced by the Prussian measure, the Hamburg Senate forcibly closed the elementary school established by Johanna Goldschmidt and Charlotte Paulsen, although Paulsen's infant school, perhaps because it was not called a kindergarten, apparently was allowed to continue. Marenholtz, who unsuccessfully attempted to use her personal influence at the Prussian court to have the ban rescinded, attributed the measure in part to an error of the Education Ministry, which had confused Friedrich Froebel with his more radical brother, Carl. The kindergarten, claimed Louise Otto, had offended those conservative groups "to whom nothing is so abhorrent as an increase in the number of citizens who can think for themselves."[8]

Both Emilie Wüstenfeld and Malwida von Meysenbug, who were outspoken in their sympathy with radical political figures, narrowly escaped arrest during this period, as did kindergarten proprietors in many cities whose institutions were forcibly closed. "The kindergarten teachers of this period went through a martyrdom that was fully equivalent to the suffering of the many men who were persecuted for their beliefs," wrote Otto. Henriette Breymann, then teaching in a girls' school in Schweinfurt, was driven from her classroom by police. The liberal humor magazine *Kladderadatsch*, the only journal of political satire to survive this wave of repression, made fun of these measures in a piece entitled "Five Minutes in a Froebel Kindergarten," portraying an oral examination administered by a Prussian policeman to kindergarten pupils. "Tinchen, are you going to renounce Communism? Pinchen, do you believe that Proudhon is Beelzebub?" Greeted with innocent laughter, the policeman turns to the teacher, "Good, Madam, I know what I shall report. The children know nothing about religion, they laugh about Communism, and as for that little song, 'The tailor's cloak has a thousand patches'—it must be about the exalted Bundestag! We *know* what to do about such subversive institutions!"9

The repression of the kindergarten was among the most conspicuous manifestations of an officially enforced return to traditional views of public/private boundaries that was intended to restore the dominance of the father in the family and the confinement of both women and small children to the home. Another such measure was the Prussian Law of Association (Vereinsgesetz) of 1850 banning women's participation in political organizations. An influential rationale for this return to tradition was provided by social theorist W. H. Riehl in a book entitled *Die Familie* ("The Family"), first published in 1855 and for many years regarded as the classic statement of the conservative view of the family. Riehl urged the restoration of the patriarchal household where the father supervised the education and moral training of the children. He specifically condemned both the aspirations of women to public activity and progressive educational trends "through which the school absorbs the home and makes it superfluous"—perhaps a direct reference to the Froebel kindergarten. At a religious service held to honor its patrons, the king and queen of Prussia, a conservative Berlin infant-school society made the connection between conservative child-rearing and monarchical authority explicit: "The king and queen," remarked the clergyman, "are, in the deepest sense, father and mother to all their children and it is an honor for children to support their parents."10

The Kindergarten Crusade

Against this background of repression and reaction, Marenholtz's continued crusade for the acceptance of the Froebel kindergarten may be seen as an act of political protest on behalf of both women and children. Within two years, Marenholtz suffered two personal tragedies. Friedrich Froebel, to whom she had become deeply attached during their brief acquaintance, died in 1852, disappointed at the seeming failure of his enterprise. In 1853, her son, Alfred, died at the age of twenty-one at the military academy. Marenholtz, who had always opposed this form of education, used his life as a metaphor for the unfulfilled potential of all children. "My life's happiness is destroyed and will remain so," she wrote, "but I shall live on, as long as God wills it, to work as much as I can, and for that which shall protect childhood from what my poor child had to suffer."[11]

With no ties to bind her to Germany, Marenholtz decided to conduct abroad the kindergarten crusade that she was now prevented from conducting in Prussia and in the other German states that had followed the Prussian lead in banning kindergartens. Marenholtz incurred the criticism of her aristocratic family for her independent life. As her niece and biographer remembered, her travels provoked "an endless storm of horror and indignation amongst relatives and acquaintances. . . . Particularly the old aristocratic aunts in Berlin and elsewhere were simply beside themselves." Her oppositional political stance was also considered very inappropriate to her class: "I was always running the risk of being associated with the Reds," she later complained. Despite the opposition of her family, Marenholtz set out on an ambitious series of journeys that took her to Belgium, Holland, France, Switzerland, England, and Italy. Although the development of the railway network had made travel easier, safer, and more respectable for women, she still faced difficulties. Her niece remarked that, in strange cities, she would often go for entire days without food because a respectable woman could not enter a restaurant alone.[12]

As an aristocrat, Marenholtz had certain advantages; wherever she went, she found acceptance in society. In Paris, for example, she called on historian Jules Michelet, who received her with utmost politeness and (according to her own reports) was soon quite captivated, both by his new acquaintance and by her message. However, Marenholtz was resolved to bring the Froebel message to people of all classes and by no means restricted her contacts to these exalted circles. In London, she tried out the kindergarten method in the "Ragged Schools," which had been set up by philanthropist Mary Carpenter. "The poorest, most neglected and ragged childen, some without parents or homes, who spend the night under doorways and bridges, behind fences and hoardings . . . are taken into these schools," wrote her biographer. In France and Belgium she spent some of her time with representatives of socialist movements, including Pierre Proudhon and some disciples of Fourier. During the years of the kindergarten ban in Prussia, Marenholtz thus created an international kindergarten movement.[13]

On her return to Prussia in 1859, she again worked for the recision of the kindergarten ban. Her success in 1860 reflected the liberalized atmosphere of the so-called new era in Prussia, which had begun in 1858 with the regency of William I. Marenholtz used the ideas drawn from her experience abroad as a basis for renewed activity in her own country. Though always idolizing the memory of Froebel (in later years his bust stood in her sitting room, covered with a velvet cloth that was removed only on special occasions), Marenholtz did not hesitate to expand and adapt his theory to a new urban and industrial setting. Her ideas on popular education, as set forth in the book *Die Arbeit und die neue Erziehung* ("Work and New Education"), published in 1864, reflected a combination of reforming liberalism and female-centered "spiritual motherhood" that would prove important to the international kindergarten movement and in the other reform movements it influenced.[14]

Marenholtz rejected some of the utopian idealism of the revolutionary period in favor of the hardheaded realism that had become a watchword among liberals of this era. Although retaining Froebel's vision of the kindergarten open to all classes as an ideal, she considered it impractical under existing circumstances. Not only did upper- and middle-class parents refuse to expose their children to the rough manners of the lower class, but the skills and intellectual development of lower-class children lagged behind those of their more privileged age-mates. Therefore she recommended the founding of *Volkskindergärten*, or free kindergartens, for the children of the urban poor. However, like other liberal reformers of the 1860s, Marenholtz saw class relations as fluid and changing rather than hardened into irreversible antagonism. She lamented the decline of the artisan into "a beast of burden, a machine, without human dignity, human worth or human consciousness." She fully shared the central belief of educational reformers in education as the key to reform; only an education starting in early childhood that encouraged the development of creativity and self-respect, she claimed, could restore the dignity of work. From a present-day perspective, the faith of upper- and middle-class reformers of this era in the saving power of education certainly seems exaggerated. However, many spokespersons for the working class during the 1860s, including the first socialist leaders, fully shared this belief in education and, as we shall see, became early supporters of the kindergarten.[15]

Although sharing many ideas that were current in the liberal movement of her time, Marenholtz nonetheless criticized, at least by implication, some aspects of liberal ideology. Her ideas provide another example of the tendency of women intellectuals to take advantage of the unresolved contradictions within a male-dominated discourse in order to define a female standpoint. German liberals during this period often struggled to reconcile conflicting beliefs in the benefits of unregulated free enterprise and the ethical responsibility of the state to promote the welfare of citizens. Marenholtz proposed kindergarten education as a partial remedy for this conflict; while encouraging individual development, it also promoted social harmony. Such values, she asserted, were necessary for all classes, not just for the poor. "We do not give our children enough opportunity to develop the virtues of community and to fulfill the duties of citizenship. . . . It is useless to expect patriotism from young people whose childhood has been spent in egotistical isolation, perhaps under the influence of parents who are motivated only by greed and perhaps encourage their children to take advantage of their fellow-citizens." The reform of child-rearing, in the home and in the school, was presented as a basis for national integration. In the kindergarten, Marenholtz wrote, the children "prepare themselves for the duties of a citizen, at whatever level of society they may be."[16]

As agents of social integration, Marenholtz designated women, especially the privileged women of the middle and upper classes, whom she called to their "true office in the great social household, as the educators of the human family." Building on Froebel's concept of the education of young women for maternal functions within and outside the home, she called for the reform of girls' secondary education, which she criticized as only an inferior imitation of boys' schooling. She insisted that education should prepare young girls for professional as well as for household tasks. Her suggested curriculum included the combination of practical and intellectual skills—physiology, psychology, natural history, universal history, and world literature as well as domestic skills and Froebel techniques. Her conception of a professional role for women extended to the creation of girls' secondary schools, staffed by a female "education society" of "married and unmarried members of the female sex." Marenholtz was thus one of the earliest advocates of two important feminist causes—the right of girls to a secondary education and the right of women to teach them.[17]

Underlying these proposals was an ethical perspective that Marenholtz defined as distinctively female and identified with women's maternal and familial roles, now given a broader scope within the "great social household." Although demanding for both sexes "the freedom and the right to develop all faculties," she believed that the abilities and roles of men and women were different and complementary, although equally important. Moreover, just as the young wife had raged against the insensitivity, cruelty, and "false independence" of the male sex, the mature woman concluded that, as "an unmistakable result" of the long-standing exclusion of women from public affairs, "the world bears a masculine stamp, which has its advantages and disadvantages," and insisted that "the present age calls for a new adjustment." For Marenholtz the mission of women was to affirm the values of nurture and community that male-dominated society had neglected.[18]

Marenholtz combined theory and practice. In 1863, she founded an organization, the Society for Popular Education. This society operated under the auspices of the Central Association for the Welfare of the Working Classes, a liberal reform organization founded in 1844, which during the 1850s and 1860s focused much of its effort on educational and child-care institutions. Having opened seven kindergartens for tuition-paying pupils, the society used the funds thus raised to found both a training institute for female kindergarten teachers and a Free Kindergarten intended specifically for the children of the poor. Unlike most Froebel kindergartens, which were open only four hours per day, the Free Kindergartens met the needs of working parents by keeping children for the full day. They differed from the already existing infant schools by introducing the Froebel methods, including directed play, physical activities, and educational games, in place of the traditional, regimented discipline. The Free Kindergartens founded by Marenholtz were imitated both in other German cities and abroad; for example, a women's group in Breslau founded twelve such kindergartens between 1861 and 1873.[19]

From the Family to the World

While Marenholtz developed a theoretical justification for a female role in the "great human household," another Froebel disciple, Henriette Breymann, attempted to educate women for such a role in the girls' school that she founded in her parents' home in 1853. Breymann, who had worked with Froebel at Liebenstein and after his death in girls' schools in Schweinfurt and Baden-Baden, felt both a longing for reunion with her family and a sense of obligation to her parents and her numerous siblings. When her father was transferred to a new pastorate in Watzum, she moved back to her parents' spacious home and set up a small boarding school for young girls, enlisting her own father and sisters as teaching staff. The school's prospectus announced that the pupils would be educated "in a Christian family for their future profession, to which nature calls every woman . . . to be the educators of children, of their own or other families." Because of limited space in the house, the number of pupils was kept to about eighteen. Relatively high tuition costs limited the enrollment to girls of upper- and middle-class background.[20]

In her school, set in the rural seclusion of a small town, Breymann developed a pedagogical approach based on maternal affection and discipline that was reminiscent of the school described by Rudolphi almost fifty years earlier. Mary Lyschinska, who was delivered to the school at the age of ten by her Polish father, remembered the intimate atmosphere. "I have never seen a home where strange children were taken in so warmly and so fully integrated into family life." The close association of girls of various ages, ranging from about ten years to late adolescence, added to the familial spirit. In addition to academic subjects such as science, geography, botany, music, English language, and religion (taught by Pastor Breymann), the girls' curriculum included sports such as ice-skating and gymnastics, very uncommon in girls' schools of the era. Despite their upper- or middle-class status, all pupils were required to participate in the domestic and outdoor work of the household. Henriette

Breymann, as a disciple of Pestalozzi, viewed such practical tasks chiefly as an essential supplement to intellectual work rather than merely as practical preparation for a future career as housewife. Lyschinska remembered the frequent outdoor expeditions, games, and social activities that reinforced the sense of "home away from home." Though serving a younger age group, the institute at Watzum resembled the Hamburg Academy in its institutional culture based on family life and in its integration of manual and intellectual work. Breymann's school was an enclave of female utopianism in a hostile world.[21]

But Breymann was not entirely satisfied with this tranquil and isolated existence and soon found a wider, more public sphere of activity by setting up courses in kindergarten methods for adult teachers and governesses, who received practical training in a kindergarten managed by her sister, Marie. The educational authorities in Braunschweig, unlike their Prussian counterparts, were very favorably disposed toward the kindergarten experiment, and Breymann was soon able to make contact with local elementary school teachers' organizations, although her hopes for the adoption of the Froebel kindergarten into the state's public school system remained unfulfilled. The professional courses, she remarked, filled a great social need, not only for trained personnel in the day care centers that were now widely established in the expanding cities, but for vocational opportunities for single women. The once-isolated institute became a center of kindergarten propaganda, and well-known kindergarten proponents such as Marenholtz were often invited to teach and lecture there. Due to the latter's extensive contacts, Henriette Breymann was invited several times to lecture in Belgium and other European countries.[22]

As a result of the considerable expansion of the school's public visibility and mission, new and larger quarters were needed, and in 1864 the school moved to a new building in Neu-Watzum outside Wolfenbüttel. The school's purpose, according to its prospectus, was the creation of a new relationship between familial and public spheres. Based on a "pious, Christian family spirit," the brochure stated, the school functioned also as "a state, a microcosmic world, in which each part is integrated into the whole. Through the fulfillment of duties in this little world, each individual is trained for her obligations in the wider world." Breymann commented on the novel combination of private and public concerns that were addressed by her curriculum. It was customary, she wrote, to educate girls for domestic life, but to educate them for the professional exercise of pedagogical skills "still sounds strange and still goes against the old prejudices."[23]

The meaning of this new form of education to a rising generation of female activists is best shown through the experience of one of Breymann's students, Hedwig Crüsemann (later Heyl), who became a colleague of her former teacher and a major leader of philanthropic and feminist organizations. Crüsemann was born in 1850 of a prosperous family in Bremen; her father was a successful businessman who eventually became the first president of the North German Lloyd shipping company. According to her own account of her childhood, she found little pleasure or meaning in her primary education, which she complained was based too much on rote learning and on academic knowledge that was remote from life. During an illness, she read Pestalozzi's *Leonard and Gertrude* and responded enthusiastically to its portrayal of a powerful woman and a practical approach to education. As a last resort, her parents sent the unruly girl to Breymann's school at Neu-Watzum, where she spent the years from 1865 to 1867. For the first time, she was exposed to a curriculum that, by making connections between academic learning and practical work, showed her that she could be powerful and effective. "The overcoming of opposites," she later wrote, "idea and practice, spirit and body, ideals and reality—that was the great task." Returning home, she found that she could use her newfound pedagogical knowledge by caring for her baby brother, "and the great problem of human education rose before me." For Crüsemann, as for the women of an older generation who have been discussed, the ideal of "spiritual motherhood" provided a framework both for a new interpretation of her own experience and for a vision of wider possibilities.[24]

Heart of the World: Spiritual Motherhood and Women's Social Mission

The work of Breymann and Marenholtz was important far beyond its limited short-term results because it contributed to the development of the more general concept of female professionalism which was the central concern of organized women's groups in the 1850s and 1860s. In the 1850s, as James C. Albisetti has pointed out, pedagogy had emerged as the first major career opportunity open to women in the German-speaking world. Though some seminars set up to train women teachers had existed for decades—the first was founded in Berlin in 1803—the number greatly expanded in the 1850s and some states introduced formal certification requirements for women teachers or expanded those that already existed. Opportunities for employment were largely limited to private institutions such as the kindergartens and girls' secondary schools; teaching jobs in public elementary schools were still largely restricted to men. The opening of careers in teaching to women at midcentury was nonetheless an important historical turning point, for such careers provided to middle-class women the first dignified and widely available means of earning an independent livelihood. These opportunities also provided what women such as Marenholtz and Breymann had sought in their own personal lives—satisfying work that provided an alternative to a marriage of convenience.[25]

Apart from the ideas of the Froebel disciples, one of the earliest rationales for such careers was developed by Luise Büchner, perhaps the best-known writer on women's educational and vocational issues of the period. Büchner, the sister of revolutionary playwright Georg Büchner, was also a friend of prominent novelist Karl Gutzkow and a supporter of the democratic liberal movement in 1848. Büchner's first major work, *Die Frauen und Ihr Beruf* ("Women and their Vocation"), published in 1856, still expressed some of aspirations of the revolutionary period, although now adapted to the constraints of reality. Like the Froebelians, Büchner made no theoretical distinction between private and public and familial and professional roles. She affirmed the paramount importance of the familial sphere, and particularly of motherhood: "It is hard to imagine," she wrote, "how holy and extensive the vocation of a true mother is, . . . the whole future is in her hands." But she argued that professional opportunities would enhance rather than erode this high ideal of family life. Büchner insisted that women must have the economic independence that would enable them to avoid marriages of convenience. Single women, she wrote, must not renounce but rather extend the motherly role. She advocated the widening of women's professional sphere to include other kinds of work besides teaching, for which she said that many girls had no talent. Like Marenholtz and Breymann, she advocated the founding of women's educational institutions, staffed by women, to educate women by both example and practical training.²⁶

Büchner's book offered an interesting contrast to Riehl's conservative treatise *The Family*, which was published at about the same time. Both authors stressed the importance of motherhood and of familial cohesion. But whereas Riehl saw the essence of woman's familial role in her subjection to male authority, Büchner saw this role as a basis of ethical autonomy and integrity. And the family, portrayed by Riehl as the foundation of political conservatism, was depicted by Büchner as a source of progressive influence. In the political world as in the household, she asserted, woman embodied the spirit of reconciliation and social harmony. "Standing above the strife of the parties, she is . . . the true protector of freedom and human rights, for Woman is the heart of the world."²⁷

German feminist movements during the years 1850 to 1864 developed in a very different political climate from the one experienced by their American counterparts. American feminism suffered no such wave of official repression as occurred in Germany. The women of Seneca Falls and others continued to hold conferences and to campaign for suffrage, married women's property rights, and other reforms throughout the decade. Such activities were obviously not possible during the 1850s for German feminists, who were forced to carry on their work abroad or in small institutional enclaves such as Breymann's school at Watzum. However, American feminist campaigns centered on "equal-rights" issues were confined to a very narrow audience and produced few lasting results. In America as in Germany, the first national or statewide feminist organizations were not founded until the 1860s. Far more widely influential among American women of this period were the works of domestic reformers, including Catharine Beecher. Like some of her German contemporaries, such as Büchner, Beecher portrayed the domestic realm both as a center of utopian harmony and as the basis of professional roles, including teaching. Beecher, too, portrayed these professions as both practical and idealistic; they provided economic opportunities for single women and spread female ethical values into the public sphere.²⁸

"Spiritual motherhood," which has often been characterized as a conservative ideology, had an oppositional and even sometimes radical significance during the period 1850–1864. In the 1850s institutions based on maternal ideology, such as the kindergarten, were repressed as harshly as organizations advocating equal rights for women. Despite the repression of women's political activities, moreover, the cause of women's rights was advanced through the development of a concept of female professionalism. This concept conflated individualistic and maternal or relational feminist ideologies. Women's right to careers, which was justified by arguments in favor of self-realization and against marriages of convenience, was in many ways a highly individualistic idea. At the same time, this idea developed from the beginning in the context of an ambitious, even utopian vision of social reform through spiritual motherhood.

Looking back in 1890 over the activities of the Froebel disciples over the past half century, feminist Jenny Hirsch paid tribute to their innovative and emancipatory significance. "Froebel, . . . who assigned to women the first and most important task in the education of the human race," wrote Hirsch, "was the one who prepared the soil upon which, here in Germany, the work for a better education for the female sex, for a widening of their employment opportunities, and for their emancipation from many legal and social restrictions has grown." In the period of German unification, this work would continue.[29]

Chapter 5
Mothers of the Nation: Spiritual Motherhood and Organized Feminism, 1865–1877

During the period from the mid-1860s to the mid-1870s, German feminists were caught up in the central political event of their time—the unification of the German states and the creation of a new nation. The ideal of spiritual motherhood as a force for the overcoming of opposites, the reconciliation of conflict, and the building of community provided the basis for a specifically female standpoint on the process of nation-building. The mid-1860s saw the rise of organized feminism on a national level. For the new feminist organizations, maternal ideology provided a philosophical link between their practical work and their broader ethical aspirations. The immediate goal, which became particularly pressing during this period, was the provision of suitable professional or vocational opportunities for the increasing number of single women who could not be supported by their families. However, many feminists insisted that the "woman question" was by no means limited to such practical aims; the right of women to work was linked to their right to participate productively in the public concerns of society and nation, often conceived as a "great social household." As in the previous decades, they stressed the interdependence of family and state and of public and private spheres. "Just as the moral strength of women is essential to the development of family life," said Henriette Goldschmidt, a prominent advocate of this viewpoint, "in the same way, women must make a wider commitment to fulfill their misssion to the national family."[1]

The feminist movements of this era must be placed in the context of the general development of German liberalism. This development was shaped by Bismarck's wars of unification, chiefly the war with Austria in 1866, resulting in the unification of the north German states into the North German Confederation, and the Franco-Prussian War of 1870–1871, resulting in the inclusion of the southern German states in a German Empire under the Prussian monarchy. Liberal spokesmen who had previously opposed royal absolutism and aspired to a parliamentary system now accepted Bismarck's authoritarian state, which, although including a representative body, the Reichstag, elected by universal male suffrage, still left most of the power over such vital matters as foreign and military policies in the hands of the Emperor. The liberal politicians and their chief constituency, the German bourgeoisie, have thus often been accused by historians of political spinelessness, and feminists have sometimes been included in that general indictment. Historians Richard Evans and Herrad-Ulrike Bussemer depict the feminists' enthusiasm for a maternalist rather than an equal-rights ideology as one sign of the political backwardness and timidity of the class to which most of them belonged. Bussemer asserts that feminist organizations retreated from an earlier struggle for equality and therefore achieved only the "integration of the women's movement into a society that was, as ever, dominated by men."[2]

As we have seen from earlier chapters, this antithesis between equal-rights and maternal ideologies is oversimplified. Earlier feminists, including equal-rights activists such as Louise Otto, had always linked the right to citizenship with a distinctively female ideal of service. Moreover, the view of the German bourgeoisie as a whole as hopelessly passive and "feudalized" has recently been challenged by British historian David Blackbourn. Blackbourn argues that the bourgeoisie, although accepting some limitations on its power at the national level, protected its status. A distinctively bourgeois and liberal political culture, supported by civic, philanthropic, and voluntary associations, flourished, especially in cities. The kindergarten movement, sponsored during this period by many such voluntary organizations, was a woman-centered contribution to this bourgeois political culture.[3]

Female kindergarten advocates played leadership roles in feminist organizations. The kindergarten movement still provided an important forum for the discussion of the relationship of the family to the broader social and political concerns of women. As this chapter will show, however, the theory and practice of spiritual motherhood was extended far beyond the miniature world of the kindergarten to inspire a new view of the relationship of women to the state. By creating female-centered alternatives to dominant, male-created ethical and political norms, feminists of this period created a basis for opposition to many forms of male privilege.

Child Care as a Professsion

The relationship between the kindergarten and feminist movements must first be seen in the context of the central practical campaign of feminists of this era—to open job opportunities to middle-class single women. This struggle for career opportunities was also a struggle to maintain the integrity of the bourgeoisie. For the untrained and unemployed daughters of the middle class, the threat of loss of status, even of proletarianization, often seemed still more fearful than the prospect of poverty or continued dependence. Better training and job opportunities, therefore, were the central objectives of two major women's organizations founded in the mid-1860s: the Allgemeiner deutscher Frauenverein (German Women's Association), founded in 1865 under the leadership of Louise Otto (who now, because of her marriage, called herself Otto-Peters), teacher Auguste Schmidt, and Henriette Goldschmidt; and the more practically oriented Verein zur Förderung der Erwerbsfähigkeit des weiblichen Geschlects (Association for the Advancement of the Work Skills of the Female Sex), also called the Lette-Verein (Lette Association) after its founder, philanthropist Adolf Lette. These organizations differed in both philosophy and purpose. The Lette Association disavowed any interest in general questions of women's emancipation and concentrated on sponsoring job-training programs. The German Women's Association was led by committed feminists and insisted that the right to work was part of a more general claim to political and social participation. "Work," declared Otto-Peters, "which will be the basis of the new society, . . . is the duty and the honor of the female sex—we therefore claim the right and the duty to work."[4]

One important source of this concept of duty and honor was the Froebelian ideology of "spiritual motherhood." Kindergarten organizations, such as Johanna Goldschmidt's Froebel Society in Hamburg, were affiliated with the German Women's Association, in which prominent kindergarten activists such as Henriette Goldschmidt, Lina Morgenstern, Auguste Weyrowitz, and many others often took leadership roles.[5]

An important goal pursued by female kindergarten advocates of this period was to make child care, whether practiced by private governesses in the home or by teachers in a kindergarten or school, into a dignified and respected profession. As Otto-Peters pointed out, the pay and status of such nurses or governesses was low and their working conditions degrading. Private child-care workers, Otto-Peters asserted, were commonly at the mercy of their mistresses, had no real authority over their often spoiled charges, were required to do menial work such as laundry and mending, and in general were treated as servants. They were also vulnerable to sexual exploitation.[6]

The purpose of extending kindergarten training to such women was twofold: to bring progressive Froebelian values into homes, and to give the governesses themselves some credentials that would entitle them to higher pay and the respect of their employers. Many training institutions were founded in the 1860s; one of the best-known was Johanna Goldschmidt's Froebel Seminar, sponsored by the newly constituted Hamburg Froebel Society in 1860. The two-year course accepted girls from the age of fourteen, trained them in such subjects as history, natural sciences, and foreign languages as well as pedagogy, and placed them in families as private governesses or in institutional kindergartens. Though far less ambitious than the Hamburg Academy for Women, which Goldschmidt had helped to found only ten years earlier, this institution was intended to serve much the same purposes—to encourage the reform of child-rearing and to give single, middle-class women the basis for economic independence. The demand among the prosperous middle class for such well-qualified child-care workers was reflected in the rapid establishment of kindergarten seminars—by 1877 twenty had been founded in various German cities, and Goldschmidt, who in the four years from 1868 to 1872 had trained five hundred students, complained that her placement service could not meet the demand for Froebel-trained employees.[7]

By insisting on the lofty mission and extensive education of these child-care workers, seminar founders such as Goldschmidt attempted to improve both the material and the social conditions of their work. Froebel's ideas on the crucial importance of the early childhood years, she wrote in 1868, showed conclusively that child care should not be left to untrained and sometimes indifferent servants: "It is thus very important to whom the care of the child is entrusted." Although she included manual occupations such as sewing in the seminar's program, Goldschmidt emphasized the academic qualifications of her students. She criticized the snobbery of leisured women who looked down on their wage-earning sisters: "The Froebel Society seeks for its graduates a position in the family which does not place them in the same category as servants. . . . If the family wants loyalty and devotion to its interest, it should accept the young girl into its midst. . . . Mothers who supervise our students in a loving and serious fashion . . . will gain the right results for their children." Professional training for child-care workers was thus also a step toward the broader goal of sisterly solidarity among middle- and upper-class women, married and unmarried. Froebelian educator Jeanne-Marie von Gayette-Georgens criticized the "false pretensions of women . . . who treat their nurses as servants rather than friends."[8]

This ideal of the mistress-servant relationship was professed by Hedwig Crüsemann, who shortly after her graduation from Henriette Breymann's school had married industrialist Georg Heyl and moved to Berlin. Hedwig Heyl, as she now called herself, did not have to work for a living, but she continued her interest in pedagogy through the rearing of her own children. When her sons were three and four years old, Heyl hired a trained kindergartner, eighteen-year-old Adelheid Ulmann, who was recommended by Breymann. Heyl asserted in her autobiography that she attempted to treat Ulmann as a companion in the joys and cares of motherhood and encouraged her to take part in the extensive social and cultural activities of the family. This story expresses the belief in the power of common female gender and maternal mission to overcome social and economic barriers that Heyl professed throughout her life; we do not know how her governess responded to the situation.[9]

Another response to the campaign for vocational training was the founding of two institutions for women in Hamburg by Emilie Wüstenfeld, who had become the head of a local organization, the Verein zur Förderung weiblicher Erwerbstätigkeit (Society for the Encouragement of Female Employment) in 1867. Wüstenfeld's effort was part of an exceedingly widespread campaign to found vocational training institutions for women. The Hamburg Society sponsored both a vocational school for school-age girls and an extension school, including a kindergarten training program, for young women who had completed their academic education. The purpose of these schools, which offered vocationally oriented curricula, was clearly practical. However, Wüstenfeld and her colleagues, as disciples of Pestalozzi, also believed that the revival of traditional female skills might restore some of the power and independence that they believed women had lost by the transfer of economic production from home to separate workplace. Wüstenfeld hoped to lay to rest the old myth "that women have no right to take part in the rich treasures of knowledge and to work together for the welfare of individuals and of society." The economic value of such vocational training was reflected in the considerable demand for it; the Hamburg institutes grew from an enrollment of thirty-six in 1867 to four hundred by 1878.[10]

Motherhood and National Unification

The practical campaign to raise the status of child-rearing was given a much broader ethical significance through the work of Henriette Goldschmidt. In 1853 Goldschmidt had moved to Russia with her rabbi husband. In the tsarist empire, the expression of liberal beliefs was dangerous. Lacking any opportunity for public activity, she found her only rewards in family life, including a loving relationship with her husband and the task of raising three stepsons. In 1859, at the age of thirty-four, Goldschmidt had returned with her family to Leipzig. Having raised her stepsons to adulthood, she soon found domestic life too narrow and directed her energies into the community activities through which she met Auguste Schmidt and Louise Otto-Peters. Her participation in the founding of the German Women's Association required the deepening of her feminist commitment. At first, she had strenuously objected to Otto-Peters's policy of excluding men from full membership in the organization, but was persuaded to change her mind in part by her husband, who insisted that the broadening of women's social role required them to develop independence.[11]

Goldschmidt, who had retained the liberal enthusiasm of her girlhood, soon linked her concern for women's social role to another political issue—the unification of Germany. The Prussian-Austrian war of 1866 had resulted in the defeat not only of Austria but of several other German states allied with Austria, including Saxony. Louise Otto-Peters, who was a native of Saxony, did not share the spirit of patriotic exultation that swept over Prussia, which now dominated the newly formed North German Confederation. She saw this German civil war, which she called a "war between brothers," chiefly as a sad reminder of the hatred and disunity within the German nation. At Otto-Peters's request, Goldschmidt spoke to the Leipzig Association for Female Education on the significance of the war to women, using the ethic of "spiritual motherhood" as a female standpoint from which to criticize the quintessentially male domain of warfare. Goldschmidt concluded by exhorting women to overcome antagonism and to build community through the power of love. "We women are created not to hate, but to love."[12]

Goldschmidt looked for some way in which women could be effective in building national unity in a state that had been created by military conquest rather than popular consensus. Soon after her speech, as her biographer recounts, she was strolling through the city and by chance came upon an inconspicuous sign indicating a kindergarten, which she visited. The woman who had devoted much of her life to child-rearing was captivated by the harmonious atmosphere: "I felt the joy that inspired the children." Goldschmidt expressed her enthusiasm through a quotation from her favorite poem, Schiller's "Ode to Joy," which had invoked joy as the force overcoming the social antagonisms imposed by custom and uniting humanity through the power of love. She immersed herself in Froebel's works and concluded that his ideal of spiritual motherhood could provide a link between women's aspirations to professional fulfillment and the broader agenda of building unity in a still-divided nation.[13]

Goldschmidt's conception of the role of woman "as member of her family, as member of her community" was further developed in her response to the Prussian victory over France in 1870–1871, which resulted in the unification of the German Empire under Prussian hegemony. Bussemer has stressed the contrast between the pacifist and antiwar spirit of Otto-Peters, portrayed as a proponent of radical feminism, and the nationalism of Goldschmidt. Certainly Goldschmidt, who was of Prussian origin (though at this time a resident of Leipzig, in Saxony), was somewhat more enthusiastic about the unification of Germany under Prussian leadership than was the Saxon-born Otto-Peters. Goldschmidt's speech on German unification touched on some nationalist themes; she criticized some German women for their uncritical sympathy for French prisoners of war and (on a more frivolous note) for their patronage of French fashion designers.[14]

Both Goldschmidt and Otto-Peters, however, protested against the mindless chauvinism and militarism of the victory celebrations. For Goldschmidt, the bloodthirsty enthusiasm of some girls who became "war-crazy, and spoke of battles and wounds and corpses as if they were flowers, toys and . . . trinkets" provided a particularly vivid example of mindless imitation of male behavior. Goldschmidt also rejected hostile stereotypes of the French, claiming that the French people were not represented by their rulers and that German women should declare solidarity with their French sisters in combating oppressive laws. She declared that women's maternal ethic should lead them to reject "one-sided nationalism" and stand for international reconciliation. The extension of the ethical perspective based on "spiritual motherhood" to the male-dominated realm of warfare and high politics was the basis for a developing concept of female citizenship. In the new Empire, the right of suffrage was based in part on the duty of military service. "Authority is masculine," asserted historian Heinrich von Treitschke, one of the most influential spokesmen for the new national consciousness. "Among other things, there is the purely physical factor . . . armed men lead, and armed men don't take orders from women." Otto-Peters ridiculed the idea that citizenship should be based only on the capacity for violence and proposed alternate qualifications, derived from the peace-keeping and community-building traditions of women. There would be no wars, she declared, if women, "with their delicate sensiblity and their capacity for love and compassion," had not been forced to disregard "the natural voice in their hearts," and to obey "laws made by men in barbaric times."[15]

Women, asserted Goldschmidt, must develop nonviolent forms of service to the nation. They must, she declared, "discover their importance in the national family. Their warmth of heart, their moral strength, properly recognized, can do more for the social question than the best constructed systems." Goldschmidt held many offices in the German Women's Association during the first twenty-five years of its existence and was one of its most conspicuous public figures. Although herself devoted first and foremost to kindergarten training, Goldschmidt immediately imagined many other applications of motherly skills to the public sphere. Of all the members of the German Women's Association, she was the most vocal in advocating the creation of both volunteer and paid positions for women in social service. Male liberals of the 1870s compensated for their lack of power on the national level through control of city and local governments. Goldschmidt envisaged a similar role for women; in 1873, she urged the participation of women in "poor relief, public nutrition programs, and supervision of orphans." She identified social service as a duty of citizenship, comparable to military service for men, and connected the increasing dignity of motherhood in the private sphere with an expanded role in the "great social household." "Just as the family only becomes worthy of its name when the woman has the honorable position of an assistant, where she is not the tool or the servant, but the complement of the man," she said in 1870, "so will our communities develop to their full potential when women become helpers in the great tasks of the time."[16]

The idea of giving women policy-making roles in social service organizations, although accepting and even affirming differences in male and female abilities, nonetheless did challenge male privilege. In the 1870s and 1880s only a few German municipalities admitted women to volunteer roles in welfare agencies, and male poor-relief workers (also chiefly volunteers) often opposed their participation. Even male reformers who recommended the use of women's talents in social services rejected their claims to policy-making roles and preferred members of the conservative Vaterländische Frauenvereine (Patriotic Women's Associations), who were willing to follow male leadership, to members of more progressive women's organizations such as the German Women's Association.[17]

The German Women's Association's agenda was also expanded to deal with biological as well as spiritual motherhood. Feminist reformers had criticized laws on marriage and divorce during the revolutionary period 1848–1850. The unification of Germany had stimulated widespread discussion of legal reform. In 1867 the German Women's Association had directed a petition to the Reichstag of the North German Confederation requesting a reexamination of the laws affecting women. In 1874, the government of the German Empire appointed a commission of jurists to draw up a uniform civil code, or Bürgerliches Gesetzbuch, for the Empire.[18]

Under the leadership of Louise Otto-Peters, the German Women's Association addressed its first petition for a change in the laws affecting women's status to the Reichstag in 1876. The central issue of this petition was the status of women in marriage and family law, specifically the rights of mothers over their children. For the national meeting of the organization in 1875, Charlotte Pape of Hannover presented a powerful position paper entitled "The Rights of Mothers over their Children." Otto-Peters, who introduced the speaker, remarked that the organization's archives held "innumerable letters of unhappy wives and mothers, who have suffered from the laws on marriage and guardianship." In all the German states, Pape explained, a mother had no right to legal control over their childen after the father's death—she could be forced to accept a guardian named in her husband's will or by a court. She had little more control during the father's lifetime. Pape cited legal cases, usually involving divorced or separated couples, in which mothers had discovered that they had no right to custody of, or even contact with, their children, whom fathers could remove from them at will. Pape ended her report with a ringing denunciation of "man-made laws that do not recognize motherhood" as "blasphemies against the law of nature, which places the child in an indissoluble relationship to the mother, when it hardly knows its father!"[19]

The German Women's Association's petition requested that "in the revision of the Civil Code the rights of women, especially in marriage and guardianship, be considered." The organization also resolved in 1875 that laws should be changed to give father and mother equal rights over decisions concerning children and that a mother who survived the father should have the right to full guardianship of her children. As historian Margrit Twellman points out, the fact that motherhood, rather than issues of property rights or financial control, was the earliest legal question addressed by the organization shows the centrality of domestic roles to women's developing consciousness during this period.[20]

This petition prompted Otto-Peters to publish a series of articles in the Association's periodical, *Neue Bahnen* ("New Avenues"), surveying the marriage laws of all the German states, "a reminder to women," she said, "of the possibly serious legal consequences that the decision to marry can bring." The petition had no immediate results. The discussion of laws on the status of women in marriage was not reopened until 1887, when the first draft of the Code was published. The petition was nonetheless important as an early effort to change the status of women through the reform of the male-dominated state, rather than through private philanthropy and educational institutions.[21]

Family and State

Another attempt to connect the welfare of children to the public and private status of women was the spread of Froebelian methods into homes and kindergarten classes. Many private kindergartens and kindergarten training programs had been founded during these years. By 1877 Prussia alone had 250 kindergartens, and the establishment of a Froebel Society in Munich in 1868 had begun the spread of the kindergarten in South Germany. The German Froebel Society, formed in 1874 from the many local societies, submitted a petition in 1876 to Prussian Minister of Education and Culture Adalbert Falk requesting the Ministry to require Froebel credentials for early childhood teachers, to incorporate kindergarten training into girls' secondary education, and to establish kindergarten classes as the lower level of elementary school systems. Falk was the leader of the *Kulturkampf*, a campaign launched in the 1870s that aimed to combat Catholic influence in all areas, but particularly in education. He probably regarded the kindergarten, which was often nonconfessional or interconfessional, as an instrument with which to undermine Catholic control over infant schools. He therefore responded that his Ministry, though not endorsing the Froebel method, had no objection to the founding of kindergartens by local education authorities.[22]

Women's activity in the kindergarten movement consisted not only of the founding and staffing of institutions, but of a broader campaign to spread Froebelian methods of child-rearing into homes. Women's writings on child care emphasized the increased autonomy and responsibility of mothers in the middle-class home. Mothers, wrote Auguste Weyrowitz, a teacher and member of the executive committee of the German Women's Association, must be educated to take over the traditional responsibility of fathers, who were now so preoccupied with their work outside the home that they could only occasionally exert a direct influence over child-rearing. Lina Morgenstern, who was born Lina Bauer in Breslau in 1825, was attracted to the Froebel movement because of both her personal experience as the mother of five and her first professional work as the author of children's stories. A follower of Marenholtz, Morgenstern served as head of the Women's Association for the Support of Kindergartens of Berlin from 1860 to 1866, and wrote one of the first advice books on the application of Froebel's ideas in the home. Her discussion of the maternal role was pervaded by Pestalozzian imagery. "A true mother," she wrote, "should be the child's sun, that warms it and brings its potential into bloom."[23]

Female kindergarten advocates explored the relationship between public and private worlds through their frequent disussions of the political implications of private child-rearing methods. A major political issue among liberals of this era was the failure of the middle class as a whole to develop a sense of social and political responsibility. Female authors often criticized prevalent child-rearing practices for encouraging the snobbery, material greed, and servile deference to authority that they believed were characteristic of their middle-class contemporaries. Morgenstern urged mothers to encourage the child's sense of social responsibility by avoiding spoiling and cultivating independence. She criticized the materialism of nouveau-riche mothers who overloaded their children with elaborate toys and expensive entertainments and suggested they offer the simple Froebel playthings as a stimulus to creativity. Maternal discipline, she insisted, must not compel obedience through external authority, but must cultivate an internalized sense of responsibility to the family and to society as a whole. Bertha Meyer, author of a series of essays on child-rearing that appeared in the periodical *Frauen-Anwalt* ("Women's Advocate"), likewise emphasized that the child's will should not be broken through authoritarian discipline, but rather trained to autonomy. "Ethical responsibility," she wrote, "has nothing to do with fear and servile dependence."[24]

By contrast to the conservative and confessionally oriented teaching methods of the elementary schools and religious preschool institutions, kindergarten pedagogy stressed the progressive values of religious tolerance, intellectual independence, and social diversity. Gentiles and Jews cooperated; the kindergarten, wrote the Jewish Morgenstern, must provide the opportunity for the children of "rich and poor, Jew and Catholic, prominent and humble to play together and to educate each other." Auguste Weyrowitz, a former governess and head of a girl's school in Berlin, warned kindergarten teachers against authoritarian approaches that did not encourage imagination, independence, and "the freedom of individual development." Furthermore, she urged elementary school teachers, whom she accused of suppressing the individuality of former kindergarten pupils, to incorporate some kindergarten methods into their own teaching.[25]

The importance of Froebelian pedagogy to the development of progressive political movements is further apparent from its influence on the first socialist writings on education. The Social Democratic party, which was founded in 1875 and scored its first major electoral success in 1878, attempted to create a new, working-class political culture in both private and public spheres. As their guiding principles, the socialists adopted the democratic and progressive values first championed, but now increasingly abandoned, by the liberal bourgeoisie. A part of this heritage was the Pestalozzian and Froebelian pedagogical tradition. Wilhelm Liebknecht, a founder and leader of the party during this era, had been a disciple of Carl Froebel, with whom he had studied in Switzerland in the 1840s. Throughout his career, Liebknecht supported the kindergarten, urging that it should be available on a public basis rather than only to "the rich and richest classes."[26]

One of the first socialist treatises that dealt specifically with education, entitled *Kindergarten und Schule als sozialdemokratische Anstalten* ("Kindergarten and School as Social-Democratic Institutions"), was published in 1877 by socialist educator Adolf Douai. Douai praised the kindergarten as an educational institution that encouraged individual development rather than obedience to authority. Moreover, he said, it inculcated the virtues of cooperation and social responsibility that parents still weighed down by traditional class and religious prejudices could not teach. Claiming that parents were "the worst possible educators of their children," Douai suggested that the training of all young children should be allotted to professional kindergarten teachers. He urged not only the establishement of free, public, and obligatory Froebel kindergartens but also the adoption of similar pedagogical methods in elementary schools. The popularity of the kindergarten among socialists was also reflected in that most famous of all socialist tracts of this period, August Bebel's *Die Frau in Vergangenheit, Gegenwart und Zukunft* ("Woman in Past, Present and Future"), first written in 1879, in which public child care, in an institution specifically called a "kindergarten," was envisaged as an important social service supporting a new status for both women and children.[27]

Thus, the kindergarten movement continued to be associated both with politically progressive ideas and with feminism during these years. It therefore provoked a strong conservative reaction. In 1873, the aristocratic Freiherr Adolf von Bissing-Beerberg founded the Oberlin Society, which spread an orthodox and sectarian model of early childhood education in the rural areas controlled by aristocrats and Protestant pastors. Although adapting some Froebelian techniques, many religious educators continued to denounce the kindergarten. Kindergarten pedagogy, complained one such educator, spread the heretical and socially disruptive doctrine that "knowledge leads to moral improvement, that knowledge and morality go together in the last analysis." The elementary school teaching profession apparently shared these attitudes.

The kindergarten developed chiefly under private auspices; despite the permissive attitude of the Prussian Education Ministry, few public-school kindergarten classes were founded in Prussia or in any of the German states.[28]

The kindergarten was also singled out as a distressing sign of the times by Pastor Philipp Nathusius, author of one of the most famous antifeminist pamphlets of the era. He decried the Froebel kindergarten as "an institution identified with the *left* wing of the women's movement [that] uses the slogans 'motherhood' and 'freedom from confessional conformity' as a kind of counter-mission [against the Church]." Denouncing feminist campaigns for improved educational and professional opportunities as threats to the family, he further called the kindergarten "a socialist institution . . . which relieves the idle mothers of the educated classes . . . of responsibility for their children." Nathusius's tract received a spirited response from Hedwig Dohm, perhaps the most radical advocate of equal rights of this era. Dohm, although focusing much of her argument on the problems of single career women, also used the maternal role as evidence of women's qualifications for higher education and professional work. Did Nathusius really think, she asked, that "less logical acuteness, less intelligence is necessary to understand and develop the soul of a child than to engage in academic study?"[29]

Despite its limited success in Germany during this period, the kindergarten movement increased in international renown. The spread of the German institution to many foreign countries was largely due to the continued tireless efforts of Marenholtz, who, for a combination of personal and professional reasons, had moved to Dresden. There in 1873 she founded an organization called the General Educational Association. The Association sponsored a seminar, called the Froebel-Stiftung, which offered two courses, a two-year program for kindergarten teachers and a shorter one for children's nurses.[30]

Marenholtz continued the international propaganda for the kindergarten that she had begun in the 1850s. In 1867, she had received a visit from eminent Boston intellectual and reformer Elizabeth Peabody, who was already a devoted Froebelian and wished to adapt the kindergarten idea to American conditions. Like Germany, the United States had recently fought a civil war; like her German contemporaries, Peabody hoped to reinforce national unity through community-building. To Peabody, as to the German kindergartners, the kindergarten seemed a miniature utopia, where individual freedom and community responsibility were reconciled. The successful transmission and adaptation of the German kindergarten to American conditions was also facilitated by Peabody's recruitment of several German teachers, including Wüstenfeld's coworker, Emma Marwedel. Two other German kindergartners, Maria Boelte (later Kraus-Boelte) and Matilda Kriege, set up the first Froebel courses in the United States and trained most of the first generation of American kindergarten teachers. Peabody made contact with many leaders of the American educational establishment, among them Henry Barnard and William Torrey Harris, who proved far more hospitable to the kindergarten idea than their German counterparts and arranged for the translation and publication of many of Marenholtz's works in the United States.[31]

The significance of the tradition of spiritual motherhood to German feminist movements of the 1860s and 1870s may be partly assessed through a comparison to Anglo-Saxon, and particularly American feminist movements. The American feminist movement of this period continued as a whole to center its efforts on the achievement of individual rights. The passage of the Fifteenth Amendment to the Constitution, which gave voting rights to freed male slaves but not to women, stimulated the founding of two organizations, the American and the National Woman Suffrage associations, both of which made suffrage the center of their programs. The German feminist organizations made no similar demands for suffrage during this era. Although advocated by some individuals, such as Otto-Peters and Dohm, suffrage was not included in the program of the German Women's Association. This difference was due to many factors, including the prevalent German tendency, strengthened during this period, to base the right of suffrage on military service. German feminists developed a conception of rights as earned rather than simply conferred by birth. "Through the education of the female sex," wrote Otto-Peters in 1872, "[and] through the spread of women's employment . . . we will prepare the foundation for the structure, of which woman suffrage will be the capstone."[32]

However, the direction of historical development in both countries was in some ways more toward the German model than toward the American. American feminists of this era, as historians William Leach and David Thelen have noted, were increasingly critical of what they termed the "unbridled individualism" of the antebellum period. They, too, came increasingly under the influence of organic social theories, most of which were imported from Europe, that conceived of rights in the context of duties to a community. American feminists, like their German sisters, began to identify the creation of community and of cooperative forms of social organization as a specifically feminine mission. Leach remarks that the Froebel kindergarten became fashionable in the United States during the 1870s because it exemplified, in microcosm, the "institutional framework of harmony and equilibrium" that reformers wished to establish in society as a whole. American women increasingly linked the achievement of suffrage with service to society. In both countries, the urban environment provided many opportunities for such service.[33]

Chapter 6
Mothers of the City: The Pestalozzi-Froebel House and the Creation of an Urban Role for Women, 1873–1900

"We have city fathers," said Henriette Goldschmidt in 1877, "but where are the mothers?" From the previous chapter, we have seen that the idea of spiritual motherhood was a fundamental influence on the development of an idea of citizenship for women in the new German national state. Increasingly, feminists' images of woman stressed uniquely female capacities for overcoming conflict, encouraging cooperation, and building community. It was a disciple of Froebel, Henriette Breymann (now, because of her marriage, calling herself Schrader-Breymann), who played the most important role in carving out for women a new field of activity in urban reform. Schrader-Breymann's work began in the Froebelian kindergarten tradition, but the massive acceleration of urban growth after 1870 provided a broader sphere of activity than had existed earlier. Under these conditions, Schrader-Breymann and her coworkers, while preserving the central idea of spiritual motherhood, developed new concepts of female professionalism and social activism. Their ideas and practical work had an important influence on the development of feminist theory and practice on many different issues during the 1880s and 1890s.[1]

During the period from 1870 to 1910, the growth of industry in the German Empire caused the massive and swift expansion of cities; whereas in 1871 there had been only eight cities with over 100,000 inhabitants, by 1910 there were thirty-three. The new cities, which first developed without any form of planning or regulation, were perceived negatively, as places of disease, ugliness, and alienation, by many new residents who had come from smaller towns. Another result of industrialization was the founding of the Social Democratic party, Marxist in theory though often more moderate in practice, which scored its first electoral success in 1878. Many upper- or middle-class Germans viewed these changes with considerable alarm; it was no longer possible to believe that proletarianization was a process that could simply be arrested or reversed. This mood of alarm was expressed in the Anti-Socialist Laws, passed by Bismarck's government in 1878, which allowed the Social Democratic party to participate in Reichstag elections but placed many restrictions on its freedom to organize. Starting in 1882, the Reichstag under Bismarck's leadership passed social insurance measures, partially funded by the government, with the express purpose of destroying socialism by preempting part of its program.[2]

The response of women such as Schrader-Breymann, Hedwig Heyl, and their colleagues to these new conditions and events was shaped by the complex interaction of class and gender consciousness. These women, their husbands, and many of their political associates had been born into the traditional commercial or professional elites of small communities. Still acting on concepts of social responsibility developed in these communities, both male and female members of this group often envisaged the solutions to social problems through the paternalistic concern of the elite for less fortunate members of the community. However, in addition to these class-specific attitudes, the motto "spiritual motherhood," denoting a gender-specific approach to social reform, was used by women to differentiate their own standpoints and interests from those of men. During this era, the trend toward the professionalization and bureaucratization of social services, whether governmental, municipal, or private, first became apparent. Women perceived this process as a threat to the charitable activities that had provided women's major center of power and influence. One strategy for preserving this influence was to push for the admission of women to bureaucracies; another was to stress the value of woman-led private institutions and charities.

"Spiritual motherhood" thus came to denote a spirit of individualized concern and compassion that was lost in an impersonal bureaucracy. The ideology reflected women's status and opportunities. This generation of women, barred from most forms of higher education, had no access to the learned sociological concepts or bureaucratic terminology used by their male contemporaries, particularly by the spokesmen for the Verein für Sozialpolitik (Social Policy Association), a prestigious group of professors and administrators who advised the government on social policy during this period. The women's responses to the urban poor tended thus to be expressed in language that was more direct and personal, and less distanced, than that of most male social scientists and officials. Moreover, some feminist reformers articulated their own sense of marginality within their own class by comparing the situation of middle-class single women to that of urban workers. In 1876, for example, Louise Otto-Peters complained that the disruption of household and social ties through urbanization had created a class of displaced single women, now threatened with poverty, unemployment, and social isolation. This perception of gender solidarity transcending class had obvious limitations; probably it was accepted by few working-class women.[3]

Whatever its limitations, however, this combination of class and gender perspectives was useful in defining the position of women reformers in relation both to their lower-class clients and to the men of their own class. Responses to clients emphasized class-based moral superiority; criticism of man-made institutions stressed compassion based on female ethical traditions and gender solidarity. Motherhood, connoting both authority and compassion, was an appropriate metaphor for this complex position. Lina Morgenstern, who during this period ran nutrition programs for the poor, expressed outrage at what she believed was the ignorance and irresponsibility of working-class mothers, to whom she referred as "poor, abandoned, irresponsible, and inexperienced." However, she and other female commentators also invoked a female-centered morality based on the sanctity of the mother-child bond in order to criticize male-dominated systems. Jeanne-Marie von Gayette-Georgens denounced the competitive capitalist economy that tore "the mothers from the cradles of their children and pulled them into the smoky, noxious atmosphere of the factories." In 1872 she reproached "that great social body, called the state" for being more concerned with "the expansion of its territory . . . than with the mothers, who should be raising citizens, scholars, heroes, workers, and artists. It [the state] . . . deprives them of their homes, forces them out on the street, even compels them to kill their children, rather than providing them with a means of supporting themselves." In 1873, Henriette Schrader-Breymann opposed the Social Darwinist arguments that were often used to justify callous indifference to suffering. "But will the human family not sink to the level of animals, or even lower, when the law of love is not respected among us? . . . In a life where we are struggling only for ourselves, don't even parents and children become rivals?"[4]

The City as Household: The Development of the Pestalozzi-Froebel House

The career of Henriette Schrader-Breymann after 1872 may be seen in the context of this tradition of female social thought and activism. As the head of the institute for women in Neu-Watzum, Henriette Breymann had met Karl Schrader; he was an attorney from a prominent Wolfenbüttel family who was active in the education society that she had founded and had advised her on some legal problems. In 1872 Breymann, now forty-five years old, married Schrader and moved with him to Berlin, where he had accepted a position as a director of the Anhalt railway system.[5]

This happy marriage, based on true emotional and intellectual congeniality, seems to have reinforced the belief of Henriette Schrader-Breymann in an ideal of gender equality based on complementary but equally valuable roles. She defined the difference between appropriate male and female occupational roles in terms not of ability but of ethical orientation. Whereas men aspired to knowledge and skills for their own sake, she speculated, women aspired to apply them to human concerns. "Not what women know or do not know, not what they can or cannot do, will make them womanly or unwomanly," she wrote. "That depends on how they use their knowledge." This conception of gender difference, though supporting some prevalent forms of discrimination, such as the exclusion of women from some "male" professions, opposed others. Its ethical rather than biological emphasis and its conception of maternal behavior as learned rather than instinctual challenged the biological determinism (based on theories of brain size and other innate characteristics) that had become fashionable among opponents of feminism in the 1870s. Most important, this argument asserted the ethical autonomy of women against conservative polemicists who still contended that woman's true virtue lay in obedience and deference to men. By contrast, Schrader-Breymann affirmed women's ethical and professional autonomy. "I certainly do not believe that women should perform exactly the same tasks as men," she wrote, ". . . but I do believe that the barriers between the sexes should fall, and that women should in every way be free of male control."[6]

Schrader-Breymann chose kindergarten and child-care work because it was one of the few fields of social activism that offered an opportunity for female leadership and some freedom from male control. As a trained kindergartner, she defined the chief social problem of the metropolis as the inadequacy of the urban environment to fulfill the custodial and developmental needs of small children. Like other reformers, she identified the children of working mothers as most at risk, and deplored the quality of available child care. Most existing child-care institutions continued to depend on private sponsorship, chiefly of church-affiliated charities, and were thus totally inadequate to meet the demand. "What are these institutions but emergency shelters?" asked another educator, Gayette-Georgens, "proofs of the disruption of German family life, and what is more depressing than the sight of a crowd of children, mostly sick and scrofulous, sitting . . . on benches, mechanically singing religious songs . . . and then driven out to a playground, often only a stretch of bare pavement, and commanded to play." The Froebelian Free Kindergarten movement, charged Henriette Schrader-Breymann, had often for lack of financial resources created similarly overcrowded and regimented institutions, which she called "caricatures of kindergartens."[7]

The first step toward the development of a more constructive alternative was the reorganization of a kindergarten society originally founded by Marenholtz, the Society for Family and Popular Education. In 1874, this society opened a free kindergarten, to which a program for the education of young women as kindergarten teachers was soon added. Finding space for the kindergarten was a problem in overcrowded Berlin. It was forced to change its location six times over the course of the first seven years and was once temporarily housed in the billiard room of a restaurant. In 1881, this problem was temporarily solved by the purchase of a house on Steinmetzstrasse in Schöneberg, a separate city in the Berlin metropolitan area, with contributions from Karl Schrader and other members of the society. The rapidly growing institution housed in this building soon became known as the Pestalozzi-Froebel House.[8]

Among the Schraders' supporters was Hedwig Heyl, who now had settled in Berlin and established a Froebel kindergarten and a school of domestic arts for her husband's employees. These enterprises, administered with the remarkable efficiency that was Heyl's most conspicuous attribute, soon came to the attention of the then Crown Princess Victoria, who was also a prominent patron of the Pestalozzi-Froebel House. In 1885 the princess persuaded Heyl to move her cooking school to the Steinmetzstrasse, where it became the basis for a School of Domestic

Arts (*Haushaltsschule*). By 1890 the programs of the Pestalozzi-Froebel House included a low-cost kindergarten enrolling 150 children from two to five years of age, an after-school crafts program, a two-year course for kindergarten teachers, shorter courses for nursemaids and childcare workers, courses in cooking and domestic arts, a school lunch program for the children of working mothers, and several other affiliated projects.[9]

At the Pestalozzi-Froebel House, Schrader-Breymann continued on a far more extensive scale the pedagogical and educational ideas that she had developed in her first institute at Watzum. The most important of these ideas was the creation of a form of institutional education based on the maternal discipline of the household rather than the coercive and patriarchal authority of the school. Class as well as gender consciousness shaped this pedagogical approach. The Pestalozzi-Froebel House prescribed middle-class familial culture, emphasizing emotional intimacy and individualized attention, as a remedy for the perceived inadequacies of the working-class household. Unlike most existing charity kindergartens, which assigned groups of up to one hundred children to one or two teachers, Schrader-Breymann's kindergarten was organized into small groups of children of different ages, which reproduced sibling groups within the family. The approach to teaching also emphasized the gender-specific ethic of spiritual motherhood. Each group was assigned to a kindergarten trainee, who thus had the opportunity to develop a truly personal and maternal rather than merely professional relationship to her charges. Such an intimate atmosphere, stated Clara Richter, who later became director of the kindergarten program, brought out the young women's "motherly talents, which would have been lost in a crowd."[10]

Much to the dismay of orthodox Froebelians such as her former friend Bertha von Marenholtz-Bülow, Schrader-Breymann almost totally abandoned Froebel's games, which she believed were rigid and authoritarian. Her own classroom routines were largely inspired by Pestalozzi's *Leonard and Gertrude*, which had described the morally elevating influence exerted by the mother in her home workshop. Schrader-Breymann involved children of both sexes in activities based on household occupations. For instance, an extended project for teachers and pupils was the making of pea soup, from the planting of the peas to the eventual cooking and eating of the soup. Schrader-Breymann, who viewed city dwellers' loss of contact with agrarian life as deeply unnatural, insisted that the children must become acquainted with gardening and the care of farm animals. The observation of such animals often required a field trip to a dairy or blacksmith's shop. Lesson plans focused each month on a different object—usually an animal or plant—and the teacher trainees were expected to provide intensive scientific and practical information on such objects. This educational program thus showed a complex of progressive and conservative attitudes, combining an awareness of new social problems with a continuing attachment to traditional small-town and rural life. One historian has called the American contemporaries and counterparts of these Germans "reformers in search of yesterday."[11]

The ideology of spiritual motherhood was both outward- and inward-turning. In the small world of the institution, Schrader-Breymann attempted to develop administrative and educational practices based on the mother-centered household. Administered, staffed, and attended by women, the institution became an enclave of female control in an era when most educational institutions, even those serving girls or women, were led by men. Although the external business of the institution was conducted by a committee consisting of seven men and seven women, the internal decisions were left to an all-female board (headed by Schrader-Breymann until her death in 1899), which delegated power over the institution's various divisions to similarly constituted sub-committees.[12]

The administrative style developed by Schrader-Breymann and her colleagues reflected their emphasis on female friendship and community. Accounts of their relationships, which were usually sentimental and idealized, probably reveal less about the down-to-earth realities of daily life than about the norms of professionalism and institutional culture to which the narrators aspired. When the Pestalozzi-Froebel House acquired a permanent home, Schrader-Breymann, who had hitherto performed much of the teaching and administration on a voluntary basis, appointed her former student and friend Annette Hamminck-Schepel as director. Their personal closeness enhanced the smooth functioning of the institution. "Annette was full of devoted and tender love for her old friend," wrote a mutual acquaintance. "Henriette was no less affectionate and often full of admiration for the way that Annette understood her ideas on female education and carried them out, often in a way that surprised Henriette." In 1892, Hamminck-Schepel retired from the director's position and was succeeded by Clara Richter, whose organizational talents were well suited to the administration of a now large and complex institution. Richter combined efficiency with what one student called "that motherly concern, which is the alpha and omega of all education." Underlying these accounts was a challenge to accepted antitheses between private and public spheres and between love and work. Unlike many of their male contemporaries, the women of the Pestalozzi-Froebel House conceived of personal and professional relationships as complementary rather than conflicting, of mutual affection among colleagues as an enhancement rather than a barrier to efficiency, and of authority as a nurturing rather than a coercive function.[13]

The reminiscences of former students suggest that some of the same spirit was encouraged among the students themselves and in their association with the teaching staff. The students in the kindergarten training program, who were required to complete a girls' secondary-school program to qualify for admission, were chiefly from the upper and middle classes. Some of these students, daughters of impoverished though respectable families, were forced to learn a profession for economic reasons; Schrader-Breymann provided scholarships for such needy students. Others came from prosperous families who strenuously objected to their aspirations to professional work. Nelly Wolffheim of the class of 1896 remarked that "in the middle class, it was not customary for young girls who 'didn't need one' to learn a profession." To young women separated physically and emotionally from their families, the institution provided a substitute family offering emotional support. Many students lived in a dormitory on an upper floor of the house in Steinmetzstrasse. "Why were we so happy?" reminisced Hanna von Prittwitz of the class of 1897. "Was it the moral seriousness of our endeavor? . . . Was it the two women who led the institution—Frau Schrader and Frau Hamminck-Schepel, and the loving atmosphere with which they surrounded us? Our happy, innocent dormitory life was full of this spirit."[14]

Unlike those of many men of their generation, whose memoirs usually stressed the unloving, impersonal, and authoritarian atmosphere of their schools, the available memoirs and reminiscences of these female students give a favorable picture of the culture of this female community. Many historians of nineteenth-century women-led institutions note that these often served as communities in which single women could develop close ties of friendship and solidarity. American historian Linda Kerber remarks that the social settlements set up in the 1880s, especially Hull House, "marked an enclosure within which women could define the terms of their most private relationships and defend themselves against social criticism."[15]

The purpose of this educational community was to prepare students for public service; as a brochure stated, to encourage "women and girls of the educated classes" to enter into "loving and natural relationships with the poorer classes." In response to the pressing demand for job opportunities for single women, the institution's preprofessional programs expanded rapidly. In 1890, 60 students were enrolled in the two-year kindergarten-training program; by 1904 the enrollment in that program had expanded to 150, and 30 attended shorter courses in child care. Schrader-Breymann's conception of female professionalism had considerable practical value. In order to meet the growing need for social services, especially for children, the original program for kindergarten teachers was expanded to include training for jobs such as "child-care specialist" and "youth worker," specifically adapted to an urban setting. The identification of needs hitherto ignored by men, and the training of women to fill them, was the beginning of an ongoing struggle to contest the control of male-dominated local governments and charitable organizations over urban social service. Schrader-Breymann devised a new role for the urban kindergarten teacher that was based on the tradition of "friendly visiting" among women's philanthropic groups and contributed to an emerging new model of professionalism, that of the female social worker. Graduates of the institution were encouraged to live in the neighborhoods where they worked and to devote not just classroom hours, but "the whole of [their] existence to the community where [they] were employed."[16]

The same conviction of the importance of household skills, when properly developed, to the urban community was expressed by Hedwig Heyl, founder of the cooking courses that later formed the basis of the School of Domestic Arts at the Pestalozzi-Froebel House. This division, where the daughter of the crown prince and princess (also named Victoria) was among the first students, soon provided a large variety of courses, chiefly in cooking but also in sewing and housekeeping. Some of these courses were intended for upper- and middle-class girls seeking general training in domestic arts, and some for elementary school graduates destined for domestic service. Though affirming the importance of some traditional female skills, Heyl's curriculum was by no means intended simply to socialize young women for conventional domestic lives. Heyl, who had served meals to her husband's employees, had noted the deterioration of nutrition among urban industrial workers. Her friend and advisor in the attempt to place cooking on a scientific basis was Josephine Mayer, who had written a cookbook (under the pen name of Marie Ernst) applying the principles of chemistry to nutrition. Mayer criticized cookbooks that taught fancy but nutritionally worthless cooking; she attempted to create nutritious recipes that were adapted to the budgets, way of life, and tastes of low-income people. Heyl wrote a popular cookbook and conducted outreach programs for women (predominantly of the working class) in the community. Her lecture for one such educational program showed a considerable understanding of the problems of working women; she outlined a simple recipe for a rice casserole that could be brought to a boil in the morning and then wrapped in pillows and left to steam until the return of the family for midday dinner.[17]

"There is no material," stated Heyl, "which provides a richer source of interesting principles, observation, and insight into cultural history than the domestic arts, if they are as deeply investigated as they deserve to be." When Heyl made these remarks in 1897, over fifteen hundred students had studied at her school during its twelve-year existence. Many of these women went on to professional work, especially teaching in domestic arts programs in girls' schools and in adult education programs.[18]

The Pestalozzi-Froebel House served as a center for many philanthropic activities. Like his wife, Karl Schrader was a tireless philanthropist who supported many organizations designed to encourage the values that he considered most important—economic independence and personal responsibility. One such organization, the Verein für häusliche Gesundheitspflege (Association for Home Health Care), which was devoted to helping low-income people care for their sick relatives at home rather than sending them to hospitals, also sponsored a program to send sick children away from the city, a supposedly unhealthy environment, to summer camp in the country. The energetic and devoted organizer of this effort was Luise Jessen, who in addition to raising her five children had worked with Wüstenfeld at the Hamburg trade school and had then moved to Berlin with her husband, Otto Jessen, who headed a trade school for boys. Luise Jessen worked as a year-round volunteer, selecting the children most in need of help, organizing the fresh-air camps, hiring teachers, and running bazaars to provide financial support. She never failed to be at the station to welcome the children back to the city after their stay in the country. From 1880 to 1908 the enrollment in the program increased from 108 to 5,247 children. Many similar programs, some inspired by Jessen's work, were founded in other cities. A close friend and coworker of Henriette Schrader-Breymann, Jessen became head of the institution's executive committee in 1904.[19]

The Pestalozzi-Froebel House continued to grow and flourish. The building on Steinmetzstrasse was soon too small for the varied programs it housed. The fund-raising program of the institution, like its internal structure and administration, depended on a network of female friendship. Elise Wentzel-Heckmann was an intimate friend of Hedwig Heyl; after their husbands died, the two women lived together and indulged a shared passion for gardening. In 1896, Wentzel-Heckmann, who had inherited a fortune and an interest in architecture from her late husband, a building contractor, endowed two new buildings, one for the domestic arts school and one for the kindergarten and kindergarten training program. These buildings, although criticized by students who missed the coziness of the Steinmetzstrasse, in fact integrated domestic and institutional space. The first floor of the kindergarten building housed an infants' nursery and a kindergarten (complete with a sun room for plants); the second was devoted to classrooms and a gymnasium; the third was residential, containing not only an apartment for the director but small rooms where students could teach groups of children in an intimate, noninstitutional atmosphere. Thus, this building exemplified the use of physical space to suit women's institutional cultures and social purposes that was an important aspect of the nineteenth-century women's movement.[20]

Motherhood, Politics, and Education

The proponents of spiritual motherhood, although insisting on female autonomy, regarded cooperation between women and men as the final goal. As Karen Offen has noted, many European feminists of this period envisaged the redemption of society not through the liberation of the individual woman but through the harmonious and egalitarian cooperation of the two genders, each working in its own fashion. The women of the Pestalozzi-Froebel House saw their own work very much as part of a wider political agenda, to be carried out in collaboration with their male partners, supporters, and colleagues. Karl Schrader, the husband of Henriette Schrader-Breymann, was elected to the Reichstag in 1881 and soon became a leading member of a minority liberal group known as the

Secession, which split off from the mainstream National Liberal party in 1882 and two years later joined with another liberal group, the Progressives, to form a new party, the Freisinnige Volkspartei (Independent People's party). This group, made up predominantly of professionals and some progressive businessmen, was deeply disaffected with Bismarck's continuing control over politics. They attributed the authoritarian structure and conservative policies of the Empire partly to the failure of the liberal bourgeoisie to play an active, independent, and responsible role in state and society. The volunteer activities of the women of this group contributed to a more general effort to create a new model of citizenship for the bourgeoisie as a basis for a renewal of its political ambitions.[21]

This political agenda was developed in a lively social circle meeting at the Schrader home. The group provided a very rare if not unique opportunity for women and men to discuss political issues in an egalitarian and collegial atmosphere. Helene Lange, a member of the group and later the leader of the German feminist movement, recalled the Schraders as the "leading figures in the political liberal movement, and also in what one could call the cultural liberal movement." The men of this movement did not regard pedagogy as a marginal, or exclusively female concern, but placed it in the center of their political agenda. "We all agreed," stated Lange, "that any change in our economic, social, and political behavior must come from the inside, through education and cultivation, through self-improvement."[22]

The combination of class and gender perspectives that informed the separate projects of the women of this group also influenced their approach to the wider world of male-dominated politics. Bismarck's national insurance program, funded by the state, employers, and workers themselves, used the authority of the state to provide a certain minimum of material security. The Schraders and their friends, opponents of Bismarck, perceived this action correctly as an attempt to weaken the liberal bourgeoisie by creating an alliance between the state and the working class. To the women, such centralized measures, carried out by a male-dominated bureaucracy, also appeared as a threat to their own control over philanthropic activities. Thus, many liberal men and women of this generation opposed state-sponsored social welfare measures. Hedwig Heyl, who first discovered her extraordinary administrative talents by organizing benefits for her husband's employees, remarked that she and her friends had always "looked on the compulsory insurance law with mistrust, because . . . I noticed a decline in the interest of employers in charitable work for their employees. . . . I often thought of Renan's saying, 'Bismarck has made Germany greater, but the Germans smaller.'" Until the end of her life, Henriette Schrader continued to criticize what she regarded as the cold impersonality of state-organized bureaucracies and to extol the familial and motherly spirit of love and personal concern. Class conflict, she wrote in 1894, could not be resolved by "external laws" but only by the "free work of love." Some of these objections to the social insurance laws were perceptive. As workers themselves were quick to point out, these measures were indeed intended to encourage political passivity and dependence on the state rather than activism. Directed chiefly at the industrial labor-force, moreover, they had little direct effect on the lot of the majority of women and children. At the same time, however, the inadequacy of "free work of love" to improve social conditions in the absence of structural change would be perceived by the next generation of bourgeois reformers.[23]

Whatever their limitations, the Schrader circle's concepts of citizenship, social responsibility, and the role of women were of central importance to the evolution of the feminist movement during the 1880s. Helene Lange, who was a member of the circle and a close personal friend of Henriette Schrader-Breymann, did more than any other individual to set the course of the mainstream women's movement from the 1880s to World War I. Lange was born in 1848 into a merchant's family near Oldenburg and lost her mother at an early age. She was raised by her father, whom she described in her autobiography as a kind, understanding, but somewhat distant parent. Although never accepting Froebelian pedagogy, which she considered too structured and confining, she regretted the lack of maternal support and advice that she had felt during her childhood. As a schoolgirl she was also much disturbed by the well-intentioned but inept and tactless attempts of a male teacher to deal with issues of sexual morality that she believed a woman teacher would have handled more effectively.[24]

As a result of her contact with feminist circles in Berlin, where she had come to train as a teacher, Lange read the German translation of John Stuart Mill's *The Subjection of Women*. Although positively impressed by many of Mill's arguments, she criticized his view of women's nature as the artificial creation of male culture. Women's nature, she insisted, was a product not of patriarchy but of women's autonomous culture; "equality," she argued, "should be demanded not because of the similarity, but because of the difference between the sexes, so that the one-sided male culture can be completed by a female culture."[25]

Lange, though not in agreement with Schrader-Breymann on every subject, based her own far more ambitious approach to educational reform on a concept of female autonomy that was obviously influenced by the older woman's ideas. In 1887, Lange took one of the earliest and most important steps in the long campaign to open teaching positions in secondary schools for girls to women by submitting a petition to the Prussian Ministry of Education. The petition was signed by Schrader-Breymann and Luise Jessen, as well as by two other members of the Schrader circle, Minna Cauer, later a prominent leader of the radical feminist movement, and Marie Loeper-Housselle, a former teacher and kindergarten activist. The accompanying statement is characterized by historian James C. Albisetti as one of the most "hard-hitting" feminist manifestos of the period. Lange indignantly denounced a recent recommendation from a male-dominated teachers' convention that girls should be educated so that German husbands should not be bored by intellectually limited wives. She saw this as just one more example of the traditional belief, which she traced to Rousseau, that women existed for the sake of men. Lange protested men's dominance over girls' secondary education and their attempts to exclude women from teaching positions. Male teachers, she said, were "much too unfamiliar with the cultural and practical environment" of their female pupils to make conventional curricular content interesting or useful to such pupils.[26]

Lange recommended instead that girls be educated to fulfill their own intellectual and ethical potential, "for themselves, as human beings," and insisted that this could only be accomplished by female teachers who could provide guidance and role-models as well as academic training. She cited Pestalozzi to affirm the importance of both love and practical experience to education, and suggested that a kindergarten be attached to each girls' secondary school. Such claims to female autonomy were clearly threatening to authority structures such as the Prussian Ministry of Education, which in response to the petition supported conservative definitions of womanly virtue as subservience to men by insisting that women should be educated only for the role of wifely "helpmate."[27]

Lange's approach to educational reform can certainly be understood in practical terms as an attempt to appeal to conventional preferences for single-sex education in order to win acceptance for women teachers. But her ideas also had a deeper philosophical significance. For Lange, the problem with women's education was not simply women's exclusion from the existing structures and curricula. These curricula themselves were male-created, the products of a one-sided male understanding of culture, and thus irrelevant to the experience and concerns of female pupils. Lange later modified her original belief in separate and female-led education in order to campaign for the admission of women to university studies. But the ideal of gender difference, or spiritual motherhood, continued to be the basis for her developing feminist critique of male-dominated culture.[28]

The approach to female education, both practical and theoretical, developed by the members of the Schrader circle found approval in high places. In the 1880s, the most prominent members of this circle were the Crown Prince Frederick and his English wife, Victoria, the eldest daughter of Queen Victoria. This couple, who were constantly embroiled in intrigues against Bismarck and his supporters, sometimes escaped from the hostile atmosphere of the Court to enjoy the company of like-minded people. Victoria believed strongly in education for women and favored practical over purely academic curricula. Her own early training by a governess who used Froebel methods probably contributed to her enthusiasm for the Pestalozzi-Froebel House, which she soon included among her multitude of charitable causes. Not merely a prestigious name on the subscription list, Victoria paid frequent, often informal visits to the institution, and she and Frederick often attended the Christmas festivities. By aligning themselves with the progressive and socially active bourgeoisie, Frederick and Victoria sought a base of political support against the reactionary military and aristocratic circle of Bismarck. Left-wing liberals such as the Schraders and their friends placed their main hopes for the liberalization of the German political system in the accession of Frederick, who had expressed admiration for the British constitutional form of monarchy. These hopes for political reform included governmental support for female education. According to Lange, another of Victoria's intimates, the future empress planned an immense institute in which academic courses preparing for secondary teaching would be held alongside courses in kindergarten pedagogy, nursing, and the new field of social work. Victoria, who insisted that all of these courses be offered in the same space, envisaged a female community that would provide an overview "of the spheres of action, which in their totality represent the entire cultural mission of women." The premature death of Frederick after only three months on the throne blighted these along with other liberal hopes.[29]

The Pestalozzi-Froebel House and a Widened Social Agenda

Despite the death of Frederick and the frustration of liberal hopes, the Pestalozzi-Froebel House continued to expand. Its development was influenced by an important transition in ideas of child development, from Froebel's own highly spiritual philosophy to the more materialistic and practical approaches that predominated in the later two decades of the century. The institution's experimentation with these new ideas of child development had international impact. Although some American kindergartners had begun to revise Froebelian methods in the 1880s, most kindergarten training programs in the United States continued to follow Froebel faithfully. Elizabeth Harrison, the head of a kindergarten training college in Chicago who visited the Pestalozzi-Froebel House in 1889, was surprised and somewhat disapproving of Schrader's extensive substitution of practical activities for Froebel games. Harrison was later won over to these methods, however, which she taught to her many students in the United States.[30]

In 1893, the institution received international publicity through an exhibit at the Chicago World's Fair, which Henriette Schrader-Breymann was prevented from attending because of her poor health. Several years later, eminent American educator G. Stanley Hall visited the Pestalozzi-Froebel House and gave a highly favorable report on its work. Although recognizing Froebel as the "morning star" of the child-study movement, Hall rejected his one-sided emphasis on spiritual development and called for methods based on a more down-to-earth understanding of the child's physical and psychological development. Hall called the Pestalozzi-Froebel House the "finest kindergarten installation in the world today." He praised its pedagogical techniques based on practical work and nature study and its emphasis on hygiene and nutrition. Hall and the American women who worked with him created a new approach to early childhood education reflecting many of the same principles and methods.[31]

The approach to social activism created by the Pestalozzi-Froebel House faced new challenges in the 1890s. The conviction of Schrader-Breymann and Heyl that the "free work of love" would create gender solidarity and solve social problems was aggressively challenged by the first organizations representing working-class women. The socialist women's groups that were formed in the 1890s objected to the involvement of middle-class women with the children of workers. In the 1890s, for example, the newspaper *Die Gleichheit* ("Equality"), which was the most widely read publication aimed at socialist women and was edited by prominent socialist Clara Zetkin, constantly emphasized the limitations of bourgeois reform efforts. Among the programs singled out for such criticism were the summer vacation programs for working-class children of the kind that were organized by the Pestalozzi-Froebel House. "The blessings that they have brought us are hardly noticeable in the midst of massive poverty," stated an editorial written in 1894. "It is impossible that a child who has become sick from constant undernourishment, from forced neglect of the most elementary requirements of health . . . should be transformed by a few weeks of vacation into a blooming, healthy creature." Rejecting such palliative measures, another editorial called for state-sponsored measures to promote the welfare of children: "It is necessary to force the existing state to take measures that will stop the unscrupulous waste of the proletariat's strength through the impoverishment of workers' children."[32]

The rising generation of bourgeois reformers shared some of the concerns, although not the overall political agenda, of their socialist contemporaries. In the 1890s and the early twentieth century, the Pestalozzi-Froebel House broadened its concerns to include the total environment, including the physical conditions, that influenced child development. And even the founding generation, although never sympathetic to socialism, proved capable of political growth in response to new conditions. Henriette Schrader-Breymann, although continuing to believe in the power of education to change behavior, nonetheless noted the inadequacy of even the most devoted maternal nurture in the hostile environment of "narrow city streets where the level of public health is very low, in a house where father and mother struggle against crushing poverty." Karl Schrader overcame his opposition to governmental intervention in the economy sufficiently to consent, albeit somewhat reluctantly, to the unification of his parliamentary group, then called the Freisinnige Vereinigung (Free-Thinking Union) with Friedrich Naumann's National Socialist Union in 1903. This party, recruited chiefly from the liberal bourgeoisie, sought to broaden the liberal program to include a more positive role for government in the provision of social security and welfare benefits.[33]

The role of state and local governments in supporting private educational and philanthropic institutions was also an important issue for the female professionals who graduated from the Pestalozzi-Froebel House, as well as from other kindergarten training programs. Unfortunately, we have no quantitative data on how many of these women went on to professional careers, or on what kinds of positions they entered, but their letters to the school's monthly bulletin indicate that almost all were hired for positions in private institutions—kindergartens, kindergarten training programs, day care centers, after-school programs, domestic arts programs—or homes. Some graduates played conspicuous roles in the improvement of services to children in various cities. For example, Erna Weigert, who had helped organize the social work program (to be described in Chapter Eleven) at the Pestalozzi-Froebel House, visited Frankfurt in 1899 to advise that city's recently established Free Kindergarten Society on the establishment of services to mothers and children. The Society later hired a permanent director from the Pestalozzi-Froebel House. Other graduates headed their own kindergartens, where they found the experience of independence and leadership exhilarating despite often difficult conditions. "A year has gone by," wrote one graduate, "and I have found so much joy and inner fulfillment in my work that I've never regretted my decision."[34]

However, because kindergarten classes continued to be supported chiefly by private funds from tuition fees and charitable foundations, the economic situation of kindergarten teachers remained very precarious. Their salaries, which in 1906 began at about fifty marks per month, were usually less than those of women elementary school teachers and were about at the level of those of the better-paid female industrial workers of the time. Working conditions, too, reflected the low status of child care as an occupation. A teacher working in a charity kindergarten reported that she had no money to buy supplies and had to collect discarded items such as string and cigar boxes from the local families. A young graduate assigned to an overcrowded urban kindergarten reported despairingly, "Froebel's games are used only to keep the children quiet." The problems suffered by young women hired as private child-care workers were still often very severe. In 1903, for instance, the liberal newspaper *Die Hilfe* ("Help") reported on an ambitious but stingy family who sought prestige by hiring a graduate of the Pestalozzi-Froebel House to care for their children and then so burdened the inexperienced girl with household tasks that she was eventually hospitalized for malnutrition and exhaustion.[35]

One possible means of raising the status of both the Froebelian approach to child-rearing and the women who practiced it was the integration of kindergarten classes into public school systems. Henriette Schrader-Breymann, who had supported this goal during her early career, increasingly retreated from it out of fear that the intimacy of the teacher-pupil relationship would be destroyed by the pressures of mass education. But the more politically oriented Henriette Goldschmidt favored it strongly. Goldschmidt, who continued to play an active role in the German Women's Association, had in 1872 also founded her own kindergarten-training institute, which was in some ways similar to the Pestalozzi-Froebel House, the *Lyzeum für Damen* (Academy for Women) in Leipzig. When the *Bund deutscher Frauenvereine* (Federation of German Women's Organizations) was founded in 1894 under the leadership of her longtime coworker Auguste Schmidt, Goldschmidt was appointed to head the organization's committee on educational questions.[36]

In 1898 she drafted a petition, to be sent to all the state governments, requesting state control of kindergarten training programs and the incorporation of required kindergarten classes into public school systems. Goldschmidt's petition struck a new and confident note—she demanded that child-rearing be recognized as an important issue not just for families, charitable organizations, and women professionals, but for government. As in her earlier writings, Goldschmidt emphasized the value of citizenship, which must be taught from the earliest years of life: "It is urgently necessary to ensure the raising of the coming generation in the interests of the state." Goldschmidt's ambitious petition, which requested not only the founding of public school kindergartens but the requirement of attendance for two years, was intended more to bring the importance of early childhood education to the attention of the public than to produce immediate results. Support from the kindergarten movement was far from unanimous; Goldschmidt's petition was opposed by the now philanthropically oriented German Froebel Society, but strongly supported by Eleonore Heerwart, the head of a kindergarten teachers' association that had been founded in 1892.[37]

The response to the petition reflected the continued prevalence in the German-speaking world of conservative attitudes toward childhood, the family, and the status of women inside and outside the home. The offensive against Goldschmidt's petition was led by the teachers; the incorporation of kindergartens into public school systems was voted down in 1899 by the annual teachers' convention in Gotha with near unanimity. The teachers opposed not only the pedagogy of the Froebel kindergarten but the entire ideology of spiritual motherhood that had sought to apply maternal values to public issues. Teacher Otto Beetz, who on this issue acted as the chief spokesperson for his professional colleagues, characterized motherhood as a function based on instinct and appropriate only to the private sphere of the home. To this maternal education, based only on the "dark impulses" of the heart, Beetz contrasted the enlightened and morally elevated masculine pedagogy of the school. He argued that the kindergarten would break down barriers between private and public spheres and thus destroy the integrity of the family. Beetz' tirade still supported the view of the home as the "shadow" of the public sphere articulated by Hegel nearly a century earlier. The continuing influence of this view was reflected in the negative responses of state governments to Goldschmidt's petition. Quite aside from the impracticality and the expense of the proposal, the Education Ministry of Saxony insisted that "the rearing and care of small children is a function of the family."[38]

The German feminist movement of this period has been called "cautious and conservative" because of its ideology based on gender difference and maternal service rather than equal rights. But a comparison to the work of American women during the same period shows that German women were sometimes regarded as innovators, and that progress in the achievement of equal rights was increasingly linked to social service. The kindergarten movement, although only one of a large number of reform movements undertaken by American women of this era, provides an instructive case study of the application of spiritual motherhood in the two societies. In the period 1870–1900, the kindergarten idea, imported from Germany, became fully Americanized. Like their German counterparts, American women supported the kindergarten as a means of bringing about moral improvement, class reconciliation, and new forms of urban community. For the many American women who founded charity kindergartens (or Free Kindergartens as they were called) in the American cities, the social and pedagogical challenge was even greater than that faced by German reformers; the American cities of this period were flooded with immigrants, whose integration into American life became a major concern of educational authorities. Largely for this reason, the school authorities in American cities did not share the conservative concern for the preservation of family life that preoccupied their German counterparts. They perceived the immigrant family as a center of alien culture rather than as a sacred zone of privacy. School authorities in America were much more willing, even eager, to incorporate kindergartens into public school systems than were authorities in Germany; by 1914, many major American cities had public school kindergartens. Thus the female reformers' basic agenda—the erosion of barriers between public and private spheres—was better adapted to the social and political conditions of America than of Germany.[39]

Another important factor was the somewhat higher status of women in American educational and political systems. Women in some American states during this period won the right to vote in local elections, a right that was exercised by very few German women. Women also predominated in the elementary school teaching profession. These gains in women's progress toward equal rights also benefited maternal causes such as the kindergarten movement. Female teachers and voters, increasingly dedicated to social motherhood as a political agenda, often used their power to support the founding of public school kindergartens. American kindergarten founders admired the work of their German counterparts. The Pestalozzi-Froebel House was an important influence on the adaptation of the American kindergarten to urban conditions, and ultimately on the settlement houses, which often sponsored kindergartens. Thus, activist women in Germany and the United States agreed on many goals, and the comparatively limited results achieved by the Germans were probably more attributable to the conservatism of German society as a whole than to the conservatism of the feminist movement itself.[40]

Part 2
Motherhood, Social Reform, and the State

Chapter 7
Mothers, Children, and the Law, 1888–1902

During the decade of the 1890s, the discourse on motherhood among German feminists was transformed by the infusion of new ideas, new issues, and new organizational strategies. Part Two will focus on several crucial transitions. The feminist organizations that were founded in the period 1888–1914 brought to the fore a new generation of activists. Many of these activists challenged the traditional ideology of "spiritual motherhood," with all its connotations of self-effacing service, and called for more assertive tactics and more ambitious goals. Such goals often went beyond the philanthropic activities described in Part One, and extended to the reform of the state. The expanding welfare state, regarded by an older generation of feminists with mistrust, appeared to the new generation in a more positive light as a favorable environment for personal emancipation and social reform. The new generation's discourse on motherhood often shifted from spiritual to biological motherhood, including sexuality, reproductive patterns, marriage, and alternative forms of the family.

However, beneath these changes was an underlying continuity. Like their predecessors, the new generation of feminists used the idea of motherhood as a metaphor for an ethical commitment that extended to both private and public worlds. During the period 1890–1914, this female-centered ethical system based on maternal values of relationship and community was adapted to the changing structures of family, society, and state.

Campaigns for reform of family and household, one of the oldest feminist issues, moved into a new phase during the 1890s. This was due in part to an event that in itself had little connection to the feminist movement—the completion of the first draft of the new Civil Code of the German Empire, which was made public in 1887 and discussed in the Reichstag in 1895 before being passed in 1896. This new legal system superseded the marriage and family laws of the various German states with a uniform code.[1]

The discussion of the legal rights of mothers, an important issue in this campaign, was shaped by the split between two factions, usually known as "moderates" and "radicals." In 1888 a new organization, the Verein Frauenwohl (Women's Welfare Association), had been founded as the women's branch of an organization known as the Deutsche akademische Vereinigung (German Academic Union) under political activist Minna Cauer. This organization, although radical and innovative, also showed considerable continuity with the past history of the movement, for Cauer, as well as Lange (who later became a leader of the moderate faction), was a member of the Schrader circle. The new group went beyond the program of the German Women's Association, which it considered too cautious, to take stands on many controversial issues. It attempted to forge relationships with working-class women's groups and, in 1895, advocated woman suffrage, which the older organizations had never officially endorsed. The new group's interest in sexual issues such as pornography and the regulation of prostitution led to broader insights into the nature and effects of male privilege in society. In 1894 the Welfare Association and many other groups were included in a new, loosely structured umbrella organization, the Bund deutscher Frauenvereine (Federation of German Women's Organizations). Both the majority of the membership and the leaders of this organization, among whom were Henriette Goldschmidt and her coworker Auguste Schmidt, adhered to traditional forms of activism and designated themselves moderates. But these leaders were challenged by the militant minority (now calling themselves progressives or radicals), who pushed for more controversial stands and more aggressive tactics. In 1899 the radicals, including the members of the Welfare Association, formed their own organization, the Verband fortschrittlicher Frauenvereine (League of Progressive Women's Organizations). Although this group remained outside the Federation until 1907, many of its individual members continued to belong to the Federation and constantly urged the radicalization of its programs.[2]

The campaign against the Civil Code was led by the radical group, which dominated the Legal Committee of the Federation, and marked the radicals' emergence into wide public visibility. Historical accounts of the moderate-radical split often hinge on a theoretical dichotomy between relational or maternal and individualist feminist ideologies; historian Bärbel Clemens, for example, contrasts the radicals' belief in sex-neutral "natural rights" with the moderates' advocacy of maternal service. The debate on the Civil Code proves that dichotomy to be oversimplified, however. Certainly, the radicals advocated the individual rights of women, but among the most essential of those rights were the rights of motherhood. Their defense of these rights was based more often on the sacredness of the mother-child bond than on the individual liberties of mothers. Their discourse on the ethical meaning of motherhood and the rights of illegitimate children, moreover, showed a marked continuity with earlier feminist writings that connected the rights of the individual mother to those of the child, and to the welfare of society.[3]

Motherhood under Patriarchy: The Protest against the Civil Code

The creation of the new Civil Code, from its initiation to its final adoption, took more than twenty years. At the time of its unification, the German Empire had only local codes developed by states that had hitherto been independent. As we have seen, the appointment of a committee to draft a new code of laws for the Empire as a whole had prompted the German Women's Association in 1876 to draw up a series of petitions to the Reichstag on various issues affecting women.[4]

By 1887, when the code was completed and made public, an expanding feminist movement resorted not just to the traditional tactic of the petition but to more aggressive froms of protest. The first feminist protest activity was the creation of numerous local legal aid centers (*Rechtsschutzstellen*), usually set up under the auspices of the Welfare Association to inform women of their legal rights. When the Federation of Women's Organizations was founded in 1894, a more centralized campaign was led by its Legal Committee, headed by Marie Stritt and Anna Simson. Simson, who was born in Breslau in 1835, had begun her career as an activist with the kindergarten movement and other educational endeavors there. Stritt, born in 1855 in Dresden, had worked as an actress and was married to an opera singer. She became active in the feminist movement in 1891, when she founded the first of the women's legal aid centers in Dresden. The Legal Committee drafted a petition for revision of the Civil Code, which was sent to the Reichstag in 1896 with twenty-five thousand signatures. When this petition was rejected, the

Committee led the most massive protest movement ever organized by a feminist organization. Stimulated by brochures and local demonstrations and lecture series, this protest brought the status of women as wives and as mothers to the forefront of public attention.[5]

The provisions of the new Code themselves did much to encourage the shift of emphasis from the public to the private status of women that marked feminist programs after 1890. In the first half of the nineteenth century, feminist authors had perceived the status of women to be higher in the private than in the public sphere. But a new generation of feminists came to the opposite conclusion, for the Code showed a substantial discrepancy between the progress of single women in the public sphere and the continued subordination of wives and mothers. The Civil Code swept away most of the traditional disadvantages of single women, who were now permitted to sign contracts, bring lawsuits, own property, and engage in commercial transactions on the same basis as men. In striking contrast were its provisions regulating marriage and the family. The new Code, although it eliminated laws that had allowed husbands to punish their wives physically and to determine when children should be weaned, was in some ways still more restrictive than the older, local codes that it superseded. Although perhaps the chief focus of this campaign was on the continuing control of the husband over his wife's property (excluding her earnings, which she was allowed to control herself) and on the restrictions on the right to divorce, the Code's definition of the mother-child relationship was also an important issue. The feminists' protest drew attention not only to the law itself but to the social conditions of inequality to which the law gave its prestigious sanction.[6]

The most basic law affecting the rights of mothers and children was the definition of "parental rights." The original local codes had shown some variation; while the Prussian General Law of 1794 had recognized only paternal power, some of the other states had theoretically given power over children to both parents, although requiring the father's will to take precedence in case of disagreement. The new Civil Code, which recognized parental rather than paternal power, appeared to support the claims of women to equal status within the family. In fact, however, the Civil Code effectively nullified the parental rights of mothers during the lifetime of the father. Of the various forms of parental power, mothers were allotted only the "personal care" of the child; the control of the child's financial affairs, education, choice of a profession, and (if underage) choice of a marriage partner was assigned to the father. Even in matters relating to the personal care of the child, the father's will prevailed if the parents disagreed.[7]

This provision was vigorously contested by both radical and moderate feminists. Marianne Weber summed up some of the moderates' objections in a commentary on the debate published in 1907. "The will of the mother must always yield to that of the father," explained Weber. "He can, if he wishes, decide entirely independently how children are to be cared for, supervised and fed, which school they should attend, which profession they should adopt, indeed he can even take them away from the mother against her will and entrust them to the care of a third party. And . . . the law gives her no right to appeal to the Guardians' Court against these decisions." Weber further remarked that the law gave paternal power priority not only over the rights of the mother but over the interests of the children. Even a father whose parental rights had been suspended because of drunkenness or insanity retained control of the children's financial affairs. If the father flagrantly abused parental power and was thus declared unfit, parental power did not pass to the mother, who the lawgivers said might be subject to his influence, but was entrusted to a male guardian. One improvement in the new Code, attributable partly to pressure from women's groups, allowed mothers to assume guardianships of their children after the fathers' deaths, but the father's will, or a court, could appoint a guardian if the mother seemed incapable of carrying out her responsibilities.[8]

As Weber pointed out, the new Code showed that many aspects of the traditional legal definition of paternal power, or *Hausgewalt*, derived from the Roman *Patria Potestas*, still prevailed. Cultural changes that had given increased authority over child-rearing to women had not changed the legal structure of the family. It was still, as Hegel had described it a century earlier, a shadow-realm, the private and despotically ruled domain of the father, of which he alone was the public representative.[9]

Feminist protests against these laws often implied that the symbiotic mother-child bond was a source of natural rights. One of the earliest feminist treatises on the new Code, written by lawyer Emilie Kempin, was introduced by a quotation from George Sand. "Society can deny maternal rights," wrote Sand, " . . . but Nature is not concerned with such opinions and you will never persuade a mother that her children do not belong to her a little more than to their father. And the children will not be convinced either." Many other authors noted the evident hypocrisy of conservative opinion that proclaimed motherhood the natural and biologically determined function of women but denied mothers the power to exercise that important task. Man-made laws, wrote Stritt, showed a continuing tendency to regard motherhood as merely a physical function and to deny its ethical importance. By demanding that the law recognize the importance of motherhood, Stritt also protested against the "dead letter" of a legal system in which women's experience was invisible. Only a law that "is fair to both [male and female] points of view can be regarded as up to date," she protested.[10]

In order to support the claims of mothers to power over their children, feminists attacked the Civil Code's concept of the family as a private realm separated from civil society, and demanded that rights of citizenship existing in the public realm be applied also in the home. Defenders of the Code claimed that the laws that alloted decision-making power to the father in cases of disagreement were necessary in order to ensure consistency in child-rearing. But why, asked some feminist commentators, should the will of the father prevail over that of the mother, who was usually much more sensitive to the children's needs? Lawyer Hermann Jastrow, who wrote a commentary on the Code specifically for women, claimed that patriarchal authority was rooted in tradition and could not be modified by law. Many feminists rejected this male-centered view of culture. The hundreds of women who came to them for advice, wrote the members of the Legal Aid Association for Women of Dresden, saw paternal power not as a hallowed tradition but as a form of "conscious and unconscious brutality" practiced by a male sex convinced of its "absolute superiority and dominance over women." Feminist protesters demanded that the family be subject to the same laws as the public sphere, where the ancient traditions of despotism had yielded to more enlightened forms of government. Their arguments drew on traditional images of the state as "great social household." Both family and nation, wrote Stritt, were communities, and both should recognize the equal rights of all citizens. "Why should only the oldest, most respected, and most intimate human community be eternally based on inequality and injustice?"[11]

The practice of equal parental power posed more difficult problems than the theory. Almost all feminist commentators insisted that both parents should have equal rights to decide about all matters concerning children, including financial affairs, education, marriage, and other matters. But what should happen when the parents disagreed? The differences of opinion among feminists on this issue highlighted some more general issues that would recur in future discussions of family law. The more traditional solution, based on theories of gender difference and separate spheres, was to allot decisions about daughters to mothers, and about sons to fathers. This approach, which was recommended by the petition of the Federation of German Women's Organizations, was praised by Marie Stritt as the "natural solution, according to simple motherly wisdom." Another solution was to call on the state to intervene in the family. Some commentators, including Weber, recommended that a public agency such as the Guardians' Court should be empowered to intervene between the parents (this proposal had also been made by the German Women's Association in 1876). The Federation's petition recommended such public intervention in cases in which the division of authority according to gender was legally unenforceable. Such a challenge to the legal barrier between public and private spheres was a major threat to the authority of fathers. Commentator Hermann Jastrow remarked sarcastically that the idea of a mother's demanding that a father await the intervention of the Guardians' Court before beating a wayward son provided more inspiration to a cartoonist than to a lawgiver.[12]

Child custody in cases of divorce was another important issue. Whereas the Prussian General Law of 1794 had permitted divorce simply on the basis of "mutual aversion," the Civil Code required proof of serious mistreatment or other offenses and the identification of a guilty party. If identified as the innocent party, the mother was awarded personal custody of the children, but the father retained all other rights, including the control of a minor child's financial assets and all decisions about education, employment, and marriage. Feminist commentators protested that the law deprived the innocently divorced woman of effective power over her children; she was forced to consult her ex-husband on almost every important child-rearing decision, and to submit to his ruling. The petition of the Federation of German Women's Organizations recommended that the parent who received personal custody of the children also be given full parental rights. Most feminists commented only indirectly on the fate of the "guilty" mother, who could be deprived of all contact with her children, by protesting the abolition of the older and more permissive divorce law, which had not required the attribution of guilt. But some, at the risk of seeming to defend misconduct, addressed the issue more directly. An article in *Die Frau*, the central organ of the Federation of German Women's Organizations, asked whether a woman who had incurred "guilt" by leaving her husband was necessarily unfit to raise her children.[13]

The clearest proof that the lawgivers were willing to sacrifice the welfare of mothers and children to the preservation of the patriarchal family was the new law concerning the rights of unmarried mothers and their children. The chief precedent for the Code, the Prussian General Law of 1794, had attempted to integrate the unmarried mother and her child into society. If she had been engaged to the father, the unmarried mother had all the rights of an innocently divorced woman, including financial support for the child. Even without such an engagement, the child was entitled to some support and to inheritance from the father in the absence of "legitimate" issue. This law, attacked by conservative jurists throughout the early nineteenth century as an encouragement to immoral behavior among lower-class women, had been changed in 1854. The new version limited the support claims of most unmarried mothers to the bare costs of delivery and allowed putative fathers to escape even this financial obligation through what was called the *exceptio plurium concumbentium*— the allegation that other men could also have fathered the child. Unlike the code of 1794, which in this situation had permitted the mother to identify the true father under oath, this provision enabled all the putative fathers to escape financial responsibility. This Prussian measure, designed to deter women from immoral behavior, was more punitive than the laws of other areas, such as Bavaria, which provided that if paternity was uncertain, all the men who could possibly be responsible were obligated to pay support.[14]

The new Civil Code did not return to the enlightened eighteenth-century precedent, but incorporated most of the punitive features of the mid-century Prussian legislation. The illegitimate child was legally considered a member only of the maternal kinship group; "the illegitimate child and its father," stated the Code, "are not considered to be related." The Civil Code improved on some earlier legislation by requiring the father to pay support "at the level of the mother's standard of living" until the child reached the age of fourteen. By retaining the *exceptio plurium*, however, the Code enabled fathers to escape this financial responsibility rather easily. The nonexistence of any legal relationship between the child and the paternal kin meant that if the father died or had no income the child received no support from the paternal grandparents. Moreover, the unmarried mother, unlike the widowed mother, did not gain full parental rights over the child, whose legal guardian was in most cases considered the maternal grandfather. This law, whatever its limitations, actually improved the status of unmarried mothers in German states where legal codes based on the Napoleonic Code allowed no paternity suits at all.[15]

The debate over this law broadened many women's awareness of the disadvantages that they suffered within the patriarchal system. Among the issues raised was the relationship between class and gender oppression. Most bourgeois feminists perceived illegitimacy chiefly as a problem affecting the urban lower classes. Because of the tendency of some pregnant women from the countryside to seek help in the city, illegitimacy rates tended to be higher in cities; while overall rates of illegitimacy for 1890 were about 9 percent of all births, rates for Berlin were 12 percent, for Leipzig 23 percent, and for Breslau 16 percent. Middle-class women were most likely to come into contact with the problems of these mothers through their involvement in social work, on a volunteer or professional basis. The attitudes of middle-class female activists toward these mothers, as toward other poor people, reflected both class and gender consciousness. Their class-related sense of moral superiority and social distance was somtimes mitigated by feelings of solidarity in the face of the irresponsible sexual behavior (*Herrenmoral*) of men of their own class. Middle-class feminists were usually indignant at the provision of the Code that set the level of child support at the mother's rather than the father's standard of living.[16]

But the sympathy of middle-class feminists for the unmarried mother sometimes arose not simply from philanthropic concern but from a closer identification. Women active in organizations assisting women and children noted that a minority of the unmarried mothers whom they helped came from the ranks of single, middle-class professional women. These women often practiced professions such as teaching and nursing in which marriage or the disgrace of unwed pregnancy meant the loss of their jobs. The fact that the fathers suffered no such penalties brought the relationship between discriminatory employment patterns and the sexual double standard into clear focus. Thus feminists of this era developed a concept of oppression that was not due primarily to class, but to patriarchy. The plight of the unmarried mother raised a host of issues—family structure, sexual mores, job discrimiation, and the conflicts between work and motherhood among both middle-class and working-class women.[17]

The campaign against the Civil Code brought the rights of unmarried women into the forefront of discussion in both branches of the feminist movement. Almost all feminist speakers, whether moderates or radicals, protested against the ease with which the law allowed fathers to evade support obligations. Failure of fathers to pay support was cited as the main reason for the extraordinarily high rates of infant mortality among the illegitimate. Likewise, almost all feminist speakers demanded the elimination of the *exceptio plurium.* The lawgivers' fear of unjustly burdening the wrong man with support obligations was indignantly dismissed by Marianne Weber; the same risk, she observed, was incurred by husbands. The petition of the Federation of German Women's Organizations demanded that the father's support payments should be set at his own, rather than at the mother's, standard of living and that the support obligation be continued until the child reached twenty-one years of age. Furthermore, the petition recommended the granting of full parental rights to the unmarried mother, with the proviso that the court could appoint an advisor for her, if necessary. Most moderate feminists, such as Weber and child-welfare activist Frieda Duensing, stopped short of recommending that the status of chidren born inside and outside the marital relationship be equalized, for fear of jeopardizing the legal status of marriage, and thus of married women and their children.[18]

Some radicals were less cautious. Marie Stritt, in a pamphlet written for the Legal Aid Center of Dresden, insisted that the illegitimate child should be entitled to the same rights to inheritance from the father as its legitimate sibling: "It is as much his [the father's] child as if it were legitimate." Moreover, she recommended that the unmarried mother should be entitled to the same parental rights as the widowed mother. Both the laws on unmarried mothers and those regulating prostitution, Stritt argued, were intended to separate women into two opposing groups—the "outcasts" living outside the patriarchal family, and the "respectable women" living within it. In the name of sisterhood, Stritt exhorted married women to refuse "this more than questionable protection, which is gained at the expense of unfortunate sisters and poor, disinherited children."[19]

Thus, moderates and radicals showed some differences of opinion on the issues raised by the Civil Code. The chief difference was in their attitudes toward the institution of marriage, upon which the radicals leveled a more aggressive attack than the moderates. Neither group, however, adopted a purely individualistic definition of rights. Both groups agreed that the individual rights of mothers were inseparable from responsibilities to their own children and to society as a whole. The "full freedom of action and civic equality" of both single and married women, stated Stritt, "is necessary in the interest of the family, in the interest of the state, to which [the married woman] makes a more important cultural contribution than the single woman, and also in the interest of all of the new social obligations . . . that today's woman must fulfill, and that she can only fulfill as a free human being."[20]

Family and State: The Protection of Children

The response of many activist women to the provisions of the Civil Code for the family led directly to an expansion of their roles in the public sphere. One of the first committees set up by the Federation of German Women's Organizations when it was founded in 1894 was the Committee on Child Protection. The work of this committee during the first years of its existence suggested some important trends in feminists' attitudes toward child protection, and more generally toward the relationship of private and public spheres and of family and state.[21]

One of the only real improvements that the Code brought about was its removal of the previous legal incapacity of women to become guardians of persons other than their own children or grandchildren. Now both single and married women could take over guardianships—with the provision, greatly resented by feminist commentators, that married women could assume this office only with the permission of their husbands. This new legal right gave women the opportunity to put their concern for the children of unmarried mothers into practice. As has been explained, unmarried mothers were not routinely given full parental rights over their own children, although they could petition the court for such rights. Some feminist reformers approved this restriction. In part, they were motivated by censorious attitudes toward the supposed irresponsibility of unmarried mothers, and in part by more practical considerations; Marianne Weber, for example, argued that unmarried mothers often lacked both the financial resources and the education to use the court system in order to obtain support payments from unwilling fathers. But the presumption that the mother's own father would function effectively as guardian was clearly inadequate to urban conditions, where the mother was often separated from family and community.[22]

The situation was complicated by the fact that the unmarried mother was often unable to care for her child, who was then placed in an institution or a foster family. The placement system that most feminists supported had been founded by physician Max Taube of Leipzig in 1883. Taube set up an agency that exercised rights of guardianship—called "professional guardianship"—over all children in institutional or foster care. Paid or voluntary representatives of the agency took the responsibility for supervising the care of the individual child and representing his or her interests. Taube and his supporters used statistics showing low rates of infant mortality among the illegitimate in Leipzig to support their approach. Whatever its advantages, this system also gave governmental agencies an unprecedented degree of authority to intervene in family life.[23]

By giving women the right to become legal guardians, the Civil Code gave them the possibility of becoming involved in this system at a more responsible level. The Committee on Child Protection distributed propaganda for the foster-child system and urged women to assume guardianships on a voluntary basis. The rationale for such work was stated in the petition of the Federation of German Women's Organizations on the reform of the Civil Code. "The unfavorable conditions in which these unfortunate [illegitimate] children grow up have the consequence that a frightening number succumb to physical sickness, and just as many to moral degeneracy," stated the petition, "and statistics show that the growing army of young criminals is recruited largely from this group." By 1911, about twelve thousand women exercised guardianships over children who were not their own in three hundred communities.[24]

Another activity of the Child Protection Committee showed its positive attitude toward the intervention of government, as well as private agencies, in family life. In 1902, the Committee formulated a petition supporting a bill originating with the Socialist party. The bill regulated the exploitation of children by their parents and guardians. In 1891, a child labor statute that had removed children from factory work had resulted in an enormous increase in the employment of children in home-based manufacturing industries and in family-owned commercial establishments, such as bakeries, taverns, and bowling alleys, that were not covered by the law. The refusal of legislators to regulate such businesses arose in part from their reluctance to interfere with the power of fathers in the private sphere, the Civil Code having given fathers absolute authority over all decisions on the employment, apprenticeship, and education of minor children.[25]

In order to counteract this highly patriarchal conception of familial authority, the Child Protection Committee argued that child-rearing was a public rather than merely a private obligation. Children, argued the petition, were "the future of our people," and thus they belonged "not simply to their parents, who can do anything that they like with them, but to the state, which in its own interest should claim the right to supervise their raising and their well-being." The law passed in 1902 imposed some new regulations on family businesses, although it still gave parents far more power over the labor of their own than of nonrelated children. Although child labor laws were often resisted by working-class parents, who resented interference with their cultural patterns and their economic strategies, they were supported by many socialist women's groups. "For the first time," commented socialist Lily Braun, "German lawgivers stepped over the walls surrounding the family circle . . . in order to protect children from exploitation."[26]

The critique of the Civil Code inspired a notable expansion of conceptions of the public and private significance of motherhood among German feminists. Criticism of the family had always been implicit in the ideology of spiritual motherhood, but earlier efforts, such as the kindergarten movements, had attempted to exert only an indirect influence on the home, and had not directly challenged familial authority. In the 1890s, however, some feminist reformers leveled a more direct attack on the existing form of the family, claiming that it did more to protect the authority of husbands and fathers than to further the welfare of women and children. But this attack on the family raised a central problem. Women and children, still without political rights, could not protect themselves; if the family did not protect them, then how could they be protected? In their arguments for professional guardianship and child labor legislation, some feminists expressed an idea that would become central to their view of motherhood for the next three decades. Motherhood and child-rearing were not only private but also public functions, they contended, and thus the state must protect mothers and children. This argument, of course, showed an important change in general views of the relationship of women's interests to the state. Whereas the genera tion active in the 1880s had seen the state as a threat to female autonomy, a younger generation affirmed the value of state-sponsored social legislation as a support to women's independence.[27]

A comparison of the evolution of feminist ideas of motherhood in Germany to those in the United States during this period suggests that, on these issues, German feminists were in some ways in advance of their American colleagues. American feminists such as Elizabeth Cady Stanton and the members of her organization, the National Woman Suffrage Association, had taken controversial stands on topics such as marriage laws and illegitimacy as early as the 1860s. But the Woodhull scandal of 1872, which identified this organization with the highly controversial cause of "free love," had brought all radical positions temporarily into disrepute. With the reunification of the two major suffrage organizations, the American and the National, in 1890, the mainstream feminist movement in America entered a conservative period during which the advocacy of controversial ideas, especially on sex or religion, was discouraged.[28]

American laws on parental rights, guardianship, and the status of illegitimate children, although varying by state, were quite similar to those of the German Civil Code. At the turn of the century, only nine states and the District of Columbia granted equal guardianship rights to both parents. In other states, legal control of most aspects of child-rearing was in the hands of fathers, who could also often appoint a guardian other than the children's mother to supervise them after his death. The laws of most states likewise declared illegitimate children not to be related to their fathers and denied them inheritance and paternal support. American feminists, although sometimes taking note of these laws, did not place legal reform at the center of the agendas of their mainstream organizations. The fact that German feminists launched wide-scale campaigns to change these laws earlier than did their American sisters was in part due to circumstances that had nothing to do with feminism; there was no attempt to create a uniform code of family law for the United States in the 1890s. However, the conservatism of the American movement on these issues was also partly due to its concentration on the achievement of suffrage, to which other causes were often subordinated. Thus, one can speculate that precisely the weakness of the suffrage movement in Germany, often assumed to have been due both to the continuance of reactionary laws restricting women's participation in politics and to the conservatism of German feminism itself, actually left room for radicalism in other areas.[29]

Chapter 8
Motherhood, Culture, and Evolution: Some New Perspectives, 1890–1914

The debate on the Civil Code was only the opening phase of a broader development of feminist ideology and practice. At the turn of the century, the upsurge in activism went along with a major reassessment of all past ideas of female nature, sexual relations, and the role of women in culture. Motherhood, in all of its ethical, scientific, cultural, and political implications, was a central theme in this flowering of feminist theory and scholarship. The main impulse for innovation came from intellectuals of the radical wing. This chapter examines the interaction of personal experience and intellectual development in the early lives of four women who were well known for their writings on motherhood—Helene Stöcker, Henriette Fürth, Lily Braun, and Adele Schreiber—and then places their ideas in a broader context.

In this as in earlier periods, women intellectuals operated within a framework defined by a dominant discourse on family, child-rearing, and the state. Both the constraints and the possibilities of this wider discourse affected their individual development. Political and cultural authority figures continued to define motherhood and childbearing as services to the state. However, the intellectual and cultural climate also changed in important ways. Views of the human personality were transformed by ideas derived from the natural sciences, and particularly from evolutionary theory. At the same time, ideas of the state were changing to encourage an ever-expanding role for government in public health and social welfare. New approaches to social policy were shaped in part by the growth of the socialist movement, which during the 1890s became a major force in politics and in intellectual life. All of the women discussed in this chapter were deeply influenced by socialism, and some belonged to both the socialist and feminist movements; Henriette Fürth, for example, was a socialist from the beginning of her political career, and both Lily Braun and Adele Schreiber became converts

In many ways, the generation to which Fürth, Schreiber, Stöcker, and

Braun belonged expressed the same values and concerns as feminists of earlier generations. They, too, emphasized the ethical significance of the mother-child bond, the integration of individualism with social responsibility, and an ideology based more on gender difference than on sameness. But they rewrote this feminist discourse in the language of their own era. The growth of socialism, the expansion of welfare legislation, and the pervasive influence of evolutionary and biological thought on all areas of culture were some of the conditions that shaped their conception of motherhood.

A New Generation: The Development of a Radical Perspective

Of these four women, three—Braun, Stöcker, and Schreiber—left autobiographical statements; on Henriette Fürth, we have only short sketches written by relatives and colleagues, and a few obviously autobiographical passages in her own works. These life stories offer an interesting contrast to those of the women discussed earlier. Many women of earlier generations had viewed biological and social (or spiritual) motherhood as equally valuable but separate alternatives, the first available only to married women and the second available chiefly to single women or to married women without dependent children. In Germany as elsewhere, the radicals of the 1890s—a small minority even of their own generation—were the first feminists to challenge this alternative. These women defined the concept of spiritual motherhood, which earlier generations had found emancipatory, as oppressive. They interpreted their own early hopes and disappointments in terms of a newly named problem—the conflict between heterosexual and maternal fulfillment, and career or intellectual aspirations.[1]

All of these women were born between 1860 and 1872: Fürth as Henriette Katzenstein in 1861, Braun as Lily von Kretschmannn in 1865, Stöcker in 1869, and Schreiber in 1872. Three came of middle-class backgrounds: Stöcker's father was a pastor in Elberfeld, Fürth's a well-off businessman in Giessen, and Schreiber's a physician in Vienna. Kretschmann, the daughter of a high-ranking army officer, belonged to the aristocracy. By contrast to the generation of privileged women born in the 1820s, this generation had some very limited professional opportunities available to them. Thus, the rebellion against the repressive conditions of respectable female existence which in the older generation had often taken the form of a generalized depression was expressed by some members of this generation through better-defined professional and educational ambitions.[2]

Motherhood and child-rearing, sometimes viewed by earlier generations as potentially empowering experiences, were regarded by these women with much more ambivalence. Schreiber, Stöcker, and Kretschmann explicitly rejected the model of female behavior represented by their own mothers; all four women chose male family members as their original role models. Schreiber aspired from early childhood to follow in her father's footsteps by becoming a physician. She blamed her mother for preventing her from fulfilling this ambition. "Whoever put an idea like that in her little head?" asked Schreiber's mother incredulously. As a result, Schreiber was limited to the desultory education usually prescribed for privileged girls. Stöcker's ambition to become an author was to some extent inspired by her highly intellectual pastor father, who despite his strict religious orthodoxy obviously permitted her to read widely, even in the works of controversial authors. Although by no means drawn to teaching as a career, Stöcker realized that teacher training was the only form of postsecondary education available to her. Her mother, burdened with the care of seven younger siblings, needed her help in the household and had little time or energy to understand her intellectual ambitions.[3]

Henriette Katzenstein, whose cultivated Jewish family was sympathetic to her intellectual ambitions, also entered teacher training. But, at least in her early adulthood, her model of professional fulfillment seems to have been her brother, who was a socialist politician and reformer. Lily von Kretschmann resented her mother, who enforced the ladylike norms of behavior that she detested. Kretschmann admired her father, an attractive though mercurial officer, and envied the male privilege that his way of life seemed to represent. Though lacking the professional aspirations of some of her middle-class contemporaries, Kretschmann criticized the snobbery of her class, aspired to social involvement, and in her youth expressed a somewhat romanticized interest in poverty and in the problems of the lower classes.[4]

Despite their adolescent resentment of their own mothers and their early emulation of male role models, however, all of these women developed models of emancipation based more on gender difference than on similarity. One reason for this was probably that they met with frustration in their attempts to imitate male models of individualism and career success. Henriette Katzenstein did not become a teacher—she married the merchant Wilhelm Fürth and over the course of the next dozen years had seven children. Stöcker fulfilled her ambition for higher education, becoming one of the first German women to obtain a university degree, but also became aware of both the enormous obstacles to women's professional success and the psychological and personal cost of overcoming them.[5]

Schreiber did not become a physician. She took a job with a private insurance company in Berlin chiefly as a means to live independently of her family. Later, she supported herself through journalism, chiefly on the limited range of subjects, including motherhood and child-rearing, upon which women were accepted as authorities. Kretschmann, although gaining some recognition as a scholar, was not able to create an independent career for herself through her own talent and energy. Her initial opportunity to publish came through her first husband, Georg von Gizycki, who edited a journal entitled *Ethische Kultur* (Ethical Culture) and encouraged his wife's intellectual ambitions by introducing her to many ideas to which her limited education had not exposed her. Thus, although rebelling against their mothers, even these exceptional women could not entirely escape from the conditions of disadvantage and dependency that had shaped their mothers' lives.[6]

For these women, new ways of understanding sexuality added another important dimension to their idea of emancipation. For earlier generations, the separation of biological from spiritual motherhood had seemed a highly emancipatory concept, justifying access to professions and to dignified single lives. But professional work, especially for teachers who were forbidden to marry, usually (although not always) meant the renunciation of marriage and motherhood. Braun, Fürth, Stöcker, and Schreiber rejected the choice between career and heterosexual fulfillment.[7]

For Braun and Stöcker, who have left the most extensive memoirs of their girlhoods, this aspect of their ideology was certainly linked to their interpretation of their own development as sexual beings. Whereas the women who grew up in the early nineteenth century had interpreted their adolescent restlessness as spiritual or religious crisis, many women of the later nineteenth century, influenced by prevailing biological theories, attributed this restlessness to puberty and awakening sexual curiosity. As an adolescent, Kretschmann resented the artificial manners, combining prudery and coquettishness, that were prescribed for an aristocratic young lady. She even fantasized about prostitutes as pioneers of emancipation. Stocker's first critique of conventional sexual morality was inspired by *Faust*, which she read as a teenager. On a girl at the beginning of puberty, she wrote, the story of the infanticide Gretchen made a frightening impression: "The dangers, the destiny that threatened a woman when love came into her life—that was shown to me in the full horror of an annihilating fate." Stöcker traced her lifelong concern for the welfare of unmarried mothers and their chidren to her highly personal identification with Goethe's heroine.[8]

The adult lives of these women show their refusal to accept the choice between personal and professional fulfillment. Henriette Furth certainly felt the conflict between her child-rearing responsibilities and her professional interests. "Let all the good mothers attack me," she wrote in 1902, "but the uninterrupted company, the constant care, supervision, and raising of a large group of children is the most strenuous work that there is. In time, all women's nervous and spiritual strength is undermined, and they lose feeling, energy, and interests." But Fürth herself, recollected her brother, Simon Katzenstein, never succumbed to this fate; she held professional conferences in the kitchen and continued work on her articles until the final weeks of her seven pregnancies. Kretschmann (then calling herself Gizycki) incurred social censure through her highly unconventional marriage in 1896 to Heinrich Braun, who was Jewish, twice-divorced, and a socialist. She regarded the birth of her son in 1897 as one of the greatest events of her life.[9]

Stöcker used her own life story to illustrate the conflict of professional and maternal aspirations. In 1899, after concluding one unhappy love affair, Stöcker met Alexander Tille, a compatriot who taught at the University of Glasgow. Although her relationship to Tille, who was married and had two children, remained an intellectual friendship, Stöcker obviously fell in love with him. Somewhat later she suddenly received a letter from him announcing the sudden death of his wife, and proposing marriage. Stöcker traveled to Glasgow to join Tille and enrolled in the university there. Faced with the prospect of giving up her studies and devoting her life to the care of two small children, she was plunged into conflict. "I had grown up in a large family," she wrote later, "and I had always thought it natural to include love, marriage, and children among my most important goals. But not yet, I pleaded inwardly. For my drive toward intellectual development, toward the development of my personality, was just as innate and natural." Stocker turned down the proposal. In 1905, at the age of thirty-seven, she fell in love with lawyer Bruno Springer, with whom she lived until his death in 1931. Because they had no children, they regarded their relationship as a purely personal commitment, needing no official sanction.[10]

Schreiber married physician Richard Krieger in 1911. Through this marriage, on which her voluminous papers give very little information, she obviously found a satisfactory solution to her needs for private fulfillment and public activity, for she described her husband as her most supportive friend, "For public consumption," she remarked in her autobiography, "all I want to say about my marriage is that, if all marriages were like it, we would have no need to reform marriage." The marriage was childless, however.[11]

For these, as for many other women, awareness of the problems posed by marriage, reproduction, and maternity led to public activism. Their approach to social problems differed from those of an earlier generation that had regarded state intervention as a threat to female autonomy. While continuing to support philanthropic activities and private charities, these women focused their attention on public policy. Often, they became involved in campaigns for legal reform inspired by the protest against the Civil Code; for example, Henriette Fürth helped to found a legal aid center for women in Frankfurt. Stöcker, Fürth, Braun, and Schreiber related legal issues to the medical and public health concerns that shaped social welfare policies during these years. Adele Schreiber became a popular author and lecturer on such topics as children in poverty, the rights of illegitimate children, child abuse, and juvenile delinquency. She traveled widely, visiting settlement houses in London and child protection agencies in Paris. Having met Cesare Lombroso, an Italian physician who attributed criminal tendencies to heredity, she began to speculate on the relationship between hereditary and environmental factors in child development. Stöcker had a long-standing interest in such questions, which she developed through her involvement in educational issues such as coeducation.[12]

As Nancy Cott has also emphasized in her study of American developments during the early twentieth century, the problems of working women in industrial as well as white-collar jobs became an increasingly important theme in the works of progressive feminists. Middle- and upper-class women who had confronted the choice between paid work and motherhood realized that working-class women often had no such choice. Braun and Fürth lectured and wrote about the problems of working mothers and were among the earliest advocates of state-sponsored maternity insurance and other benefits for these mothers.[13]

Like many other radical feminists of similar background, these four women regarded most bourgeois feminist groups as timid and reformist, and sympathized with the Social Democratic party. However, with the exception of Fürth, whose brother was a socialist, they hesitated to join that party because of personal and intellectual barriers to communication between classes. Schreiber, who had read Bebel's *Woman and Socialism* at the age of eighteen, attended a socialist women's meeting in Vienna but was denied entry; what was a physician's daughter doing there? When she moved to Berlin in the 1890s, the German Social Democratic party's women's groups proved somewhat more receptive, and she gave several lectures on working mothers before a group headed by prominent organizer Ottilie Baader. But, perhaps scarred by her earlier rejection, she did not join the party until 1918, preferring to work with the radical feminist movement. Braun, as an aristocrat, faced great difficulty in winning the trust of her fellow socialists after joining the party in 1895. Stöcker never joined any party, but her sympathy for some socialist ideas was always apparent.[14]

Feminists of this generation encountered the problems raised by class and gender differently from their predecessors. Women of the mid-nineteenth century had worked among an urban lower class that was not yet politically organized and could therefore be considered a fitting object of educational and philanthropic attention. The socialist women's groups rejected that kind of interest. Clara Zetkin, editor of a socialist women's weekly entitled *Die Gleichheit* ("Equality"), shared much the same class and educational background as many middle-class feminists; she had attended a teacher-training seminar headed by moderate feminist Auguste Schmidt. She nonetheless insisted on a "clean division" between bourgeois and socialist women and accused the former of taking only a halfhearted and patronizing interest in working-class women. Moreover, she considered feminism itself a diversion from the more important task of working toward the socialist revolution that would resolve both class and gender conflicts.[15]

Radical feminists at the turn of the century, although facing these changed conditions, used strategies that were in some ways similar to those of their predecessors. Both Braun and Fürth were leaders of a minority faction within the socialist women's movement that urged solidarity among bourgeois and socialist women. Largely as a result of their efforts, the first Socialist Women's Conference, held in 1900, decided to allow individual socialist women to work in feminist organizations, although refusing other forms of cooperation. Looking for issues that would appeal to women of all classes, Braun bitterly criticized bourgeois feminist organizations' emphasis on issues such as higher education and professional opportunities, which she considered of interest only to the middle and upper classes. By contrast, she declared motherhood, child welfare, and family structure to be the great unifying concerns of women. "Motherhood," she wrote, "is indeed the culmination of womanhood, and no so-called emancipation will put an end to the slavery of women as long as one pregnant woman groans under her burden, as long as one new mother must strain her exhausted body at work, or as long as one neglected baby cries for its mother." Once again, as in 1848, the joys and sorrows of motherhood and the sacred mother-child bond were hailed as a basis for overcoming class differences and forging gender solidarity.[16]

Motherhood and Evolution

Before turning to the practical work and political strategies of these women, it is necessary to look at the intellectual basis of their new view of motherhood. One of the major differences between most radical feminists of this period and their moderate colleagues was the former group's strongly scientific orientation. At the turn of the century, the context for the scientific discussion of motherhood was provided by hereditarian and evolutionary theories. Hereditarian thought, especially as it contributed to the new field of eugenics, had many negative implications for women. But these theories, which were diverse, controversial, and susceptible to revision, also provided opportunities for female intellectuals to develop a woman-centered counterdiscourse on the relationship of biology to culture.

One form of hereditarian thought that was very important to many women of this era, including some of those mentioned here, was the field of child psychology. A major proponent of this field was psychologist Wilhelm Preyer, author of an often-reprinted book, *Die Seele des Kindes* (The Mind of the Child), published in 1882. Preyer argued that most of the child's personality traits, including capacities for speech, learning, emotion, and moral judgment, were the result of heredity rather than maternal teaching. In a lecture given at the Victoria Lyceum, a well-known educational institution for women, he asserted that "knowledge of human nature helps very little," in child-rearing, because "everything is already there in potential that later emerges." He laid more emphasis upon careful observation of the child than on pedagogy, which could have only a limited effect upon innate tendencies. A powerful reinforcement to hereditarian theories of childhood at the turn of the century was a book by the Swedish author Ellen Key entitled *The Century of the Child*, which was widely read among feminists. Key, an enthusiastic Darwinian, urged mothers to respect children's innate tendencies and to avoid constricting and confusing them through intrusive pedagogical techniques.[17]

During this period, child-rearing manuals shifted their emphasis from pedagogical to medical concerns, urging mothers to rely on physicians for advice on all aspects of child development. Women's activities in areas such as child welfare and child labor legislation certainly affirmed the general concern for children's physical health. At the same time, the new theories called into question the importance of the mother's pedagogical role, which earlier generations had extolled as a major source of women's ethical authority. If the child's personality were determined chiefly by heredity, then the mother's most important contribution was simply the passive transmission of desirable hereditary traits.[18]

Moreover, this view of motherhood as a purely biological function was also developed by the field of eugenics. This field, given its name by British biologist Francis Galton in 1883, first attracted wide interest in Germany in the 1890s and was publicized by the Society for Racial Hygiene, founded in 1905 by Alfred Ploetz. The goal of eugenics was defined as the improvement of the biological quality of human populations through the application of the science of heredity. Eugenic theory, at least according to many of its most prestigious proponents, had many deeply antifemale implications. Prominent eugenicists such as Wilhelm Schallmayer, the winner of a prize offered by the Krupp firm in 1903 for his essay *Vererbung und Auslese* ("Heredity and Selection"), argued that modern civilization encouraged biological degeneration. He laid much of the blame on recent improvements in the status of women. Access to educational and professional opportunity, he contended, had encouraged the most able women to engage in activities that impaired, limited, or wholly destroyed their biological fitness for motherhood.[19]

Among the most influential of many essays on this theme was that of neurologist Paul Möbius, whose *Uber den physiologischen Schwachsinn des Weibes* ("On the Physiological Feeble-Mindedness of Women") was published in 1900 and by 1906 had been reprinted in eight editions. Möbius contended that women's intellectual inferiority was due directly to the maternal role to which the ineluctable laws of evolution had destined them. Defining motherhood as an animal and instinctive function, Möbius argued that women were on a lower evolutionary level than men, and thus incapable of abstract reasoning. Such theories completely discounted feminists' high estimation of motherhood as a source of moral and cultural authority. Indeed, Möbius contemptuously dismissed women's ethical insights as weak-minded sentimentality; only men understood the abstract principles of justice. He concluded rather inconsistently that if women attempted to engage in intellectual or professional work, which he had claimed that they were unable to do, they would risk sterility and thus endanger the future of the human race. Even before widespread concern about declining birthrates had added to the public impact of such ideas, they were often used to oppose advances in women's educational and career opportunities and to advocate women's confinement to the household.[20]

Despite this barrage of antifeminist propaganda, however, many feminist intellectuals of this period chose to revise rather than abandon the Darwinian framework. To many feminists of this era, notably Helene Stöcker, the advantages of Darwinism as a worldview seemed to outweigh its possible problems. From adolescence, Stöcker had believed that Christianity, which she identified with life-denying sexual asceticism, was the major cultural obstacle to the emancipation of women. The pastor's rebellious daughter thus welcomed Darwinism as a refutation of the doctrine of original sin—if human nature was shaped essentially by heredity, then how could it be said to be sinful? As an adult, Stöcker became a member of an organization called the Monist League, which used evolutionary theory to oppose the Christian ethical theories that separated body and spirit and to advocate alternative principles based on the acceptance of physical drives as an essential aspect of human nature.

Stöcker integrated the ideas of philosopher Friedrich Nietzsche with those of Darwin. Nietzsche also rejected Christianity and proposed an alternative ethical system affirming biological and spiritual evolution, or self-transcendence. He regarded sexuality as a means to self-transcendence through the production of ever-higher human types. Stöcker combined biological and philosophical theory to develop what she termed the "New Ethic," based on the acceptance of sexuality as a positive and creative aspect of human nature.[21]

Stöcker, enthralled with the liberating potential of these new ideas, constantly argued against prevailing misogynist and androcentric interpretations. Among such interpretations were not only those of Nietzsche himself, who regarded feminism with vitriolic hostility, but those of her close friend Tille. Tille's book, *Von Darwin bis Nietzsche: ein Buch Entwicklungsethik* ("From Darwin to Nietzsche: A Book of Evolutionary Ethics"), published in 1895, advocated improving the human race by abandoning Christian mercy in favor of a tough-minded ethic encouraging unrestrained competition and the elimination of the biologically unfit. In his discussion of the future evolution of the human race, moreover, Tille mentioned women only twice, once to condemn the middle-class wife's selfish fear of childbirth, and once to remark that the new ethic must use "the woman, the mother, as its most important instrument." This male-centered view of evolution denied women's social importance and relegated them to the status of breeders. "An instrument?" wrote Stöcker, "and the goal is . . . the man? And this is supposed to be a progressive ideology? It takes us back before the Christian era, to our ancestors, who gave women only one function—to bring forth strong men."[22]

The challenge to women intellectuals of this period was thus in many ways similar to that faced by earlier generations—to subvert a male-dominated discourse by reconstructing it to provide a more usable meaning. They found a basis in alternative interpretations of evolutionary theory, usually known as reform Darwinism. Reform Darwinists speculated that cooperation had been more important than competition to the survival and development of species. Influenced by German biologist Wilhelm Bölsche, they considered the ability to work cooperatively toward the creation of a humane and rational environment among the most important of the adaptive traits through which the human species from the beginning had controlled its own evolution. British sexologist

Havelock Ellis used this view of evolution as a basis for an alternative view of eugenics, termed by historian Daniel J. Kevles the "social-radical," as distinguished from the "mainline," school. Unlike mainline eugenicists such as Tille and Schallmayer, who identified social reform as a cause of biological degeneration, Ellis and his colleagues regarded genetic and environmental improvements as part of the same "movement toward social amelioration which has been going on for more than a century."[23]

Within the framework of reform Darwinism, feminist theorists created their own woman-centered view of the evolution of civilization. The mother-child bond, that primary relationship reconciling self and other, was identified as the source of the cooperative and altruistic traits that drove human evolution. This was a rewriting of Pestalozzian theories of the mother-child bond as the source of social morality. In an intellectual climate pervaded by genetic and evolutionary theories, this primal bond was traced to the beginning not only of the individual life but of human society itself.

Theories of primeval matriarchy, as first developed by classical scholar Johann Jakob Bachofen and revised by socialist ideologues such as Friedrich Engels and August Bebel, provided one important basis for this woman-centered view of biological and social evolution. Bachofen's ponderous but profoundly innovative work, *Das Mutterrecht* ("Mother-Right"), published in 1861, was a study of the civilization of the archaic Greeks. From the mythology and naming customs of this civilization, which he mistakenly identified as one of the oldest in the world, he concluded that the original form of the family must have been created by women, who in the beginning had played a leading role not only in the family but in society as a whole. Bachofen portrayed the mother-child bond as the origin of all altruism, and women thus as the originators of all social ethics. However, he saw this maternal ethic as primitive and instinctual and regarded the triumph of the more abstract spirit of patriarchy as an essential step in the progress of civilization. Both Engels and Bebel popularized Bachofen's theory in widely read books that became authoritative sources for socialist theories of the family. Although portraying matriarchy as a primitive and undeveloped form of society, they depicted the overthrow of matriarchal power not as the triumph of enlightenment but as the origin of all oppression, "the world-historical defeat of the female sex."[24]

Feminist theorists turned Bachofen on his head, identifying mother-centered norms with enlightenment rather than backwardness, and proclaiming their continued validity. "In the most primitive forms of human society," wrote Ellen Key, "the relationship between mother and child contains the origins of those customs and beliefs through which the altruistic and sympathetic feelings of humanity are developed to a new strength and a greater extent." Like Bachofen, Key traced the origins of the family to mothers, who had taught men to love and protect their children. By picturing the family as originally a mother-headed unit that only later expanded to include fathers, feminist authors argued against laws (as found, for example in the Civil Code) that enforced male supremacy. "What confronts us as inviolable and universally valid is not marriage, this contract regulating sexual relations, but motherhood alone," wrote Fürth, "the creative principle underlying all that is."[25]

Many feminist theorists argued that evolution was produced by cultural as well as biological development. The highest stage of human evolution, argued socialist Oda Olberg, would be the transition from a competitive to a cooperative way of life, which could only be brought about through the cultural contributions of women. Debates on the implications of this theory for the contemporary status of women showed the influence of three influential thinkers, Ellen Key, the American Charlotte Perkins Gilman, and Olive Schreiner, who was born in South Africa but spent much of her adult life in England.[26]

In "The Misuse of Women's Energy," given as a lecture in Sweden in 1895 and published in Germany in 1898, Key warned that women's distinctive role in culture was endangered by what she identified as the mistaken aims of the feminist movement. Women's energy, she claimed, was best used for motherhood; the encouragement of careers, higher education, and work outside the home for women would lead them to imitate men, thus depriving the younger generation and society as a whole of their salutary influence. Key, who argued for many improvements in women's status, such as suffrage, the reform of marriage and divorce laws, and payment for housework, nonetheless insisted that women's careers outside the home should be limited to work that used specifically motherly talents. Because she rejected imitative or assimilationist models of emancipation, Key has sometimes been classified as an antifeminist by historians of later generations. But Key's view of women's work supported a separatist conception of women's culture that had many radical implications. A fervent pacifist who in 1900 accurately predicted a century of unprecedented carnage, she identified the nurturing and nonviolent traditions of women—which she traced to the maternal role—as the only countervailing force to male aggression. She opposed female participation in male professions as the diversion of oppositional female energies to serve male authority structures.[27]

Feminist arguments against Key's controversial tract affirmed rather than contested her exalted view of motherhood as a culture-bearing force. Maternal energies, they contended, should not be restricted to the household but should be extended to all aspects of social life, including a broad range of industrial, professional, and political activities. Among the prominent exponents of this expansive view were Schreiner and Gilman; the latter's central work, *Women and Economics*, was translated into German by Marie Stritt in 1901. Both Schreiner and Gilman portrayed women as the creators of culture, including religion, science, and industry. These ideas appealed to moderate as well as radical feminists; Helene Lange objected to Gilman's criticism of marriage but endorsed her general view of history. Mothers, she agreed, had indeed been the original community builders, the civilizers of men and the creators of the "community consciousness" on which all social progress was based.[28]

Lily Braun, like Gilman, took issue with contemporary social scientists who had identified the family as a center of conservatism and tradition; she portrayed it instead as a locus of technological progress. She speculated that the first invention, fire, was used to create the domestic hearth and that the most important of early technologies, such as cooking and weaving, were invented by women within the family. Braun pictured the height of home industry in the Middle Ages, when the mother controlled an extensive network of industrial enterprises: the household, she wrote, "comprised entire building complexes, in which male and female serfs carried out their manifold duties. Their labor created means to satisfy not only the needs of the moment but also those of generations to come." According to Braun, mothers had played an active historical role that combined productive and reproductive functions. Only the introduction of the machine and the separation of home and workplace had consigned mothers to economic dependency and technological backwardness.[29]

Thus feminist theorists at the turn of the century neither rejected nor uncritically accepted contemporary evolutionary theories; instead, they engaged in a counterdiscourse that subverted androcentric biases and created new, feminist interpretations. To the arguments of male scientists that the exclusion of women from public life had benefited the evolutionary process, they responded that, on the contrary, cultural evolution had been retarded by the absence of women's contributions. This idea was ubiquitous in the writings of feminists of this era, even of those who did not place motherhood and child welfare issues in the center of their agenda. In her pamphlet, *Die ethische Seite der Frauenbewegung* ("The Ethical Side of the Women's Movement"), Anita Augspurg, a lawyer and journalist who was a conspicuous figure in many of the radical organizations, identified the women's movement as the most important positive influence on the development of culture. Men and women, she asserted, made different but equally important contributions to evolution; human society "must deteriorate, when either factor is missing." The "stinking swamp of corruption" into which present-day urban society had fallen, she asserted, was the result of the exclusion of women from policy-making roles. Augspurg, one of the most daring advocates of individual rights such as suffrage, nonetheless did not identify the achievement of such rights as an end in itself. The highest stage of human evolution, she insisted, was not individualism but cooperation. Another prominent figure in the radical wing, Minna Cauer, took the same view of women's role in the evolutionary process; women's mission, she asserted, was to overcome conflict and to create harmony, "understanding, reconciliation, compromise, decency, and morality. Rise up," she exhorted her comtemporaries, "your duties are holy."[30]

Motherhood and Career

Such inquiries into the historical role of women in culture encouraged not just absorption in the past, but new hopes for the future. During this period the utopian strain in feminist thought, which had flowered briefly in 1848, once again emerged conspicuously. Women, declared Helene Stöcker, must become "people with a strong, unbroken will to live, who have courage for great responsibility." A central utopian aspiration of this generation was toward a harmonious combination of motherhood and career. As we have seen, this was a major personal problem for the women discussed in this chapter; it also became one of their most important political issues.[31]

Feminist ideas on careers and motherhood developed in the context of a larger public discourse on married women and work. Since the 1890s, the number of married women in the paid work force was thought to be increasing—a perception that seemed to be borne out by a survey taken in 1907. In fact, the statistics of the 1907 survey were misleading and the percentage of married women workers remained fairly stable; in 1895 about 31 percent of all working women were married, as compared to about 33 percent in 1907. Changes such as the development of the textile industry, which led to a concentration of women laborers in cities, and a growing number of educated women entering the professions were nonetheless widely taken as evidence of a problem, indeed a crisis. The work of married women, especially of mothers, was regarded by reformers on both left and right as fundamentally unnatural and dangerous to the stability of family and state. Solutions to this perceived problem differed according to the class of the worker. The response of reformers to perceived increases in married industrial workers was regulation; in 1891 federal laws forbade night work for women and limited their working hours. Professional workers such as teachers, however, were often forbidden to combine marriage and career. State laws dating from earlier in the century that required the dismissal of female teachers and other female public employees when they married were upheld and expanded during this period.[32]

One side of the debate on motherhood and career was stated in a widely read work, *Mutterschaft und Geistige Arbeit* ("Motherhood and Intellectual Work"), by Helene Simon and Adele Gerhard. Its authors, like the figures discussed earlier, were involved in both bourgeois feminist and socialist movements. Helene Simon, born in Berlin in 1862, was a reformer whose interest in the problems of working women was inspired both by the British Fabians (especially by Beatrice Webb) and by economist Gustav Schmoller, whose lectures she had audited. Gerhard, a childhood friend of Simon, was a socialist and a creative writer. Simon was a single career woman; Gerhard combined her intellectual interests with marriage and the care of two children. The two women undertook a "psychological and sociological study" based on interview data and correspondence with four hundred professional women who were also mothers. Most of these were middle-class women in such fields as journalism, the arts, music, literature, and science; some were political activists. The authors justified their focus on middle-class occupations by arguing that the problems of working-class mothers could be solved by social legislation relieving them of the necessity to work.

But for women in intellectual profesions, entered for self-fulfillment rather than for economic survival, the problem had no such clear solution. Could such professional self-fulfillment be combined successfully with the spiritually demanding obligations of motherhood?[33]

The authors, although arguing vigorously against theories such as those of Möbius and others that the biological demands of motherhood made women unfit for intellectual work, depicted the psychological burdens of motherhood as more serious than the physical. In an argument that was clearly influenced by Ellen Key, Gerhard and Simon claimed that the biological mother was the only person qualified to raise her child. Child-care workers—governesses, kindergarten teachers, nursemaids, even older relatives—were dismissed as inadequate substitutes. The "spiritual power that is expressed through the devotion and strength of motherly influence," the authors asserted, could not be reproduced by a hireling. This intense emotional and psychological commitment, they continued, usually left little room for any other demanding intellectual interest. "Almost any kind of intellectual work," they wrote, "imposes conditions that make a harmonious combination with the motherly vocation impossible. In most cases, simultaneous commitment to motherhood and intellectual activity leads to conflict." Gerhard and Simon concluded that only women with exceptional talent were justified in overcoming this conflict in order to make a uniquely valuable contribution to culture. In all other cases, motherhood itself, when rightly understood and practiced, was a sufficiently complex and valuable function to occupy a woman's total intellectual energy.[34]

This idealized motherly role was not understood as purely private, however. Like Webb, Gerhard and Simon believed that the modern state had so eroded the barriers between public and private spheres that a responsible commitment to motherhood necessitated public involvement. They thus became early advocates of suffrage for women. "And thus, the capacity of woman for political activism seems attributable to the fact that motherhood, which drains her productive capacity, also strengthens her spiritual powers and her understanding. . . . Her task is to apply the insights gained from her individual experience to public concerns. The uniqueness of motherly experience shows the value of women's entry into legislative bodies."[35]

Responses to this book from reviewers across the political spectrum showed that its central theme, motherhood and career, attracted wide public attention. Conservatives, ignoring the authors' advocacy of woman suffrage, used the book to support traditional restrictions on women's work. Even some socialists, including Reichstag deputy Edmund Fischer, used the authors' data to reassess their party's earlier support of women's employment opportunities and to extol traditional family life. August Bebel claimed that the problems of intellectual women were due less to gender than to economic oppression, which impaired the intellectual development of both sexes and could only be remedied by the overthrow of capitalism. Socialist women such as Wally Zepler criticized the authors' pessimistic acceptance of existing conditions; although suggesting that the conflict between career and motherhood might someday be solved through social change, Gerhard and Simon had not explored such possibilities.[36]

A more energetic commitment to new solutions, however, was shown by the radical wing of the feminist movement. The issue of career and motherhood arose at the International Women's Conference of 1904, where the Prussian elementary school teachers' organization invited their colleagues from other nations to a discussion on the subject of "The Married Teacher." The central issue was the so-called marriage ban imposed by state laws requiring the dimissal of married or pregnant teachers. The ideas of Charlotte Perkins Gilman, who spoke at this session, clearly influenced many of the speakers.[37]

As in the debate over the Civil Code, the opponents of the marriage ban combined strongly individualistic and strongly maternalist arguments. Former teacher Maria Lischnewska called celibacy a deformation of the human personality; "an unmarried life," she insisted, "is always somehow an incomplete and imperfect existence." The right to individual happiness included not only the right to heterosexual fulfillment (for respectable women permitted only within marriage) but to motherhood. "The motherly instinct is her [woman's] strongest instinct," declared Lischnewska. "She wants to see her own children." "Freedom and joy in sexual life," she continued, promoted not only individual but also social welfare. Celibacy clauses deprived society of qualified teachers and damaged the quality of the next generation by excluding able women from motherhood. This viewpoint was widely supported by other radical feminists. "This law discriminates against women," wrote Helene Stöcker, "and especially against the most capable and healthy women; it hurts not only women, but also men, children, and the state." Lily Braun asserted that "the loss of these women to motherhood is very harmful to the human race." Defenders of the rights of married teachers also argued that pupils' respect for motherhood would be increased by exposure to pregnant teachers.[38]

These arguments were more popular among radical feminists than among the rank and file of teachers, made up primarily of single women who feared the competition of their married colleagues for scarce job opportunities. Partly for this reason, laws requiring the dismissal of married teachers remained on the books in most German states. Many moderate feminists, including Helene Lange, defended the right of married teachers to a job, but personally opposed the employment of mothers. Under existing conditions, as Lange and others saw, the combination of child-rearing and career clearly posed overwhelming practical problems. To create new possibilities for women's self-fulfillment and economic self-sufficiency, broader cultural changes were necessary.[39]

The best-known proponent of utopian solutions to the conflicts of work and career was Lily Braun, whose picture of the household as the original center of human culture and community-building we have already examined. Because the tasks once performed in the household had been transferred to a separate workplace, Braun proposed changes in household structure to allow women, particularly mothers, to pursue jobs and careers without carrying the "double burden." This problem was experienced by middle-class intellectuals and artists as well as factory workers. "A painter cannot spend time in the kitchen," Braun wrote. "A writer cannot always be getting up to see if the soup is burning." Braun pointed out that the emancipation of the middle-class woman must follow inevitably from that of her working-class counterpart, whose socialist self-consciousness no longer tolerated the degrading conditions of domestic service. Like Gilman, she thus imagined a new form of domestic life, located in a new living unit known as the *Einküchenhaus*, or "one-kitchen house," a cooperative containing about sixty residential units, a central kitchen equipped with automatic dishwashers, a laundry providing automatic washing machines, and an all-day kindergarten. These services, staffed by trained professionals, would enable female tenants to combine career and motherhood.[40]

This idea, which had also been proposed by Gilman, became popular in radical feminist circles. Lischnewska suggested it in her speech to the Women's Conference as one possible living arrangement for married teachers. Another strong endorsement came from Hedwig Dohm. At the age of seventy, this veteran feminist, who since the 1870s had written with unequaled wit and cogency on women's issues, had obviously decided, like her American contemporary Elizabeth Cady Stanton, not to become conservative with age. In a book published in 1903, entitled *Die Mütter* ("The Mothers"), Dohm gently ridiculed authors such as Key, Gerhard, and Simon and their reverential cult of mother-love. Motherhood, she insisted, did not automatically confer sainthood. Many mothers were exceedingly unqualified parents, and children were often better off in the hands of trained child-care workers. Dohm, herself the mother of five, saw no reason why the mother's pursuit of a career should harm her children; on the contrary, she argued, many children would be better off if their mothers were too busy to fuss over them. Why not found special boarding schools, she proposed, where children, free of their parents' idiosyncracies, could be raised according to the best and most scientific principles? Dohm predicted that when women had the vote they would create such institutions.[41]

However, most responses to Braun's utopian proposals were disapproving. Headlines in the conservative press denounced the "barracks utopia" and the "socialist rabbit-hutch." Even most feminists showed extreme reluctance to undermine the familial roles upon which most women still depended. Käthe Schirmacher, during this period a leader of the Verband fortschrittlicher Frauenvereine (Federation of Progressive Women's Organizations), argued that future forms of the household should not encourage women to abandon housework and motherhood, but should rather create a higher status for these functions. Schirmacher recommended pay for housework and insisted that the moral influence of mothers could not be reproduced by machines or institutionalized living arrangements. Marianne Weber, who took the same view of maternal duties, also objected that the proposed condominium would be much too expensive for working-class people, especially working women, to operate. Weber suggested part-time work, four to five hours a day, for mothers of dependent children. But she acknowledged that such a schedule, although possible for some professionals who worked from home offices, could not confer economic independence on women, most of whom would continue to depend on marriage.[42]

The response from Braun's fellow socialists was hardly more positive. Clara Zetkin, although agreeing that the double burden oppressed women, supported her male comrades' conviction that this, like all other forms of oppression, could only be abolished through a thorough restructuring of the economic system. Zetkin, whose hostility to Braun had personal as well as political motives, accused her rival of using frivolous utopianism to divert the energies of working women from revolutionary struggle. Zetkin further contended that working-class families were attached to conventional home life. Such conservatism was also expressed by a reviewer for *Die Gleichheit*, who feared that the sharing of facilities, even among comrades, would give rise to "conflict and hatred." In a thoughtful assessment of the conflict between Zetkin and Braun, Jean Quataert has characterized the former as a revolutionary oriented toward long-term, radical change, and the latter as a reformist working toward more limited objectives. However, in some ways Braun's vision of social change, which demanded the transformation of culture as well as economic structures, was more ambitious than the purely external and public conception developed by Zetkin. In the tradition of feminism as well as utopian socialism, Braun saw the interdependence of private and public spheres, and realized that one could not be transformed without the other.[43]

Although usually rejecting utopian projects, reformers in both socialist and feminist movements continued to search for more practical solutions to the problems of working mothers. Among these was the founding of publicly supported kindergartens, open for the entire working day. Along with many socialist women, Braun expressed considerable dissatisfaction with church-supported infant schools "in which children learn Bible verses and pious songs and are exposed to all sorts of patriotic nonsense. . . . In short, they are completely estranged from their parents." At the Mannheim (Socialist) Party Congress of 1906, women delegates declared themselves in favor of tuition-free child-care facilities and debated whether these institutions should be supported by municipal welfare authorities or by privately organized groups of socialist parents. Simon Katzenstein, a prominent child-welfare activist and the brother of Henriette Fürth, announced the formation of an experimental socialist kindergarten in Charlottenburg. The socialist kindergarten, staffed by teachers chiefly from middle-class backgrounds, lasted only a year before being closed by the police in 1907 as a subversive institution, chiefly because it refused to celebrate patriotic holidays such as the Emperor's birthday.[44]

Another strategy, often adopted by socialist deputies to municipal governments, was to urge public support for existing Froebelian kindergartens, which they preferred to religiously supported institutions.

Municipal subsidies were granted to privately run kindergartens in many cities, including Berlin and Munich, during this period, although most kindergarten funding still came from tuition and private foundations. In Frankfurt, a municipal subsidy to the local Free Kindergarten Association was enthusiastically supported by socialist members of the City Council, including Max Quark, later a Reichstag deputy. Despite her opposition to cooperation with bourgeois women's organizations, Zetkin herself, who was a graduate of a teacher-training seminar, showed considerable sympathy for progressive educational ideals, such as that of the kindergarten. In a major speech on socialist child-rearing at the Mannheim Party Congress of 1906, she cited that still-authoritative text, Pestalozzi's *Leonard and Gertrude*, in support of a balanced combination of intellectual and manual training and a curriculum stressing social responsibility and community. Despite the conflicts between socialist and feminist approaches to social change, there were also areas of agreement and possibilities for cooperation.[45]

The expansion of concepts of professionalism to include married women raised some new problems, which to this day have yet to be resolved. One centered on the development of attitudes toward heterosexuality. In order to defend the right of married women to careers, feminists such as Stöcker, Braun, and Lischnewska had created a new vision of emancipation that rejected celibacy as a deformation of the personality and glorified heterosexuality and motherhood. This new definition implicitly called into question the single lives of many of their fellow feminists and female professionals who lived with female partners. As Lillian Faderman has pointed out, the designation of such relationships as "lesbian" by sexologists of the 1890s had subjected them to a new stigma. Stöcker and Schreiber, along with many of their colleagues, had been involved since 1901 with a committee headed by sexologist Magnus Hirschfeld that advocated the elimination of Paragraph 175, which forbade homosexual acts between males. In 1909, legal reformers advocated the extension of Paragraph 175 to females. In 1911, the Berlin branch of the League for the Protection of Mothers, an organization headed by Stöcker, held a public protest meeting in Berlin, which was so well attended that they called another. Helene Stöcker argued in the periodical that she edited, *Die Neue Generation* ("The New Generation"), that legal prohibitions against female homosexuality would disrupt the lives of single professional women by making them vulnerable to denunciation and police persecution. As Faderman remarks, this was a remarkable and historic occasion, probably the first on which a feminist organization openly defended the rights of lesbians. Such opposition to legal discrimination, however, did not imply a full acceptance of these relationships. Stöcker described female partnerships, sexual and nonsexual, chiefly as another unhealthy result of laws and customs that prevented professional women from forming relationships with men. She strongly implied that such relationships would become less common when legal restrictions on marriage for professional women had been abolished. An unintended result of the incorporation of heterosexual and maternal fulfillment into feminist definitions of emancipation was the privileging of heterosexuality over other sexual or social choices.[46]

Another problem has resulted from the failure of utopian schemes, such as the "one-kitchen house," which remained controversial and were therefore not widely implemented. In the absence of such changed living arrangements, the new definition of self-fulfillment, including both profession and family life, demanded enormous efforts on the part of women. Many feminists of this era were overoptimistic about the ability of women, aided by such marvelous technological advances as electricity, to bear this new burden. In the electrified home, wrote socialist Oda Olberg, housecleaning could consume at most thirty minutes a day. The importance to women of their child-rearing roles as a basis for empowerment is suggested by the almost total lack of interest on the part of both radical and moderate feminists in conceptualizing an expanded role for fathers in the practical work of child-rearing. Thus, it is to this generation, in Germany and in other Western societies, that we owe the invention of the "supermom."[47]

Radical Feminism: Continuity and Change

The growth of radical feminism in the 1890s has often been described as a break with the past traditions of feminist movements. Certainly, there were some significant innovations: the attempt at an alliance between bourgeois and socialist movements, a critique of traditional forms of familial and sexual morality, and new definitions of emancipation combining career and marriage. However, there were also important elements of continuity. The radicals, although criticizing the ethic of spiritual motherhood, preserved and even exalted the idea of a female ethic based on the nurturing role and the mother-child bond. They recast these traditional ideas in the vocabulary and conceptual framework of their own era, modifying and broadening them to respond to new conditions, including the increase in career opportunities for women, the growth of the welfare state, and the growing prominence of medical and reproductive issues in public discourse.[48]

The German feminists' ideas on motherhood in modern society were part of an international discourse shaped by Swedish, British, and American as well and German theorists. The works of Ellen Key, Charlotte Perkins Gilman, and Olive Schreiner influenced the debate on private and public motherhood as much in the United States as in Germany. Karen Offen has also noted the predominance of maternal over equal-rights ideology in the feminist movements of many other Western societies during this period. Aileen Kraditor, one of the earliest historians of the American suffrage movement, describes maternalism chiefly as a concession to political expediency; maternal service seemed a less radical basis for political claims than equal rights. More recent works, such as Barbara Leslie Epstein's account of the women's temperance movement, explore the potentially radical implications of domestic ideology. Of course, maternalist ideology served a strategic purpose in Germany as well as the United States. However, the example of the German radicals shows that maternalist arguments may by no means simply be correlated to political conservatism, conformity, and caution. Motherhood, in its medical, biological, ethical, and social implications, was a much more conspicuous issue on the far left than on the right of the German bourgeois feminist movement during this period. The language of biology, evolution, and eugenics was appropriated and used much more extensively by left-wing feminists such as the ones described here than by their more conservative or moderate colleagues. The next chapter will describe the further development of these ideas through theoretical and practical work.[49]

Chapter 9
Motherhood as Right and Duty: The Campaign against Infant Mortality, 1904–1914

"Today the Germans, and not least the German women," remarked British sexologist Havelock Ellis in 1910, "awaking from a long period of quiescence, are inaugurating a new phase of the woman movement, based on the demands of woman as mother, and directed to the end of securing for her the right to control and regulate the personal and social relations which spring from her nature as mother or possible mother." Ellis, a member and enthusiastic supporter of the Bund für Mutterschutz (League for the Protection of Mothers), thus paid tribute to the innovative role of this organization during the prewar period. By 1905, the year of the organization's founding, motherhood in all its legal, ethical, and cultural implications had become the focus for a public debate among widely diverse groups within German society. The immediate cause of this upsurge of concern was the perceived crisis arising from a decline in the birth rate, which had been noticed since the 1890s but did not become a major political issue until the first years of the twentieth century. The debate on declining birthrates affected both feminist ideology and strategies. Motherhood in relation to the state became the central issue in German feminist ideology and activism during these years, far surpassing suffrage in importance. The League for the Protection of Mothers played a major role in defining the public debate on this issue.[1]

The League, in which the four women discussed in the previous chapter played prominent roles, was widely criticized by moderate feminists for its radicalism. And yet the issues it confronted were not new: Pestalozzi's tract, *On Legislation and Infanticide*, eighteenth-century Prussian legislation on the status of unmarried mothers and their children, and the recent debate on the Civil Code had established connections among infant mortality rates, the rights of mothers, and the status of women. The League's critique of monogamous marriage and its advocacy of what was often called free love were indeed innovative. However, contrary to the assertions of their critics in the moderate feminist movements, the leaders of the League did not base this new morality primarily on individualist claims to self-determination or self-fulfillment. Rather, their positions on sexual morality arose directly out of concern for the welfare of mothers and children, expanded to include the hitherto neglected households of unmarried mothers.

The activities of middle-class women, allied with physicians and officials, in programs designed to combat infant mortality among lower-class children have been criticized, most recently by historian Ute Frevert, as part of an officious campaign to impose middle-class ideas on hygiene and proper child-rearing methods on lower-class women. Such efforts, she strongly implies, were designed to protect and reinforce the power-structure and class system of the German Empire. But the history of the League for the Protection of Mothers shows that women's child welfare work did not always express or reinforce conservative attitudes; it could sometimes provide the basis for radical criticism of authority, whether political, familial, or religious.[2]

The League for the Protection of Mothers

At the turn of the century, both the intellectual and the practical efforts of German feminists of many different political orientations focused on new ways of understanding the relationship of familial structure to broader social and political issues. For some, including Stöcker, Schreiber, Braun, and Fürth, even radical organizations were still far too cautious in their approach to such issues as child-rearing, reproductive and sexual problems, and new forms of social support for motherhood. The League of Progressive Women's Organizations was still heavily influenced by the abolitionist movement, which in its fight against legalized prostitution upheld standards of sexual purity for both genders and resisted any relaxation of those standards. Stöcker related her disagreement with some of the leaders of this organization to the differences in their personal as well as their political choices. She described Minna Cauer, the president of the Union of Progressive Women's Organizations, as an effective and courageous advocate of the rights of women in the public sphere who had "repressed everything that had to do with erotic life and did not wish to be reminded of it." She added that two other leaders of that group, Anita Augspurg and Lida Gustava Heymann (who were lifelong domestic partners), "belonged to that type of woman for whom any relationship to a man meant a betrayal of the ideals of the women's movement." Another member of the same group, former teacher Maria Lischnewska, proved more receptive, and agreed to join Stöcker in the founding of a new organization devoted specifically to issues affecting motherhood and reproduction.[3]

Stöcker and Lischnewska faced the competition of another organization headed by an elementary school teacher who used the pen name Ruth Bré. Bré, herself the child of unmarried parents, wished to found a utopian community for unmarried mothers and their children. Stöcker, who disapproved of this scheme, described Bré as a "totally undisciplined person" who was "a little crazy." However, along with several influential male sexual reformers, she joined the organization that Bré had founded in 1904, the League for the Protection of Mothers, and transplanted it early in 1905 to Berlin. Among the founding members meeting were Adele Schreiber, Lily Braun, Helene Stöcker, Henriette Fürth, and Frieda Duensing.[4]

In public debates on motherhood, infant welfare, and reproduction, the League for a brief period acquired an importance that was utterly disproportionate to its very limited membership. Despite establishing branches in ten German cities, it remained a very small organization—its total membership in 1908 was only about thirty-eight hundred. Even this small group was highly fragmented—some branches, for example, wished to concentrate wholly on philanthropic projects and rejected the leadership's ambitious programs of sexual reform. The leadership itself, moreover, splintered in 1908, partly because of a bitter dispute between Stöcker and Schreiber, which resulted in the latter's departure, along with many of her colleagues, including Henriette Fürth, to found her own organization. Nonetheless, especially during the period from 1905 to 1910, the League's program became a central focus of debate within feminist organizations and often among the general public as well. The organization's impact was due chiefly to the high visibility of its leaders. Stöcker edited the organization's journal, first under the title of *Mutterschutz* ("The Protection of Mothers") and then *Die Neue Generation* ("The New Generation"). The journal contained not only her own hard-hitting essays but contributions from eminent authors, including many men, such as psychiatrist Sigmund Freud; sexologists Alfred Moll, Havelock Ellis, and Magnus Hirschfeld; politician Friedrich Naumann; and birth-control advocate Johannes Rutgers (to name only a very few examples). Schreiber was a tireless lecturer, who gained sensational publicity that was increased by occasional prohibitions by the police. Her speeches, along with the League's annual conferences, were always widely reported in the press. Editorial commentators were usually unfavorable, sometimes even scandalized. But the League's leading spokespersons nonetheless changed the terms of the debate on motherhood by introducing controversial and previously taboo issues so forcefully that many other speakers were forced to take a stand on them. Among these were leaders not only of the feminist movement but of the conservative political and medical establishments, whose public positions on such issues as infant mortality and mothers' welfare was often motivated, at least in part, by their desire to counteract the League's radical propaganda.[5]

The League for the Protection of Mothers, although representing a small minority within the German and international feminist movements, thus influenced the development of feminist ideology throughout the Western world during this period. The program of the League was the first major attempt to create a specifically feminist approach to the new possibilities and problems presented by increased governmental intervention in the previously private sphere of child-rearing and reproduction. The first stage in the creation of the League's program was its response to the major child welfare issue of the period—the problem of infant mortality.

Infant Mortality and the Politics of Motherhood

The League's conception of the rights and duties of mothers can only be understood in the context of a widespread public discussion of maternal behavior. This new preoccupation with motherhood was in part a response to international tensions. The government of William II, who had ascended to the throne in 1888, had failed to renew Bismarck's treaty with Russia; the resulting alliance between Russia and France and subsequent agreements between both of these nations and Great Britain aroused German fears of "encirclement" and of a European war. Moreover, the expansion of Germany's influence on the European continent and overseas became an increasingly popular cause among all segments of society, but particularly among the intellectual elite, after 1900. This revival of imperial ambition, however, coincided with the demographic transition that resulted in declining birthrates throughout the Western world. Crude birthrates in the German Empire, having reached a peak (37.6 per 1,000 population) in the postwar period 1876–1880, had declined to 35 by 1902, and to about 30 by 1912. These figures, although by present-day standards very high, caused great concern. Politicians, military figures, and moralists pointed to the danger from Russia, where birthrates remained high, and to the example of France, where, they argued, low birthrates were linked to military weakness and cultural decadence.[6]

Among both health ministry officials and private citizens, a heightened concern for population growth was first expressed through concern with the infant death rate. "We believed that the high mortality rate of children in their first year was the result of natural selection which eliminated the weaker constitutions," wrote Carl von Behr-Pinnow, a prominent Berlin physician and infant-welfare advocate in 1911. "Now we know that it is a great national misfortune." International competition also acted as a stimulus toward reform; the German infant mortality figure of about 20 per 100 live births in 1903 was considerably higher than the figures published by Finland (12.7), France (13.7), and England (13.2), and was surpassed only by the figures for such economically backward countries as Russia (27) and Austria (21.5).[7]

Of all possible interpretations for these statistics, both governmental and medical authority figures chose those that placed responsibility upon mothers. Explanations stressing such social causes as poor housing and sanitation were superseded at the turn of the century by an almost exclusive emphasis upon the importance of breast-feeding. A flood of propaganda, put out by both governmental and charitable organizations, urged women to breast-feed their babies. "Attention, mothers, if you value the lives of your children," proclaimed a leaflet published by the Society for Prevention of Infant Mortality, "every mother should try to nurse her child herself!" These exhortations often expressed the controlling and moralizing purpose that Ute Frevert has criticized; a statement issued by the Health Ministry in 1906 blamed the decline of natural feeding on women's "love of comfort and fear of injury to their bodies." But social control was not the only rationale for this campaign. Indeed, politicians and reformers of all persuasions, including many feminists and socialists, regarded the encouragement of breast-feeding as an important measure in the struggle against infant mortality. They responded to a diagnostic trend that attributed an increasing percentage of infant deaths to diarrheal ailments, from about 15 percent in 1880 to about 25 percent by 1900, when these diseases were identified as the most common single cause of infant death. The frequency of such deaths in the hot summer months indicated that many were due to spoilage of milk, for which no adequate storage yet existed. Many studies, including one carried out in Berlin in 1903, showed that about 20 percent of all bottle-fed but only about 7 percent of all breast-fed babies died in their first year.[8]

Many politicians and activists, including both feminists and socialists, fully supported infant-welfare programs set up by local governments and private organizations. For mothers who were not able to nurse, these organizations attempted to make available supplies of uncontaminated cow's milk, at the same time instructing mothers on its storage and preparation. Adele Schreiber estimated that the number of such centers, offering pure milk as well as advice and medical services, increased from 4 in 1900 to 251 in 1910. Some of these centers offered financial aid (*Stillprämien*) to mothers who agreed to breast-feed their babies and to bring them regularly to be examined. A new institution, the Kaiserin-Auguste Viktoria House, was founded in 1909 and served as a center both of philanthropic activity and of infant-welfare research. The involvement of the empress and of the conservative medical establishment in infant welfare resulted in part from their anxiety at the radical propaganda of the League for the Protection of Mothers, to which they wished to create a conservative alternative. Socialist deputies to the Berlin City Council in 1905 approved such measures in principle, although deploring their inadequacy. "Social reform is being prescribed to us in homeopathic doses," objected one Socialist deputy, "but at least the ice is now broken . . . we hope that great results will follow these limited ones."[9]

Such limited and philanthropic measures could do little to remedy the underlying causes of infant mortality. The major contribution of the League for the Protection of Mothers to this general discourse was to recognize and publicize to the feminist movement as a whole the need for changes in the legal and economic status of mothers and children. The opening manifesto of the League protested against measures that were narrowly aimed at the welfare of children without any consideration of their mothers. "All protection of children that does not at the same time protect mothers is inadequate," stated the manifesto, "for the mother is the source of the child's life and essential to its survival. Whatever guarantees her rest and care during her delivery, ensures her economic security in the future, and shields her from the scorn . . . of her fellow human beings, creates the basis for the welfare of the child. . . . This is the aim of the League for the Protection of Mothers."[10]

The League's activists connected the status of women to the welfare of children by emphasizing a dimension of the infant-mortality problem—the death rates among illegitimate infants—that they claimed had been given insufficient attention. By contrast to the overall figure of about 20 percent for the children of married parents, about 34 percent of all infants born of unmarried mothers (thus 70 percent more) died in the first year of life. The statistics on death rates for illegitimate infants fully exposed the emptiness of official moralizing about maternal duty. Obviously, observed Adele Schreiber, mere moral pressure on these mothers to breast-feed their children was useless, for the difficulty of collecting child support meant that they were forced to seek employment soon after childbirth. Schreiber's view was later confirmed by the heads of privately and publicly sponsored infant welfare clinics, who noted that despite the offer of financial support for breast-feeding, few unmarried mothers were in a position to take advantage of their services.[11]

The approach of Schreiber and her colleagues in the League to the problems of the unmarried mother differed considerably from that of more traditional organizations such as the Federation of German Women's Organizations. As we have seen, the Child Welfare Committee of this organization supported the so-called Leipzig system, which arranged the placement of illegitimate children in foster homes, under the supervision of an agency that assumed the responsibility of legal guardian. Max Taube of Leipzig, the founder of this system and a respected authority on foster care, declared that illegitimate children were often better off with foster families than with their own mothers, whom he described as irresponsible and mentally deficient. Although supporting some aspects of the foster home system, Schreiber objected passionately to this negative view of the single mother. She asserted that the problems of single-parent families were due not to the deficiency of the mothers but to a system of morality that deprived the mother of rights, subjected her to "every kind of ostracism and contempt," and forced her to "entrust the child shortly after its birth to strangers in order not to be disgraced by the open acknowledgment of her motherhood."[12]

Before she joined the League, Schreiber had become a leader of a campaign to establish homes for unmarried mothers and their children. These homes enabled mothers to care for their children and work at the same time. This philanthropic activity eventually brought Schreiber and other mothers' rights activists into conflict with prevailing standards of sexual morality. Most existing maternity homes took only married women, and those few that were open to unmarried mothers often regarded them as "fallen women" and subjected them to patronizing religious rhetoric. In 1904, Schreiber cooperated in the founding of a home in Berlin that encouraged a far more positive attitude toward unmarried mothers. "It is a disgrace to our culture," she said, "that women are forced to conceal the maternity of which they should be proud. No woman can 'fall from virtue' through motherhood." The founding of homes for unmarried mothers that enabled mother and child to stay together was the major philanthropic activity of the local branches of the League.[13]

By aggressively criticizing conventional moral prejudice against unmarried mothers, Schreiber and her colleagues advocated a "New Ethic" that seemed very radical to most of her contemporaries. At the same time, however, she preserved the traditional female ethic that affirmed the mother-child bond as the basis of social and cooperative virtues. Schreiber praised motherhood in both its biological and spiritual forms as a redemptive social force. Linking biology to culture, she insisted that the experience of breast-feeding was necessary to the child's moral as well as physical development. The problems of modern society, she asserted in 1904, were due largely to the "loosening of the mother-child bond." As a basis for this sweeping argument, she used studies that claimed that illegitimate children were more likely than others to become criminals or dependent adults. Schreiber reversed conventional arguments that blamed the failings of illegitimate children on the immorality of their mothers, and claimed instead that the deprivation of maternal affection produced their antisocial behavior.[14]

As the debate on the Civil Code had shown, the status of unmarried mothers and their children was integrally linked to the existing family structure. Practical work thus led inevitably to a more theoretical critique of the legal, social, and political aspects of the mother-child relationship. The first of these discussions erupted over the utopian schemes of Ruth Bré, the founder of one of the two organizations that had later combined to become the League for the Protection of Mothers. Bré insisted that the status of the unmarried mother could not possibly be improved without the creation of a new relationship between family and state. Rejecting conventional, negative views of mother-headed households, she extolled such households as the continuation of the oldest and most valid familial tradition, matriarchy. Instead of the existing child-support system, which placed these households in an inferior status to father-headed "legitimate" families, she demanded that the state should support communities of mothers and children. Bré's proposal, although controversial and extreme, reflected a more general tendency of feminist reformers to call in the state as substitute for an absent or irresponsible father. The community itself, which existed for a short time, failed for lack of financial support.[15]

Another reason for its failure was the opposition of many members of the League, including Stöcker, Schreiber, and Fürth. Bré's opposition to maternity homes in the city and her romantic insistence on locating mothers and children in the countryside seemed to them impractical in an urban society. They also objected that matriarchy, a primitive form of the family, should be replaced by new forms that included fathers in an egalitarian partnership. In the first edition of the periodical *Mutterschutz*, Stöcker proclaimed that the reform of the family, which she described as the "holy trinity of father, mother, and child," was the aim of the organization. Disagreement on this as well as on other issues prompted Bré's resignation from the League, which continued under the leadership of a committee headed by Stöcker.[16]

Although rejecting utopian solutions, the League embarked on an extensive campaign to create a theoretical and practical basis for new forms of the family. Harking back to the recent protest against the family law provisions of the Civil Code, members of the League used the plight of the "illegitimate" to show that existing forms of the family protected the rights of fathers rather than the welfare of mothers and children. "For men wrote these laws," said Schreiber in 1904, "men have passed judgment on the problems of women, which will always be foreign to them." In place of this man-made system, members of the League argued for a new ethic centered on love rather than law. Stöcker, the chief theorist of this new ethic, argued along with Nietzsche that existing systems of morality purporting to arise from eternal and God-given principles actually reflected only power relationships—in this case, the power of men over women. It was time, she said, to throw over these outmoded ideas in favor of a code of ethics based on the most important earthly value—the value of human life itself. The highest goal, wrote Stöcker, was to "cultivate the love of life in all its forms—to place the stamp of eternity on our lives—to live, as if one were to live forever." As the ultimate expression of that "highest of all mysteries, the origin of life," she proposed the image of mother and child. In Stöcker's essays on sexual reform, the unmarried mother emerged as a new icon celebrating the triumph of life-giving nature over the dead formalism of man-made systems.[17]

The importance of the mother-child relationship was a central theme in the League's debates on sexual morality. At a conference held in 1908, the assembled delegates of the League summed up the views that they had expressed over the past three years by proposing that the children of unmarried parents be given all of the rights of legitimate children, including the right of inheritance from the father. As a corollary to this demand, they called for other forms of legal recognition for "free"—that is, nonmarital—relationships. This sensational advocacy of "free love" was widely noted in the press and provoked vociferous protest from conservative clergy and politicians.[18]

The leaders of the moderate feminist movement, who had previously avoided these controversial issues, were forced to take a stand on them. Helene Lange denounced the radicals for their "unfettered individualism," but her arguments in fact reflected some shared premises. For her, too, the mother-child bond was a paramount consideration. She defended the institution of marriage particularly for the sake of children, who would otherwise be deprived of parental care and security. The majority of the Federation of German Women's Organizations concurred with Lange's viewpoint; the organization's position paper of 1907 stated that "both man and woman are responsible for upholding marriage as the highest form of sexual relationship." The intent to protect the interests of married mothers and their children was also evident in the Federation's very cautious stance on the status of illegitimate children, for whom it demanded only an increased level of paternal support, rather than rights to inheritance or to membership in the father's family. Opposition to the League's program came from left as well as right. Socialist spokeswoman Klara Zetkin also identified the radicals' program as anarchic and individualistic, and defended monogamous marriage as a protective institution for mothers and children. All of the participants in this acrimonious debate, while disagreeing on many issues, took the rights and duties of motherhood as well as the rights of the separate individual as the basic premise of their arguments.[19]

Feminists of all shades of opinion took advantage of official concern over the numbers and health of the new generation to argue for a widened role for the state in supporting motherhood. Chief among the threats to the health of illegitimate and legitimate children alike was the economic pressure on mothers to work outside the home. The problems of working mothers had become a cause of widespread concern in an era when the number of married women in the work force was perceived as dramatically increasing. In the debate on protective legislation for working women, including restrictions on working hours, dangerous occupations, and the employment of expectant and new mothers, arguments based on the rights of mothers prevailed over those based on the rights of women as individuals. Protective measures were acknowledged to be a threat to women's right to make individual choices. But both bourgeois and socialist women's organizations increasingly concluded that the rights of individuals must sometimes yield to the paramount right to motherhood. The socialist groups, who had opposed protective legislation in the 1880s, changed their position at the party conference in 1893 and demanded protective legislation to support "the role of mother, which is so important to the future of society." "Nothing is so detrimental to the rights of women," wrote Lily Braun, "as the disregard for motherhood, the pressure to neglect her children." The widespread acceptance of this view was expressed through the practical campaign for the widening of state-supported maternity insurance.[20]

The idea of maternity insurance was not new, for the German Empire already had a system of state-supported maternity benefits. As early as 1878 the employment of mothers in the first three weeks after childbirth had been forbidden. By 1903 this mandatory maternity leave had been lengthened to six weeks, and support for this period was furnished by state-subsidized insurance agencies at one half to one third of the worker's average daily wage. But both Lily Braun and Henriette Fürth, two of the earliest advocates of expanded maternity insurance, pointed out that most working women could not live on only a fraction of their usual wage, and were thus forced to circumvent the regulations by engaging in domestic industry. Moreover, only a minority of women workers—those employed in industry—were subject to the mandatory coverage, which excluded larger groups, such as agricultural workers, domestic workers, home workers, and the unemployed spouses of workers. Only a considerable improvement of coverage, therefore, would enable women to combine work and motherhood without damage to their own and their children's health. In 1901, Braun advocated the extension of the mandatory maternity leave from six weeks before to six weeks after the birth, the payment of benefits at the level of the full daily wage, the provision for medical care and a hospital stay if needed, and additional financial support for breast-feeding mothers. Fürth advocated all of these benefits over a considerably longer period—six weeks of pregnancy and twelve of maternity leave. These proposals represented a compromise between the short-term and long-term interests of both women and children. Braun, who agreed with physicians and some socialist authors that babies should ideally be breast-fed for more than six weeks, nonetheless feared that insistence on a longer maternity leave would imperil the job security, and thus the long-term survival, of women workers.[21]

The ideas of Braun, Fürth, and many others were expressed in a petition drawn up by the League for the Protection of Mothers and submitted to the Reichstag in 1907, when many reforms of the state-sponsored insurance system were being discussed. The League's petition appealed to the legislators' concern for military strength by pointing out that high rates of infant mortality and the poor health of surviving children directly affected the number of new military recruits, and thus the quality of the army. While recognizing the employment of mothers as a cause of this problem, the petition defended the right of women to work, which it called "a necessary result of our economic development." The petition called on the state to protect the health of the younger generation by enabling women to combine gainful employment and motherhood. The expansion of maternity coverage was also supported by a wide range of feminist organizations, including the Federation of German Women's Associations, the socialist women's groups, and the League of Progressive Women's Organizations, as well as the Social Democratic party itself. The breadth of this support showed the value of motherhood as an issue transcending class and political differences. Despite this substantial support, the actual reforms, which were enacted in 1911 and put into effect in 1914, were disappointing. The new insurance code lengthened the total period of pregnancy and maternity leave from six to eight weeks, and included previously unprotected occupational groups. But the level of support remained low, and medical expenses and support payments for breast-feeding were included as optional rather than mandatory benefits.[22]

Despite these limitations, maternity insurance benefits in Germany continued to surpass those provided by other major Western countries. Many contemporary commentators pointed to declining rates of infant mortality—from 22 per 100 live births in 1890 to about 16 by 1910—as proof of the effects of increased official and philanthropic concern for infant welfare. The steady decline especially in diarrheal diseases among the causes of infant death after 1900 may have been due at least partially to efforts to encourage breast-feeding and to provide a purer milk supply. Frevert speculates that the educational efforts of middle-class women had some beneficial effects on the health of lower-class mothers and children.[23]

The campaign for mothers' rights shows how completely many members of this generation had accepted an idea that the older generation—that of Schrader-Breymann and Heyl—had found more problematic: the assumption by the state of functions that had traditionally been performed by the family. Historian Jean Quataert has claimed that the German Empire's social policies served chiefly to reinforce patriarchal family structure by allotting benefits to male wage earners as heads of household. The idea of maternity insurance, paid directly to mothers, departed from this pattern by supporting the independence of mother-headed families. Through their demand for maternity insurance and for other social benefits, the feminists of the League increasingly envisaged the state in the role of extended family. New approaches to social policy often harked back to traditional conceptions of the state as "great social household." "We must now recognize," wrote Ellen Key, an enthusiastic supporter of the League, in 1909, "that the relationships between parents and children are no longer a purely private affair, but that the new generation must become the focus of social policy."[24]

In Germany during this period, many women activists conceived of women's citizenship as an entitlement to social benefits more than (as in the English-speaking world) as the right to vote. Social benefits, moreover, were conceived not primarily as an individual right but as a reward for the performance of a duty. This argument became central to the campaign for suffrage as well as for welfare benefits. As we have seen, suffrage for women had been advocated by individual feminist leaders since the 1870s, and was endorsed by the Social Democratic party, under the leadership of August Bebel, in 1891. The first feminist organization devoted specifically to suffrage agitation, the Deutsche Verein für Frauenstimmrecht (German Woman Suffrage Association), however, was not founded until 1902, and the Federation of German Women's Organizations did not fully endorse this goal until 1907. Full-fledged campaigns for woman suffrage were not possible until the repeal, in 1908, of the Association Laws, which had barred women in some states from membership in political parties and from attendance at political meetings. As early as 1896, Helene Lange had attributed the low status of German women in relation to their English-speaking counterparts to the militarism of German society, where the right to vote was widely believed to be earned through military service rather than granted as a right. The feminists' emphasis on motherhood as an essential contribution to society and to military strength must be seen in this context. "In the competition of peoples," said Schreiber in 1912, "that nation will win which does not waste the strength of its mothers."[25]

Suffrage advocates did not simply accept male definitions of citizenship, but often criticized and revised them. As Karen Offen has remarked, feminists at the turn of the century envisaged female political activity as a means of changing the metaphorical "gender" of a state that had traditionally been identified with the masculine strength and authority. The demand for state support for motherhood and child-rearing was a demand for a change in the image and function of the state. In 1903, Lily Braun, who was a strong advocate of suffrage, envisaged a change in the state's metaphorical "gender" through an image of a peaceable female army devoted to nurture rather than violence. "I see a procession of women. They march with steady pace and heads held high. They are unarmed; they carry their children in their arms." When the Reichstag refused full funding for the maternity-insurance benefits proposed by the coalition of women's organizations in 1911, Adele Schreiber, a strong suffrage advocate, drew attention in her many public speeches to the ironic contrast between the generosity of the Reichstag deputies toward the military and their callous neglect of the needs of women and children and asserted that only the achievement of woman suffrage could change the state's man-made policies.[26]

International responses to the League for the Protection of Mothers showed that feminist movements centered on motherhood and child welfare were not considered more cautious, conservative, or conventionally feminine than those centered on equal rights. Many American feminists regarded the German organization as a vanguard of radicalism and daring. Certainly suffrage and maternal issues were intertwined for the American feminists—their most common argument during this period was that women needed the right to vote in order to apply their distinctively female ethical and cultural values to the male-dominated sphere of politics. But the specifically maternal issues that occupied the center of German feminist programs during these years were given comparatively little attention by American feminist organizations such as the NAWSA (National American Women Suffrage Association). Some American feminists criticized these priorities, which they saw as an accommodation to conservative women's groups, and looked to Germany and Scandinavia, and especially to the League for the Protection of Mothers, for more stimulating and advanced ideas. German feminists, asserted philosopher Ethel Sturges Dummer, were more radical than their American colleagues because they "would change not only law but custom, would reverse the attitude of mind toward marriage." Dummer's friend Katherine Anthony, an admirer of Ellen Key, praised the League for creating a "new science of womanhood" which attempted neither to preserve traditional ideas nor to imitate men. Anthony attempted to introduce some of the League's main ideas, such as equal status for illegitimate and legitimate children, into the programs of American feminist movements, but without much success. The international publicity given to the League's ideas was another sign of the extensive, though brief, influence of this tiny organization.[27]

The League's campaign against infant mortality, which envisaged a new relationship between family and state, raised serious ethical and practical issues. If motherhood was a contribution to the state, and the basis of women's claim to citizenship, then to what extent did the state have the right to control and regulate mothers' behavior? If the state were asked to assume the protective function previously assigned to the father, then would it not also assume the father's authority? Conservative feminists, who were still attached to traditional models of family privacy, were more apt to perceive these problems than their radical colleagues. "Healthy human instinct," reflected social worker Alice Salomon, "must rebel against the one-sided definition of motherhood as a social function." What would be the consequences, Salomon asked, if the state put this idea into practice and "laid on women the duty—or the right—to bear children for the state"? The debate on the rights of women to reproductive choice, which briefly preoccupied the feminist movement as a whole in 1908, showed that this problem remained unresolved.[28]

Chapter 10
Motherhood as Choice: The Campaign for Reproductive Rights, 1908–1914

The campaign against infant mortality had expressed a conception of the relationship of women to the state that was based on a synthesis of old and new ideas, of ethical values centered on motherhood and new expectations of state involvement in maternal and child welfare. These ideas influenced the debate among diverse groups within German feminist movements upon a new but related theme—reproductive rights and responsibilities. The League for the Protection of Mothers was the first major feminist organization, not only in Germany but in the Western world, to place the issues of birth control, abortion, and eugenic legislation on its public agenda. In 1908, the Legal Committee of the Federation of German Women's Organization submitted a resolution to the organization's annual meeting recommending the total deletion of the federal law prohibiting abortion, Paragaph 218 of the Civil Code. Although this proposal was voted down by the majority of delegates to the Federation's 1908 convention in Breslau, the debate at the convention represented a high point of the feminist movement's interest in reproductive issues, which were widely discussed throughout the period from 1904 to 1914.

The attempt to formulate a feminist approach to reproduction caused deep division and bitter hostility within the German feminist movement, but the debate as a whole revealed underlying agreement as well as diversity. Both advocates and opponents of abortion rights and birth control balanced rights against responsibilities. All saw reproduction as a concern for society and state as well as the individual. Thus, none of the speakers took purely individualistic positions; even the most fervent defenders of women's right to self-determination could also support the state's right to intervene in reproductive decision-making in order to preserve population quality. To some recent historians, notably Richard Evans, this latter argument seems to foreshadow the policies of totalitarian states. However, these ideas should be seen in the context not of some future form of the state but of the state these women experienced. As we have seen from the previous chapter, the right of privacy that protected father-headed households often seemed to threaten, not to guarantee, the rights of women and children. State intervention in the familial sphere, whether in reproduction or in child-rearing, could sometimes be justified as a protection of the rights of women. A tradition of feminist discourse that questioned conventional public/private boundaries and linked rights to duties, the self to the other, and the individual to the community emerged here in its most complex and problematic form.

Motherhood: Choice or Destiny

The creation of a feminist standpoint on reproductive rights was in part a response to increasing governmental control of reproductive decision-making. Despite the steady decrease in rates of infant mortality, population growth rates continued to decline, and the surplus of births over deaths decreased. Therefore, governments increasingly combined campaigns to save infant lives with coercive measures to increase the birthrate itself. The abortion statute of the Criminal Code, Paragraph 218, was enforced ever more stringently; the number of convictions for this offense, although still representing only a tiny portion of the total number of abortions, rose from 411 in 1902 to 1,648 in 1914.[1]

This effort to raise birthrates posed a more direct threat to women's autonomy than did the campaign against infant mortality. Whereas infant mortality had been attributed partly to environmental conditions, falling birthrates were blamed directly on moral degeneracy, especially that of women. Because family limitation was clearly most successfully practiced among the middle class, physicians, politicians, and moralists attacked middle-class women, the group who had benefited most from recent progress in opening educational and professional opportunities to women. The feminist movement was denounced for allegedly encouraging middle-class women to refuse motherhood. "Humanity, our race, our culture needs a progeny as numerous as possible, born of the most competent and talented women," stated one widely quoted article. "Thus feminism, which conflicts with these goals, must be condemned."[2]

This rhetoric, despite its viciously antifeminist tone, acknowledged the public importance of women's private choices. It thus provided a context for the public discussion of subjects such as sexuality and reproductive behavior, which had previously been considered private and taboo. Radical feminists' positions on these issues were often influenced by the international birth control movement, known in Germany chiefly by its British name, "neo-Malthusianism." Advocates of neo-Malthusianism such as British sexologist Havelock Ellis and Dutch physician Johannes Rutgers denied that a decline in crude rates of population growth posed a threat to the vitality or success of Western culture. Instead they interpreted this trend as a sign of progress toward rational control over reproduction, careful nurture, and increasing attention to the individual development of each child. This idea was enthusiastically supported by Ellen Key, who argued in *The Century of the Child* that the most important of parental duties was the rational planning of reproduction. "Civilization," she wrote, "should make man conscious of an end and responsible in all these spheres in which up to the present he has acted without responsibility." Thus the theories on which German feminists based their conception of reproductive rights linked these rights to parental responsibility, and the welfare of women as individuals inseparably to that of children and the "new generation."[3]

On a practical as well as a theoretical level, the concern of German feminists with family limitation arose directly out of their involvement with child welfare issues. Marie Baum, who worked as the head of a private child welfare agency in Düsseldorf, stressed the relationship between smaller families and increased investment in each child. Families who controlled their fertility, she wrote, regarded "every child . . . as a possession of high value, whose preservation justified every kind of exertion, because the new pregnancy was not simply willed by God, but by the individual." Studies published in Stöcker's periodicals, *The Protection of Mothers* and *The New Generation*, documented the fact that, among poor families, rates of infant and child mortality could be correlated directly to large numbers of children and short birth intervals. Sociologist Rudolf Goldscheid, who influenced both Stöcker and Fürth, argued that evolutionary progress now required the abandonment of the wasteful reproductive patterns of plant and other animal species for a "human economy" based on quality rather than quantity.[4]

The first major debate on reproductive rights to involve the feminist movement as a whole was held in November 1908 at the Annual Convention of the Federation of German Women's Organizations in Breslau. The central issue was a resolution recommending the complete deletion of Paragraph 218, which prohibited abortion, from the Civil Code. The resolution was introduced as part of a package of suggestions for legal reform by the Federation's Legal Committee, then headed by Marie Stritt. Stritt had served as president of the Federation since 1899 and was also an enthusiastic member of the League for the Protection of Mothers. However, in 1908 the members of the Legal Committee, who represented chiefly the radical organizations, faced a new political constellation within the Federation. As a direct reaction to the anticipated vote on the proposal of the Legal Committee, the moderate members had invited a large, conservative religious organization, the League of Protestant Women, to join the organization. The presence of the Protestant women as well as representatives of other religious organizations, such as the Federation of Jewish Women, guaranteed in advance the defeat of the Legal Committee's recommendation that the antiabortion law be abolished, but also ensured that the widest possible variety of bourgeois feminist positions, from religious conservatism to radicalism, would be represented in the debate.[5]

In order to appreciate the structure, limits, and possibilities of this wide-ranging feminist discourse on reproductive issues, we must first see what all of the members agreed on. The proposal for the legalization of abortion was presented as part of a package of suggestions for legal reform. The laws to be reformed included some specifically affecting women and others affecting the moral and sexual welfare of children and young people. Thus, motherhood, both biological and spiritual, was portrayed from the outset as both a right and duty; "if they [women] care about their rights to be equal members of society," commented the Federation's newsletter, "then they also care about their duty, to work for . . . morally endangered young people, whose natural and committed protectors they are." Most of the Legal Committee's proposals called for the strengthening of laws protecting vulnerable women and girls from various kinds of abuse, especially sexual abuse, by men; they concerned the raising of the age of consent, the protection of underage girls from sexual exploitation by guardians or teachers, and abolition of laws regulating prostitution, along with stronger punishment of brothel-keepers. All of these proposals, with modifications, were accepted by the entire assembly. Thus sexuality and reproduction were portrayed by all participants in this discussion as areas not of freedom, pleasure, and self-determination for women but rather of vulnerability and oppression. This view reflected the common experiences of many of these women, conservative and radical, whose introduction to feminist activism had come through social work or from work in the many legal-aid centers set up to advise women.[6]

The same theme was taken up in the discussion, beginning the next day, of another law, Paragraph 217, the law penalizing infanticide. This law already took the desperate situation of unmarried mothers into consideration by prescribing a lighter penalty for the murder of an illegitimate child by its mother than for the murder of a legitimate one. The Legal Committee proposed an amendment: the father of the child should share in the penalty if "it can be established that he bears any responsibility, even moral responsibility." This proposal, which was accepted unanimously, established several premises for the far more controversial discussion that followed. Unwanted pregnancy was established as a disastrous and life-threatening situation for women and children, caused by the irresponsibility of men. In the absence of familial and social support, the choice to avoid motherhood was clearly made not in freedom, but under terrible constraint.[7]

The relationship of abortion to infanticide—both similarities and differences—was a subtext of the immediately ensuing discussion of abortion rights. Camilla Jellinek, a member of the Legal Committee who had set up legal advice centers (*Rechtsschutzstellen*) for women in Heidelberg, opened the debate by arguing that the two acts were different, indeed, antithetical. The law recognized personhood only from birth; moreover, the legalization of abortion would reduce the frequency of infanticide. "What reason would a woman have to go through with a pregnancy and then to strangle it [the infant] after birth?" she asked. Jellinek's emphasis on the difference between abortion and infanticide was partly strategic. The majority of the Legal Committee had decided not to recommend the abolition of Paragraph 219, the law penalizing persons performing abortions. Only early abortions could be performed unassisted. Jellinek, who personally disapproved of this law, nonetheless defended it by asserting that women's revulsion against infanticide would always lead them to prefer early to late abortions. "Any woman with healthy feelings . . . knows the difference between getting rid of a little egg and an embryo whose movements she has begun to feel." Thus legalization was justified through the authority both of man-made legal traditions and of specifically female experience. Jellinek's speech emphatically asserted reproductive self-determination but also portrayed the abortion decision as an expression of maternal responsibility—a value that was shared by all members of her audience.[8]

Abortion was not entirely dissociated from infanticide, however. Speakers on both sides of the issue agreed on seeing both actions largely as desperate responses to the sexual victimization of women by men—the central theme of the previous discussion. They argued chiefly over whether legalized abortion would increase or lessen such victimization. This argument reflected a broader disagreement on the role of the family. Conservative feminists believed that the patriarchal family, whatever its injustices, was still the best protector of the interests of women and children. The separation of sexuality from pregnancy seemed to them to encourage men to exploit women sexually without pressure toward commitment. Paula Müller, head of the League of Protestant Women, argued that legalization would encourage the "degradation of women" by promoting an "increase in indulgence and irresponsible behavior," and Bertha Pappenheim, of the Federation of Jewish Women, declared that the legalization of abortion would protect men, not women. Radical women were critical of the family, declaring that family law protected the patriarchal family rather than women themselves. Referring to laws that made evasion of paternal child support very easy, Käthe Schirmacher, of the League of Progressive Women's Organizations, asserted that women were already so vulnerable that the legalization of abortion could hardly make the situation worse. "Men have the pleasure," she concluded, "and women have the burden." ("Der Mann hat die Lust und die Frau hat die Last.") The law that placed such a disproportionate share of responsibility on women should at least permit them a choice about continuing pregnancy.[9]

Another area of basic agreement among speakers on both sides of the issue was on the importance of motherhood and maternal responsibility as ethical values, but the two sides disagreed on the relationship of abortion to such maternal responsibility. Whereas physician Agnes Bluhm deplored the frivolity and selfishness of women who wished to avoid motherhood, radical feminist Helene Stöcker argued that the abortion decision could in some cases be a responsible one. "Couldn't the mother of a numerous family in fact be expressing love for her children by deciding against another addition to the family?"[10]

The social dimension of reproductive behavior, its significance not only to the family but to the community and state, was taken very seriously by all speakers. All accepted the state's interest in the quantity and quality of its population, and this point was much more strongly made by the radicals, advocates of the welfare state, than by the conservatives and moderates who still defended the role of the family. The only radical to oppose legalization, retired teacher Maria Lischnewska, was also the only speaker to take an aggressively nationalist stand, urging that population growth was necessary for the success of the German "cultural mission." This was a very different, and far more "modern" rationale for prohibition than the Christian morality urged by the conservatives. More "modern" also was Lischnewska's orientation toward medical rather than moral considerations; she made an exception for abortion according to the "eugenic indication" and recommended that cases of this sort be decided by a board of physicians. And Lischnewska linked the duty of mothers to the state to the state's own duty to give "woman . . . as the mother of the human race . . . the position that she deserves." Opponents of Lichnewska took issue less with her concern for population growth than with her assumption that the prohibition of abortion would itself achieve the desired end. "The population," argued Jellinek, echoing the neo-Malthusian rhetoric of the contemporary birth control movement, "is affected, not just by the number of births, but by the rate of infant mortality caused by neglect and infanticide."[11]

Within this discourse on social responsibility and maternal experience, some arguments based on pure civil-liberties doctrine were also heard. Stöcker asserted that the individual did not exist for the state, but the state for the individual, and Jellinek defined "the control of one's own body" as among the "rights of the free personality."[12]

The problems faced by the proponents of legalization in reconciling strong beliefs in both individual liberties and social responsibility were clearly revealed by Adele Schreiber. Although the Federation excluded socialist women's organizations, Schreiber, as a strong socialist sympathizer, claimed that she spoke from the point of view of working-class women. She argued that the penalties for abortion fell chiefly on working-class women, while more prosperous women, who refused "the duty of motherhood out of self-indulgence and hedonism," were hardly ever affected. She also criticized abortion prohibitions because they were hypocritical; a state which, for lack of protective factory legislation, allowed "the mass murder of fetuses in some industries" was not justified in imprisoning individual women for the same action. But Schreiber was surely aware that her position conflicted with that of many leading socialist women, including Clara Zetkin. Some prominent socialist women, although opposed to Paragraph 219, condemned the campaign for birth control and abortion rights as irresponsible individualism, which might benefit individual mothers but could not help the working class as a whole. They themselves emphasized the need to eliminate the social conditions causing abortion by state-sponsored protective legislation for working women and benefits to mothers and children. Schreiber clearly shared these concerns. Rather than asserting abortion as an individual right, she portrayed it chiefly as a social problem—an unfortunate but inevitable response to an oppressive social order. This left open the question: if this oppressive and unjust order were ended, if the state were to fulfill its responsibilities to women and children, would it then be justified in prohibiting abortion in the interests of population policy?[13]

The assembly, having heard the arguments for and against legalization, voted against the Legal Committee's proposal for the abolition of the antiabortion statute, Paragraph 218. There was, the organization's newsletter reports, a "strong minority," but the actual figures were not given. This vote has been interpreted by Richard Evans and Barbara Greven-Aschoff as a victory of conservatism over radicalism within the feminist movement. But the substitute motion that was accepted was in some ways modern (here "modernity" is not identified with progress), suggesting some guidelines that are very similar to those that were eventually adopted in the Federal Republic of Germany. The motion, introduced by Lischnewska, proposed a lighter penalty and also exceptions to the law made to save the life of the mother and to prevent the birth of a defective child, the "eugenic indication" (or *Notlagenindikation*). Contemporary West German law has added a "social indication." These indications were to be established by a committee of physicians "on which women have a seat and a voice." This proposal indicates two crucial changes in feminists' views of abortion. Abortion was now regarded as a medically assisted rather than a private, self-assisted action, and the basis for decision-making was now defined not as Christian or secular ethics but as the judgment of legal and medical professionals. Strikingly modern, as well, was the role assigned to professional women, who were now placed in the position of helping, counseling, judging, and controlling less privileged women. The Federation did not discuss the abortion issue again until after the war, largely because, as a result of the 1908 debate, Marie Stritt was ousted from the presidency in

1910 and replaced by the more conservative Gertrud Bäumer. Disagreements on the abortion issue also disrupted the League for the Protection of Mothers and led to the resignation of some of its members.[14]

During the immediate prewar period, the remaining members of the League identified themselves increasingly with the international birth control movement. In 1911, a German Neo-Malthusian Committee was formed with a membership drawn almost entirely from the League, which hosted an International Neo-Malthusian Conference in 1912. Governments responded to such developments with increased coercive pressure. In 1912 the Prussian government asked all local officials to report on the incidence of birth control and abortion in their districts. In 1913 stiffer federal laws were proposed limiting the sale of contraceptive devices. These measures were justified by a flood of inflammatory rhetoric. "The vulture of depopulation spreads its wings over the German Empire," warned one right-wing pamphlet.[15]

Marie Stritt worked to establish links between the largely male-dominated birth control movement and the women's movement. She argued that reproductive self-determination was a basic right without which all others were meaningless; woman had finally realized the "entire unacceptability of the role of a childbearing machine." But the synthesis of feminism and neo-Malthusianism presented problems. Neo-Malthusians, in the tradition of British economist Thomas Robert Malthus, regarded the reduction in numbers as the only cure for poverty, and thus opposed social programs such as maternity insurance, which they feared would encourage population growth. Therefore, socialist leaders, including Zetkin, took a dim view of the birth control movements and supported welfare benefits designed to help working mothers bear and rear children. Feminists with strong socialist sympathies, such as Stöcker and Schreiber, attempted to support both social reform and birth control. Stöcker, for example, insisted that feminists did not wish to discourage childbearing, but only unwanted pregnancy enforced by "punishments, punishments, punishments!"[16]

The first wide-scale socialist campaign supporting birth control was not intended as a protest against the oppression of women, but only against the military buildup of the immediate prewar years. In 1913, socialist physicians Alfred Moses and Julius Bernstein called on socialist women to refuse to bear children who would only provide cannon fodder for imperialist wars. Most feminist birth control advocates, including

Braun, Schreiber, and Fürth, opposed this "birth strike." They had based their entire program on cooperation with the state, hoping that it would be transformed through the growing power and influence of women. Even though the failure of the suffrage campaign had disappointed them, these women insisted that motherhood was a patriotic duty. In 1915, after the outbreak of war, Henriette Fürth commented bitterly on a Reichstag debate on legislation imposing stiffer penalties on the sale of contraceptives. The debate, she complained, was conducted entirely by "men who, without consideration for our rights and our welfare, demand children and more children. How will they compel us?" But she nonetheless concluded, "We will be the mothers whom the Fatherland needs."[17]

Population Quality

The feminists' attempt to create new definitions of motherhood as both right and responsibility extended to the concern for population quality, as formulated during this period by the eugenics movement. Many historians have seen the interest of feminists of this era in eugenics as a sign of right-wing and racist tendencies. Richard J. Evans identifies the increasing prominence given to eugenic issues after 1908 as the chief sign of a disastrous decline of liberalism in the feminist movement. Heinz Niggemann characterizes Henriette Fürth, although she was a socialist and a Jew, as a "fringe phenomenon" and a precursor of National Socialism. Marie-Luise Janssen-Jurreit sees feminist eugenic theory as only a chapter in the deplorable history of scientific racism. Amy Hackett takes a more balanced but still basically apologetic view of Stocker's enthusiasm for eugenics. Recent West German historians have defended Stöcker's interest in eugenics by explaining it away as an attempt to win the support of male physicians or, in the words of Heide Soltau, as a mere "temporary collaboration with clearly reactionary tendencies that later contributed to Fascism." Most of these accounts do not deal with other outspoken feminist advocates of eugenics during this period, such as Braun, Schreiber, and Fürth.[18]

Many of these judgments, which identify the eugenics movement chiefly with the political right, do not take into account the left-wing and progressive branches of the movement, described in Chapter Eight. Left-wing reformers, including many feminists, often argued throughout this period that the emancipation of women would not damage, but rather enhance, the quality of the next generation. They had used this argument to justify many improvements in women's legal and social position.[19]

The most important feminist use of eugenic theory was to justify criticism of patriarchal marriage patterns, especially parental control over the marriage choices of young women. Opposition to marriages of convenience, which since the beginning of the nineteenth century had been justified on ethical grounds, was now also supported by hereditarian theory. Much literature on marriage during this era, whether scientific or popular, warned against the danger to offspring of unions based merely on social or economic factors without regard to the fitness of the partners for parenthood. The "right of a child to choose his parents," stated Ellen Key, was the most important right of the new generation.[20]

Feminists of all shades of opinion used such arguments in order to support the decision of young women to delay marriage and to seek professional training. Professional training, asserted authors such as Lily Braun, Grete Meisel-Hess, and many others, would not deter women from marriage and reproduction but would enable them to marry for love instead of economic convenience. Following many social-radical eugenic theorists, including Wilhelm Bölsche, Havelock Ellis, and Ellen Key, they took an exalted view of romantic love as a biological force promoting evolutionary development by encouraging genetically favorable unions. They criticized conventional marriage laws that subjected women to the power of men as injurious not just to individual women but to the quality of the new generation. These laws, they argued, discouraged the fittest and strongest women, who would transmit the most favorable hereditary traits, from marrying and ensured that the new generation would be borne and raised by weaker and more docile women.[21]

Arguments for the rights of unmarried mothers and their children were also buttressed by eugenic theories. Disagreement on the interpretaton of these theories caused a split within the League for the Protection of Mothers and exposed it to criticism by the hard-liners of the eugenics movement. In its opening manifesto, the League had characterized illegitimate children as "valuable offspring" whose preservation would enhance the quality of the population. Ruth Bré, the original founder of the League, had proposed that only healthy mothers should be admitted to her proposed community of mothers and children. The refusal of Stöcker and her colleagues to agree to such selective measures was one of the grievances that prompted Bré to resign from the League. The League's policies were also criticized by influential eugenicist Alfred Ploetz, editor of the *Review of Racial and Social Biology*. Ploetz, who was a member of the League and a friend of Stöcker, argued that nondiscriminatory philanthropy was worthless from a eugenic point of view; only the selection of the fittest mothers for help would lead to real biological improvement. The leadership of the League, although not rejecting Ploetz's position on principle, argued against it on what they termed practical grounds—that not much was known about hereditary disease, that the health of the absent father was as important as that of the mother, and that environment could be just as important as heredity to the formation of character. By stressing the interaction of heredity and environment, feminists objected to the hard-line hereditarian theories that were often used at this time to justify the downgrading of social reform and the enforcement of coercive and punitive approaches to social problems.[22]

Many concrete legislative proposals by the League for the Protection of Mothers and other feminist organizations called on the state to protect both women and children from threats to their welfare posed by irresponsible male behavior. One of the first of these campaigns was for the legal requirement of a health examination before marriage. This proposal was widely regarded during this era as a drastic interference with the right of privacy that protected sexual behavior from public scrutiny. But, for many female activists, both radicals and moderates, this was a prime example of a definition of privacy that protected only husbands and fathers while exposing women and chldren to danger and exploitation. Elsbeth Krukenberg, who was active in the abolitionist and temperance movements, laid responsibility both on parents and on women themselves to investigate the health of prospective spouses before marriage. The enthusiasm for premarital health examinations was largely due to the example of the United States, admired as a progressive and scientifically enlightened society, where several states had recently enacted laws requiring such examinations. But unlike some American reformers, most members of the League for the Protection of Mothers did not favor the legal prohibition of marriages to those afflicted with hereditary ailments, but instead encouraged education of such couples to voluntary reproductive responsibility.[23]

The result of this campaign, which was supported by numerous other organizations, was a petition submitted to the Health Office in 1917 advocating the distribution of an informational pamphlet to all newly married couples. The leaflet advised a premarital health examination and warned of the transmission of hereditary disease. The Imperial Health Ministry had doubts about even this very mild measure—in 1917 a committee of the Ministry warned against "severe interference with personal liberty"—but a law requiring the distribution of the leaflet was passed in 1920.[24]

Another important demand of the League for the Protection of Mothers was for the addition of sex education to school curricula—the subject of a petition submitted to the Reichstag in 1906. This proposal, like the recommendation of premarital health examinations, called for the injection of state authority into a traditionally private concern chiefly in order to protect women, who too often were reared in enforced sexual ignorance. The League for the Protection of Mothers envisaged a far more extensive program of sex education than was recommended by most prominent male eugenicists. Wilhelm Schallmayer, for example, urged sex education only for adolescent boys, chiefly in order to warn them against the dangers of disease. The League's petition to the Reichstag, by contrast, advocated a program of sex education in the public schools for children of both sexes. This curriculum, they insisted, should stress the positive aspects of sexuality rather than its dangers. Fürth contended that such education would benefit both mothers and their offspring by teaching that "each human being should strive . . . to become so strong and perfect in body and spirit as to produce a new and better generation." This petition evidently received no response and Furth remarked regretfully in 1920 that little had been done beyond a few lectures to members of secondary school senior classes, most of which were all male.[25]

Another way the population-quality argument was used to support women in their right to make responsible reproductive choices was the feminists' advocacy of access to contraception and legalized abortion in order to avoid the transmission of hereditary disease. The idea that the state should take measures to discourage the unfit from reproduction was shared by almost all groups concerned with population policy, even by many who opposed the use of contraception and abortion by healthy people. Feminist advocates of legalized abortion presented it as a means toward voluntary exercise of reproductive responsibility. Parents, Stöcker asserted, now had the means to prevent the individual suffering and social burden caused by the birth of handicapped children. "There are cases when the production of a child would be a crime," she wrote in 1906. "Society must answer for every defective life. . . . It takes the consequences, therefore it should prevent it."[26]

Even the opponents of legalized abortion within the Federation argued for abortion according to the so-called eugenic indication when parents were afflicted by conditions, such as alcoholism, venereal disease, and mental retardation, that were thought to be hereditary. Such recommendations, once again, called on state authority to intervene in the private sphere in order to protect women and children. Alcoholism, sexual promiscuity, and its result, venereal disease, were regarded by female reformers of this era as forms of male immorality by which women and children were victimized. For example, several speakers in the 1908 debate stated or strongly implied that drunkenness (viewed as an entirely male vice) was often the cause of marital rape and unwanted pregnancy. What of the married woman, asked Camilla Jellinek, "who cannot get away from a drunken husband?" Some speakers in the 1908 debate attempted to broaden the eugenic indication to include environmental as well as purely hereditary factors. Meta Hammerschlag, a prominent member of the League for the Protection of Mothers, stated that, as malnutrition was a major cause of low population quality, the fact that a mother could not feed another child should be reason enough for an abortion under the eugenic indication.[27]

Although the vast majority of feminist opinions on reproductive rights in this era stressed moral responsibility, some also recommended new forms of compulsion. Feminists such as Schreiber, who had vehemently resisted the interference of the state with the abortion decision, nonetheless advocated the compulsory sterilization of individuals afflicted by a few conditions believed to be hereditary. At the 1908 convention of the Federation of German Women's Organizations, Adele Schreiber, who as we have seen was a strong opponent of Paragraph 218, also advocated the prevention of mental retardation through the internment of retarded individuals and some criminals in humane colonies where they would be prevented from reproducing.[28]

How could advocates of individual reproductive rights, including the right of abortion, also argue in favor of such an unprecedented level of state interference in reproductive decision-making? The belief in eugenic sterilization, although later associated with National Socialist reproductive policies, was not considered a right-wing idea at this time; it was widely held by progressive segments of public opinion and by the left wing of the feminist movement to which Schreiber and Fürth belonged. As we have seen, feminists of all shades of opinion saw reproduction as a responsibility as well as a right, and accepted the state's interest in the quantity and quality of population. Fürth, although not in favor of total legalization, argued for broadened access to abortion according to medical, eugenic, and social indications. She believed that the community, which must take an increased responsibility for the survival and welfare of weak and diseased individuals, must have the right to prevent the birth of such individuals, even at the cost of a "terrible infringement on the liberties of individuals." "What is more immoral," asked Fürth, "to allow sick or genetically damaged people to produce numerous offspring, or to recognize their right to sexuality but not to reproduction?" Schreiber's proposal for the internment of the mentally retarded was part of a package of legislative recommendations for the protection of retarded children and the prevention of mental retardation. Though such a measure might seem "monstrous" to many people, she said, it would be less cruel to individuals, and probably more beneficial to society, than many other measures designed to promote social welfare, such as military conscription and capital punishment.[29]

These proposals, supported by many Jewish and socialist feminists (Schreiber and Fürth belonged to both groups), were free of the open racial and class prejudice that motivated the Nazis' compulsory sterilization program. As historian Sheila Weiss has noted, however, many proposals made by the eugenicists of this period, although not explicitly racist, still created the basis for later racist policies. Certainly, the feminists aimed chiefly at enhancing the value and quality of life through increased reproductive responsibility, the elimination of disease, and the rational use of medical resources. But their basic ethical stance, in which individual and collective interests, and rights and duties, were inseparable had left them poorly prepared to deal with potential conflicts between individual liberty and social welfare. Inexperienced with the practical consequences of compulsory sterilization laws, they failed to consider what we now realize was the crucial question of how, by whom, and upon whom they would be enforced.[30]

Conclusion: Public and Private Power

Thus feminists at the turn of the century applied ethical conceptions of public and private motherhood to a host of new problems, among them reproductive rights and the preservation of population quality. Some of these positions seem contradictory and problematic, advocating both individual autonomy and increased state control. Historian Richard J. Evans has assumed that even the radical feminists simply capitulated to the increasingly right-wing and militaristic atmosphere of the German state after 1908, and that their interest in eugenics reflected a decline of liberalism. However, German feminists' view of reproductive rights had never been based on liberal notions of individual freedom, which to them seemed inadequate to protect the welfare of women and children. They could justify even a certain measure of state intervention in reproductive decision-making as a legitimate extension of the state's responsibility for solving social problems.[31]

Evans connects the ideas of the German feminists to illiberal tendencies that he identifies as specifically German. But the inspiration for many of the ideas that he finds most problematic came not from Germany but from the United States. German eugenicists of all shades of opinion, in fact, looked to the New World as a golden land of exemplary scientific legislation and lamented the comparatively conservative attitude of German public opinion. Indeed, the very receptive attitude of some American state governments to this kind of legislation contrasts markedly with the scrupulous reserve of prewar German officials, who rejected proposals to introduce such legislation in Germany. In 1907, Indiana became the first American state to enact laws permitting the involuntary sterilization of institutionalized criminals, and by 1914 several states had passed such legislation. These laws tended to be supported by progressive and scientific opinion; opposition came chiefly from conservative Christians. The fact that compulsory sterilization was not always repugnant to the liberal conscience was shown most clearly in 1926 by the case of *Buck* v. *Bell*, in which Supreme Court Justice Oliver Wendell Holmes, a famous liberal, upheld a Virginia sterilization law on the grounds of "a compelling state interest in preventing the procreation of children who will become a burden to the state." Holmes justified this measure as an extension of the state's responsibility for public health. "The principle that sustains compulsory vaccination," he wrote, "is broad enough to cover cutting the Fallopian tubes." Certainly the advocacy of compulsory sterilization can be seen as a disastrous but by no means a distinctively German error.[32]

Moreover, as Linda Gordon and others have explained, arguments for reproductive rights in the United States, the center of equal-rights feminism, were not primarily individualistic during this era but reflected many of the same state-oriented and collectivist attitudes that were expressed by the German feminists discussed here. Margaret Sanger, an enthusiastic eugenicist, tells us in her memoirs that she considered "birthrate control," "race control" and "population control" before settling on "birth control" as the proper designation for her movement. As studies of birth control movements in other Western societies show, very few advocates of reproductive rights—even among the most ardent feminists—adopted arguments based purely or even chiefly on the rights of women as individuals, without reference to the welfare of community, nation, or new generation. In this context, the German feminist movement—and not only the radical organizations—stands out for its relative advancement and daring, not for its conservatism. Margaret Sanger complained that, when she first began her campaign for birth control in 1913, American feminist organizations would have nothing to do with such a controversial issue. British feminist organizations, also focused on suffrage, shared the same reluctance. The German Federation of Women's Organizations, by contrast, at least confronted the issues, if only as a prelude to excluding them from future agendas. Seen in this light, the debate of 1908 was a step forward. Reproductive issues could not be excluded from feminist theory and practice, and this debate had created a vocabulary, a conceptual framework, and a precedent for the discussions that were resumed during the postwar years.[33]

Feminist theorist Carol Brown has identified a central problem in women's history over the past century—the development of a "public patriarchy" that, while freeing women from some constraints of the patriarchal family, makes them more subject to the state. Certainly the German feminists, in linking individual reproductive decisions to national population policies, fell into this trap. The state, as they were soon to see, was also a patriarchy, which certainly did not operate in the interests of women and children. However, the questions that they raised are still debated by feminists in our own day. Some feminist theorists have complained that the liberal concept of privacy is ultimately an inadequate theoretical justification for reproductive rights because it provides no basis for social, as opposed to individual, responsibility for children. How can women, asks American Rosalind Pollack Petchesky, "negotiate between the social (yet personal) need to extend responsibility for reproduction to men and the state and the personal (yet social) need to defend their control over the terms and conditions of reproduction?" Radical advocates of birth control and abortion rights were not the only feminists to face the problems posed by the extension of state control into aspects of life previously regarded as private. The next chapter will show that moderate feminists engaged in other areas of social activism encountered the same issues.[34]

Chapter 11
Motherhood and Social Reform: The Careers of Alice Salomon, Anna von Gierke, and Frieda Duensing, 1890–1914

The prewar period, 1908–1914, saw a great expansion of women's involvement in child welfare issues. We have seen that the campaign against infant mortality hinged on a view of motherhood as both individual right and social responsibility. The idea of motherhood as the basis of a public contribution was enormously expanded by the women who worked during this era to create volunteer and professional roles for women in new areas of public involvement, including communally sponsored child-care programs, school reform, and the new municipal juvenile court systems. This chapter will focus chiefly on three women—Alice Salomon, Anna von Gierke, and Frieda Duensing—who attempted to devise new forms of coordination between women's traditional charitable activities and governmental agencies.[1]

After the election of Gertrud Bäumer to the presidency of the Federation of German Women's Organizations, this group increasingly distanced itself from the controversial reproductive-rights and sexual-reform programs that had been advocated by the radicals. This trend was also due to the great increase in the organization's membership, consisting chiefly of conservative women, which resulted from the repeal of laws restricting women's political activities in 1908. During the period from 1910 to 1914, the chief influence within the movement as a whole was returned to the moderate wing, to which Salomon, Gierke, and Duensing belonged. Salomon and Gierke became prominent spokespersons within the Federation on children's and social issues. Duensing was less directly involved with the organization, but her ideas and activities had considerable influence within it. These women's work showed more direct continuity with older traditions of feminist activism than that of their radical contemporaries. Unlike the radicals, they preferred environmental to hereditarian theories of human behavior, and their sexual ethics remained conservative.

However, unlike the previous generation of female social reformers, they called on the state to advance the welfare of the new generation and envisaged new forms of cooperation between women's community activities and state or local agencies, such as schools, child welfare programs, and justice systems. This work acquired a new political significance in the context of the campaigns for woman suffrage, which gained increased support after 1908. The moderate branch of the feminist movement, headed by Helene Lange and Bäumer, believed that suffrage would eventually be granted to women when they had proved their usefulness to society. Female suffrage, they asserted, must follow on the development of female citizenship. Adopting the model of female citizenship first developed by Henriette Goldschmidt in the 1860s, they urged women to create a distinctive role for themselves as "mothers of the community."[2]

Some accounts of women's work in social reform during this period, including that of Christoph Sachsse, portray women professionals and volunteers as merely reinforcing agendas set by the men of their class. But Salomon, Gierke, and Duensing, although certainly acting as members of their class, nonetheless insisted on the importance of their identity as women. They did not fit smoothly into male-dominated bureaucracies geared to social reform, but often advocated alternative approaches that they defined as female, especially an individualized relationship to clients and a special concern for the interests of women and children. For all three of these women, class and gender identities were sometimes harmonious and sometimes conflicting.[3]

The female citizen, stated Lange, must achieve "an organic relationship between the traditional sphere of women and her public functions." Both the lives and the work of these women were devoted to the integration of public and private spheres through new roles for women and new forms of cooperation between family and state. But their work raised some new problems: How should the relationship between public and private worlds be defined? The careers of Salomon, the period's most influential advocate of a widened social role for women, and of Gierke and Duensing, who applied this maternalist ideal to new forms of activity, illustrate these new dilemmas.[4]

Education for Motherhood: Alice Salomon and the Profession of Social Work

The autobiographies of professional women often express a conception of the relationship of work and personal life that is fundamentally different from that of their male counterparts. Alice Salomon, the best-known of many founders of social work as a female profession during this period, saw work not as a polar opposite of domestic life but as an alternative focus for nurturing talents.

Salomon, born in Berlin in 1872, was the energetic and intellectual daughter of a once-prosperous Jewish family who had been plunged into genteel poverty by the death of the father. Salomon's account of her early life was centered on female relationships, especially to her mother and to a beloved younger sister who died in childhood. Her only rewarding work during her youth was the care of her nieces and nephews. By extending this interest in child care into charity work she received her first harsh intiation into the world of urban poverty and ultimately discovered her vocation for social work. In 1893, she joined the Frauen-und Mädchengroppen für soziale Hilfsarbeit (Women's and Girls' Social Work Groups), a committee promoting women's involvement in social welfare which developed a training program held at the Pestalozzi-Froebel House. This program derived much of its inspiration from the older tradition of kindergarten pedagogy, and much of its theoretical and practical content concerned children's issues. The curriculum integrated practical work in kindergarten pedagogy with courses responding to newer interests such as infant hygiene, child labor, and family law. Salomon developed a close relationship with Jeannette Schwerin, an older woman who led the social work program. After Schwerin's death she took over her position.[5]

Salomon, who unlike her contemporaries Helene Stöcker and Lily Braun remembered a total lack of childhood curiosity about sex, retained a rather conservative attitude toward sexual ethics and the family throughout her life. She attributed her failure to marry to traditional factors, such as her lack of beauty and fortune, as well as to her dedication to her work. Like many professional women of this era, she found emotional support chiefly through relationships to women, including her mother and her female friends and colleagues. Unlike her radical contemporaries, she did not actively protest against the celibacy imposed by custom on the single professional woman, but accepted it regretfully. "Disappointment in love," she wrote, "is one of the saddest experiences, sadder than the death of a loved one. For years, I could not see a woman with a child without being reminded of my lost hopes." At the age of thirty-four, Salomon became one of the first women to earn a doctoral degree from the University of Berlin, where she had studied with some of the most prominent profesors of the social sciences.[6]

Despite her impressive qualifications, she regarded her career not as an imitation of male professional patterns but as the expression of the specifically female, or motherly, energies that might otherwise have been expended on her own children. Salomon's concept of social motherhood showed the continuing influence of Pestalozzi and Froebel, who had stressed close attention to the child's individual development as the most important source of motherly wisdom. Central aspects of this maternal mentality were a mistrust of abstract and schematic approaches to human problems and a preference for individualized and contextual judgments. Salomon was suspicious of all political movements that overrode individual differences in favor of ideological purity. Her intense sympathy with the suffering of striking workers in the town of Crimmitschau in 1904 led her to reject all parties' responses to the strike—the smugness of liberals, the self-interested greed of conservatives, and the enraged extremism of socialists. "Even if I hadn't been in the women's movement," she wrote, "my experience of social work would have led me to join those women who believe that there is no value in the world except human life, and that life must be honored and protected."[7]

Salomon had no sentimental illusions that class conflicts could be overcome by individual acts of charity. She had considerable sympathy for the Social Democratic party, seriously considered joining it, and was actively recruited by prominent socialist leader August Bebel. Her justification for her opposition to socialism was based more on gender than on class identity. She was unwilling to commit herself to a political ideology that discouraged communication between women of different classes. This attitude was shared by her mentor, Schwerin, who was one of the first bourgeois feminists to advocate cooperation between bourgeois and socialist women's groups. Schwerin responded to the hostility of socialist leaders such as Zetkin by pointing out that all women were subject to oppression, regardless of class. "Women against women, mothers against mothers," she declared in 1896, "that would be unheard-of in the history of the human race." But Salomon, who supported Schwerin, was nonetheless fully aware of the problematic aspects of her position. When she and her coworkers founded clubs for working women, she was personally attacked by Braun for trying to wean these women away from socialism by encouraging friendly relations with middle-class women. While rejecting the attack, Salomon remained troubled by the questions that her socialist critic had raised: "Can social work help to create a better world? Isn't it just a palliative or a compromise? Reform or revolution—which way should we go?"[8]

Salomon's concept of organized motherhood was an attempt to respond to these concerns by proposing a distinctive role for middle-class women in overcoming class conflict. Her ideas on this subject were, as Sachsse points out, heavily influenced by those of male reformers of her own and previous generations, especially by the British philosophers Thomas Carlyle and John Ruskin and her mentor at the University of Berlin, Gustav Schmoller. All of these thinkers had rejected atomistic views of the individual and laissez-faire liberalism and urged an active role for government in promoting social responsibility among the privileged classes. Salomon's sources also included feminist authors such as Olive Schreiner and Charlotte Perkins Gilman. These theorists attributed their generation's lack of social responsibility to a distortion of the evolutionary process which had allowed males to control the public realm, including cultural and economic life, while confining women to the private sphere. Like Schreiner, who characterized the position of middle-class women as "sex parasitism," Salomon saw the enforced idleness of middle-class women as a major cause of class conflict. Instead of causing resentment through their irresponsibility and conspicuous consumption, she said, these women should apply their talents to the task of social reconciliation.[9]

Along with many social scientists of this era, Salomon had great faith in the rational reorganization of society as the solution to social problems. At the same time, however, she questioned the value of the abstract and schematic models proposed by male academics and reformers. Social reform, she insisted, must be shaped by female responsiveness to individual needs. Salomon, like many city dwellers, harked back nostagically to the neighborly virtues of small towns. She urged contemporary women to apply the community-building powers of women, once employed in households and villages, to the task of class reconciliation in the city. Like the feminists of 1848, who had rejected violence and called instead for a transformation of society through education, Salomon and her contemporaries also advocated the peaceful evolution of society to new forms of cooperation. Such cooperation, they asserted, could only be achieved through the release of female energies hitherto unnaturally confined to the family into a wider, public sphere of usefulness.[10]

Salomon saw an opportunity to encourage a new sense of responsibility among young women in the reform of female secondary education. The prospect of the regular admission of women as matriculated students to universities in Prussia (they had already been admitted in many other German states) led in 1908 to the extensive reorganization of girls' public secondary schools. In addition to schools preparing young women for university admission, educational policymakers envisaged alternative schools offering a general education to students who had completed girls' secondary schools (*Höhere Töchterschulen*, from which girls graduated at sixteen) but were not destined for academic higher education. The first curricula proposed for such schools, ultimately known as *Frauenschulen* ("women's schools"), had been an unsystematic combination of superficial academic courses and domestic training. Salomon, a strong advocate of serious academic education for girls, was shocked by this plan. The Female Teachers' Association shared her outrage: "If there had to be a special type of female secondary school," wrote Salomon, then the teachers "at least wanted one with a central idea."[11]

At the urging of the Female Teachers' Association, Salomon formulated a model curriculum based on the courses in social work that she had led at the Pestalozzi-Froebel House. Her proposed curriculum aimed to cultivate a serious sense of social purpose among middle-class women who were destined for lives as housewives and community volunteers by cultivating skills suitable to both domestic and community activities. She designed courses focusing on social science fields such as politics, economics, and modern history. Underlying her pedagogical approach to these complex fields were the values of interdependence and organic connection derived from family life: "Only the feeling of one's own dependency on others can awaken a sense of social responsibility, the sense of being a citizen who has a stake in the life of the nation." Practical work, she insisted, must reinforce this theoretical lesson; a kindergarten serving disadvantaged children should be attached to each school. She hoped that the housewives of the future would thus be rescued from "sex parasitism" and encouraged to take a constructive role in the community. She viewed this form of education not as an inferior substitute for more "serious" academic training but as a novel synthesis of individual and social concerns, of "the claims of the world and those of the individual, which so many people today are attempting to reconcile."[12]

Salomon's ambitious ideas for the new girls' secondary school were not fulfilled; the new, nonacademic secondary schools offered only a disjointed combination of domestic and vocational training. However, the educational policymakers did carry out one long-standing goal of the moderate feminist movement by making kindergarten training, according to methods developed at the Pestalozzi-Froebel House, an optional subject at these new schools. Thus, despite the failure of the plans made by the Empress Victoria in 1888 for the spread of kindergarten education, the kindergarten had gained some measure of governmental support. In response to the widespread demand for kindergarten teachers and Froebel-trained governesses, the Prussian government in 1911 fulfilled the demand that representatives of the kindergarten movement had made since 1899 for a standardized state examination for kindergarten teachers.[13]

Thus Salomon's conception of female social involvement did not fit smoothly into the agendas of male reformers and received only very limited official support. In order to put her educational ideals into effect, she founded a private institution—the first fully developed school of social work in the German-speaking world. The Soziale Frauenschule (Women's School of Social Work) opened in 1908 in space provided by the Pestalozzi-Froebel House and acquired its own building in 1914. Salomon saw the role of the female social worker, whether paid or volunteer, as "the assumption of duties for a wider circle which are usually performed by the mother in the home." She claimed that the special fitness of women for social work lay in their understanding of individual and familial problems. This capacity, whether innate or "the product of a century-long division of roles based on power relationships," accounted for women's effectiveness in jobs requiring interpersonal communication. These abilities were well suited to the jobs as caseworkers to which women were now sometimes admitted, especially in agencies involving children. They worked under the supervision of men, whom Salomon considered better qualified to be administrators.[14]

Salomon, however, did not encourage her students to conform to male expectations. On the contrary, she asserted, women's interest in social problems arose from the critical standpoint of a historically oppressed group. Because they had no part in creating existing systems, she claimed that women lacked "the holy reverence for the existing order of things that makes so many men blind and indifferent to terrible abuses in economic life and in government." Their disadvantaged situation had also endowed women with a "natural" sympathy for women and children, the chief victims of social problems. The two-year curriculum of the Soziale Frauenschule encouraged an interest in public policy as well as individual casework; the first year offered training chiefly in child care and pedagogy, the second in more publicly oriented fields such as economics, social ethics, and family law. In 1914, thirty-three students attended the first-year and sixty the second-year program (for which the first was not a required prerequisite); seventy-three more students took continuation courses offered in the evening.[15]

The concept of professional training in social work proved popular and influential; by 1913 there were fourteen such schools in the German Empire, administered by private and church-related groups. One of these was the Lyzeum für Damen (Academy for Women) opened by kindergarten advocate Henriette Goldschmidt in Leipzig in 1911. Goldschmidt, now eighty-six years of age, was still an enthusiastic Froebelian and modeled her institution on the Hamburg Academy for Women, which she remembered from 1848. But she also showed intellectual flexibility by adapting Froebelian theory to the newer doctrines of child study developed by modern psychologists. Child development, she wrote, recapitulatied the various stages of human evolution, which had begun with individual self-consciousness, progressed through the learning of complex skills, and culminated in the devolopment of cooperative forms of social organization. As nurturers of their own families and of "the great human household," Goldschmidt wrote in 1911, women were the agents of this process of evolution. The curriculum integrated kindergarten training with training for social work and included modern fields such as child psychology along with the study of the nineteenth-century philosophical and literary traditions to which Goldschmidt herself continued to be devoted.[16]

Although some feminists questioned Goldschmidt's designation of this institution as a *Hochschule*, or institution of higher education, arguments for the admission of women to more rigorous forms of higher education, including universities, were often based on similar views of women's mission. Sociologist Marianne Weber wrote that women's contribution to the evolution of scholarship, particularly in the social sciences, must reflect their distinctive system of values. Women, she explained, had remained close to emotional reality and to practical experience. By bringing this perspective to the social sciences, which were now dominated by male tendencies to abstraction and overgeneralization, Weber hoped that women scholars would prevent the degeneration of scholarship into rigidity and narrow specialization.[17]

German women of this era often compared their own efforts to create an active role for educated women in urban society to the British and American settlement house movements, from which they derived much of their inspiration. The social work schools were clearly similar to the settlement houses in important ways. In both nations, activist women shared a basic intellectual orientation toward organic and communitarian views of society, a dedication to the integration of familial and public virtues, and a pervasive nostalgia for the supposed neighborly virtues of small-town life. To a certain extent, the social work schools, like the settlement houses, also attempted to provide a communal life for single women, who were often uprooted from their families of origin. Salomon sometimes found herself in the position of mediator between between prospective students and their mothers, who often opposed their professional ambitions. "It was a time," she recollected, "when an analogy to the traditional father-son struggle often occurred between mothers and daughters. . . . The mothers were not familiar with professional and public life. . . . They could not enter this promised land and often could not even see its attractiveness." In her relationship to these young women, Salomon finally found an appropriate nurturing and maternal role. "In my marriageable years I had wished for a dozen daughters . . . now all of these students were my adopted daughters."[18]

The development of social work as a field in Germany and the United States reflected important differences between the cultures and political structures of the two nations. Although some German reformers founded urban settlements—the most famous example was the Hamburg Volksheim (People's House) established in 1901 by pastor Theodor Classen—the movement did not become nearly so widespread in Germany as in the English-speaking world. German observers noted that the American settlements flourished in part because of the underdeveloped and disorganized state of American city governments and social services. Volunteers such as the women of Hull House furnished forms of assistance that in German cities were often provided by communal, municipal, or other public authorities. They further remarked that the pedagogical and educational programs of the settlements, obviously needed in the ethnically diverse American cities, were less necessary in German cities where the population was far more stable and homogeneous. The superior organization of German city governments and the orderly atmosphere of German cities were widely praised by reformers of all nations, including Americans, who deplored the comparatively primitive state of their own municipal governments. Precisely because of their disorganization, however, American cities provided opportunities for active female involvement and leadership that were lacking in the male-dominated German municipal bureaucracies. By the early years of the twentieth century these German public welfare agencies had begun to hire women as social workers, but women were seriously underrepresented and had little opportunity to influence policy. As the example of Salomon has shown, women still exercised their greatest power chiefly in private organizations that they themselves founded or headed. Anna von Gierke and Frieda Duensing were both leaders of such organizations.[19]

Child Care—Public or Private? Anna von Gierke and the Charlottenburg Youth Center

Many of the graduates of both social work schools and kindergarten-training insitutes went on to found or to staff new institutions offering services to children. Among the best known and most widely imitated of these was the Charlottenburg Youth Center, founded by Anna von Gierke and supported by funds from private sources and the municipal government of Charlottenburg, a city adjoining Berlin.[20]

Anna von Gierke, born in 1874 as the oldest daughter of legal scholar Otto von Gierke, left school in 1890 at the usual age of sixteen. Although she enjoyed the domestic tasks of a homebound daughter, including the care of her numerous brothers and sisters, she soon felt the need of a broader sphere of activity. For her, as for her contemporary

Alice Salomon, this activity was volunteer work; Gierke first worked in a child-care center in a distant area of Berlin. In 1894, Helene Weber (mother of Max Weber) provided Gierke with a more convenient workplace near her home in Charlottenburg by recruiting her as a volunteer in a new after-school center for schoolgirls, modeled on the one that Hedwig Heyl had established for the daughters of her husband's employees. The center was supported by an organization headed by the mayor of Charlottenburg and including Heyl and Weber. It soon expanded into new quarters and added a kindergarten and domestic-arts class.[21]

At this point Gierke, who acted as the administrator of this increasingly complex program, decided that she needed specialized training, and subsequently attended the kindergarten-training program of the Pestalozzi-Froebel House in 1897. She returned as head of the Youth Center, with the modest salary of one hundred marks a month, which surpassed that of the average kindergarten teacher. In 1901 the Youth Center added a boys' after-school program and in 1907 it took over a school lunch program for the needy pupils of the Charlottenburg public schools. For this service, the Center received a financial subsidy from the municipal government of Charlottenburg, which also donated land for a new building. As school classes often were dismissed by noon, the Youth Center provided after-school care as well as lunch. This service was specifically intended to serve the needs of families headed by working women who could not care for their children during the afternoon. As assistants, Gierke recruited a professional kindergarten teacher and graduate of the Pestalozzi-Froebel House, Martha Abicht, and a large group of volunteers (sixty by 1902) composed largely of young, middle-class graduates of female secondary schools.[22]

The Youth Center responded to several central concerns of social reformers of the period—the regulation of child labor and the protection of the health and moral well-being of children and young people. The child labor law of 1891 prohibited the employment of school-age children in industry and thus created the need for child care while parents were at work. The founders of the Youth Center, however, recognized that this legislation had not brought an end to child labor, which was now employed by family businesses rather than factories. "The incomplete statistics that we have," read the opening statement of the Youth Center Association in 1891, "show that in Charlottenburg alone there are 226 school children working on the street at five o'clock in the morning. . . . The Association cannot, of course, itself provide the money that the overburdened children must earn at the cost of their health and moral development, but it seeks to contribute to their wellbeing through influence on their parents, through teaching, nurture and training and through the provision of good nutrition for growth and development." Such concerns were shared by the Prussian government, which in 1908 established a Central Youth Agency (Zentrale für Jugendpflege), based in a private charitable organization, the Central Welfare Agency (Zentralstelle für Volkswohlfahrt). Meanwhile, many school systems set up medical and nutrition programs for pupils; the Charlottenburg system, in which Gierke participated, was particularly well known for such efforts.[23]

Gierke attempted to improve the physical health and moral character of Charlottenburg school children through educational approaches developed in the Pestalozzi-Froebel House. She tried to avoid an institutional atmosphere and to provide the orderly and harmonious environment that she assumed was lacking in the children's homes. Lunch was served at small tables, each decorated with flowers. Children received training in domestic tasks in order to both cultivate useful work skills and encourage a sense of community responsibility. Like other reformers engaged in youth work during this period, Gierke believed strongly in the morally uplifting potential of manual labor. Re-creating the atmosphere of Gertrude's workroom, as portrayed in Pestalozzi's still popular novel, Gierke assigned housekeeping tasks to both boys and girls. With the help of a local bank, she and the staff also set up savings accounts for the children. "Visitors note the happiness and orderly behavior of the children," wrote Gierke in a yearly report. "This is the result of our effort to give the children a home, for which they work, and where they become secure members of a household where they belong because they have learned to love their duties."[24]

Gierke, however, remained troubled by the implications of her work and struggled to reconcile her own commitment to public child-rearing with the conservative views of family life with which she had been raised. Her father, Otto von Gierke, had devoted his life to the study of Germanic legal traditions that defined society as an organic unit rather than a collection of individuals. As a member of the committee appointed to compile the new Civil Code, Otto von Gierke had defended the traditional powers of the family, which he attempted to preserve from public intrusion. In an essay of 1911, his daughter asserted that her own work reinforced such familial values; Pestalozzian and Froebelian pedagogy taught the same spirit of organic unity and cooperation as was taught by the family. She advised her teachers to base discipline not on individual confrontation but on peer-group influence. The educator, she stipulated, must strive to create "not only individuals as such, but parts of a greater social organism."[25]

Historians such as Jürgen Reulecke and Paul Weindling have interpreted the involvement of voluntary and governmental agencies in youth welfare during this period as a massive effort, prompted by fear of criminality and socialist tendencies among working-class youth, to establish state control over child-rearing. But Gierke, although influenced by such ideas, also had reservations (probably inspired partly by her father's ideas and partly by her training in the Pestalozzi-Froebel House) about state intervention in child-rearing. It was a problem, she wrote, "how far public child care should interfere with family life, and what role it should assume in welfare policy." She was therefore exceedingly careful to accept only the children of genuinely needy parents into her program. This selective policy was motivated not primarily by financial limitations but by her belief that easily available child care might encourage "a decline of parental responsibility, an increase in work by mothers outside the home, and the weakening of family ties." So anxious was she about these possible consequences that she insisted on taking part in the school system's selection of school social workers in order to ensure that her own guidelines were followed. Although full of sympathy for mothers who worked in order to support their children, Gierke sternly reproached those who seemed to be using the Center's services to enable them to earn money for mere "luxuries" or to engage in recreational activities. Gierke's approach to institutional child care thus showed a mixture of class and gender consciousness: her sense of moral superiority to working-class mothers combined with her concern with preserving the values of domestic life, which she regarded as a female sphere of influence, from encroachment by the state.[26]

As we have seen, other feminists of this era took a less positive attitude toward family privacy and saw the household as an oppressive rather than a protective environment for women and children. Frieda Duensing's ideas provided a contrast to those of Gierke but centered on the same basic dilemma—the proper boundaries between public and private spheres and between family and state.

Parents, Children, and the State: The Work of Frieda Duensing

Frieda Duensing, one of the first German women to study law, combined legal expertise and philanthropic energy to formulate new definitions of the relationship of parents, children, and the state. Duensing acted as head of a private agency, the Zentralstelle für Jugendfürsorge (Central Agency for Youth Services), later Deutsche Zentrale für Jugendfürsorge (German Central Agency for Youth Services), which coordinated volunteer and professional efforts on behalf of abused and delinquent children. In the course of her work, Duensing speculated frequently on the proper scope and limits of parental authority over children. Unlike the conservative Gierke, who upheld traditional boundaries between family and state, Duensing developed legal arguments for increased state intervention in families in order to protect children from abuse and neglect. For Duensing as for many of her contemporaries, the protection of children was closely linked to the protection of women. As Linda Gordon, a historian of American women, has observed, the definition of domestic violence as a crime against women as well as children was largely due to the efforts of feminist reformers, especially of those engaged in child welfare work. In Germany, Duensing made a major contribution to this process of definition.[27]

Born in 1864 in Diepholz, near Hannover, of a well-off family, Frieda Duensing experienced a childhood of unusual freedom and grew up with the ambition to be a writer. But she was disappointed and often depressed at her lack of creative talent. "Again, I felt the lack of creative inspiration," she wrote in her diary at the age of twenty-three. "I have a plenitude of ideas and thoughts, sometimes great and good, but as soon as I try to find a form for them, they elude me. . . . I expect more from myself than I can achieve, a sad state." As a substitute for the abstract creativity of art, she turned to the more human and contextual creativity of education: "If she could not create eternal values," wrote her political colleague, Anton Erkelenz, "she wished to communicate her own . . . inexhaustible knowledge and her understanding of human beings to youth, so that she could have an influence on the future." Throughout her career, Duensing defined women's cultural role as the application of creative energy to human concerns.[28]

When the death of her father forced her to find some form of professional work, she qualified as an elementary school teacher at the Lehrerinnenseminar (Teachers' Seminar) in Hannover, but soon found the classroom a confining environment and longed for a wider sphere of activity. Duensing's decision to lead a single life was motivated by a strong desire for independence: "I could never subordinate myself to a man," she reflected in 1903. But she did not rebel against every aspect of the female familial role. Like Salomon, she saw her professional life as an alternative focus for specifically female, or maternal, energies. When her best friend gave birth to a child, Duensing, who served as godmother, reflected on motherhood as a form of creativity. There were various ways, she wrote in 1903, for a woman to achieve—by giving birth to a child, by creating a work of art, or by undertaking some form of public service. Her failure to achieve the first two possibilities had motivated her to attempt the third.[29]

Even before she became a conscious feminist, Duensing had become passionately concerned with the problems of poor women and children. As a volunteer worker in her small rural community, she attempted to help a mother and her children who had been abused and then abandoned by the male head of their household. Duensing requested help for the family from the local clergyman, only to be told that charitable assistance must be made conditional on the abusive man's returning to his wife and children—in order, he pompously declared, to uphold the institution of Christian marriage. Duensing thus became convinced of the inadequacy of existing familial, religious, and legal structures to protect vulnerable women and children. For Duensing as for so many other female activists, women's and children's issues were linked: "Whoever has seen the frightful suffering of innocent women and children," she said to her friend, Ricarda Huch, "will never again be able to laugh."[30]

In her attempts to help poor women and children, Duensing encountered the same barriers to communication between classes, including mistrust of middle-class reformers, that had confronted other feminists such as Schreiber, Stöcker, and Salomon. Duensing's concept of spiritual motherhood was based on a strong sense of class superiority. The lower classes, she wrote in 1893, were like children who desired only material benefits instead of the education in moral and spiritual values that would bring about a more permanent improvement in their lives. She criticized the German Social Democratic party for what she termed its emphasis on material rather than spiritual values, and for its encouragement of class conflict. But Duensing's mistrust of German socialism, which in the 1890s still professed a rigidly Marxist and revolutionary doctrine, arose from gender as well as class consciousness. Like Salomon, she mistrusted dogmatic and rigid approaches to social problems, and urged sensivity to individual needs. She identified this individualized approach as specifically female and maternal. "She scorned theory as a purely male creation," recollected her friend Ludwig Curtius. "She always began with the individual."[31]

In the 1890s she traveled to England, where she responded quite favorably to Fabian socialism, which was based on class cooperation rather than antagonism, and on an evolutionary rather than revolutionary view of social change. The nearest nonsocialist German equivalent to this British movement was Pastor Friedrich Naumann's National Social movement, which united liberalism with social activism. Duensing, like Bäumer and Salomon, supported Naumann, but she also perceived the weakness of this movement's base of support and was reluctant to identify herself too closely with the male-dominated political party system.[32]

Duensing, who went to Zürich to study law in 1903, had both practical and intellectual grounds for choosing this field. Legal expertise, she assumed, would enhance her effectiveness as a social reformer and provide the basis for a theoretical synthesis of the rational spirit of man-made laws with the female ethic. The existing legal system, she complained, was "miserable because it was created by men in whom logic and the will to power had stifled love." Her dissertation, completed in 1903, exemplified a developing feminist perspective on man-made laws by discussing the legal nature of the parent-child relationship. The feminist critique of the Civil Code had indirectly protested against child abuse by challenging the private despotism of the father over the familial sphere. Duensing's argument, by specifically exploring the limits of the parent's right to discipline the child, created a pioneering legal definition of criminal child abuse. As justification for public intervention in the family, Duensing used the common argument based on child-rearing as public as well as private responsibility, defining child abuse as a crime "directed against the state itself."[33]

In 1904, after she had completed her studies and briefly observed Leipzig's model foster care program, Duensing accepted a position in Berlin as administrative head of the organization then known as the Central Agency for Youth Services. The agency, which in addition to

Duensing had only two other administrative employees, was set up in response to the widely perceived need for some coordination among an enormous variety of child welfare agencies. Duensing coordinated the efforts of workers, predominantly volunteers but also some professionals, among whom were many graduates of social work programs such as Salomon's School of Social Work; in her first years in office, Duensing supervised sixty charitable organizations and forty institutions for children. She also provided legal advice, chiefly on laws pertaining to paternal child-support obligations and to guardianship, which had recently been redefined to permit women to become legal guardians of children not related to them. In 1905, Duensing cooperated in the founding of the Association of Female Guardians, which encouraged women volunteers to undertake the care and supervision of endangered or abused children. As the administrator of the Central Agency for Youth Welfare, Duensing was also involved in many other Berlin youth welfare programs, including those centered on the prevention of infant mortality, the care of homeless or neglected children, day care services, and many others. In 1907, Duensing combined her work for the Berlin agency with the leadership of a national organization, the Deutsche Zentralverein für Jugendfürsorge (German Central Association for Youth Services), which gathered information and organized conferences on youth work throughout the German Empire. Duensing merged the two agencies under the name Deutsche Zentrale für Jugendfürsorge (German Central Agency for Youth Services). She also edited the agency's journal, *Jugendwohlfahrt* ("Youth Welfare"). She headed the organization only until 1911; the job proved exhausting. After her retirement she remained active as a consultant and lecturer and held several teaching appointments at the Pestalozzi-Froebel House, Salomon's School of Social Work, and many other institutions.[34]

In her opening speech as administrator of the German Central Agency for Youth Services she advocated the coordination of private with state and municipal welfare services. The spirit of social responsibility, personal concern, and ethical commitment expressed through private charity, she insisted, must not be stifled through the cold bureaucracy of the welfare state. "We encourage the development of our national life in the cooperation of public and private activities; we fight against the impersonal indifference and apathy that lets everything be done through the state and its employees and paid for by taxes." Duensing's defense of private charities, which were often led by women, against the inroads of male-dominated bureaucracies recalls the arguments of an older generation of reformers, including Schrader-Breymann and Heyl. At the same time, she called for state measures, including legal reforms, to support private charity.[35]

Of all the causes in which Duensing was involved, three—spouse abuse, child abuse, and juvenile court work—best show her conception of a new role for the state in the protection of women and children. During this era, child abuse and neglect had become a prominent issue among reformers. This development came relatively late—whereas the United States had a Society for the Prevention of Cruelty to Children in 1874, the German Empire did not have such an organization until 1899. During the 1890s, state welfare laws were changed to empower welfare authorities to remove children from homes considered unsatisfactory, and this power was also granted to the states by the Civil Code adopted in 1900. The chief criterion for removal was the severe abuse of parental—chiefly paternal—power. "If the spiritual or mental well-being of a child is endangered by the father's abuse of his right to care for the personal needs of the child," the law read, " . . . the Guardians' Court can order that the child be placed in a suitable family or in an institution." The new laws set much broader criteria for the removal of children from homes considered unsatisfactory than earlier laws had permitted. Leaders of child welfare agencies responded enthusiastically to these new possibilities; in Prussia, the number of children and youths removed from their homes rose from 7,787 in 1901 to 10,358 in 1912. Duensing regarded these developments with considerable ambivalence. She approved of the new laws and regretted that children could be removed only if abuse had actually occurred, and not when it seemed likely. But she warned against unjust applications. In one case, for example, she had called for a suspension of the protective-custody proceedings because the problem was not parental neglect but "bitter, hopeless poverty. . . . The love between parents and children was not extinguished, but merely buried under countless frightful anxieties and pressures." Moreover, the removal of children from abusive fathers could also victimize innocent mothers. While approving of child-protective services, she feared the consequences, especially for women, of their administration by male bureaucrats.[36]

As Duensing had noted long before she came to Berlin, child abuse and spouse abuse usually went together. The latter theme, however, had previously been spoken of by feminists chiefly indirectly, through campaigns on issues such as divorce, temperance, birth control, and the spread of venereal disease. Duensing addressed the problem more directly in a speech delivered to an annual convention of the Center for Youth Services in 1911, entitled "The Protection of the Family from the Drunken Father." Although her theme was of interest to many reform movements, she declared at the outset that she would approach this problem from a female perspective: "Not from the point of view of the general problem of alcoholism or of legal reform . . . but only from the point of view of the woman . . . and I will repeatedly emphasize this point of view." She based her speech on a case study. A local woman, driven to insanity by repeated mistreatment by a chronically alcoholic husband, had murdered her five children and then unsuccessfully attempted to kill herself. The woman, who had been honest and hardworking, had repeatedly appealed for protection to the police and the welfare authorities. Duensing enumerated the existing remedies for this situation—such as the short-term confinement of the man or the removal of the family to another city—and showed that they often entailed more serious consequences for the woman and children than for the father. As to the removal of the abused children from the home by child-welfare authorities (the most commonly adopted solution), Duensing insisted that this was often a gross violation of the rights of the mother: "What humane person could possibly take responsibility for taking children away from mothers such as Frau Friedrich?" Such coldhearted officials, Duensing said, must be "men in the municipal agencies, who know nothing of the life and suffering of these women."[37]

She argued that the system should take measures not against the mother and children but against the abusive father himself, who still seemed to enjoy privileged status. "If I wear a loose hatpin, or if a worker carries a spade without a protective covering, the police intervene, but when a crazy drunkard poses a constant hazard to his surroundings, it refuses to intervene. It's as if a magic shield surrounds this man, as if some privilege protects him." Duensing concluded with a plea to her audience of lawyers and municipal officials to create legal mechanisms for the arrest and long-term imprisonment of such alcoholics.[38]

By linking the crimes of spouse abuse and child abuse to drunkenness, Duensing appealed to the widespread support for temperance in the moderate women's movement. Perhaps partly for that reason, child abuse became an increasingly prominent issue on the agenda of the Federation of German Women's Organizations. At the Annual Meeting of 1908 the Legal Committee of the League of German Women's Associations proposed several legislative measures, some of which were first suggested at a conference organized by Duensing in 1907, to protect retarded children from abuse or exploitation. In 1910 the Child Protection Committee and the organization as a whole endorsed a petition that had originated with Duensing's agency. The petition, addressed to the Reichstag, advocated the strengthening of a proposed law on child abuse by widening the upper age limit of victims from fourteen to eighteen and permitting the prosecution of members of the household who were not related by blood to the child. By stipulating that psychological and emotional abuse, which was considered more common than physical mistreatment in middle- and upper-class families, should be penalized, the petition also acknowledged that child abuse could occur at all levels of society. The petition was illustrated by many individual case studies drawn from Duensing's extensive files. Clearly, although rape and sexual abuse were referred to only in veiled language, these measures were designed to protect underage girls from those crimes. In 1912 the annual convention of the Federation took an important step toward the inclusion of spouse abuse in its legislative agenda by voting unanimously to appoint a committee to draft legislation protecting women and children from alcoholic husbands and fathers.[39]

Duensing's most important contribution to child welfare services was her attempt to create a role for female social workers, both volunteer and professional, in the expanding juvenile court system. The juvenile court system in Germany, based on American and British models, was initiated by a court founded in Frankfurt in 1908; such courts were soon founded in other German cities. The juvenile justice system required a preliminary hearing before the trial to explore the defendant's family situation, which the judge could take into account in sentencing. Social workers were trained to investigate and then to report to the judge on the personal situations of accused juveniles. Duensing, who was called upon to train and coordinate the efforts of these juvenile court workers, viewed this as a nearly ideal form of male-female collaboration in the "great social household." "The juvenile court and the juvenile-court social worker," she wrote in 1909, "belong together like husband and wife; their activities in the administration of justice enhance and reinforce each other as do mother and father in the household."[40]

The creation of the juvenile court system has sometimes been interpreted chiefly as a measure of social control. As historian Detlev Peukert has pointed out, the determination of punishment based on the personality and social background of the accused, requiring investigation of the family, was an invasion of family privacy and a danger to the rights of young defendants. However, another historian, Linda Gordon, points out that familial privacy did not protect women and children. Gordon's study of American child-protective agencies points out that, especially in cases of child abuse, social workers often acted as advocates for lower-class women and children against male relatives.[41]

Duensing's view of the juvenile-court workers illustrated both of these possibilities—the controlling and the protective. Her attitude toward working-class families was sometimes fearful and intolerant; in the poor neighborhoods of Berlin, she warned in 1905, "a fertile garden of coarseness, evil and crime is growing around us." She advised social workers sent to visit a young defendant's home to show a friendly and sympathetic interest in the family while at the same time keeping an eye out for any aspects of the environment that could have fostered the child's antisocial tendencies. "Imagine yourself in the position of these people, represent their interests," counseled Duensing, "but still be as cunning as serpents." Such official scrutiny of working-class homes is interpreted by Peukert as an attempt by the state to control the private lives of its citizens.[42]

However, Duensing also urged the social worker to function as the child's advocate against the state. Thus, although in general approving of the juvenile justice system, she also criticized some of its authoritarian tendencies. Duensing argued that the social worker should not be responsible for gathering evidence to support a conviction—that function should be left to the prosecutor. She further insisted that the social worker report directly to the judge—whose function she portrayed as primarily pedagogical—rather than to the prosecutor. Moreover, she outspokenly disputed the belief of some authorities on juvenile justice that, because the hearing was not a trial in the formal sense, the role of the defense attorney should be eliminated. On the contrary, she asserted the juvenile's right to legal representation and envisaged the social worker as a potential witness for the defense. As usual, she cited an individual case to illustrate the social prejudice that could influence verdicts and sentencing. An errand boy had been encouraged by his companion, a *Gymnasium* (elite high school) student, to shout insults at a passing teacher and had been found guilty and sentenced to a fine. The social worker had been outraged at the absence of a defense. "If a defense attorney had pointed out the triviality of the offense and the absence of malicious intent and had asked those present if they had ever shouted insults at teachers in their youth, the sentence would have come out differently."[43]

Alice Salomon had expressed the hope that female social workers would be especially effective in understanding the problems and representing the interests of female clients and juvenile-court defendants. Duensing, too, often advocated the interests of women against social welfare and court bureaucracies, and urged the workers at her agency to do the same. According to Duensing's own accounts—we do not know what her clients thought—female social workers could be effective with young female offenders. A young girl accused of theft, recounted Duensing, had confided to a female social worker that "she had been instigated to sexual misconduct and to other offenses by male relatives since the age of fifteen. She only reported this after the social worker had pledged absolute secrecy. The social worker testified for the defense and [the girl] got a light sentence." As Linda Gordon has remarked of American child-protective agencies, Duensing's agency was sometimes used by the clients themselves in order to gain advantages. Duensing herself remarked that her clients often urged her to take unruly or mistreated children into protective custody and were disappointed if she refused.[44]

Like the prevention of child abuse, juvenile justice was recognized by the mainstream of the women's movement as an appropriate field for women's involvement. A resolution by the Federation of German Women's Organizations in 1910 demanded the participation of women on juries in juvenile cases. As a rationale for such participation, the resolution described the distinctive ethical and psychological aspects of the mother-child relationship in terms reminiscent of Pestalozzi. "No one any longer denies that a mother, through close relationships with her children, through her constant association with them and her supervision of their behavior has a deeper understanding of the . . . most intimate impulses of the child's soul and of the bodily and spiritual needs of children than the father who is involved in professional work outside the home." The resolution went on to recommend that the "motherly insight and the judgment of educationally experienced women" would be indispensable to the juvenile-court judge.[45]

Organized Motherhood: A Basis for Female Citizenship

The creation of a distinctively female form of citizenship based on organized motherhood did not achieve the objective envisaged by Lange and Bäumer—the attainment of woman suffrage. Of course, the political work of the radical feminists, who favored a more direct and aggressive approach, was no more successful. In Prussia, where votes in state and local elections were still weighted according to wealth, class divisions proved an obstacle to the woman suffrage movement, which in 1912 split into two factions, one supporting equal suffrage and the other advocating suffrage for women on the same terms as men. But organized motherhood nonetheless provided an extremely useful basis for defining the expanding sphere and interests of middle-class women during the prewar era. This ideology connected the two important areas of feminist activism—the family and the public world. It validated the experience and ethical insights gained by women in the family and encouraged their application to new areas of public policy. It provided a standpoint from which middle-class women could define themselves in relation to lower-class clients and to men of their own class. Moreover, it could be adapted to a wide variety of positions: conservative defense or radical criticism of the family, authority over or solidarity with lower-class women, claims to participation in, or independence from, male-dominated bureaucracies. It provided a basis from which a still-disenfranchised group could interpret, criticize and influence the political system. "From every form of social work," stated a resolution of the Annual Meeting of the Federation of German Women's Organizations for 1912, "there is a direct link to larger political issues. . . . The women's movement has shown women that there is nothing in the modern state that is not connected to broader circumstances, that from each individual activity, from each individual destiny the threads run to the general political life of our people."[46]

Conclusion

We have traced the history of an idea—the idea of motherhood—and a movement—the women's movement in Germany—over a period of more than a century. This story, which begins in the small-town settings of the first kindergartens or the rural world of Henriette Breymann's instititute and ends in the industrialized and urban environments of Gierke's Youth Center and Salomon's Women's School of Social Work, shows the effects of extensive cultural, social, and economic change. But all of the major figures and the movements that they helped found nonetheless shared certain ideas. They attributed to women certain distinctive qualities derived from the experience and traditions of maternal nurture. The basis established for this view of female nature changed with changing conceptions of the relationship of biology to culture, from the primarily ethical and spiritual emphasis of the first half of the nineteenth century to the strongly evolutionary and biological orientation of the second half, and particularly of the last two decades. But the development of an ethical perspective based on motherhood nonetheless shows strong elements of continuity.

Women brought to the public sphere the values developed in the private realm. The most important of these was an ethical system emphasizing relationship and affiliation, often contrasted to allegedly male traits such as competitiveness and individualism. This approach to ethics was often symbolically expressed through a specifically and uniquely female experience, the mother-child bond. The comments of psychologist Carol Gilligan on the outlook of some contemporary women also describes the perceptions of many nineteenth-century German feminists: "The experiences of inequality and interconnectedness, inherent in the relation of parent and child, then give rise to the ethic of justice and care, the ideals of human relationship—the vision that self and other will be treated as of equal worth, that despite differences in power things will be fair; the vision that everyone will be responded to and included, that no one will be hurt." The realization of these values in society was often symbolized through the image of the "great social household," where divisions between private and public spheres, home and world, would be overcome through new forms of cooperation. The preceding chapters have not discussed all of the uses of these ideas, but have concentrated on their application to issues affecting mothers and children. But they have also emphasized the central and increasing importance of such issues to the development of feminist movements as a whole.[1]

The idea of women's social role thus developed has often been portrayed as simply conservative. It was, in fact, both backward- and forward-looking, seeking to preserve positive aspects of women's traditional work as well as to open up new possibilities for work in the professions and social reform. Discourses on public and private motherhood encompassed the most radical as well as the most conservative positions taken by feminists of this era. Some historians have emphasized what they see as a dramatic change in feminist ideology and practice with the rise of the first radical organizations in the 1880s. Although not denying the significance of this change, I have also emphasized elements of continuity among periods and wings of the movement, and have shown that the radicals chiefly developed and expanded, rather than rejected, older ideas of public and private motherhood. Some historians have compared the feminist movements of the English-speaking world, identified with liberalism and equal rights, and those of continental Europe, characterized by maternalist or relational arguments. Although this contrast is useful, I have pointed out that American as well as German feminists used both types of arguments in ways that were usually complementary rather than contradictory.

These developments in feminist theory and practice have been placed in two contexts—in that of German national history and culture, and in that of feminism as an international movement. Thus I will focus here on the significance of this story to our understanding of both the history of Germany and that of feminism as a whole.

Feminism and German History: An Epilogue

The significance of German feminism before 1914, and particularly of its orientation toward maternal ideology, to the course of German history has recently been explored in a widely read work, Claudia Koonz's *Mothers in the Fatherland*. Concentrating on the history of women under Nazism, Koonz also emphasizes what she sees as the close relationship between the ideals of nineteenth-century feminist movements and those of National Socialism. The National Socialist state, Koonz argues, "was the nineteenth-century feminists' view of the future in nightmare form. The earliest crusaders for women's rights had believed passionately in their distinct female nature and concluded that their political participation and legal equality would elevate the level of public debate, redirect the government toward more humane concerns, and calm male leaders' warlike predisposition." One would not normally think of the National Socialist state as in any way supportive of such aspirations. But Koonz nonetheless sees a connection; she claims that the maternalist theory and practice of prewar feminism encouraged the acceptance and even the enthusiastic affirmation of the Nazi regime by women. "At the heart of this vision," writes Koonz of German feminism, "lay a dream of a strong man and a gentle woman, cooperating under the stern guidance of an orderly state." The feminists' emphasis on mother-love as a source of power, Koonz further implies, encouraged a view of female virtue that was limited to the private sphere (to which she refers as a female *Lebensraum*) and separated from political concerns. Koonz's interpretation resembles those of some other historians, such as Richard J. Evans, who also sees German feminists' emphasis on maternal as opposed to equal-rights ideology as an example of more general tendencies in German bourgeois culture that encouraged the rise of National Socialism.[2]

These assertions of continuity between prewar feminism and National Socialism raise two basic questions. Did the National Socialist state represent, in any essential way, the fulfillment of prewar feminists' aspirations? And were German feminists' ideas sufficiently different from the ideas of their counterparts in other countries to be identified as causes of a uniquely German development, National Socialism?

Koonz claims that the idea of motherhood upon which much of the prewar German feminist movement had been based was an essentially private and separatist one, encouraging women to care for their own families while ignoring the larger world of politics. "Mothers as mythical angels in the house," reflects Koonz in a paragraph linking the ideas of a Nazi activist to nineteenth-century feminist precedents, "have preserved idealism, love and faith while men made war, killed and exploited." But, as the preceding chapters have shown, most prewar German feminists had specifically rejected purely private views of motherhood and had often linked their commitment to motherhood to a new vision of the relationship of public and private worlds. Much more than equal-rights doctrine, maternal feminism had provided the first, powerful rationale for women's emergence into public roles in the professions and in social reform. Koonz is right that the public sphere in which women worked was exceedingly narrow and defined by the limits that society imposed on females. However, many feminists worked constantly and against heavy opposition to expand these limits. Although often limited in their practical effectiveness to the home, the kindergarten, and the female-led institution or agency, most feminists did not regard these fields of activity as isolated from the male-dominated public world. Women used the limited authority over child-rearing and motherhood that was granted to them by culture as a basis for entry into public discourse and activity on much broader issues of politics, social reform, and public policy.[3]

During the wartime and Weimar periods, many forms of social activism that had been developed by private women's organizations were incorporated into the state. All of the women described here who were still alive during the war adapted their activities to the new conditions of wartime. Most of them supported the war effort, although often with deep reservations. Salomon, although sympathetic to the peace movement, agreed to work for the National Women's Service, an organization that coordinated social services to women. Heyl and Fürth both worked in nutrition programs, the first on a national level, the latter in her home city of Frankfurt. Gierke was appointed in 1916 as head of a national Committee on Children's Services. Duensing ran a kindergarten in Berlin before leaving in 1916 for Munich, where she founded her own school of social work in 1919. Schreiber, too, continued active in children's services and with the Red Cross. Governmental support for many of these services was increased; the women's movement, as historian Bärbel Clemens remarks, had become almost a separate department of the government. The aspirations of nineteenth-century feminists for a powerful and transformative role in the state seemed to some to have been realized. Partly for this reason, some prominent feminists, including Gertrud Bäumer, the president of the Federation of German Women's Organizations, were enthusiastic about the war effort.[4]

However, maternal ideology was by no means identified with patriotism; on the contrary, it also provided the most powerful rationale for the opposition to the war of a minority of feminists, including Helene Stöcker, Anita Augspurg, Lida Gustava Heymann, and Bertha von Suttner. When war broke out in 1914, one of the long-standing goals of the League for the Protection of Mothers, the widening of maternity-insurance benefits, was fulfilled; benefits were improved and extended to the female dependents of servicemen. But Stöcker realized that these measures were motivated by expediency rather than by any real concern for mothers and children. Along with women of many nations who were members of the International Women's League for Peace and Freedom, Stöcker evoked women's commitment to the giving and nurturing of life as a basis for female pacifism. She continued active in the pacifist movement after the war. "Above all, it is the responsibility of a movement directed to woman, who as mothers have a special concern for life, to explore the implications of this point of view," said Stöcker in 1921. "It is in the nature of woman, of the sex that gives life, to support all measures that serve, preserve, and elevate life, and that promise to safeguard culture and peace." Thus, by 1914, the discourse on motherhood was so prevalent and powerful in the feminist movement that it encompassed the widest possible spectrum of positions, from strident nationalism to pacifism.[5]

Women who had won the right to vote in 1918, largely as a result of their work for the war effort, had high hopes for the new Weimar Republic. Indeed, the National Assembly, elected to draw up the constitution for the new state, was the first national representative body in German history to have been elected by women as well as men; 10 percent of its delegates (a total of 37, spread across the whole spectrum of parties) were women. Several of the women discussed in the preceding chapters entered politics during this period; Schreiber went to the Reichstag as a socialist (Social Democratic party) delegate, Bäumer as a liberal (German Democratic party), and Gierke as a conservative (German Nationalist party), while Fürth was elected to the city council of Frankfurt and Heyl to the city council of Charlottenburg. As Alice Salomon remarked, the Weimar constitution was the first in the world to result from the collaboration (although a highly unequal one) of men and women. The completed constitution showed the influence of these female delegates by opening the way for many of the legal reforms for which prewar feminists had worked. As they had been during the prewar period, feminists were deeply divided on these issues. The section entitled "Basic Rights and Duties of Germans" committed the new state to the protection of motherhood, to the welfare of children, and to the creation of "equal conditions for spiritual, physical, and social development" for illegitimate and for legitimate children. The very inclusion of this latter issue showed the influence of radicals such as Schreiber; however, the conservative women overruled a stronger statement calling for equal legal rights for the illegitimate. The constitution stated that marriage, as the "basis of family life and of the preservation and increase of the state," should be based on the "equal rights of both sexes." Furthermore, the constitution provided that "men and women have basically the same rights and duties." This clause also reflected a compromise. Whereas socialist and left-wing liberal women had favored the removal of the word "basically," which they rightly feared might allow many exceptions, more conservative delegates of both sexes insisted on a wording that would permit the reintroduction of military conscription (then forbidden by the Versailles Treaty). The Weimar constitution, although not a radical document, thus reflected many feminist aspirations, not to a private *Lebensraum*, but toward an improved status for mothers and children in a state that empowered women. This view of the state, while expansive, was highly democratic and was intended as a decisive break with previous German authoritarian state traditions.[6]

As in other countries, the immediate postwar period saw the high point of women's political participation. During this period, the development of the welfare state also seemed to promise the fulfillment of prewar feminist agendas. In 1922, the Imperial Law on the Welfare of Youth committed the federal government to the support of a wide range of services to children and youth. In 1924, the responsibility for these welfare services was shifted to local governments, many of which set up special youth agencies (*Jugendämter*). These were often modeled on the private agencies developed by women such as Gierke and Duensing.[7]

However, the hopes that feminists had placed in the Weimar Republic proved as illusory as those of other liberal or left-wing groups. The legal reforms that would have been necessary to improve the status of illegitimate children, reform marriage laws, and ensure the rights of women in family and workplace were never enacted. The financial basis for the creation of services for children and young people was completely destroyed by the catastrophic inflation of 1922–1924. Among those services were kindergartens, which remained in private hands and, despite the urging of socialist educators, were never incorporated into public school systems. Social workers did not fulfill Salomon's vision of female power and influence in public policy, but were often victims of discrimination and of the hostility of male bureaucrats. Desirable jobs in social work, including juvenile-court work and youth services, were increasingly taken by men. The League for the Protection of Mothers continued its work until 1933, but its campaigns to repeal laws against abortion, also supported by Communist women's organizations, were unsuccessful.[8]

The failure of these programs was partly due to the declining participation of women in electoral politics; a decreasing percentage of women voted, and politicians soon learned that they did not vote as a bloc and were more likely to vote for conservative than for left-wing parties. Arguments that feminist movements created preconditions for the rise of Nazism imply that feminism was an important force in politics during the final years of the Weimar Republic. In reality, feminism was at a low point of its political influence. At the same time, the rhetoric and policies of the Federation of German Women's Organizations, reflecting the political atmosphere of the period, shifted steadily to the right. This trend was due partly to the influence of the large, conservative organizations that had joined the Federation in the period from 1908 to 1910, such as the Protestant Women's Organization, and during the 1920s, such as the National Housewives' League and the National Rural Housewives' League. In addition, the politics of the Federation were increasingly shaped by the many women's professional associations, most of which had joined after 1920. These groups were more concerned with their own interests than with broadly feminist issues. Thus, the conservatism of the Federation during these years was due less to its prewar history and ideology than to its postwar development. Even by abandoning most of its previous goals, the Federation could not keep its membership—the two conservative housewives' organizations withdrew in 1932. While deploring the weakness of the Federation, Evans does not suggest that it would have been more effective had it been, according to his criteria, more truly feminist—that is, liberal and individualistic—for liberalism was an unpopular ideology during the Weimar period, and liberal parties steadily lost votes. As a result of the Nazi seizure of power in 1933, both the Federation, which voted to disband itself, and the League for the Protection of Mothers were dissolved.[9]

As evidence of continuity between the aims of German feminism and National Socialism, both Koonz and Evans point to the similarity between the rhetoric of feminist leaders and that of the Nazis. Both feminists and Nazis, they emphasize, stressed the organic relationship of the individual to the state, and both lauded the family as a cell of that great social organism. During the Weimar period, the Federation's use of the term *Volksgemeinschaft* ("people's community"), which had not been used by prewar feminists, suggested right-wing, although not necessarily

National Socialist, tendencies, and some leaders, including Gertrud Bäumer, expressed anti-Semitic prejudice. In a more general sense, however, the discourse on the organic state was vast and varied, and its meaning was not fixed by any one set of speakers. During the nineteenth century and the prewar period, as we have seen, this general discourse had encompassed an enormous variety of positions, both left- and right-wing. The Nazis provided the classical example of the organization of power through the appropriation and redefinition of language. "The world of speech and desires," asserts Michel Foucault, "has known invasions, struggle, plundering, disguises, ploys." Alice Salomon, who as an ardent liberal and a Jew could not be suspected of any sympathy at all for National Socialism, remarked ironically on the National Socialists' new construction of traditional language. She had based her own code of ethics on the duty of the individual to serve the state and was appalled to hear a Nazi speaker use the same words that she had used in a speech supporting a liberal candidate. "It is strange enough," she remarked in her autobiography, "that exactly the same words, 'the welfare of the people and our own welfare' later became a slogan of the National Socialists. . . . Nobody could have foreseen what was to come."[10]

Did the National Socialists fulfill some aspects of the prewar feminist agenda? Some of their measures seemed similar to those recommended by some feminists. The National Socialists took measures to encourage population growth by providing loans to newly married couples of proper racial background—although these allowances were paid to fathers rather than mothers—and forgave a certain percentage of the loan for each child. They increased maternity insurance benefits. During wartime, they provided state support to the racially qualified mothers of illegitimate children. They introduced measures designed to achieve their own conception of population "quality," including the requirement of a health examination before marriage, the legalization of abortion according to the "eugenic indication," and compulsory sterilization for certain diseases and conditions believed to be hereditary. As Evans notes, they appealed to intellectuals, including some feminists, by seeming to appropriate ideas that had been considered very advanced during the prewar period. But the similarity to feminist ideas was more apparent than real. The small group of feminists who had supported eugenic selection policies before World War I had laid their chief emphasis on reproductive responsibility rather than coercion. Quite contrary to the prewar radicals' recommendations, the Nazis made access to birth control more difficult and prohibited voluntary sterilization. Above all, the racial and class biases of the Nazi program would have been abhorrent to most prewar feminists.[11]

The continuity between these policies and prewar feminist recommendations chiefly shows not that prewar feminists somehow anticipated the rise of the totalitarian state, but rather that they did not. In their enthusiasm for the expansion of the welfare state, which they saw chiefly as a protective agency for vulnerable women and children, they did not foresee the danger to individual rights that such expansion would pose. Their failure to foresee these dangers showed the ethical and practical weaknesses of a view of citizenship that saw individual rights and duties to the state as inseparably linked. However, whatever the errors of the German feminists on these "population quality" issues, they cannot be regarded as links in a causal chain (*Sonderweg*) leading inevitably to National Socialism. As we have seen, reformers in other cultures had much the same ideas, which led certainly to abuses of human rights—in the United States between 1907 and 1964 about 64,000 persons were subjected to compulsory sterilization, compared to 320,000 in Germany between 1933 and 1939—but not to totalitarian reproductive policies such as those of the Third Reich.[12]

The discontinuities between Nazi and prewar feminist goals are more striking. For prewar feminism, the concept of organized motherhood had expressed aspirations to empowerment involving expanded professional and policy-making roles and ultimately, for most feminists, full political participation. The National Socialists, although not denying women the vote, reduced them to powerlessness within the state by limiting their educational and professional opportunities until first the rearmament program and later wartime conditions created a demand for female labor. The Nazis also denied women access to most political offices and positions of leadership. As Koonz points out, women's political activities were regarded by National Socialist leaders as completely unimportant—certainly women did not succeed in winning public respect for their concerns or in transforming or even in significantly affecting the male-dominated state through female influence.[13]

As Gisela Bock has shown, moreover, the Nazi regime did not support but rather specifically opposed many aspects of prewar maternalist ideology. At the center of prewar feminists' aspirations to public influence or power was compassion, particularly for the weak and defenseless. Of all ethical values, this was the one that the Nazis most explicitly detested. Most feminists, from the generation of 1848 to that of 1914, denied that motherly concern should be reserved for one's own children, or for children of one's own social class or religion. Koonz's frightening picture of the Nazi mothers who "gazed at their own cradles, children, and 'Aryan' families" while making life "unbearable and then impossible for racially unworthy citizens" represents not the realization, but the negation, of prewar feminists' social ethic, expressed though the metaphor of the "great social household." In fact, as Bock points out, Nazi authorities specifically warned against maternal compassion for all children, even the racially or genetically "unworthy," as an obstacle to the effective implementation of their policies. For this reason, they insisted that decisions on the sterilization of underage children be allotted to fathers rather than mothers, and excluded women physicians from sterilization proceedings. As far back as the 1840s, moreover, most women's organizations that were in any way identified with feminism (apart from specifically confessional ones) had encouraged cooperation between Jewish and Christian women and had encouraged the teaching of religious tolerance in kindergartens and schools. Clearly, some characteristics of prewar bourgeois feminism, chiefly its not always uncritical acceptance of the strident nationalism of the period and its strong, sometimes questioned, bias in favor of middle-class interests and values, made some feminists susceptible to the National Socialist message. But if the prewar feminsts had succeeded in realizing their goal—a society oriented toward nuture and compassion, and toward female concerns—National Socialism could not have existed.[14]

A further argument against a view of prewar German feminism as a direct cause of National Socialism is that feminism, although influenced by national culture, also developed in much the same way throughout the Western world. American feminist movements at various periods in their history had shown almost as much strident nationalism as their German counterparts, and considerably more overt racism. In the 1920s American feminists faced an atmosphere that was in some ways more hostile to feminism and to social reform than that of the Weimar Republic before 1930. While the central prewar organization in Germany, the Federation of German Women's Organizations, held together until 1933, its American counterpart, the National American Woman Suffrage Association, dissolved in 1919, making way for two successor organizations, the National Women's Party and the League of Women Voters. Whereas German feminists succeeded at least in inserting guarantees of equal rights into their constitution (even though they had little practical effect), American feminists did not even succeed in passing an Equal Rights Amendment through Congress. The failure of this effort in 1923 was due in part to the opposition of many women's organizations, such as the League of Women Voters. As in Germany, the political power of women was greatest in the early 1920s and was expressed most successfully through the passage of child welfare measures. In the United States, the most significant of these was the Sheppard-Towner Federal Maternity and Infancy Act of 1921, which provided federal matching funds for local maternal and infant welfare programs. However, by 1929 the political power of women had declined to such an extent that Congress refused to renew the program, which was denounced by right-wing politicians as dangerously "socialistic." Enthusiasm for feminism fell off conspicuously among the younger generation, some of whom showed the same enthusiasm for domestic values as the German housewives' organizations. But the result of these developments was not, as in Germany, the conversion of large numbers of women to fascism. Rather, the political energies of women were revitalized by the New Deal, which encouraged a new generation of female reformers. Thus the energies of organized motherhood could be enlisted to serve democracy as well as totalitarianism. In Germany, many such careers, including those of Salomon, Stöcker, Schreiber, Gierke, and many others were cut short by National Socialism. As Barbara Greven-Aschoff concludes, society often changes women more than women change society.[15]

By questioning such teleological interpretations of history, I do not intend to deny the importance of inquiries into the roots of National Socialism. Teleological approaches to this as to other historical developments, however, too often assume that words and ideas retain fixed meanings through time, and that continuity of language and ideas thus implies continuity of meaning and intention. Language and ideas, however, acquire meaning only in context. I have therefore chosen to evaluate such ideas, strategies, and ethical choices in the context experienced by the historical actors themselves—the prewar feminists who are the subjects of this study.

Feminism as Ideology and Experience

I have also taken a contextual approach to the history of feminism. My central assumption has been that words, concepts, and ideas cannot be judged according to ethical or political criteria that claim to be universal, but take on significance only from the discourse in which they are formulated. Thus, feminism and feminist movements cannot be understood simply in terms of their success in achieving specific objectives defined by historians of later generations. They must be understood more broadly, as symbolic and conceptual frameworks created by women in order to understand, interpret, and change their world. The concepts used by women, as by other speakers, are never freely chosen by individuals, but developed within the language and conceptual frameworks provided by a specific culture and period. Speech is a social rather than a simply individual act; if an individual wishes to change culture, she must nonetheless conceptualize such change within existing language and discourse. Thus, efforts to change culture are nonetheless burdened and limited by it. The history of feminist movements repeatedly shows the use of established words and images to express altered meanings; this is as true of the American equal-rights feminists, who found their inspiration in the Declaration of Independence, as of their German contemporaries, who cited Pestalozzi. Both groups accepted the important texts of their culture, but as critical, even as resisting readers; by receiving them, they also revised and transformed them.[16]

Essential to the development of a feminist standpoint was a definition of "woman" that included distinctive ethical and political as well as physical characteristics. The creation of such a definition has always been a major problem for feminism; women are such an enormously diverse group that no one political ideology can define them all. The definitions that have been created by feminist movements, whether based on gender similarity or difference, have thus always been specific to classes or groups of women. The maternalist ideology of German feminism was originally created by a specific group of women from the upper and middle classes, who at a specific period in history experienced motherhood, and the cultural values attached to it, as empowering. Their use of these experiences to create a definition of "woman" purporting to be universal expressed class as well as gender identity.[17]

Certainly, such hegemonic and falsely universal claims did not go unchallenged; politically organized working-class women often criticized the limitations of bourgeois feminists' approach to social problems, as well as their patronizing behavior. The interaction, and sometimes conflict, of gender and class as aspects of female identity has been a recurring theme of this study. However, the appeal to the common experience of motherhood was not wholly unsuccessful; of all the issues raised by feminists during the nineteenth and early twentieth centuries, maternal and child welfare occasioned the greatest degree of agreement, even sometimes of cooperation, between socialist and bourgeois women. Even those socialist women who declined to cooperate with bourgeois feminism often favored similar reforms, such as maternity insurance and protective legislation, and similar child-care institutions. The integration of socialist women into public welfare work and policy-making during the wartime period and during the Weimar Republic also shows the appeal of this approach to female activism to working-class as well as middle- and upper-class women. An ideology based on the "joys and sorrows of motherhood" could not, of course, overcome class antagonisms, but ideologies stressing such equal- rights issues as suffrage were no more successful, in Germany or elsewhere.[18]

A definition of ideology as a symbolic framework interpreting the experience and aspirations of a specific group must lead to a reappraisal of the way in which feminism, particularly in Germany, has often been understood. Historians have attempted to classify feminist movements by identifying them with mainstream, that is male-dominated, political movements; Evans, as we have seen, derives feminism from liberalism and Greven-Aschoff from both liberalism and socialism. This method of classification, however, is clearly imperfect, for as these historians constantly point out, feminists often deviated from these political paradigms. The women described in this study, although until 1908 excluded from political parties, certainly took many of their ideas from the political movements of their time; some identified themselves as liberals, some as socialists, and at least one as a conservative. Despite their political diversity, however, they tended to share one attitude—a marked discomfort with and resistance to established political ideology. Sometimes this resistance was expressed through an insistence on an individualized and personal as opposed to an abstract and rule-oriented approach to individuals and issues; sometimes it was expressed more explicitly. The "central dogma" of the woman social worker, said Frieda Duensing, should be "never to sacrifice human beings to a principle and always to struggle against principles that victimize people, as the greatest sin." Ideologies created by men in order to interpret their own experience were inadequate to express women's views of politics, which were based on a very different social position and experience.[19]

The position of women within mainstream political ideologies highlights the broader problem of women's relationship to all male-defined conceptual structures. "For women," writes literary critic Rachel Blau du Plessis, "existing in the dominant structure of meanings and values that structure culture can be a painful, or amusing, double dance, clicking in, clicking out—the divided consciousness." As we have seen from the women described here, women often perceived the intersection and relationship of public and private worlds differently from their male contemporaries. The antitheses that defined nineteenth-century male political thought—family and state, emotion and reason, love and work—were often challenged by women who explored the political dimensions of personal experience and applied familial values to public concerns. As Catherine N. Prelinger has also pointed out, German feminist movements, like their counterparts in other countries, had a strong utopian tradition that reflected gender-based political ideals and aspirations and can be related, but not completely assimilated, to other political ideologies.[20]

How successful were the theory and practice of public and private motherhood in improving the status of women? Clearly, the practical results were very limited, at least in the short term. Feminist reformers did not succeed in gaining large-scale public funding for child care, in effecting significant changes in family law, in increasing social benefits to mothers and children, in attaining reproductive rights, or in greatly changing the funding priorities of the state. However, they did contribute to the long-term realization of these goals by helping to create a rationale for women's public involvement and new professional and organizational roles that supported such involvement. By 1914, the activities of women's organizations, even small and radical ones such as the League for the Protection of Mothers, sometimes had a major influence on public opinion, and woman leaders were sometimes consulted on issues of public policy and appointed to official committees. Along with the opening of educational opportunities to women, the creation of roles for women in social services must be counted as among the greatest successes of the prewar feminist movement. This public role was limited; it was centered almost wholly on maternal, child welfare, and educational issues, including those described here. But the limited scope of women's public role was not due, as Koonz sometimes implies, to a specifically German preference for maternalist over equal-rights ideology. Women's public roles developed in much the same way in the United States, where the mainstream feminist movement was centered much more on suffrage and much less on social welfare and maternal issues than in Germany. There, too, women gained their greatest influence in connection with social welfare issues, particularly those related to mothers and children.[21]

Much of the criticism leveled against the ideas and political strategies of earlier feminist movements by historians of the late twentieth century reflects the ideology of the feminist movement of the 1960s and 1970s, exemplified in its leading texts such as Betty Friedan's *The Feminine Mystique* and Shulamith Firestone's *The Dialectic of Sex*. For this generation of feminists, domestic and maternal roles were in themselves the source of women's oppression. Friedan characterized the middle-class household as a "comfortable concentration camp," in which motherhood was chiefly a form of vicarious gratification for the mother's own frustrated drive for self-fulfillment. Firestone saw the "interrelated myths of femininity and childhood" chiefly as instruments of the oppression of both women and children, and called for the freeing of women from the "tyranny of reproductive biology." The first historians of women often reproached past generations of feminists for not sharing these ideas.[22]

But these late-twentieth-century positions, like nineteenth-century statements on spiritual motherhood, represented not a quintessential feminist orthodoxy but the response of a specific group of women to specific historical conditions. These included improved control over reproduction, smaller families, longer life spans, widening economic opportunities, and the accompanying decline in the importance and status of domestic work. Responding to these changed conditions, the American feminist movement of the 1960s and 1970s attacked not only the reactionary "feminine mystique" of the 1950s but earlier feminist ideologies based on gender difference and spiritual motherhood. The escape from earlier, female-identified domestic and professional spheres and the exploration of new vocational and private options became the most widely publicized goals of feminist movements in these decades.[23]

Maternal ideologies and maternal issues have by no means become obsolete, however. In the practical realm, some feminists of the 1980s, particularly in the United States, have criticized the recent emphasis of American feminism on purely equal-rights issues at the expense of social issues, particularly concerning maternity and child care. They draw a dismal contrast between the total lack of national maternity insurance in the United States and the much more fully developed welfare policies of Western European nations, among them West Germany. On a more theoretical level, psychologists such as Carol Gilligan and Nancy Chodorow have speculated that, despite recent social changes, women still tend to conceive of the relationship between reason and emotion and between private and public concerns differently from men. According to Gilligan, women's ethical decisions are typically based on affiliative and individualized rather than abstract and rule-oriented systems of values. Chodorow traces these psychological characteristics to the relationship of daughters to mothers, which she claims requires less separation than that of sons to their mothers, and therefore encourages women to develop views of the world based more on relationship and affiliation and less on competitive individualism than those of men. Whatever the merits of these theories—and they have proved very controversial—they show the continuing conviction of some feminist scholars that familial and maternal roles exert a positive influence on women's public and private behavior. The feminist utopianism of our own time—including antiwar, ecological, religious, and many other movements—also often uses maternal imagery to express a standpoint that is identified as distinctively female. For example, philosopher Sara Ruddick proposes the theory and practice of motherhood—what she calls maternal thinking—as a basis for new, nonviolent approaches to social and international conflicts. Thus in our own day, as in an earlier period, equality and difference often prove to be complementary rather than contradictory themes in feminist ideology and practice.[24]

Notes

Introduction

1. Helene Lange, *Lebenserinnerungen* (Berlin, 1930), 111–112.
2. Some discussions of maternalism and its role in German feminist movements are: Catherine N. Prelinger, *Charity, Challenge and Change: Religious Dimensions of the Mid-Nineteenth-Century Women's Movement in Germany* (Westport, Conn., 1987); Barbara Greven-Aschoff, *Die bürgerliche Frauenbewegung in Deutschland, 1894–1933* (Göttingen, 1981), 31–44; Herrad-Ulrike Bussemer, *Frauenemanzipation und Bildungsbürgertum: Sozialgeschichte der Frauenbewegung in der Reichsgründungszeit* (Weinheim, 1985), 185–233; Richard J. Evans, *The Feminist Movement in Germany, 1894–1933* (London, 1976), 24–32 and passim; Irene Stoehr, "Organisierte Müttelrichkeit: Zur Politik der deutschen Frauenbewegung um 1900," in Karin Hausen, ed., *Frauen suchen ihre Geschichte: Historische Studien zum 19. und 20. Jahrhundert* (Munich, 1983), 224–247.
3. Carol Gilligan, *In a Different Voice: Psychological Theory and Women's Development* (Cambridge, Mass., 1982), 26–73.
4. On contextualism versus present-mindedness in intellectual history see David Harlan, "Intellectual History and the Return of Literature," *American Historical Review* 94 (June 1989): 593–598, and David A. Hollinger, "The Return of the Prodigal: The Persistence of Historical Knowing," *American Historical Review* 94 (June 1989): 610–622; on continuity in German history see David Blackbourn and Geoff Eley, *The Peculiarities of German History: Bourgeois Society and Politics in Nineteenth-Century Germany* (Oxford, 1984), 1–33 and passim; on continuity in women's history see Karen Offen, "Defining Feminism: A Comparative Historical Approach," *Signs: Journal of Women in Culture and Society* 14 (Autumn 1988): 119–157.
5. On objectivity see Martin Jay, "Should Intellectual History Take a Linguistic Turn?" in Dominick LaCapra and Steven L. Kaplan, eds., *Modern European Intellec- History: Reappraisals and New Perspectives* (Ithaca, N.Y., 1982), 94–96; on history as a dialogue see Harlan, "Intellectual History," 603–604.
6. Richard J. Evans, "The Concept of Feminism: Notes for Practicing Historians," in Ruth-Ellen Joeres and Mary Jo Maynes (eds.), *German Women in the Eighteenth and Nineteenth Centuries: A Social and Literary History* (Bloomington, Ind., 1986), 255; Evans, *The Feminist Movement in Germany*, 116–145, and Evans, "Liberalism and Society: The Feminist Movement and Social Change," in Evans, *Rethinking German History: Nineteenth-Century Germany and the Origins of the Third Reich* (London, 1987), 221–247.
7. Claudia Honegger and Bettina Heinz, eds., *Listen der Ohnmacht: Zur Sozialgeschichte weiblicher Widerstandsformen* (Frankfurt, 1984), 45; Aileen Kraditor, *The Ideas of the Woman Suffrage Movement, 1890–1920* (New York, 1965; reprinted 1971), 38–64.
8. Amy K. Hackett, "The Politics of Feminism in Wilhelmine Germany, 1888–1918" (Ph.D. diss., Columbia University, 1977), v; Greven-Aschoff, *Die Bürgerliche Frauenbewegung*, 194; Prelinger, *Charity, Challenge and Change*; Bärbel Clemens,

Menschenrechte haben kein Geschlecht! Zum Politikverständnis der bürgerlichen Frauenbewegung (Pfaffenweiler, 1988); Elisabeth Meyer-Renschhausen, *Weibliche Kultur und soziale Arbeit: Eine Geschichte der Frauenbewegung am Beispiel Bremens, 1810–1927* (Cologne, 1989), 1–11.

9. Herrad-Ulrike Bussemer, *Frauenemanzipation und Bildungsbürgertum*, 185–223; Renate Bridenthal, Atina Grossmann, and Marion Kaplan, eds., *When Biology Became Destiny: Women in Weimar and Nazi Germany* (New York, 1984), xiii; Claudia Koonz, *Mothers in the Fatherland: Women, the Family and Nazi Politics* (New York, 1987), xx.

10. Cf. Heide Soltau, "Erotik und Altruismus: Emanzipationsvorstellungen der Radikalen Helen Stöcker" in Jutta Dalhoff, Uschi Frey, and Ingrid Scholl, eds., *Frauenmacht in der Geschichte* (Düsseldorf, 1986), 65–82; Clemens, *Menschenrechte haben kein Geschlecht!*, 42–47; see also a reference work, Daniela Weiland, ed., *Geschichte der Frauenemanzipation in Deutschland und Österreich: Biographien, Programme, Organisationen* (Düsseldorf, 1983), from which Hedwig Heyl, Bertha von Marenholtz-Bülow, Anna von Gierke, Frieda Duensing, Charlotte Paulsen, Johanna Goldschmidt, and many other figures important in feminist movements but identified with maternal issues are omitted. Women's contributions to social work and social reform are described in Prelinger, *Charity, Challenge and Change*; Christoph Sachsse, *Mütterlichkeit als Beruf: Sozialarbeit, Sozialreform und Frauenbewegung, 1871–1929* (Frankfurt, 1986); Susanne Zeller, *Volksmütter: Frauen im Wohlfahrtswesen der zwanziger Jahre* (Düsseldorf, 1987); and Ilka Riemann, *Soziale Arbeit als Hausarbeit: Von der Suppendame zur Sozialpädagogin* (Frankfurt, 1985). But other recent works on social reform and child welfare, such as Detlev J. K. Peukert, *Grenzen der Sozialdisziplinierung: Aufstieg und Krise der deutschen Jugendfürsorge von 1878 bis 1932* (Cologne, 1986); Franz Josef Krafeld, *Geschichte der Jugendarbeit: Von den Anfängen bis zur Gegenwart* (Weinheim, 1984); and Jürgen Reulecke, "Bürgerliche Sozialreformer und Arbeiterjugend im Kaiserreich," *Archiv für Sozialgeschichte* 22 (1982): 299–329, make no mention of the contributions of women, and a new work on the kindergarten movement, Günter Erning, Karl Neumann, and Jürgen Reyer, *Geschichte des Kindergartens*, 2 vols. (Freiburg im Breisgau, 1987), mentions some of the contributions of women to this movement but does not discuss their role in any detail.

11. Koonz, *Mothers in the Fatherland*, 31; Joan Wallach Scott, *Gender and the Politcs of History* (New York, 1988), 176–177; Gisela Bock, "Challenging Dichotomies: Theoretical and Historical Perspectives on Women's Studies in the Humanities and Social Sciences," EUI Working Paper No. 89/139 (Florence, 1989), 16–17; Linda S. Alcoff, "Cultural Feminism vs. Poststructuralism: The Identity Crisis in Feminist Theory," *Signs* (Spring 1988): 405–436; see also Jane Flax, "Political Philosophy and the Patriarchal Unconscious: A Psychoanalytic Perspective on Epistemology and Metaphysics," in Sandra Harding and Merrill B. Hintikka, eds., *Discovering Reality* (New York, 1983), 245–275.

12. Michel Foucault, "Nietzsche, Genealogy, History," in *The Foucault Reader*, edited by Paul Rabinow (New York, 1984), 76–100; see also Mark Poster, "The Future According to Foucault," in LaCapra and Kaplan, eds., *Modern European Intellectual History*, 137–152.

13. Offen, "Defining Feminism," 152, 126; the early histories are Anna Plothow,

Die Begründerinnen der deutschen Frauenbewegung (Leipzig, 1907); and Lina Morgenstern, *Die Frauen des 19. Jahrhunderts: Biographische und culturhistorische Zeit- und Charactergemälde*, 3 vols. (Berlin, 1888–91); Nancy Cott, *The Grounding of Modern Feminism* (New Haven, 1987), 3–10.

14. Meyer-Renschhausen, *Weibliche Kultur und soziale Arbeit*, 13–20; Carroll Smith-Rosenberg, *Disorderly Conduct: Visions of Gender in Victorian America* (New York, 1985), 266; see also Foucault, "Truth and Power," in *The Foucault Reader*, edited by Rabinow, 51–77; Chris Weedon, *Feminist Practice and Poststructuralist Theory* (Oxford, 1987), 107–135; John E. Toews, "Intellectual History after the Linguistic Turn: The Automomy of Meaning and the Irreducibility of Experience," *American Historical Review* 92 (October 1987): 890–891; and Xavière Gauthier, "Is there Such a Thing as Women's Writing?," in Elaine Marks and Isabelle de Courtivron, eds., *New French Feminisms: An Anthology* (Brighton, Sussex, 1980), 161–164.

15. Michel Foucault, *The History of Sexuality: Volume I, An Introduction*, trans. Robert Hurley (Paris, 1976; reprinted New York, 1980), 95–102; Toril Moi, *Sexual/Textual Politics: Feminist Literary Theory* (London, 1985), 158; Scott, *Gender and the Politics of History*, 25–26.

16. Hackett, "The German Women's Movement and Suffrage, 1890–1914: A Study of National Feminism," in Robert J. Bezucha, ed., *European Social History* (Lexington, Mass., 1972), 362–364; Greven-Aschoff, *Die bürgerliche Frauenbewegung*, 37–44; Offen, "Defining Feminism," and "Liberty, Equality and Justice for Women: The Theory and Practice of Feminism in Nineteenth-Century Europe," in Renate Bridenthal, Claudia Koonz, and Susan Stuard, eds., *Becoming Visible: Women in European History*, 2nd ed. (Boston, 1987), 335–373.

17. Cf. Hackett, "The German Women's Movement and Suffrage," 364; Offen, "Liberty, Equality and Justice," 339.

18. Nancy C. M. Hartsock, "The Feminist Standpoint: Developing the Ground for a Specifically Feminist Historical Materialism," in Sandra Harding, ed., *Feminism and Methodology: Social Science Issues* (Bloomington, Ind., 1987), 170. On the relationship between subjectivity and culture see Nancy M. Theriot, *The Biosocial Construction of Femininity: Mothers and Daughters in Nineteenth-Century America* (New York, 1988), 7–24; Toews, "Intellectual History," 892–908; Weedon, *Poststructuralist Theory*, 12–42; and Gilligan, *In a Different Voice*.

19. On class implications of feminist ideology, cf. Renate Bridenthal, "'Professional' Housewives: Stepsisters of the Women's Movement," in Bridenthal, Grossman, and Kaplan, eds., *When Biology Became Destiny*, 154.

20. Joan Kelly, "The Doubled Vision of Feminist Theory," in *Women, History and Theory: The Essays of Joan Kelly* (Chicago, 1984), 58; see also see Scott, *Gender and the Politics of History*, 24; and Linda Kerber, "Separate Spheres, Female Worlds, Woman's Place: The Rhetoric of Women's History," *Journal of American History* 75 (June 1988): 10–39.

Chapter 1. From Authority to Nurture

1. Betty Gleim, *Erziehung und Unterricht des weiblichen Geschlechts: Ein Buch für Eltern und Erzieher* (Leipzig, 1810), 93; on background of German philosophy

see Maurice Mandelbaum, *History, Man and Reason: A Study in Nineteenth-Century Thought* (Baltimore, 1971), 163–218; on the maternal role see Karin Hausen, "Family and Role Division: The Polarization of Sexual Stereotypes in the Nineteenth Century—An Aspect of the Dissociation of Work and Family Life," in Richard Evans and W. R. Lee, eds., *The German Family* (London, 1981): 51–83.

2. Compare the discussions of American parallels in Nancy Cott, *The Bonds of Womanhood: Woman's Sphere in New England, 1780–1835* (New Haven, 1971), and Linda K. Kerber, *Women of the Republic: Intellect and Ideology in Revolutionary America* (Chapel Hill, N.C., 1980).

3. Edward Shorter, "Die Wandel der Mutter-Kind Beziehungen zu Beginn der Moderne," *Geschichte und Gesellschaft* 1 (1975): 257–287, and "Maternal Sentiment and Death in Childbirth: A New Agenda for Psycho-Medical History," in Patricia Branca, ed., *The Medicine Show: Patients, Physicians and the Perplexities of the Health Revolution in Modern Society* (New York, 1977), 72–73. On motherhood in early modern and modern times, see Elisabeth Badinter, *Mother Love: Myth and Reality: Motherhood in Modern History* (Paris, 1980), and Lloyd de Mause, "The Evolution of Childhood," in de Mause, ed., *The History of Childhood* (New York, 1974), 1–73.

4. Mary Lindemann, "Maternal Politics: The Principles and Practice of Maternity Care in Eighteenth-Century Hamburg," *Journal of Family History* 9 (Spring 1984): 44–63; Michel Foucault, *The History of Sexuality: Volume I, An Introduction*, trans. Robert Hurley (New York, 1980), 115–178.

5. On the status of unmarried mothers see Dirk Blasius, *Ehescheidung in Deutschland: Scheidung und Scheidungsrecht in historischer Perspektive, 1794–1945* (Göttingen, 1987), 100–103; Marianne Weber, *Ehefrau und Mutter in der Rechtsentwicklung: eine Einführung* (Tübingen, 1907), 340; and Marilyn Chapin Massey, *Feminine Soul: The Fate of an Ideal* (Boston, 1985), 31–48.

6. Prussian legislation on parental rights and duties is quoted and discussed in Jurgen Schlumbohm, ed., *Kinderstuben: Wie Kinder zu Bauern, Bürgern, Aristokraten wurden, 1700–1850* (Munich, 1983), 42–61; Susan Groag Bell and Karen M. Offen, eds., *Women, the Family and Freedom, The Debate in Documents*, 2 vols. (Stanford, 1983), 2: 31–39; Weber, *Ehefrau und Mutter*, 334–341; Doris Alder, "Im 'wahren Paradies der Weiber?' Naturrecht und rechtliche Wirklichkeit der Frauen im preussischen Landrecht," in Viktoria Schmidt-Linsenhoff, ed., *Sklavin oder Bürgerin? Französische Revolution und neue Weiblichkeit* (Frankfurt, 1989), 206–221.

7. G.F.C. Wendelstädt, *Uber die Pflicht gesunder Mütter, ihre Kinder selbst zu stillen* (Marburg, 1798), 6, 7; see also D. Christ. Wilh. Hufeland, *Guter Rath an Mütter über die wichtigen Punkte der physischen Erziehung der Kinder in den ersten Jahren* (Berlin, 1799); on breast-feeding, see Weber, *Ehefrau und Mutter*, 113; Massey, *Feminine Soul*, 36–37; and Lindemann, "Love for Hire: The Regulation of the Wet-Nursing Business in Eighteenth-Century Hamburg," *Journal of Family History* 6 (Winter 1981): 379–395; and Ute Frevert, *Woman in German History: From Bourgeois Emancipation to Sexual Liberation*, trans. Stuart McKinnon-Evans (Oxford, 1988), 46–47.

8. On the Philanthropists see Jürgen Reyer, *Wenn die Mütter arbeiten gingen . . . : Eine sozialhistorische Studie zur Entstehung der öffentlichen Kleinkinderziehung in Deutschland* (Cologne, 1983), 109–122; Schlumbohm, *Kinderstuben*, 47–62, and Reyer, *Wenn die Mütter arbeiten gingen*, 109–122.

9. Christian Gotthilf Salzmann, *Konrad Kiefer, oder Anweisung zu einer vernünftigen Erziehung der Kinder: Ein Buch fürs Volk* (Langensalza, 1901), excerpted in Johannes Prüfer, ed., *Quellen zur Geschichte der Kleinkinderziehung* (Frankfurt, 1911), 66–73; Christian Gotthilf Salzmann, *Uber die wirksamsten Mittel, Kindern Religion beizubringen*, (Leipzig, 1787), quoted in Prüfer, *Kleinkinderpädagogik* (Leipzig, 1913), 37. On play in the eighteenth-century family see Barbara Beuys, *Die deutsche Familie: Neue Bilder aus der deutschen Vergangenheit* (Reinbek, 1980), 320–324.

10. Joachim Heinrich Campe, *Sittenbüchlein für Kinder* (Braunschweig, 1788); Elisabeth Blochmann, *Das "Frauenzimmer" und die "Gelehrsamkeit": Eine Studie über die Anfänge des Mädchenschulwesens in Deutschland* (Heidelberg, 1966), 26–41; Peter Petschauer, "From Hausmutter to Hausfrau: Ideals and Realities in Late Eighteenth-Century Germany," *Eighteenth-Century Life* 8 (1982): 73–81; and Marion W. Gray, "Prescriptions for Productive Female Domesticity in a Transitional Era: Germany's *Hausmutterliteratur*, 1780–1840," *History of European Ideas* 8 (1987), 413–426. None of these works devotes much attention to prescriptions for child-rearing, nor do they include Pestalozzi's works among the body of literature that they discuss. On Campe's educational approach see Reyer, *Wenn die Mütter arbeiten gingen*, 122; and Christa Kersting, "Prospekt fürs Eheleben: Johann Heinrich Campe: Väterlicher Rath für meine Tochter," in Schmidt-Linsenhoff, ed., *Sklavin oder Bürgerin?*, 373–390.

11. Johann Heinrich Pestalozzi, *Wie Gertrud ihre Kinder lehrt*, in *Pestalozzis sämtliche Werke*, ed. Emanual Dejung, Walter Guyer and Herbert Schonbaum, 18 vols. (Berlin and Leipzig, 1930), 13:311. On Pestalozzi's life and career see Kate Silber, *Pestalozzi: The Man and his Work*, 3rd ed. (New York, 1973); and Johann Heinrich Pestalozzi, "Brief an einen Freund über den Aufenthalt in Stans," in *Pestalozzis Lebendiges Werk*, 2:109–119.

12. Silber, *Pestalozzi*, 226–235; Pestalozzi, *Über Gesezgebung und Kindermord*, in *Pestalozzis sämtliche Werke*, 9:160–165.

13. Pestalozzi's response to the events of his time is expressed in many essays, notably "An die Unschuld, den Ernst, und den Edelmut meines Zeitalters und meines Vaterlandes," *Heinrich Pestalozzis Lebendiges Werk*, 2:332–362; on transition from contractarian to organic theories see Mandelbaum, *History, Man and Reason*, 163–218. On individualism and relationship in Western political theory see Jane Flax, "Political Philosophy and the Patriarchal Unconscious: A Psychoanalytic Perspective on Epistemology and Metaphysics," in Sandra Harding and Merrill B. Hintikka, eds., *Discovering Reality: Feminist Perspectives on Epistemology, Metaphysics, Methodology and Philosophy of Science* (Boston, 1983), 245–231.

14. Pestalozzi, *Wie Gertrud ihre Kinder lehrt*, 342, 345. On Pestalozzi's attutudes toward women see Massey, *Feminine Soul*, 49–64; on his educational theories see Helmut Heiland, "Erziehungskonzepte der Klassiker der Frühpädagogik," in Günter Erning, Karl Neumann, and Jürgen Reyer, eds., *Geschichte des Kindergartens: Entstehung und Entwicklung der öffentlichen Kleinkinderziehung in Deutschland*, 2 vols. (Freiburg im Breisgau, 1987), 2:148–184.

15. Pestalozzi, *Lienhard und Gertrud: Ein Buch für das Volk, Heinrich Pestalozzis Lebendiges Werk*, vol. 1. Part One of the novel was published in the 1780s, but subsequent sections appeared throughout the 1790s.

16. Ibid., 318–319; "Die Schule des Leutnants Glülphi," in *Heinrich Pestalozzis Lebendiges Werk*, 3:68–93.

17. Theodor Gottlieb von Hippel, *On Improving the Status of Women*, trans. and ed. Timothy F. Sellner (Detroit, 1979), 84.

18. Ibid., 89, 93.

19. Kerber, *Women of the Republic*, 265–287.

20. On German and British bourgeoisie see Jürgen Kocka, ed., *Bürger und Bürgerlichkeit im 19 Jahrhundert* (Göttingen, 1977); Barbara Duden, "Das schöne Eigentum: Zur Herausbildung des bürgerlichen Frauenbildes zur Wende vom 18. zum 19. Jahrhundert," *Kursbuch* 47 (1977): 125–140; Ute Frevert, "Bürgerliche Meisterdenker und das Geschlechterverhältnis: Konzepte, Erfahrungen, Visionen," in Frevert, ed., *Bürgerinnen und Bürger: Geschlechterverhältnisse im 19. Jahrhundert* (Göttingen, 1988), 17–48.

21. On public/private boundaries see Ute Daniel, "Offentlich-privat: begriffsgeschichtlich Entwicklung einer Lebensnorm oder: Dr. Jekyll und Mr. Hyde für Jedermann," unpub. typescript. I am grateful to the author for allowing me to read this unpublished article. See also Jean Bethke Elshtain, *Public Man, Private Woman: Women in Social and Political Thought* (Princeton, 1981), 170–178.

22. Johann Gottlieb Fichte, *Addresses to the German Nation* (paperback ed. New York, 1968), 39; G.W.F. Hegel, *Phenomenology of Mind*, 2 vols., trans. and with an introduction by J. B. Baillie (London, 1910), 2:445. On Fichte see also Massey, *Feminine Soul*, 88–91, and Ernst J. G. Bergmann, *Fichte der Erzieher* (Leipzig, 1928), 303–309. On Hegel see Joan Landes, "Hegel's Conception of the Family," in Jean Bethke Elshtain, ed., *The Family in Political Thought* (Amherst, Mass., 1982), 126–139.

23. Jean Paul Richter, *Levana, or the Doctrine of Education* (London, 1891), 230, 227. For a commentary on Jean Paul's view of childhood see Prüfer, ed., *Quellen*, 140–153.

24. On changes in the family see Michael Mitterauer, *The European Family: Patriarchy to Partnership from the Middle Ages to the Present*, trans. Karla Oosterveen and Manfred Horziner (Chicago, 1982), 48–70; Ingeborg Weber-Kellermann, *Die deutsche Familie: Versuch einer Sozialgeschichte* (Frankfurt, 1975), 102–118; Karl Neumann, "Kinder und Eltern: Die bürgerliche Familie als Leitbild, gesellschaftliche Widersprüche und die Vermittlungsfunktion der öffentlichen Kleinkinderziehung," in Neumann, Erning and Reyer, eds., *Geschichte des Kindergartens*, 2:135–146; Frevert, *Women in German History*, 15–17. On female virtues see Cott, *The Bonds of Womanhood*, 197–206 (summary of her conclusions); Blochmann, *Das Frauenzimmer*, 63–68; and James C. Albisetti, *Schooling German Girls and Women: Secondary and Higher Education in the Nineteenth Century* (Princeton, 1988), 3–22.

25. On the domestic sphere in literature see Jane Tompkins, "Sentimental Power: *Uncle Tom's Cabin* and the Politics of Literary History," in Elaine Showalter, ed., *New Feminist Criticism: Essays on Women, Literature and Theory* (New York, 1985), 81–104; on women's literary perspectives see Showalter, "Feminist Criticism in the Wilderness," in *Feminist Criticism*, 259–266.

26. Amalie Holst, geb. von Justi, *Über die Bestimmung des Weibes zur Höheren Geistesbildung*, edited by Bertha Rahm (Berlin, 1802, reprinted Hamburg, 1984), 38, 90.

27. Ibid., 39, 114.

28. Carroll Smith-Rosenberg, "The Female World of Love and Ritual: Relations between Women in Nineteenth-Century America," *Signs* 1 (Autumn 1975): 1–29; Caroline Rudolphi, *Gemälde weiblicher Erziehung*, 2 vols. (Heidelberg, 1815), 1:90–91. On Rudolphi's career and influence see Blochmann, *Das Frauenzimmer*, 68–71; and Albisetti, *Schooling German Girls and Women*, 16–17.

29. Rudolphi, *Gemälde*, 2:59; 1:240–248.

30. Ibid., 2:61–63; on Rudolphi's influence see Blochmann, *Das Frauenzimmer*, 69; Schwarz's opinion was expressed in his introduction to the 1815 edition, xxxi.

31. Betty Gleim, *Erziehung und Unterricht des weiblichen Geschlechts: ein Buch für Eltern und Erzieher* (Leipzig, 1810), 5, 45, 50. On Gleim's life and career see Blochmann, *Frauenzimmer*, 70–76; August Kippenberg, *Betty Gleim* (Bremen, 1882); and Elisabeth Meyer-Renschhausen, *Weibliche Kultur und soziale Arbeit: Eine Geschichte der Frauenbewegung am Beispiel Bremens* (Cologne, 1989), 20–43; Albisetti, *Schooling German Girls and Women*, 17–18.

32. Gleim, *Erziehung*, 84, 62, 67, 91.

33. On professions see ibid., 102–110, and Blochmann, *Frauenzimmer*, 77–78.

34. Ruth Dawson, "'And This Shield Is Called—Self-Reliance': Emerging Feminist Consciousness in the Late Eighteenth Century," in Ruth-Ellen B. Joeres and Mary Jo Maynes, eds., *German Women in the Eighteenth and Nineteenth Centuries: A Social and Literary History* (Bloomington, Ind., 1986), 157–174, takes another view of this issue.

35. Froebel's recollections are contained in an autobiographical fragment, entitled (in English translation) "Letter to the Duke of Meiningen," in Henry Barnard, ed., *Papers on Froebel's Kindergarten, with Suggestions on Principles and Methods of Child Culture in Different Countries* (Hartford, Conn., 1881), 21–48; on Froebel's biography see Robert B. Downs, *Friedrich Froebel* (Boston, 1978).

36. Froebel, "Letter to the Duke of Meiningen," 33–40. Froebel was influenced particularly by F.W.J. Schelling, *Bruno: Or On the Natural and Divine Principle of Things*, trans. Michael G. Vater (Albany, 1984); see also John Herman Randall, *The Career of Philosophy*, 2 vols. (New York, 1962–1965), 1:247–275; for another discussion of intellectual influences on Froebel see Massey, *Feminine Soul*, 147–154.

37. Froebel, "Letter to the Duke of Meiningen," 40–48; on his military experiences, 45.

38. Froebel, *Mutter und Koselieder: Dichtung und Bilder zur edlen Pflege des Kindheitslebens* (Vienna and Leipzig, 1883), 14 (translation by author). See also Massey, *Feminine Soul*, 150–154.

39. Froebel, *Entwurf eines Planes zur Begründung und Ausführung eines Kindergartens* (Leipzig, 1840), 29. Among many statements of Froebel's pedagogical philosophy is Froebel, "Education by Development," in *The Second Part of the Pedagogics of the Kindergarten, or his Ideas Concerning the Play and Playthings of the Child*, trans. Josephine Jarvis (New York, 1899). For a fuller account of Froebel's pedagogy and the early history of the kindergarten see Erning, Neumann, and Reyer, eds., *Geschichte des Kindergartens*, 1:46–57, and Heiland, "Erziehungskonzepte," 163–166.

40. For an account of the use of women in religious preschool education see Catherine N. Prelinger, "The Nineteenth-Century Deaconessate in Germany: The Efficacy of a Family Model," in Joeres and Maynes, eds., *German Women in the*

Eighteenth and Nineteenth Centuries, 215–219; Froebel, *Second Part*, 161. Froebel, *Die Menschenerziehung: Die Erziehungs, Unterrichts- und Lehrkunst angestrebt in der allgemeinen deutschen Erziehungsanstalt zu Keilhau* (Leipzig, 1826) 49; Wichard Lange, "Reminiscences of Froebel," in *Papers on Froebel's Kindergarten*, 84. On the history of the kindergarten, Ann Taylor Allen, "Spiritual Motherhood: German Feminists and the Kindergarten Movement, 1840–1914," *History of Education Quarterly* 22 (Fall 1982): 319–340.

41. Froebel, quoted in Henriette Goldschmidt, *Bertha von Marenholtz-Bülow: Ihr Leben und Wirken im Dienste der Erziehungslehre Friedrich Froebels* (Hamburg, 1896), 5, 1; *Second Part*, 170.

42. Froebel, "Entwurf eines Planes," 1; For early history of kindergarten see Allen, "Spiritual Motherhood," 319–323; Gunnar Heinsohn, *Vorschulerziehung in der bürgerlichen Gesellschaft* (Frankfurt, 1974), 50–62; Erika Hoffmann, *Vorschulerziehung in Deutschland: Historische Entwicklung im Abriss* (Witte, 1971), 37–38; on participation of women in *Gutenbergfest* see Carola Lipp, "Frauen und Öffentlichkeit: Möglichkeiten und Grenzen politischer Partizipation im Vormärz und in der Revolution 1848," in Lipp, ed., *Schimpfende Weiber und patriotische Jungfrauen: Frauen im Vormärz und in der Revolution, 1848/49* (Baden-Baden, 1985), 280–81.

43. Kerber, *Women of the Republic*, 265–288

Chapter 2. The Personal and the Political

1. On discourse and resistance see Michel Foucault, *The History of Sexuality: Volume I, An Introduction*, trans. Robert Hurley (New York, 1980), 95; and Toril Moi, *Sexual/Textual Politics: Feminist Literary Theory* (London, 1985), 155.

2. On individual and familial experience in conflict see Carl Degler, *At Odds: Women and the Family in America from the Revolution to the Present* (New York, 1980).

3. Ruth-Ellen Boettcher Joeres, "Self-Conscious Histories: Biographies of German Women in the Nineteenth Century," in John C. Fout, ed., *German Women in the Nineteenth Century: A Social History* (New York, 1984), 172–196; on the familial culture of the early nineteenth century see Ute Frevert, *Women in German History: From Bourgeois Emancipation to Sexual Liberation*, trans. Stuart McKinnon-Evans (Oxford, 1988), 63–72.

4. On Wüstenfeld's childhood see Marie Kortmann, *Emilie Wüstenfeld: Eine Hamburger Bürgerin* (Hamburg, 1927), 7–13, and Kortmann, *Aus den Anfängen sozialer Frauenarbeit* (Berlin, 1913), 1–3; and Catherine N. Prelinger, *Charity, Challenge and Change: Religious Dimensions of the Mid- Nineteenth-Century Women's Movement* (New York, 1986), 55–63. Other biographical materials on Wüstenfeld may be found in the Familienarchiv Wüstenfeld: Nachlass Emilie Wüstenfeld, Staatsarchiv Hamburg. Information on Meysenbug's childhood may be found in her autobiography, Malwida von Meysenbug, *Memoiren einer Idealistin*, 2 vols., in Berta Schleicher, ed., *Malwida von Meysenbugs Gesammelte Werke*, 5 vols. (Stuttgart, 1922), 1:7–8.

5. Anna Wohlwill, "Charlotte Paulsen," in *Schule des Paulsenstifts* (Hamburg, 1900) 1–3; Fritzi Liecks, "Charlotte Paulsen, geb. Thornton" in *100-Jahr-Feier in der Charlotte-Paulsen-Schule* (Hamburg, 1949), 8–11. Other biographical materials on Paulsen are "Schule des Paulsen-Stifts," Staatsarchiv Hamburg. I am much indebted to

Prelinger for her advice on finding materials on the Hamburg women, and for her constructive and valuable criticism of my earlier work. On Marenholtz-Bülow see Bertha von Bülow-Wendhausen, *The Life of the Baroness von Marenholtz-Bülow*, 2 vols. (New York, 1901), 1:47–61. This personal reminiscence, written by a niece who worked intensively with Marenholtz, contains extensive excerpts from her journals. Henriette Goldschmidt, *Bertha von Marenholtz-Bülow: Ihr Leben und Wirken im Dienste der Erziehunglehre Friedrich Froebels* (Hamburg, 1896), 3–7, and Maria Müller, *Frauen im Dienste Froebels* (Leipzig, 1928), 3–95.

6. Johannes Prüfer and Josefine Siebe, *Henriette Goldschmidt: Ihr Leben und Ihr Schaffen* (Leipzig, 1922), 1–5. Johannes Prüfer worked closely with Goldschmidt in Leipzig, and much of this biography is based on personal conversations.

7. Mary Lyschinska, *Henriette Schrader-Breymann: Ihr Leben aus Briefen und Tagebüchern zusammengestellt und erläutert*, 2 vols. (Berlin and Leipzig, 1922), 1:1–64. This biography was written by Schrader-Breymann's student and coworker, and contains extensive excerpts from letters, diaries, and journals.

8. Wohlwill, "Charlotte Paulsen," 4–5; Liecks, "Charlotte Paulsen," 9–10, 5–7.

9. Bülow-Wendhausen, *The Life of the Baroness*, 1:77–82, 136; Goldschmidt, *Bertha von Marenholtz-Bülow*, 7–8; Ida Hahn-Hahn, *Gräfin Faustine* (Berlin, 1845), 244, quoted in Renate Möhrmann, *Die andere Frau: Emanzipationsansätze deutscher Schriftstellerinnen im Vorfeld der Achtundvierziger-Revolution* (Stuttgart, 1977), 105.

10. Bülow-Wendhausen, *The Life of the Baroness*, 1:113, 115; Goldschmidt, *Bertha von Marenholtz-Bülow*, 9.

11. For an extensive discussion and statistics on infant and child mortality, see Jürgen Schlumbohm, *Kinderstuben: Wie Kinder zu Bauern, Bürgern und Aristokraten wurden, 1700–1850* (Munich, 1983), 23–41; Caroline Rudolphi, "An eine trauernde Mutter," in *Gemälde weiblicher Erziehung*, 2 vols. (Heidelberg, 1915), 1:xxxix; Wohlwill, "Charlotte Paulsen," 6.

12. Kortmann, *Emilie Wüstenfeld*, 17–25.

13. Prüfer and Siebe, *Henriette Goldschmidt*, 14; Lyschinska, *Henriette Schrader-Breymann*, 1:23.

14. Lyschinska, *Henriette Schrader-Breymann*, 1:30–32

15. Malwida von Meysenbug, *Memoiren*, 1:45, 109; on religion and social consciousness see Prelinger, "Prelude to Consciousness: Amalie Sieveking and the Female Association for the Care of the Poor and Sick," in Fout, ed., *German Women in the Nineteenth Century*, 118–134.

16. Bülow-Wendhausen, *The Life of the Baroness*, 1:101, 136–137, 156.

17. Ibid., 1:121.

18. Ibid., 1:123. On Saint-Simonianism and its effects on German feminist authors see (among many other sources) Möhrmann, *Die andere Frau*, 30–39 and 60–117.

19. Ronge is quoted in Alexandra Lotz, "Die Erlösung des weiblichen Geschlechts: Frauen in deutschkatholischen Gemeinden," in Carola Lipp, ed., *Schimpfende Weiber und patriotische Jungfrauen: Frauen im Vormärz und in der Revolution 1848/49* (Baden-Baden, 1985), 235, 237; on German Catholicism, see Prelinger, *Charity, Challenge and Change*, 88–94 and passim. Because Prelinger has given such thorough attention to German Catholicism, I will treat it only briefly here.

20. Sabine Rumpel, "Thäterinnen der Liebe: Frauen in Wohltätigkeitsvereinen," in

Lipp, ed., *Schimpfende Weiber*, 310–338; Prelinger, "Prelude to Consciousness," 118–132.

21. For some information, unfortunately very brief, on Goldschmidt's life and other writings see Prelinger, *Charity, Challenge and Change*, 61–66.

22. Johanna Goldschmidt, *Rebekka und Amalie: Briefwechsel zwischen einer Israelitin und einer Adeligen über Zeit- und Lebensfragen* (Leipzig, 1847), 21, 25.

23. Kortmann, *Emilie Wüstenfeld*, 29; Wohlwill, "Charlotte Paulsen," 6–8. See also Prelinger, *Charity, Challenge and Change*, 79–104.

24. Bülow-Wendhausen, *The Life of the Baroness*, 1:153,136; see also Goldschmidt, *Bertha von Marenholtz-Bülow*, 7–10.

25. Prüfer and Siebe, *Henriette Goldschmidt*, 12–44.

26. Meysenbug, *Memoiren*, 1:139, 144, 145. On the influence of Feuerbach see also Prelinger, "Religious Dissent, Women's Rights and the Hamburg *Hochschule fur das weibliche Geschlecht* in Nineteenth-Century Germany," *Church History* 45 (1976): 43–52.

27. Lyschinska, *Henriette Schrader-Breymann*, 1:52–23, 64, 86.

28. Ibid., 1:60, 80. On the Rudolstadt convention see also Prelinger, *Charity, Challenge and Change*, 92–93, and Ann Taylor Allen, "Spiritual Motherhood: German Feminists and the Kindergarten Movement, 1848–1911," *History of Education Quarterly* (Fall 1982): 324–325.

29. Barbara Berg, *The Remembered Gate: Origins of American Feminism: The Woman and the City, 1800–1860* (New York, 1878), 268; Linda K. Kerber, *Women of the Republic: Intellect and Ideology in Revolutionary America* (Chapel Hill, N.C., 1980), 265–288; see also the comments of Prelinger, *Charity, Challenge and Change*, 169–172.

Chapter 3. Spiritual Motherhood and Revolution

1. *Frauen-Zeitung*, August 11, 1849, excerpted in Ute Gerhard, Elisabeth Hannover-Drück and Romina Schmitter, eds., *Dem Reich der Freiheit werb'ich Bürgerinnen: Die Frauen-Zeitung von Louise Otto* (Frankfurt, 1979), 127.

2. On varieties of feminist ideology see the introduction to Gerhard, Hannover-Drück and Schmitter, eds., *Dem Reich der Freiheit*, 18–19; and Ute Frevert, *Women in German History: From Bourgeois Emancipation to Sexual Liberation*, trans. Stuart McKinnon-Evans (Oxford, 1988), 73–82.

3. On preschool education see Sabine Rumpel, "Täterinnen der Liebe: Frauen in Wohltätigkeitsvereinen," in Carola Lipp, ed., *Schimpfende Weiber und patriotische Jungfrauen: Frauen im Vormärz und in der Revolution, 1848/49* (Baden-Baden, 1985), 206–231, and Gunnar Heinsohn, *Vorschulerziehung in der bürgerlichen Gesellschaft: Geschichte, Funktion, aktuelle Lage* (Frankfurt, 1974), 50–62.

4. On urban working-class childhood see Jürgen Schlumbohm, ed., *Kinderstuben: Wie Kinder zu Bauern, Bürgern, Aristokraten wurden, 1700–1850* (Munich, 1983), 213–302.

5. Ann Taylor Allen, "Gardens of Children, Gardens of God: Kindergartens and Day-Care Centers in Nineteenth-Century Germany," *Journal of Social History* 19 (Spring 1986): 433–437; many other sources are given in the notes to that article. See also

Günter Erning, Karl Neumann, and Jürgen Reyer, eds., *Geschichte des Kindergartens: Entstehung und Entwicklung der öffentlichen Kleinkinderziehung in Deutschland*, 2 vols. (Freiburg im Breisgau, 1987), 1:29–43 and 2:18–22, and Reyer, *Wenn die Mütter Arbeiten gingen . . . : Eine sozialhistorische Studie zur Entstehung der öffentlichen Kleinkinderziehung in Deutschland* (Cologne, 1983), 197–202. On Fliedner's pedagogy see Catherine N. Prelinger, *Charity, Challenge and Change: Religious Dimensions of the Mid Nineteenth-Century Women's Movement in Germany* (New York, 1987), 167–169. As kindergartens and day-care institutions were not parts of local public school systems, no systematic statistics were kept by state governments.

6. Prelinger, *Charity, Challenge and Change*, 92–93; Allen, "Spiritual Motherhood: German Feminists and the Kindergarten Movement, 1848–1911," *History of Education Quarterly* (Fall 1982): 324–325.

7. Mary Lyschinska, *Henriette Schrader-Breymann: Ihr Leben aus Briefen und Tagebüchern zusammengestellt und erläutert*, 2 vols. (Berlin and Leipzig, 1927), 1:80, 81.

8. For the text of the teachers' petition see Erika Hoffmann, *Vorschulerziehung in Deutschland: Historische Entwicklung im Abriss* (Witten, 1971), 97; Lyschinska, *Henriette Schrader-Breymann*, 1:81.

9. On the contrast between kindergarten and *Bewahranstalt* see Allen, "Gardens of Children, Gardens of God," 437–439; Breymann's criticism of Froebel's methods is in Lyschinska, *Henriette Schrader-Breymann*, 1:78.

10. Doris Lütkens, "Brief einer Mutter," in Doris Lütkens, ed., *Unsere Kinder: Vereinsschrift oder literarische Sprech-Saal fur Eltern, Lehrerinnen, Kindergärten-und Gärtnerinnen und Vorsteher von Kleinkinderschulen und Warteschulen jeder Art* (Hamburg, 1849), 186; Alwine Middendorff, "Kindergarten-Chronik des Instituts Lütkens in Hamburg," in Lütkens, ed., *Unsere Kinder*, 86.

11. Lütkens, "Der Kindergarten," in Lütkens, ed., *Unsere Kinder*, 32.

12. Wilhelm Middendorff, *Die Kindergärten: Bedürfnis der Zeit, Grundlage einigender Volksbildung: Der deutschen Nationalversammlung zur Würdigung vorgelegt* (Blankenburg bei Rudolstadt, 1848), 8–9, 14.

13. Middendorff, *Die Kindergärten*, 44. On German liberalism see Leonard Krieger, *The German Idea of Freedom: History of a Political Tradition* (Boston, 1957), 252–261.

14. Prelinger, *Charity, Challenge and Change*, 139–144; *Frauen-Zeitung*, May 4 and July 6, 1850, excerpted in Gerhard, Hannover-Drueck, and Schmitter, eds., *Dem Reich der Freiheit*, 251 and 282.

15. Jürgen Reulecke, *Sozialer Frieden durch soziale Reform: Der Centralverein für das Wohl der arbeitenden Klassen in der Frühindustrialisierung* (Wupperthal, 1982), 17–21.

16. Marie Kortmann, *Emilie Wüstenfeld, Eine Hamburger Bürgerin* (Hamburg, 1927), 27–32.

17. Prelinger, "Religious Dissent, Women's Rights and the Hamburg *Hochschule für das weibliche Geschlecht* in Nineteenth-Century Germany," *Church History* 45 (1976): 43–45; Prelinger, *Charity, Challenge and Change*, 95–100; Sabine Hering-Zalfen, "Uber die Schwierigkeit, eine Hochschule zu gründen," in *Sozialpadagogik im Wandel: Geschichte, Methoden, Entwicklungen* (Kassel, 1984), 65–68; Elke Kleinau,

"Die 'Hochschule für das weibliche Geschlecht' und ihre Auswirkungen auf die Entwicklung des höheren Mädchenchulwesens in Hamburg," *Zeitschrift für Pädagogik* 36 (1990): 121–126.

18. Diesterweg to Goldschmidt, 15 October 1849, reprinted in Hugo Gotthard Bloth, *Adolph Diesterweg: Sein Leben und Wirken für Pädagogik und Schule* (Heidelberg, 1966), 264; Prelinger, *Charity, Challenge and Change*, 93.

19. Malwida von Meysenbug, *Memoiren einer Idealistin*, 2 vols., in *Malwida von Meysenbugs Gesammelte Werke*, edited by Berta Schleicher, 5 vols. (Stuttgart, 1922), 1:186–187. For more on Meysenbug's role see Rudolf Kayser, "Malwida von Meysenbugs Hamburger Lehrjahre," *Zeitschrift des Vereins für hamburgische Geschichte*, 28 (1927): 117–127.

20. Carl Froebel and Johanna Froebel, geb. Kuestner, *Hochschulen für Mädchen und Kindergärten als Glieder einer vollständigen Bildungsanstalt, welche Erziehung der Familie und Unterricht an der Schule verbindet*, Hamburg, 1850, 1–7. This pamphlet and other materials relating to the *Hochschule* are held in Familienarchive, Nachlass Emilie Wüstenfeld, "Hamburger Bildungsverein deutscher Frauen und Hochschule für das weibliche Geschlecht," Staatsarchiv Hamburg. See also Prelinger, "Religious Dissent," and *Charity, Challenge and Change*, 128–134.

21. Carl Froebel, *Hochschulen für Mädchen*, 5; see also Reyer, *Wenn die Mütter arbeiten gingen*, 222–227.

22. Carl Froebel, *Hochschulen für Mädchen*, 1–7; on the Saint-Simonians and their theories of gender difference see Claire Goldberg Moses, *French Feminism in the Nineteenth Century* (Albany, 1984), 41–61.

23. Johanna Froebel, "Der Kindergarten in seiner sozialen Bedeutung," in *Hochschulen für Mädchen*, 25–42; Johanna Froebel to Amalie Sieveking, in *Hochschulen für Mädchen*, 48.

24. The curriculum of the *Hochschule* is outlined in "Höhere Bildungsanstalt für das weibliche Geschlecht in Hamburg," 7–8, Nachlass Emilie Wüstenfeld, vol. 5; Carl Froebel, *Hochschulen für Mädchen*, 11–18; Meysenbug, *Memoiren*, 1:194–196, 202–203; see also Prelinger, *Charity, Challenge and Change*, 97, and Kleinau, "Die 'Hochschule für das weibliche Geschlecht,'" 126–127.

25. Adolph Diesterweg, "Der Frauen-Verein in Hamburg," *Sämtliche Werke*, edited by Artur Buchenan, Eduard Spranger, and Hans Stettbacher, 10 vols. (Berlin, 1971), 9:142–154; on the forced closing see Hering Zalfen, "Uber die Schwierigkeit, eine Hochschule zu gründen," 71–73; Prelinger, "Religious Dissent," 53–55, and Kleinau, "Die 'Hochschule für das weibliche Geschlecht,'" 129–130.

26. On American women's colleges and teacher training see Helen Lefkowitz Horowitz, *Alma Mater: Design and Experience in the Women's Colleges from their Nineteenth-Century Beginnings to the 1930s* (New York, 1984), 9–27; on the absence of private colleges for women in Germany see James C. Albisetti, *Schooling German Girls and Women: Secondary and Higher Education in the Nineteenth Century* (Princeton, 1988), 199–203.

27. Gerhard, Hannover-Drück, and Schmitter, eds., *Dem Reich der Freiheit*, 18–19.

28. Louise Otto-Peters, *Frauenleben im deutschen Reich: Erinnerungen aus der Vergangenheit mit Hinweis auf der Gegenwart* (Leipzig, 1876), 15, 17; "Georgine" (real

name of correspondent is not known), *Frauen-Zeitung*, 18 August 1849, in Gerhard, Hannover-Drueck, and Schmitter, eds., *Dem Reich der Freiheit*, 132–133.

29. On Otto's ties to the German Catholics see Prelinger, *Charity, Challenge and Change*, 106–110; "Aufruf an die deutschen Frauen," *Frauen-Zeitung*, 22 December 1849, in Gerhard, Hannover-Drueck, and Schmitter, eds., *Dem Reich der Freiheit*, 189.

30. Lyschinska, *Henriette Schrader-Breymann*, 1:80.

31. On the Wüstenfeld and Traun divorces see Kortmann, *Emilie Wüstenfeld*, 40–41, and Prelinger, *Charity, Challenge and Change*, 64–65, 126–145; and Kleinau, "Die 'Hochschule für das weibliche Geschlecht,'" 129.

32. Johanna Froebel to Luise Dittmar, in Carl and Johanna Froebel, *Hochschulen für Mädchen*, 51–52.

33. Bertha von Bülow-Wendhausen, *The Life of the Baroness von Marenholtz-Bülow*, 2 vols. (New York, 1901) 1:132; Louise Otto, "Die Demokratinnen," *Frauen-Zeitung*, 22 December 1849, in Gerhard, Hannover-Drueck, and Schmitter, eds., *Dem Reich der Freiheit*, 202. On the response of female writers of the era to George Sand see also Renate Möhrmann, *Die andere Frau: Emanzipationsansätze deutscher Schriftstellerinnen im Vorfeld der Achtundvierziger-Revolution* (Stuttgart, 1977), 49–59.

34. Lyschinska, *Henriette Schrader-Breymann*, 1, 107.

35. Johanna Froebel to Luise Dittmar, in Karl and Johanna Froebel, *Hochschulen für Mädchen*, 52; Otto, *Frauen-Zeitung*, 21 April 1849, quoted in Gerhard, Hannover-Drueck, and Schmitter, eds., *Dem Reich der Freiheit*, 17.

36. Linda K. Kerber, *Women of the Republic: Intellect and Ideology in Revolutionary America* (Chapel Hill, 1980), 265–288.

37. "Declaration of Sentiments," in Alice S. Rossi, ed., *The Feminist Papers From Adams to de Beauvoir* (New York, 1974), 417, 419; Ellen Carol DuBois, *Feminism and Suffrage: The Emergence of an Independent Women's Movement in America, 1848–1969* (Ithaca, N.Y., 1978), 21–52.

Chapter 4. The Great Social Household

1. Donald K. Rohr, *The Origins of Social Liberalism in Germany* (Chicago, 1963), 158–164; Thomas Nipperdey, *Deutsche Geschichte, 1800–1866: Bürgerwelt und starker Staat* (Munich, 1983), 718–732; James J. Sheehan, *German Liberalism in the Nineteenth Century* (Chicago, 1978), 79–122.

2. Fritzi Liecks, "Charlotte Paulsen, geb. Thornton," in *100-Jahr-Feier in der Charlotte Paulsen Schule* (Hamburg, 1949), 10; Elke Kleinau, "Die 'Hochschule für das weibliche Geschlecht' und ihre Auswirkungen auf die Entwicklung des höheren Mädchenschulwesens in Hamburg," *Zeitschrift für Pädagogik* 36 (1990): 130–132.

3. Liecks, "Charlotte Paulsen," 10, 14–15; see also other materials in "Schule des Paulsen-Stifts," Staatsarchiv Hamburg; cf. Catherine N. Prelinger, *Charity, Challenge and Change: Religious Dimensions of the Mid-Nineteenth-Century Women's Movement in Germany* (Westport, Conn., 1987), 84–85.

4. Bertha von Bülow-Wendhausen, *The Life of the Baroness Marenholtz-Bülow*, 2 vols. (New York, 1901), 1:159, 158–162; Bertha von Marenholtz-Bülow, *Reminiscences of Friedrich Froebel*, trans. Mary Mann (Boston, 1877), 1–2.

5. Marenholtz-Bülow, *Reminiscences*, 2, 3.

6. Bülow-Wendhausen, *The Life of the Baroness*, 1:226; Adolph Diesterweg to Johanna Goldschmidt, 15 October 1849, reprinted in Hugo Gotthard Bloth, *Adolf Diesterweg: Sein Leben und Wirken für Pädagogik und Schule* (Heidelberg, 1966), 264. See also Henriette Goldschmidt, *Bertha von Marenholtz-Bülow: Ihr Leben und Wirken im Dienste der Erziehungslehre Friedrich Froebels* (Hamburg, 1896), 41.

7. Bülow-Wendhausen, *The Life of the Baroness*, 1:193; Marenholtz-Bülow, *Reminiscences*, 130–131.

8. Louise Otto, *Das Recht der Frauen auf Erwerb: Blicke auf das Frauenleben der Gegenwart* (Hamburg, 1866), 99; Marenholtz-Bülow, *Reminiscences of Friedrich Froebel*, 197–201. On police repression of kindergartens and other educational institutions see Prelinger, *Charity, Challenge and Change*, 161–165; Ann Taylor Allen, "Spiritual Motherhood: German Feminists and the Kindergarten Movement" *History of Education Quarterly* 22 (Fall 1982): 325–326; and Allen, "Gardens of Children, Gardens of God: Kindergartens and Day-Care Centers in Nineteenth-Century Germany," *Journal of Social History* 19 (Spring 1985): 440.

9. On Wüstenfeld's problems during this period see Marie Kortmann, *Emilie Wüstenfeld, Eine Hamburger Bürgerin* (Hamburg, 1927), 53, and Prelinger, *Charity, Challenge and Change*, 163; Otto-Peters, *Das Recht der Frauen auf Erwerb*, 99; *Kladderadatsch* 3, no. 36 (1851): 142.

10. Wilhelm Heinrich Riehl, *Die Familie* (Stuttgart, 1855), 349; "Predigt zur Jahresfeier des Vereins für die Beförderung der Klein-Kinder-Bewahranstalten," 13 November 1854, in Zentrales Staatsarchiv, Rep. 191, nr. 17, Ministerium für Volkswohlfahrt, Erziehungsanstalten und Vereine, Merseburg. On other educational measures of the 1850s see Hans-Georg Herrlitz, Wulf Hopf, and Hartmut Titze, *Deutsche Schulgeschichte von 1800 zur Gegenwart: eine Einführung* (Frankfurt, 1981), 30–58.

11. Bülow-Wendhausen, *The Life of the Baroness*, 1:206–207, 217, 219; and Marenholtz-Bülow, *Reminiscences*, 288–297.

12. Bülow-Wendhausen, *The Life of the Baroness Marenholtz-Bülow*, 1:226, 231. For more stories of traveling women see Wulf Wülfing, "On Travel Literature by Women in the Nineteenth Century: Malwida von Meysenbug," in Mary Jo Maynes and Ruth-Ellen Joeres, eds., *German Women in the Eighteenth and Nineteenth Centuries: A Social and Literary History* (Bloomington, Ind., 1986), 289–304.

13. Bülow-Wendhausen, *The Life of the Baroness*, 1:236, 234, 238; see also Marenholtz-Bülow, *Die Arbeit und die neue Erziehung nach Froebels Methode* (Berlin, 1864), 414–419.

14. Goldschmidt, *Bertha von Marenholtz-Bülow*, 50; Allen, "Spiritual Motherhood," 326.

15. Marenholtz-Bülow, *Die Arbeit und die neue Erziehung*, 7, 60–65; Nipperdey, *Deutsche Geschichte*, 739. Marenholtz's ideas on education may be compared to those of some of the utopian socialists; for example Charles Fourier, *Le Nouveau Monde Industriel et Sociétaire*, introduction by Michel Butor (Paris, 1973), 214–251; and Jonathan Beecher, *Charles Fourier: The Visionary and His World* (Berkeley, 1986), 260–266.

16. Marenholtz-Bülow, *Die Arbeit und die neue Erziehung*, 30; Rohr, *Social Liberalism*, 158–161.

17. Marenholtz-Bülow, *Women's Educational Mission: Being an Explanation of Froebel's System of Infant Gardens* (London, 1855), 3, 80. On women teachers in girls' secondary schools see James C. Albisetti, "Could Separate be Equal? Helene Lange and Women's Education in Imperial Germany," *History of Education Quarterly* 22 (Fall 1982): 301-318.

18. Marenholtz-Bülow, *Die Arbeit und die neue Erziehung*, 339.

19. On the Society for Popular Education see Bülow-Wendhausen, *The Life of the Baroness*, 1:370-371; Jürgen Reulecke, *Sozialer Frieden durch soziale Reform: Der Centralverein für das Wohl der arbeitenden Klassen in der Frühindustrialisierung* (Wupperthal, 1983), 248-260; Günter Erning, Karl Neumann, and Jürgen Reyer, eds., *Geschichte des Kindergartens: Entstehung und Entwicklung der öffentlichen Kleinkinderziehung in Deutschland*, 2 vols. (Freiburg im Breisgau, 1987), 1:50-52.

20. The history of the school at Watzum is recounted in Arnold Breymann, *Festschrift zum 50-jährigen Bestehen des Breymannschen Instituts* (Braunschweig, 1906), 9-14.

21. The memoirs of Mary Lyschinska are excerpted in Breymann, *Festschrift*, 65-71 (quotation 67); on Breymann's attitude toward practical tasks see Breymann, *Festschrift*, 18; and Henriette Schrader-Breymann, "Die Hauswirtschaftliche Bildung der Mädchen in den ärmeren Klassen," in *Kleine Pädagogische Texte* (Berlin, 1930), 30, 63-65

22. Breymann, *Festschrift*, 11-15.

23. Breymann, *Festschrift*, 25-26, 23. On the school at Neu-Watzum and its significance, see James C. Albisetti, *Schooling German Girls and Women: Secondary and Higher Education in the Nineteenth Century* (Princeton, 1988), 66.

24. Hedwig Heyl, *Aus Meinem Leben* (Berlin, 1925), 5, 7; Heyl's letters from school are also quoted in Breymann, *Festschrift*, 81-92.

25. Albisetti, *Schooling German Girls and Women*, 58-92.

26. Luise Büchner, *Die Frauen und Ihr Beruf* (Frankfurt, 1856), 97.

27. Wilhelm Heinrich Riehl, *Die Familie* (Stuttgart, 1855), 323-351; Büchner, *Die Frauen und ihr Beruf*, 117.

28. Miriam Gurko, *The Ladies of Seneca Falls: The Birth of the Women's Rights Movement* (New York, 1974), 108-207; Ellen Carol DuBois, *Feminism and Suffrage: The Emergence of an Independent Women's Movement in America, 1848-1868* (Ithaca, N.Y., 1978), 21-52; Kathryn Kish Sklar, *Catharine Beecher: A Study in American Domesticity* (New Haven, 1973); Nancy Hoffman, *Woman's True Profession: Voices from the History of Teaching* (Old Westbury, N.Y., 1981), 3-5, 36-45.

29. Jenny Hirsch, *Geschichte der 25-jährigen Wirksamkeit 1866 bis 1891 des unter dem Protektorat Ihrer Majestät der Kaiserin und Königin stehenden Lette-Vereins zur Förderung höherer Bildung und Erwerbsfähigkeit des weiblichen Geschlechts* (Berlin, 1891), 14.

Chapter 5. Mothers of the Nation

1. Henriette Goldschmidt, *Die Frauenfrage innerhalb der modernen Culturentwicklung: Vortrag gehalten zur Eröffnung des Frauentages zu Hannover am 17 September, 1877* (Hannover, 1877), 14.

2. Richard Evans, *The Feminist Movement in Germany 1894–1933* (London, 1976), 26–27; Herrad-Ulrike Bussemer, *Frauenemanzipation und Bildungsbürgertum: Sozialgeschichte der Frauenbewegung in der Reichsgründungszeit* (Weinheim, 1985), 169–185, 250; Dietlinde Peters, *Mütterlichkeit im Kaiserreich: Die bürgerliche Frauenbewegung und der soziale Beruf der Frau* (Bielefeld, 1984); Jürgen Reyer, *Wenn die Mütter arbeiten gingen . . . : Eine sozialhistorische Studie zur Entstehung der öffentlichen Kleinkinderziehung in Deutschland im 19. Jahrhundert* (Cologne, 1983).

3. David Blackbourn and Geoff Eley, *The Peculiarities of German History: Bourgeois Society and Politics in Nineteenth-Century Germany* (Oxford, 1984), 190–206.

4. Luise Otto, *Das Recht der Frauen auf Erwerb: Blicke auf das Frauenleben der Gegenwart* (Hamburg, 1866). On the employment crisis see Bussemer, *Frauenemanzipation*, 49–53; and Elisabeth Meyer-Renschhausen, *Weibliche Kultur und soziale Arbeit: Eine Geschichte der Frauenbewegung am Beispiel Bremens, 1810–1927* (Cologne, 1989), 73–106.

5. Louise Otto-Peters, *Das erste Vierteljahrhundert des allgemeinen deutschen Frauenvereins, gegründet am 18. Oktober in Leipzig* (Leipzig, 1890), 3–13 (quotation p. 5); Jenny Hirsch, *Geschichte der 25jährigen Wirksamkeit der unter dem Protektorat Ihrer Majestät der Kaiserin und Königin Friedrich stehenden Lette-Vereins zur Förderung höherer Bildung- und Erwerbsfähigkeit des weiblichen Geschlechts* (Berlin, 1891); Anna Plothow, *Die Begründerinnen der deutschen Frauenbewegung* (Leipzig, 1907) 45–60; Bussemer, *Frauenemanzipation*, 101–123; James C. Albisetti, *Schooling German Girls and Women: Secondary and Higher Education in the Nineteenth Century* (Princeton, 1988), 99–104.

6. On status of child-care workers, see Otto, *Das Recht der Frauen auf Erwerb*, 26; Jeanne-Marie von Gayette-Georgens, *Die Frauen in Erwerb und Beruf: Zwölf Vorträge* (Berlin, 1872), 140–141.

7. On Goldschmidt's career see "Johanna Goldschmidt," *Hamburger Zeitung*, 10 November 1910. Her seminar is described in her yearly reports in Hamburger Froebel-Verein, Boxes 861–862, Staatsarchiv Hamburg. On kindergarten training see Dr. Franz, *Die Berufswahl der Frau* (Görlitz, 1877), 99–110; and Ann Taylor Allen, "Spiritual Motherhood: German Feminists and the Kindergarten Movement," *History of Education Quarterly* 22 (Fall 1982): 329.

8. Goldschmidt is quoted in "Johanna Goldschmidt"; on status of trained governesses see Goldschmidt, "Bericht über die Tätigkeit des Hamburger Fröbel-Vereins," *Der Frauen-Anwalt* 4 (1873):149; Gayette-Georgens, *Die Frauen im Erwerb und Beruf*, 142.

9. Hedwig Heyl, *Aus meinem Leben* (Berlin, 1925), 16, 20.

10. Marie Kortmann, *Emilie Wüstenfeld: Eine Hamburger Bürgerin* (Hamburg, 1927), 101–106; Margarete Schecker, *Die Entwicklung der Mädchenberufsschule* (Weinheim, 1963), 56–58; quotation from Wüstenfeld is from *Der Frauen-Anwalt*, 1878, cited in Schecker, *Entwicklung*, 56. See also Albisetti, *Schooling German Girls and Women*, 99–104.

11. Johannes Prüfer and Josefine Siebe, *Henriette Goldschmidt: Ihr Leben und ihr Schaffen* (Leipzig, 1922), 45–48; on use of biographies and autobiographies, see chapter 2 above.

12. Goldschmidt's speech on the Prussian-Austrian War is reported in *Neue Bahnen* 1 (1866): 117; Otto-Peters, "Frauenpflichten im Kriege," *Neue Bahnen* 1 (1866): 110.

13. Prufer and Siebe, *Henriette Goldschmidt*, 55–56.

14. Henriette Goldschmidt, *Die Frau in Zusammenhang mit dem Volks- und Staatsleben* (Leipzig, 1871), 1–30. This is a speech that she delivered before the Women's Organization of Kassel; Louise Otto, "Krieg," *Neue Bahnen* 5 (1870): 122; see also "Sieg," *Neue Bahnen* 5 (1870): 138; Heinrich von Treitschke, *Politics*, edited by Hans Kohn (New York, 1963), 115. Contrast between Otto and Goldschmidt is in Bussemer, *Frauenemanzipation*, 185.

15. Goldschmidt, "Die Frau im Zusammenhang mit dem Volks- und Staatsleben," 18, 28; Otto-Peters, "Sieg," 122.

16. Goldschmidt, *Die Frauenfrage eine Kulturfrage*, 14; Otto-Peters, *Das erste Vierteljahrhundert*, 35.

17. Bussemer, *Frauenemanzipation*, 241–250; on the opposition to women in welfare agencies see Christoph Sachsse, *Mütterlichkeit als Beruf: Sozialarbeit, Sozialreform und Frauenbewegung, 1871–1929* (Frankfurt, 1985), 146 and Meyer-Renschhausen, *Weibliche Kultur*, 120–126.

18. On the decision of the German Women's Association to take up the cause of legal reform see Emilie Kempin, *Die Stellung der Frau nach den zur Zeit in Deutschland gültigen Gesetzes-Bestimmungen sowie nach dem Entwurf eines Bürgerlichen Gesetzbuches für das deutsche Reich* (Leipzig, 1892), e.

19. Otto-Peters is quoted in Kempin, *Die Stellung der Frau*, i; Charlotte Pape, "Die Rechte der Mütter auf ihre Kinder," *Neue Bahnen* 11 (1876): 9–12, quotation 11; the petition is quoted in Otto-Peters, *Das erste Vierteljahrhudert*, 37.

20. Margrit Twellmann, *Die deutsche Frauenbewegung: Ihre Anfänge und erste Entwicklung, Quellen, 1843–1889*, 2 vols. (Meisenheim, 1972), 2:207.

21. Otto-Peters is quoted in Kempin, *Die Stellung der Frau*, h.

22. On the statistics on kindergartens and training schools see Franz, *Berufswahl der Frau*, 100–102; and Reyer, "Entwicklung der Trägerstruktur in der öffentlichen Kleinkinderziehung," in Günter Erning, Karl Neumann, and Jürgen Reyer, eds., *Geschichte des Kindergartens*, 2 vols. (Freiburg, 1987), 2:40–68; for an outline of the Froebel societies' petition see 103; see also Allen, "Gardens of Children, Gardens of God," *Journal of Social History* 19, no. 3 (Spring 1986): 443.

23. Auguste Weyrowitz, *Wer hilft der Mutter ihre erziehliche Aufgabe zu lösen?* (Berlin, 1871), 26–27; Lina Morgenstern, *Das Paradies der Kindheit: Lehrbuch für Mütter, Kindergärtnerinnen und Erzieherinnen* (Regensburg, 1904), 53.

24. Morgenstern, *Paradies*, 56; Bertha Meyer, *Von der Wiege bis zur Schule an der Hand Friedrich Froebels* (Berlin, 1884), 182, 287.

25. Morgenstern, *Paradies*, 38; Weyrowitz, *Wer hilft der Mutter*, 31.

26. Wilhelm Liebknecht, *Wissen ist Macht—Macht ist Wissen und andere bildungspolitische Ausserungen*, edited by Hans Brumme (Berlin, 1968), 123; on Liebknecht's relationship to Carl Froebel see Raymond H. Dominick, *Wilhelm Liebknecht and the Founding of the German Social Democratic Party* (Chapel Hill, N.C., 1982), 24–27.

27. Adolf Douai, *Kindergarten und Volksschule als sozialdemokratische Anstalten* (Leipzig, 1876), 1976; August Bebel, *Die Frau in der Vergangenheit, Gegenwart und*

Zukunft (Zurich, 1883), 182; see also Ulrich Bendele, *Sozialdemokratische Schulpolitik und Pädagogik im wilhelminischen Deutschland: Eine sozialhistorisch-empirische Analyse* (Frankfurt, 1979), 21–27.

28. Johannes Hubener, "Das Verhältnis des Kindergartens zur christlichen Kleinkinderschule," (Gotha, 1888), 264, quoted in Erning, ed., *Quellen zur Geschichte der öffentlichen Kleinkinderziehung. Von den ersten Bewahranstalten bis zur vorschulischen Erziehung der Gegenwart* (Kastellaun and Saarbrücken, 1976), 136; Adolph Freiherr von Bissing-Beerberg, *Die grundlegende und gemeindepflegende christliche Kleinkinderschule, nicht nur nützlich, sondern nothwendig* (Leipzig, 1874); see also Heike Flessner, *Untertanenzucht oder Menschenerziehung? Zur Entwicklung öffentlicher Kleinkinderziehung auf dem Lande* (Weinheim and Basel, 1971); and Allen, "Come, Let Us Live with Our Children: Kindergarten Movements in Germany and America," *History of Education Quarterly* 28 (Spring 1988): 41–43.

29. Philipp Nathusius-Ludom, *Zur "Frauenfrage"* (Halle, 1871), 78; Hedwig Dohm, *Was die Pastoren denken* (Berlin, 1872; reprinted Zürich, 1986), 37.

30. On Marenholtz's institute in Dresden, see Bertha von Bülow-Wendhausen, *The Life of the Baroness von Marenholtz-Bülow*, 2 vols. (New York, 1901) 2:474–504.

31. Ruth M. Baylor, *Elizabeth Palmer Peabody, Kindergarten Pioneer* (Philadelphia, 1965), 103–104; on Peabody's background and ideas see Bruce Ronda, ed., *Letters of Elizabeth Peabody, American Renaissance Woman* (Middletown, Conn., 1984); see also Allen, "Come, Let Us Live with Our Children"; on roles of Boelte and Marwedel see Michael Steven Shapiro, *Child's Gardens: The Kindergarten Movement from Froebel to Dewey* (University Park, Penna., 1983), 29–45.

32. Otto-Peters, *Der Frauen-Anwalt* 6 (1875–76), 288, quoted in Twellmann, *Die deutsche Frauenbewegung*, 1:207; on American suffrage movement see Ellen Carol DuBois, *Feminism and Suffrage: The Emergence of an Independent Women's Movement in America, 1848–1868* (Ithaca, N.Y., 1978), 79–202.

33. On the development of organic views of society among American feminists of this era see William Leach, *True Love and Perfect Union: The Feminist Reform of Sex and Society* (New York, 1980), 133–174, quotation 333; and David P. Thelen, *The New Citizenship: The Origins of Progressivism in Wisconsin, 1885–1900* (Columbia, Mo., 1972). On comparisons between views of the state among European and American feminists see Karen Offen, "Liberty, Equality and Justice for Women: The Theory and Practice of Feminism in Nineteenth-Century Europe," in Renate Bridenthal, Claudia Koonz, and Susan Stuard, eds., *Becoming Visible: Women in European History* (Boston, 1987), 335–375.

Chapter 6. Mothers of the City

1. Henriette Goldschmidt, *Die Frauenfrage innerhalb der modernen Culturentwicklung, Vortrag gehalten zur Eröffnung des Frauentages zu Hannover, September, 1877* (Hannover, 1877), 14.

2. On attitudes to city life and social problems see Andrew Lees, *Cities Perceived: Urban Society in European and American Thought* (New York, 1985).

3. Christoph Sachsse, *Mütterlichkeit als Beruf: Sozialarbeit, Sozialreform und Frauenbewegung, 1871–1929* (Frankfurt, 1985), 17–94; on liberalism see Peter Gilg,

Die Erneuerung des demokratischen Denkens im wilhelminischen Deutschland (Wiesbaden, 1969), 88–137 and James J. Sheehan, *German Liberalism in the Nineteenth Century* (Chicago, 1978), 250–255; Louise Otto-Peters *Frauenleben im deutschen Reich, Erinnerungen aus der Vergangenheit mit Hinweis auf der Gegenwart* (Leipzig, 1876), 15–18.

4. Lina Morgenstern, *Der Beruf des Weibes* (Berlin, 1871), 30; Jeanne-Marie Gayette-Georgens, *Die Frauen im Erwerb und Beruf* (Berlin, 1872), 102; Henriette Schrader-Breymann, *Pädagogische Schriften*, in *Kleine Pädagogische Texte*, 5 vols. (Berlin, 1930), 5:22. On women in community service see Amy Hackett, "The German Women's Movement and Suffrage, 1890–1914: A Study of National Feminism," in Robert J. Bezucha, ed., *Modern European Social History* (Lexington, Mass., 1972), 354–386; Dietlinde Peters, *Mütterlichkeit im Kaiserreich: Die bürgerliche Frauenbewegung und der soziale Beruf der Frau* (Bielefeld, 1984), 168–172; Jürgen Reyer, *Wenn die Mütter arbeiten gingen . . . : Eine sozialhistorische Studie zur Entstehung der öffentlichen Kleinkinderziehung im 19. Jahrhundert in Deutschland* (Cologne, 1983), 154–158; and Ute Frevert, *Women in German History: From Bourgeois Emancipation to Sexual Liberation*, trans. Stuart Mc-Kinnon-Evans (Oxford, 1988), 102–106.

5. On Schrader-Breymann's career in Wolfenbüttel see Arnold Breymann, *Festschrift zum 50-jährigen Bestehens des Breymannschen Instituts* (Braunschweig, 1906), 29–35; and Martha Genzmer, *Anna Vorwerk: Ein Lebensbild* (Wolffenbüttel, 1910), 49–55; on her marriage to Karl Schrader see Mary Lyschinska, *Henriette Schrader-Breymann: Ihr Leben aus Briefen und Tagebüchern zusammengestellt und erläutert*, 2 vols. (Berlin and Leipzig, 1922).

6. Schrader-Breymann, *Pädagogische Schriften*, 10; Lyschinska, *Henriette Schrader-Breymann*, 2:114.

7. Gayette-Georgens, *Die Frauen*, 102; Schrader-Breymann, *Padagogische Schriften*, 27; Schrader-Breymann, *Der Volkskindergarten im Pestalozzi-Froebel Haus* (Berlin, 1890), 30.

8. On the early history of the Pestalozzi-Froebel House and the acquisition of the building on Steinmetzstrasse see Lyschinska, *Henriette Schrader-Breymann*, 2:1–30.

9. Hedwig Heyl, *Aus Meinem Leben* (Berlin, 1925), 29–33; Schrader-Breymann, *Volkskindergarten*, 1–3.

10. Clara Richter, "Das erweiterte Gruppensystem im Pestalozzi-Froebel Haus," *Vereins-Zeitung des Pestalozzi-Froebel Hauses* 5 (January 1890): 4–7, and Richter, *Bilder aus dem Kinderleben des Pestalozzi-Froebel Hauses* (Berlin, 1904), 29–47. For another account see Günter Erning, Karl Neumann, and Jürgen Reyer, eds., *Geschichte des Kindergartens: Enstehung und Entwicklung der öffentlichen Kleinkinderziehung in Deutschland*, 2 vols. (Freiburg im Breisgau, 1987), 1:54–57.

11. On domestic occupations in kindergarten see Richter, *Bilder aus dem Kinder-Leben*, 29–47; on monthly lesson plan see Schrader-Breymann, *Volkskindergarten*, 19–25; On small-town attitudes of American reformers, see Brenda Kurtz Shelton, *Reformers in Search of Yesterday: Buffalo in the 1890's* (Albany, N.Y., 1976).

12. The organization of the administration is described in Schrader, *Volkskindergarten*, 3–5.

13. Selma Althoff, *Henriette Schrader und das Pestalozzi-Froebel Haus* (Berlin, 1898), 17; Lyschinska, *Henriette Schrader-Breymann*, 2:16–17; comment on Richter is

in Hildegard von Gierke, "Aus der Geschichte des Pestalozzi-Froebel Hauses," unpub. typescript, n.d., Archive of the Pestalozzi-Froebel Haus, West Berlin.

14. Wollfheim is quoted in von Gierke, "Aus der Geschichte des Pestalozzi-Froebel Hauses." On relationships between women of this era see Carroll Smith-Rosenberg, "The Female World of Love and Ritual: Relations between Women in Nineteenth-Century America," *Signs* 1 (Autumn 1975): 1–29.

15. Linda K. Kerber, "Separate Spheres, Female Worlds, Women's Place: The Rhetoric of Women's History," *Journal of American History* 75 (June 1988): 34. Compare accounts of women's colleges as female communities in Helen Lefkowitz Horowitz, *Alma Mater: Design and Experience in the Women's Colleges from their Nineteenth-Century Beginnings to the 1930s* (Boston, 1984). For male accounts of secondary-school experience see James C. Albisetti, *Secondary-School Reform in Imperial Germany* (Princeton, 1983), 36–56.

16. Purpose of the Pestalozzi-Froebel House was stated in Schrader-Breymann, *Der Volkskindergarten*, 3; Lyschinska, *Henriette Schrader-Breymann*, 2:16.

17. On Marie Ernst and her approach to cooking see Heyl, "Marie Ernst," in *Bahnbrechende Frauen: herausgegeben auf Anlass der Ausstellung "Die Frau im Haus und Beruf" vom deutschen Lyzeum-Club* (Berlin 1912), 142–151; Heyl, *ABC der Küche* (first edition Berlin 1892; 10th ed. Berlin, 1910); Heyl, "Ansprache bei der Versammlung der Mütter der Volksschülerinnen," *Vereins-Zeitung des Pestalozzi-Froebel Hauses* 15 (July 1900): 2–3.

18. Heyl, "Die Bildungsanstalt für Hauswirtschaft im Pestalozzi-Froebel Haus," in *Vereins-Zeitung des Pestalozzi-Froebel Hauses* 12 (April 1897): 53; see also Margarete Schecker, *Die Entwicklung der Mädchenberufsschule* (Weinheim, 1963), 89–107.

19. On Karl Schrader's philanthropic activities see the various materials in Nachlass Karl Schrader, 240, N I, nr.1; N IV, nr.2; N V, nr. 12; N VII, nr. 2, vol. 2, Niedersächsisches Staatsarchiv, Wolfenbüttel; on Jessen see "Luise Jessen: Gedenkblatt gewidmet von dem Berliner Verein für Ferienkolonien," in Nachlass Karl Schrader, 240, N I, nr. 5 and "Luise Jessen" in *Bachnbrechende Frauen*, 133–136. Compare accounts of urban reform movements in Klaus Bergmann, *Agrarromantik und Grosstadtfeindschaft* (Meisenheim, 1970), 135–163; and Lees, *Cities Perceived*, 82–90 and 142–149.

20. Heyl, *Aus Meinem Leben*, 62–64, and Heyl, "Das neue Pestalozzi-Froebel Haus," *Vereins-Zeitschrift des Pestalozzi-Froebel Hauses* 12 (January 1897): 3–4.

21. On the political beliefs and activities of the Schrader-Barth circle see Gilg, *Die Erneuerung des demokratischen Gedankens*, 88–137; and Sheehan, *German Liberalism*, 204–271; on feminism and liberalism see Hackett, "The German Women's Movement and Suffrage, 1890–1914," 362–363.

22. Helene Lange, *Lebenserinnerungen* (Berlin, 1930), 136.

23. Heyl, *Aus Meinem Leben*, 22; Schrader-Breymann, *Pädagogische Schriften*, 114. On Bismarck's social insurance program see Florian Tennstedt, *Sozialgeschichte der Sozialpolitik in Deutschland, vom 18 Jahrhundert bis zum Ersten Weltkrieg* (Göttingen, 1981), 137–151.

24. Lange, *Lebenserinnerungen*, 25–48.

25. Ibid., 111–112.

26. *Die Hohere Mädchenschule und ihre Bestimmung* (Berlin, 1887), 19. On the his-

tory and significance of this pamphlet see James C. Albisetti, "Could Separate be Equal? Helene Lange and Women's Education in Imperial Germany," *History of Education Quarterly* 22 (Fall 1982): 301–318.

27. *Die Hohere Mädchenschule*, 26, 23; on the response of the Prussian Ministry see Albisetti, "Could Separate be Equal?" 306.

28. On the struggle for female secondary and higher education, see James C. Albisetti, *Schooling German Girls and Women: Secondary and Higher Education in the Nineteenth Century* (Princeton, 1988), 136–167.

29. Lyschinska, *Henriette Schrader-Breymann*, 2:32–33; Heyl, *Aus Meinem Leben*, 29–32; Bertha von der Lage, *Kaiserin Friedrich und ihr Wirken für Vaterland und Volk* (Gera, 1888), 19–49; on Victoria's plans for female education see Lange, *Lebenserinnerungen*, 140–141, and Albisetti, *Schooling German Girls and Women*, 156–157.

30. Elizabeth Harrison, *Sketches along Life's Road*, edited by Carolyn Sherwin Bailey (Boston, 1930): 120–122.

31. G. Stanley Hall, "The Pedagogy of the Kindergarten," in *Educational Problems*, 2 vols. (New York, 1911), 1:16–17. On the exhibition at the Chicago World's Fair in 1893 see "The Exhibit of the Pestalozzi-Froebel House of Berlin," *Kindergarten Magazine* 6 (1893–94): 8–12, and Paul Nathan, "Uber Grotemeyers Kinderbilder," *Die Nation*, 25 November 1893; see also Ann Taylor Allen, "Come, Let Us Live with Our Children: Kindergarten Movements in Germany and the United States, 1840–1914," *History of Education Quarterly* 28 (Spring 1988): 23–46, and Michael Steven Shapiro, *Child's Garden: The Kindergarten Movement from Froebel to Dewey* (University Park, Penn., 1983), 107–130 and 151–193.

32. *Die Gleichheit* 4 (1894): 23; *Die Gleichheit* 2 (1892): 140. quoted in Anna-E. Freier, *"Dem Reich der Freiheit sollst Du Kinder gebären": Der Antifeminismus der proletarischen Frauenbewegung im Spiegel der "Gleichheit", 1891–1917* (Frankfurt, 1981), 66, 67.

33. Schrader-Breymann quoted in Lyschinska, *Henriette Schrader-Breymann*, 2:566; on Schrader's later career see Hugo Preuss, "Karl Schrader als Politiker," *Die Hilfe*, 15 May 1915, and obituaries in Nachlass Karl Schrader, 240, N I, nr. 4. See also Dieter Düding, *Der Nationalsoziale Verein, 1896–1903: Der gescheiterte Versuch einer parteipolitischen Synthese von Nationalismus, Sozialismus und Liberalismus* (Munich, 1972), 180–193.

34. *Dritter Jahresbericht des Vereins fur Volkskindergärten* (Frankfurt, 1899), 1–2; "Bericht aus einem schlesischen Kindergarten," *Vereins-Zeitung des Pestalozzi-Froebel Hauses* 20 (January 1905): 5.

35. Käthe Heintze, "Beitrage zur Geschichte des deutschen Kindergartens," unpub. ms. n.d., Archive of the Pestalozzi-Froebel House; *Die Hilfe*, 5 April 1903. On status of kindergarten teachers see Allen, "Spiritual Motherhood: German Feminists and the Kindergarten Movement, 1840–1914," *History of Education Quarterly* 22 (Fall 1982): 336, and Helene Lange and Gertrud Bäumer, eds., *Handbuch der Frauenbewegung*, 5 vols. (Berlin, 1906), 4:189

36. Plothow, *Begründerinnen*, 105; Johannes Prufer and Josefine Siebe, *Henriette Goldschmidt: Ihr Leben und ihr Schaffen* (Leipzig, 1922), 156–160.

37. Prüfer and Siebe, *Henriette Goldschmidt*, 111–112; text of petition, 112. A text

of this petition is also held in the Archiv des Bundes deutscher Frauenvereine, 10/1, Karton 48, "Bildungs- und Erziehungsfragen," Deutsches Zentralinstitut für soziale Fragen, Berlin.

38. The response of the teachers' convention and Beetz's pamphlet are extensively quoted in Prüfer and Siebe, *Henriette Goldschmidt*, 120–129. The response of the Saxon government is the only response to this petition that has been preserved; "Königlich-Sächsisches Ministerium des Kultus und öffentlichen Unterrichts an Frau Auguste Schmidt," 26 August 1899, Archiv des Bundes deutscher Frauenvereine, 10/1, Karton 48, "Bildungs- und Erziehungsfragen. See also Reyer, *Wenn die Mütter arbeiten gingen*, 196–203.

39. Richard J. Evans, *The Feminist Movement in Germany, 1894–1933* (London, 1976), 30; on comparisons between German and American kindergarten movements see Allen, "Come, Let Us Live with Our Children."

40. Allen, "Come, Let Us Live with Our Children," 40–47. For a discussion of the relationship between equal-rights and "relational" feminism see Karen Offen, "Defining Feminism: A Comparative Historical Approach," *Signs* 14 (Autumn 1988): 118–157.

Chapter 7. Mothers, Children, and the Law

1. On the new code see Michael John, *Politics and the Law in Late Nineteenth-Century Germany: The Origins of the Civil Code* (New York, 1989).

2. On the development of new organizations see Barbara Greven-Aschoff, *Die bürgerliche Frauenbewegung in Deutschland, 1894–1933* (Göttingen, 1981), 87–107.

3. Bärbel Clemens, *"Menschenrechte haben kein Geschlecht: Zum Politikverständnis der bürgerlichen Frauenbewegung* (Pfaffenweiler, 1988), 119–130; see also Greven-Aschoff, *Die Bürgerliche Frauenbewegung*, 94–95; Richard J. Evans, *The Feminist Movement in Germany, 1894–1933* (London, 1976), 42–43; and Ute Frevert, *Women in German History: From Bourgeois Emancipation to Sexual Liberation*, trans. Stuart McKinnon-Evans (Oxford, 1988), 113–117.

4. On Civil Code see Dirk Blasius, *Ehescheidung in Deutschland, 1794–1945: Scheidung und Scheidungsrecht in historischer Perspketive* (Göttingen, 1987), 128–145. On Otto-Peters' campaign see Emilie Kempin, *Die Stellung der Frau nach dem zur Zeit in Deutschland gültigen Gesetzes-bestimmungen sowie nach dem Entwurf eines bürgerlichen Gesetzbuches für das deutsche Reich* (Leipzig, 1892), d–m. Otto-Peters's articles are in *Neue Bahnen* 9 (1876): nos. 15, 16, 17, 18, 19, 20, 21.

5. Olga von Beschwitz, *Begleitschrift zu der Petition des Bundes deutscher Frauenvereine an den Reichstag betreffend das Familienrecht des neuen bürgerlichen Gesetzbuches für das deutsche Reich* (Frankenberg, 1899); on protest see Evans, *The Feminist Movement in Germany*, 13–22; Amy K. Hackett, "The Politics of Feminism in Wilhelmine Germany, 1890–1918," (Ph.D. diss., Columbia University, 1977), 465–470; and Ute Gerhard, "'Bis an die Wurzel des Übels: Rechtsgeschichte und Rechtskämpfe der Radikalen," *Feministische Studien* 3 (May 1984), 77–98; on Anna Simson see Anna Plothow, *Die Begründerinnen der deutschen Frauenbewegung* (Leipzig, 1907), 178–179; on Stritt see Hackett, "The Politics of Feminism," 236–245.

6. On rights of single and married women under the Code see Blasius, *Ehescheidung*, 128–145.

7. On parental rights see Marianne Weber, *Ehefrau und Mutter in der Rechtsentwicklung: Eine Einführung* (Tübingen, 1907), 443–468; R. Hinsberg, "Das Erziehungsrecht der Mutter," *Die Frau* 5 (February 1898): 257–263; Emilie Kempin, *Die Stellung der Frau*, passim; Hermann Jastrow, *Das Recht der Frau nach dem bürgerlichen Gesetzbuch: Dargestellt für die Frauen* (Berlin, 1897), 98–103; Hackett, "The Politics of Feminism," 461.

8. Weber, *Ehefrau und Mutter*, 462, 445–450.

9. Ibid., 453.

10. Kempin, *Die Stellung der Frau*, 10; Weber, *Ehefrau und Mutter*, 443.

11. G. Planck, *Die rechtliche Stellung der Frau nach dem bürgerlichen Gesetzbuche* (Göttingen, 1899), 27; Jastrow, *Das Recht der Frau*, 18; Rechtschutzverein für Frauen in Dresden, *Das deutsche Recht und die deutschen Frauen; Kritische Beleuchtung des Entwurfs eines bürgerlichen Gesetzbuches für das deutsche Reich* (Dresden, 1895), iv–vii; Marie Stritt, *Das bürgerliche Gesetzbuch und die Frauenfrage: Vortrag gehalten auf der Generalversammlung des BDF in Hamburg* (28 October 1898), 5.

12. Stritt, *Das bürgerliche Gesetzbuch*, 13; Beschwitz, *Begleitschrift*, 5; on guardians' court see *Das deutsche Recht und die deutschen Frauen*, 26; Jastrow, *Das Recht der Frau*, 98; Weber, *Ehefrau und Mutter*, 453;

13. Weber, *Ehefrau und Mutter*, 453–457; von Beschwitz, *Begleitschrift*, 10; Edmund Friedeberg, "Die Unterhaltungspflicht nach dem bürgerlichen Gesetzbuch," *Die Frau* 7 (1899/1900): 455–457.

14. For extensive background on the history of laws concerning illegitimate children see Weber, *Ehefrau und Mutter*, 340–341, Blasius, *Ehescheidung*, 98–101, and Kempin, *Die Stellung der Frau*, passim. Also see chapter 1 above.

15. On the Civil Code's regulation of the status of illegitimate children see Weber, *Ehefrau und Mutter*, 561–571, Blasius, *Ehescheidung*, 101–110, and Jastrow, *Recht der Frau*, 169–176; on states under Napoleonic Code see Hackett, "The Politics of Feminism," 463.

16. On rates of illegitimacy see entry under "Uneheliche Kinder" in Max Taube et al., eds., *Enzyklopädisches Handbuch des Kinderschutzes und der Jugendfürsorge*, 2 vols. (Leipzig, 1911), 2:298; for reactions of middle-class women see, for example, Alice Salomon, *Charakter ist Schicksal: Lebenserinnerungen*, trans. Rolf Landwehr (Weinheim, 1984), 35.

17. Adele Schreiber, "Uneheliche Mütter," in Adele Schreiber, ed., *Mutterschaft: Ein Sammelwerk für die Probleme des Weibes als Mutter* (Munich, 1912), 257–277; Max Marcuse, *Uneheliche Mütter* (Berlin, 1906), 79–88.

18. For example, laws on illegitimacy were discussed at the International Women's Conference of 1904; "Internationaler Frauenkongress," *Dresdener Anzeiger*, 18 June 1904; Marcuse, *Uneheliche Mütter*, 73–79; Weber, *Ehefrau und Mutter*, 565; *Das deutsche Recht und die deutschen Frauen*, 28.

19. Stritt, *Das bürgerliche Gesetzbuch*, 15.

20. Ibid., 4.

21. See archive of Kommission für Kinderschutz, Archiv des Bundes deutscher

Frauenvereine, 2/IX/5, Karton 9, Deutsches Zentralinstitut für soziale Fragen, West Berlin.

22. Laws on professional guardianship are discussed in Weber, *Ehefrau und Mutter*, 570.

23. See entry under "Berufsvormundschaft" in Taube et al., eds., *Enzyklopädisches Handbuch*, 75–77; Jenny Apolant, *Stellung und Mitarbeit der Frau in der Gemeinde* (Leipzig, 1910), 20–36 and 84–86; for other evaluations of this system see Detlev Peukert, *Grenzen der Sozialdisziplinierung: Aufstieg und Krise der deutschen Jugendfürsorge von 1878 bis 1932* (Cologne, 1986), 97–115; Christoph Sachsse, *Mütterlichkeit als Beruf: Sozialarbeit, Sozialreform und Frauenbewegung* (Frankfurt, 1985), 70–79; and Ilka Riemann, *Soziale Arbeit als Hausarbeit: Von der Suppendame zur Sozial-Pädagogin* (Frankfurt, 1985), 90–110.

24. Flugblatt, herausgegeben von der Kommission fur Kinderschutz, Kommission für Kinderschutz, Archiv des Bundes deutscher Frauenvereine, 2/IX/5, Karton 9; Apolant, *Stellung und Mitarbeit der Frau in der Gemeinde*, 36. For the experiences of one of these female guardians, see Marie Baum, *Rückblick auf mein Leben* (Heidelberg, 1950), 120–127.

25. On child labor legislation see Klaus Saul et al., eds., *Arbeiterfamilien im Kaiserreich: Materialien zur Sozialgeschichte in Deutschland, 1871–1914* (Frankfurt, 1982), 203–213.

26. Petition des Bundes deutscher Frauenvereine zur Regelung der Erwerbsarbeit der Kinder, Archiv des Bundes deutscher Frauenvereine, 2/IX/5, Karton 9, Deutsches Zentralinstitut für soziale Fragen, West Berlin; Lily Braun, *Die Frauen und die Politik* (Berlin, 1903), 17.

27. For another view of the transition from social service to social legislation in the program of German feminists see Evans, *The Feminist Movement in Germany*, 35–38, and Sachsse, *Mütterlichkeit als Beruf*, 105–125.

28. On the politics of the American suffrage movement see Nancy Woloch, *Women and the American Experience* (New York, 1984), 307–369.

29. For a very useful account of American feminists' positions on familial and maternal issues in this era see Mary Madeleine Ladd-Taylor, "Mother-Work: Ideology, Public Policy and the Mothers' Movement, 1890–1930" (Ph.D. diss., Yale University, 1986), 171–184. I am grateful to the author for making a copy of her dissertation available to me.

Chapter 8. Motherhood, Culture, and Evolution

1. On German feminism see see Barbara Greven-Aschoff, *Die Bürgerliche Frauenbewegung in Deutschland, 1894–1933* (Göttingen, 1981), 31–69; on comparative American developments see Nancy F. Cott, *The Grounding of Modern Feminism* (New Haven, 1987), 11–51.

2. On Fürth see Marie Juchacz, *Sie lebten für eine bessere Welt* (Berlin, 1955), 91–95, and various shorter materials in Stadtarchiv Frankfurt Am Main, "Henriette Fürth: Personalakten"; some of Fürth's letters are held in the "Kleine Kollektion Henriette Fürth," Internationaal Instituut vor Socialgeschiednis, Amsterdam. On Lily

Braun see Alfred Meyer, *The Feminism and Socialism of Lily Braun* (Bloomington, Ind., 1986); and Jean H. Quataert, *Reluctant Feminists in German Social Democracy, 1885–1917* (Princeton, 1979); on German socialist women see Heinz Niggemann, *Emanzipation zwischen Sozialismus und Feminismus: Die sozialdemokratische Frauenbewegung im Kaiserreich* (Wupperthal, 1981). Helene Stöcker wrote an autobiography entitled "Lebensabriss," unpublished typescript in Box 1, Helene Stöcker Papers, Swarthmore Peace Collection, Swarthmore College. This collection also contains other short biographical sketches. On Stöcker's life see also Amy Hackett, "Helene Stöcker: Left-Wing Intellectual and Sex Reformer," in Renate Bridenthal, Atina Grossmann, and Claudia Koonz, eds., *When Biology Became Destiny: Women in Weimar and Nazi Germany* (New York, 1984), 109–130. Schreiber's early life is described in several short, unpublished typescripts held in Nachlass Adele Schreiber, vol. 1, Bundesarchiv Koblenz. A useful reference work on the lives of all of these women, and many others, is Daniela Weiland, *Geschichte der Frauenemanzipation in Deutschland und Österreich: Biographien, Programme, Organizationen* (Düsseldorf, 1983).

3. Schreiber described her attempt to enter medical school in "Lebenslauf" (unpub. typescript, n.d.) in Nachlass Adele Schreiber, vol. 1; Stöcker described her relationship to her mother in "Vom Kampf um das Frauenstudium" (unpub. typescript, n.d.) in Box 1, Helene Stöcker Papers.

4. Juchacz, *Sie lebten für eine bessere Welt*, 91; Bertha Badt-Strauss, "Ein Kapitel aus einer vergangenen Welt: Henriette Fürth—eine jüdische Sozialpolitikerin in Deutschland," *Frankfurter Allgemeine*, 9 May 1958; Meyer, *Lily Braun*, 1–24.

5. Juchacz, *Sie lebten für eine bessere Welt*, 92; Helene Stöcker, "Vom Kampf um das Frauenstudium"; for more on women and higher education see James C. Albisetti, *Schooling German Girls and Women: Secondary and Higher Education in the Nineteenth Century* (Princeton, 1988), 93–167.

6. Schreiber, "Lebenslauf;" Meyer, *Lily Braun*, 20–22; Quataert, *Reluctant Feminists*, 76–83.

7. On celibacy as a requirement for women's careers see Albisetti, "Women and the Professions in Imperial Germany," in Ruth-Ellen Joeres and Mary Jo Maynes, eds., *German Women in the Eighteenth and Nineteenth Centuries: A Social and Literary History* (Bloomington, Ind., 1986), 103.

8. Meyer, *Lily Braun*, 5–15; Quataert, *Reluctant Feminists*, 76–83; Stöcker, "Lebensabriss," Chapter 1, and pp. 30–33.

9. Henriette Fürth, *Die Fabrikarbeit verheirateter Frauen* (Frankfurt, 1902), 15; Badt-Strauss, "Ein Kapitel aus einer vergangenen Welt"; Meyer, "The Radicalization of Lily Braun," in John C. Fout, ed., *German Women in the Nineteenth Century* (New York, 1984), 220–222; Meyer, *Lily Braun*, 17–18.

10. Stöcker chronicled her time in Glasgow and her relationship to Tille in "Lebensabriss," chapter 3, quotation pp. 9–10.

11. Schreiber's laconic comment on her marriage is in "Lebenslauf." Unfortunately, she said nothing more about her married life for public consumption.

12. Some of Schreiber's articles from this period are: "Leiden und Rechte des Kindes," *Die Frau* 8 (1899/1900): 5, 243–244; "Kindliche Martyrer und jugendliche Verbrecher," *Die Frau* 8 (1898/99): 364. Her lecture, "Aus dem dunklen Land der

Kinder," is described in many newspaper clippings in Nachlass Adele Schreiber, vols. 9–12, including one from *Vorwärts*, 14 January 1905. On Stöcker and coeducation see "Vom Kampf um das Frauenstudium."

13. Cott, *The Grounding of Modern Feminism*, 32–35; some of Fürth's early works are: "Die Ehefrage und der Beruf: Sozialstatistische Betrachtungen," *Die Frau* 3 (1897/98): 710–712; "Die Berichte der preussischen Fabrikinspektoren," *Die Frau* 4 (1898/99): 40–42; "Die Idee des Rechtsschutzes fur Frauen und ihre Verwirklichung in Frankfurt am Main," *Die Frau* 4 (1898/99): 5, 398–399; and *Die Fabrikarbeit verheirateter Frauen* (Frankfurt, 1902); Lily Braun, *Die Frauenfrage: Ihre geschichtliche Entwicklung und wirtschaftliche Seite* (Leipzig, 1901).

14. On socialism and feminism see Quataert, *Reluctant Feminists*; Schreiber's early experiences with socialist organizations are described in her "Lebenslauf"; on Braun's conversion to socialism see Meyer, "The Radicalization of Lily Braun," 230–231.

15. On attitude of Zetkin toward bourgeois feminism see Meyer, *Lily Braun*, 51–52; Quataert, *Reluctant Feminists*, 127–136; and Anna-E. Freier, *Dem Reich der Freiheit sollst Du Kinder gebären: Der Antifeminismus der proletarischen Frauenbewegung im Spiegel der "Gleichheit," 1891–1917* (Frankfurt, 1981), 81–92.

16. Juchacz, *Sie lebten fur eine bessere Welt*, 93; Lily Braun, *Die Frauenfrage*, 12; Meyer, *Lily Braun*, 66–67.

17. Wilhelm Preyer, *Die geistige Entwicklung der ersten Kindheit, nebst Anweisungen für Eltern, dieselbe zu beobachten* (Stuttgart, 1893), 2; Ellen Key, *The Century of the Child* (New York, 1972), 106–191 and passim.

18. On the medicalization of child-rearing as reflected through mothers' advice literature, see Yvonne Schutze, "Die gute Mutter—Zur Geschichte des normativen Musters Mutterliebe," in Maria-Eleonora Karsten and Hans-Uwe Otto, eds., *Die Sozialpädagogische Ordnung der Familie*: *Beitrag zu Wandel familärer Lebensweisen und sozialpädagogische Intervention* (Weinheim, 1987), 45–67; Jürgen Reyer, "Kindheit zwischen privat-familiärer Lebenswelt und öffentlich veranstalteter Kleinkindererziehung," in Günter Erning, Karl Neumann, and Jürgen Reyer, eds., *Geschichte des Kindergartens: Enstehung und Entwicklung der öffentlichen Kleinkinderziehung in Deutschland*, 2 vols. (Freiburg im Breisgau, 1987), 2: 232–284; and Ute Frevert, "The Civilizing Tendency of Hygiene: Working-Class Women under Medical Control in Imperial Germany," in Fout, ed., *German Women in the Nineteenth Century*, 320–344. On the transition from an environmental to a biological concept of motherhood see Linda Gordon, *Woman's Body, Woman's Right: A History of Birth Control in America* (New York, 1976), 176.

19. For more general background on the eugenics movement and women see Ann Taylor Allen, "German Radical Feminism and Eugenics, 1900–1918," *German Studies Review* 11 (February 1988): 31–56; Sheila Faith Weiss, *Race, Hygiene, and National Efficiency: The Eugenics of Wilhelm Schallmayer* (Berkeley, 1987); and Paul Weindling, *Health, Race and German Politics between National Unification and Nazism* (New York, 1989), 61–304; on the shift to a medical and biological view of women's issues see the very stimulating study of women's ideology in the United States in Nancy M. Theriot, *The Biosocial Construction of Femininity: Mothers and Daughters in Nineteenth-Century America* (New York, 1988), 107–118.

20. P. J. Möbius, *Über den physiologischen Schwachsinn des Weibes* (Halle, 1922),

1–13; on the public impact of these and similar ideas see Albisetti, *Schooling German Girls and Women*, 168–203.

21. Stöcker, "Lebensabriss," chapter 1, pp. 15–33; see also Hackett, "Helene Stöcker," 119; Heide Schlüpmann, "Radikalisierung der Philosophie: Die Nietzsche-Rezeption und die sexualpolitische Publizistik Helene Stöckers," *Feministische Studien* 1 (1984): 10–38; and Heide Soltau, "Erotik und Altruismus: Emanzipationsvorstellungen der Radikalen Helene Stöcker," in Jutta Dalhoff, Uschi Frey, and Ingrid Scholl, eds., *Frauenmacht in der Geschichte* (Düsseldorf, 1986), 65–81.

22. Alexander Tille, *Von Darwin bis Nietzsche: Ein Buch Entwicklungsethik* (Leipzig, 1895), 231; Helene Stöcker, "Liebesbrief einer modernen Frau," (unpub. typescript, n.d.) Box 1, Helene Stöcker Papers; on Tille see Weindling, *Health, Race and German Politics*, 110–111.

23. On reform Darwinism and the influence of Bölsche see Alfred E. Kelly, *The Descent of Darwin: The Popularization of Darwinism in Germany, 1890–1914* (Chapel Hill, N.C., 1981); Havelock Ellis, *Sex in its Relation to Society* (Philadelphia, 1910), 576; Daniel J. Kevles, *In the Name of Eugenics: Genetics and the Uses of Human Heredity* (New York, 1985), 65–67.

24. Johann Jakob Bachofen, *Myth, Religion and Mother Right: Selected Writings of J.J. Bachofen*, trans. Ralph Manheim (Princeton, 1967); Friedrich Engels, *The Origins of the Family, Private Property and the State in the Light of the Researches of Lewis H. Morgan*, trans. Alex West (New York, 1972); August Bebel, *Die Frau und der Sozialismus* (Stuttgart, 1922), 20–55; for more on matriarchal theories see Eleanor Leacock, "Women in Egalitarian Societies," in Renate Bridenthal, Claudia Koonz, and Susan Stuard, eds., *Becoming Visible: Women in European History* (Boston, 1987), 15–40.

25. Ellen Key, *Missbrauchte Frauenkraft: Ein Essay* (first ed., 1898; reprinted Berlin, 1911), 23; Henriette Fürth, "Mutterschaft und Ehe," *Mutterschutz* 1 (1905): 8, 267.

26. Oda Olberg, *Das Weib und der Intellektualismus* (Berlin, 1902), 38.

27. Key, *Missbrauchte Frauenkraft*, 67–73; for another interpretation of Key's text see Kay Goodman, "Motherhood and Work: The Concept of the Misuse of Women's Energy," in Joeres and Maynes, eds., *German Women in the Eighteenth and Nineteenth Centuries*, 110–135.

28. Olive Schreiner's central work, *Woman and Labour* was not published until 1911, but she stated its central argument in an article, "The Woman Question," first published in 1899 and reprinted in Carol Barash, ed., *An Olive Schreiner Reader* (London and New York, 1987), 63–100; Charlotte Perkins Gilman, *This Man-Made World, or Our Androcentric Culture* (New York, 1911); Helene Lange, review of *Women and Economics*, *Die Frau* 9 (1901): 18.

29. Lily Braun, *Frauenarbeit und Hauswirtschaft* (Berlin, 1901). This essay is translated and excerpted in Meyer, ed. and trans., *Selected Writings on Feminism and Socialism: Lily Braun* (Bloomington, Ind., 1987), 3–27; quotation p. 5. See also the same idea as expressed by Henriette Fürth in *Fabrikarbeit*, 5–7.

30. Anita Augspurg, *Die ethische Seite der Frauenbewegung* (Minden, 1893), 7, 10; Minna Cauer, *Die Frau im 19. Jahrhundert* (Berlin, 1898), 137; on Darwinism in the radical feminist movement see Bärbel Clemens, *Menschenrechte haben kein*

Geschlecht: Zum Politikverständnis der bürgerlichen Frauenbewegung (Pfaffenweiler, 1988), 42–63.

31. Helene Stöcker, *Die Liebe und Die Frauen* (Minden, 1908), 9; on similar American developments see Cott, *The Grounding of Modern Feminism*, 40–47.

32. On married women's work see Barbara B. Franzoi, *At the Very Least She Pays the Rent: Women and German Industrialization, 1871–1914* (Westport, Conn., 1985), 17–39, on protective legislation, 60–81; on prohibitions against married teachers see Albisetti, *Schooling German Girls and Women*, 175–178.

33. On the biographies of Simon and Gerhard see Sabine Klöhn, *Helene Simon (1862–1947): Deutsche und britische Sozialreform und Sozialgesetzgebung im Spiegel ihrer Schriften und ihr Wirken als Sozialpolitikerin im Kaiserreich und in der Weimarer Republik* (Frankfurt, 1982), 1–72 and 238–242; Adele Gerhard and Helene Simon, *Mutterschaft und geistige Arbeit: Eine psychologische und soziologische Studie. Auf Grundlage einer internationalen Erhebung mit Berücksichtigung der geschichtlichen Entwicklung* (Berlin, 1901), 6–7.

34. Gerhard and Simon, *Mutterschaft und geistige Arbeit*, 29, 319.

35. Ibid., 238.

36. Robert Wilbrandt, "Mutterschaft und geistige Arbeit," *Schmollers Jahrbuch* 25 (1901): 765–768; Edmund Fischer, "Die Familie," *Sozialistische Monatshefte* 9 (1905): 534; August Bebel, "Mutterschaft und geistige Arbeit," *Die Neue Zeit* 19 (1900/01): 45–47; Wally Zepler, "Mutterschaft und geistige Arbeit," *Sozialistische Monatshefte* 5 (1901): 803–814, quoted in Klöhn, *Helene Simon*, 252–253.

37. *Die Verheiratete Lehrerin: Verhandlungen der ersten internationalen Lehrerinnen-Versammlung in Deutschland* (Berlin, 1905), 7–10; see also Albisetti, *Schooling German Girls and Women*, 175–178; the text of Gilman's remarks has apperently not been preserved.

38. *Die Verheiratete Lehrerin*, 15, 20, 22; Helene Stöcker, "Von neuer Ethik," *Mutterschutz* 1 (1905): 79; Braun, *Die Mutterschaftsversicherung: Ein Beitrag zur Frage der Fürsorge für Schwangere und Wöchnerinnen* (Berlin, 1906), 23; *Die Verheiratete Lehrerin*, 25–26.

39. Negative responses of teachers are expressed in *Die Verheiratete Lehrerin*, 7–10, 53–58; see also Albisetti, *Schooling German Girls and Women*, 175–178.

40. Braun, *Frauenarbeit und Hauswirtschaft*, 16 and passim. For background on Braun's proposal in the context of her career, see Freier, *Dem Reich der Freiheit sollst Du Kinder gebären*, 53–64; and Quataert, *Reluctant Feminists*, 107–127.

41. See the speech of Maria Lischnewska in *Die verheiratete Lehrerin*, 24–25; and Maria Lischnewska, "Die wirtschaftliche Reform der Ehe," *Mutterschutz* 2 (1906): 227; Hedwig Dohm, *Die Mütter: Ein Beitrag zur Erziehungsfrage* (Berlin, 1903), 145–147. On Dohm and her ideas about child-rearing and motherhood see Julia Meissner, *Mehr Stolz, Ihr Frauen! Hedwig Dohm, eine Biographie* (Düsseldorf, 1987), 87–93. Cf. Henriette Fürth, *Die Hausfrau: eine Mongraphie* (München, 1914), 66.

42. Freier, *Dem Reich der Freiheit*, 58–59; Käthe Schirmacher, *Die Wirtschaftliche Reform der Ehe* (Leipzig, 1906), 11–18; Marianne Weber, *Beruf und Ehe: Die Beteiligung der Frau an der Wissenschaft* (Berlin, 1906), 3–8; for background on Marianne Weber see Günther Roth, "Marianne Weber and her Circle," introduction to Marianne Weber, *Max Weber* (New Brunswick, N.J., 1988).

43. Zetkin's response is discussed in Quataert, *Reluctant Feminists*, 120–124, 127–136; and Freier, *Dem Reich der Freiheit*, 53–64, quotation p. 57; review by Frieda Wulff appeared in *Die Gleichheit*, 1901, 55, quoted in Freier, *Dem Reich der Freiheit*, 57.

44. Braun, *Frauenarbeit und Hauswirtschaft*, 18; Katzenstein's speech is in *Protokoll über die Verhandlungen des Parteitages der Sozialdemokratischen Partei Deutschlands, abgehalten zu Mannheim, sowie Bericht über die 4. Frauenkonferenz* (Berlin, 1906), 407–408. The brief career of the socialist kindergarten is described in "Das Vandalentum der Ara Studt," *Die Neue Gesellschaft* 3 (1907): 15, excerpted in Klaus Saul, Jens Flemming, Dirk Stegmann, and Peter-Christian Witt, eds., *Arbeiterfamilien im Kaiserreich: Material zur Sozialgeschichte in Deutschland, 1871–1914* (Düsseldorf, 1982), 265–266.

45. *Auszug Protokolle des Magistrats der Stadt Frankfurt am Main*, 12 July 1904, Stadtarchiv Frankfurt am Main; see also *Dritter Jahresbericht des Vereins für Volkskindergärten* (Frankfurt, 1899); Zetkin's speech was transcribed in *Protokoll über die Verhandlungen des Parteitages*, 347–350. For more material on the funding of kindergartens see Brigitte Zwerger, *Bewahranstalt, Kleinkinderschule, Kindergarten: Aspekte nichtfamiliärer Kleinkinderziehung in Deutschland im 19. Jahrhundert* (Weinheim, 1982), 60; and Jürgen Reyer, "Entwicklung der Trägerstruktur in der öffentlichen Kleinkinderziehung," in Günter Erning, Karl Neumann, and Jürgen Reyer, eds., *Geschichte des Kindergartens*, 2 vols. (Freiburg, 1987), 2:40–66.

46. Lillian Faderman and Brigitte Eriksson, eds. and trans., *Lesbian-Feminism in Turn-of-the-Century Germany* (Iowa City, 1980), ii–v; Helene Stöcker, "Die beabsichtigte Ausdehnung des #175 auf die Frau," *Neue Generation* 5 (1909), 110–121; Ilse Kokula, "Der linke Flügel der Frauenbewegung als Platform des Befreiungskampfes homosexueller Frauen und Männer," in Dalhoff et al., eds., *Frauenmacht in der Geschichte*, 46–64.

47. Oda Olberg, "Polemisches über Frauenfrage und Sozialismus," *Sozialistische Monatshefte* 9 (1905): 304.

48. This view of radical feminism was expressed by Helene Lange, *Lebenserinnerungen* (Berlin, 1930), 225; on radicalism as a break with the past see also Richard J. Evans, *The Feminist Movement in Germany, 1894–1933* (London, 1976), 35–48.

49. On the meaning of the Key-Gilman debate in the United States see Cott, *Grounding of Modern Feminism*, 40–41, and Mary Madeleine Ladd-Taylor, "Mother-Work: Ideology, Public Policy and the Mothers' Movement, 1890–1930" (Ph.D. diss., Yale University, 1986), 141–154; Aileen S. Kraditor, *The Ideas of the Woman Suffrage Movement, 1890–1929* (New York, 1965; reprinted 1971), 38–64; Barbara Leslie Epstein, *The Politics of Domesticity: Women, Evangelism and Temperance in Nineteenth-Century America* (Middletown, Conn., 1981). For a more general discussion of maternalist thinking in European suffrage movements see Karen Offen, "Liberty, Equality and Justice for Women: The Theory and Practice of Feminism in Nineteenth-Century Europe," in Bridenthal, Koonz, and Stuard, eds., *Becoming Visible*, 335–374.

Chapter 9. Motherhood as Right and Duty

1. Havelock Ellis, *The Task of Social Hygiene* (Boston, 1914), 95. For a comparative perspective on women's participation in the debate on falling birthrates see Karen

Offen, "Depopulation, Nationalism and Feminism in Fin-de-Siècle France," *American Historical Review* 89 (June 1984): 648–676.

2. Ute Frevert, "The Civilizing Tendency of Hygiene: Working-Class Women under Medical Control in Imperial Germany," in John C. Fout, ed., *German Women in the Nineteenth Century: A Social History* (New York, 1984), 320–344.

3. Helene Stöcker, "Lebensabriss," unpublished typescript, Box 1, Helene Stöcker Papers, Swarthmore College Peace Collection, Swarthmore College; this account is on pp. 4–5 of the chapter headed "B.F.M."; see also Richard J. Evans, *The Feminist Movement in Germany, 1894–1933* (London, 1976), 115–118.

4. Stöcker, "Lebensabriss," "B.F.M.," 11. On the founding and complex history of the *Bund für Mutterschutz* see Bernd Nowacki, *Der Bund für Mutterschutz, 1905–1933* (Husum, 1983); Christl Wickert, Brigitte Hamburger, and Marie Lienau, "Helene Stöcker und der Bund für Mutterschutz," *Women's Studies International Forum* 5 (1982): 611–618; and Evans, *The Feminist Movement in Germany*, 115–145.

5. On membership figures for the *Bund für Mutterschutz* see Evans, *The Feminist Movement*, 129; on the impact of its propaganda see Evans, *The Feminist Movement*, 131; Ann Taylor Allen, "Mothers of the New Generation: Adele Schreiber, Helene Stöcker, and the Evolution of a German Idea of Motherhood," *Signs: Journal of Women in Culture and Society* 10 (Spring 1985): 418–438; and Heide Soltau, "Erotik und Altruismus: Emanzipationsvorstellungen der Radikalen Helene Stöcker," in Jutta Dalhoff, Uschi Frey, and Ingrid Scholl, eds., *Frauenmacht in der Geschichte* (Düsseldorf, 1986), 65–82; on responses of medical establishment see Paul Weindling, *Health, Race and German Politics Between National Unification and Nazism* (Cambridge, 1989), 205–207.

6. Sheila Faith Weiss, *Race Hygiene and National Efficiency: The Eugenics of Wilhelm Schallmayer* (Berkeley, 1987), 127–135; John E. Knodel, *The Decline of Fertility in Germany, 1871–1939* (Princeton, 1974), 38–39; see also Marie-Luise Janssen-Jurreit, "National-Biologie, Sexualreform, und Geburtenrückgang: Über den Zusammenhang von Bevölkerungspolitik und Frauenbewegung um die Jahrhundertwende," in Gabriele Dietze, ed., *Die Überwindung der Sprachlosigkeit: Texte aus der neuen Frauenbewegung* (Darmstadt and Neuwied, 1978), 139–173; Anna A. Bergmann, "Von der unbefleckten Empfängnis zur Rationalisierung des Geschlechtslebens: Gedanken zur Debatte um den Geburtenrückgang vor dem ersten Weltkrieg," in Johanna Geyer-Kordesch and Annette Kuhn, eds., *Frauenkörper-Medizin-Sexualität: Auf dem Wege Zu einem neuen Sexualmoral* (Düsseldorf, 1986), 129–131.

7. Quotation from Karl von Behr-Pinnow is in Kaiserin Auguste-Viktoria Haus, *Säuglingsfürsorge in Gross-Berlin, III internationaler Kongress fur Säuglingsschutz* (Berlin, 1911), 6; for statistics see Hallie Kintner, "The Causes of Infant Death in Germany, 1880–1933," unpub. paper delivered at the Social Science History Association, 31 October 1987. I am grateful to the author for letting me use this unpublished paper.

8. "Mütter, beachtet!" (June 6, 1904); "Bayern, Entschliessung des Kgl. Staatsministeriums," (12 September 1907), and "Preussisches Ministerialerlass, " (16 June 1908). All of this pamphlet literature is held in Reichsgesundheitsamt, R/86, 2376, vol. 1, "Bekämpfung der Kindersterblichkeit," Bundesarchiv Koblenz. On diagnosis see Kintner, "Causes of Infant Death"; on nursing and bottle-feeding see Henriette Fürth,

Die Mütterschaftsversicherung (Jena, 1911), 23; and Weindling, *Health, Race and German Politics*, 203–205; Frevert, "The Civilizing Tendency of Hygiene."

9. Arthur Keller and C. J. Klumker, *Säuglingsfürsorge und Kinderschutz in den europäischen Städten* (Berlin, 1912) 1212–1214; Adele Schreiber, "Ergänzende Einrichtungen der öffentlichen Fürsorge," in Schreiber, ed., *Mutterschaft: Ein Sammelwerk für die Probleme des Weibes als Mutter* (Munich, 1911), 327; Kaiserin-Auguste-Viktoria Haus, *Säuglingsfürsorge in Gross-Berlin*; Berlin, Stadtverordneten-Versammlung, Stenographische Berichte, 2 March 1905. For another socialist child welfare, and especially on infant mortality, see Otto Rühle, *Das proletarische Kind: Eine Monographie* (Berlin, 1911), 5–63; on the founding of the Kaiserin Auguste-Viktoria House see Weindling, *Health, Race and German Politics*, 203–205.

10. "Bund für Mutterschutz," *Archiv für Rassen- und Gesellschaftsbiologie* 2 (1905): 164; see also Nowacki, *Bund für Mutterschutz*, 10.

11. For statistics on illegitimate children's mortality see Carl von Behr-Pinnow, *Erhaltung und Mehrung des Nachwuchses*, Reichsgesundheitsamt, R/86, 2375, vol. 2, Bundesarchiv Koblenz; Adele Schreiber, *Pflanzstätten der Mutterliebe*, 1904, reprint in Nachlass Adele Schreiber, vol. 31, Bundesarchiv Koblenz. On unmarried mothers and child welfare services see Franz Rott, *Umfang, Bedeutung und Ergebnisse der Unterstützungen an stillende Mütter* (Berlin, 1914), 50–51. Rott was the head of infant services for the Kaiserin Auguste-Viktoria Haus.

12. On the foster care system see Max Taube, "Ziehkinder," Max Taube et al., eds., *Enzyklopädisches Handbuch des Kinderschutzes und der Jugendfürsorge*, 2 vols. (Leipzig, 1911), 2:409–410; Schreiber, "Pflanzstätten der Mutterliebe," 1.

13. Schreiber, "Pflanzstätten der Mutterliebe." On the alternative homes that Schreiber helped found see Max Marcuse, *Uneheliche Mütter* (Berlin, 1906), 69–72. Compare the accounts of the homes for unwed mothers and their children founded by Jewish women's organizations in Marion Kaplan, *The Jewish Feminist Movement in Germany: The Campaigns of the Jüdischer Frauenbund, 1904–1938* (Westport, Conn., 1979), 134–135.

14. Schreiber, "Pflanzstätten der Mutterliebe," and "Uneheliche Kinder," in Schreiber, ed., *Mutterschaft*, 357–377.

15. On Ruth Bré and her experiment see "Ruth Bré und der Bund für Mutterschutz" unpub. typescript, Nachlass Adele Schreiber, vol. 17; Nowacki, *Bund für Mutterschutz*, 17–20; Evans, *The Feminist Movement in Germany*, 71–100; Soltau, "Erotik und Altruismus," 73–74.

16. Helene Stöcker, "Die Ziele der Mutterschutzbewegung," in *Die Liebe und die Frauen* (Minden, 1908), 181–183; see also see Amy Hackett, "Helene Stöcker: Leftwing Intellectual and Sex Reformer," in Renate Bridenthal, Atina Grossmann, and Marion Kaplan, eds., *When Biology Became Destiny: Women in Weimar and Nazi Germany* (New York, 1984), 112–119; Irene Stoehr, "Fraueneinfluss oder Geschlechtsversöhnung? Zur 'Sexualdebatte' in der deutschen Frauenbewegung um 1900," in Geyer-Kordesch and Kuhn, eds., *Frauenkörper*, 159–190; and Ilse Kokula, "Der linke Flügel der Frauenbewegung als Plattform des Befreiungskampfes homosexueller Frauen und Männer," in Dalhoff et al., eds., *Frauenmacht in der Geschichte*, 46–64.

17. Schreiber's speech was reported in the *Dresdener Anzeiger*, 27 November 1904; Stöcker, "Von neuer Ethik," *Mutterschutz* 2 (1906): 4.

18. Stöcker, "Unsere erste Generalversammlung," *Mutterschutz* 3 (1907): 78.

19. Helene Lange, "Feministische Gedankenanarchie," in Gertrud Bäumer, ed., *Frauenbewegung und Sexualethik* (Heilbronn, 1909), 50; Bund deutscher Frauenvereine, *Grundsätze und Forderungen der Frauenbewegung*, 1907, Archiv des Bundes deutscher Frauenvereine, 10/I, Karton 48, "Bildungs- und Erziehungsfragen," Deutsches Zentralinstitut für soziale Fragen, West Berlin; reprinted in Susan Groag Bell and Karen Offen, eds., *Women, the Family and Freedom: the Debate in Documents*, 2 vols. (Stanford, 1983), 2:102–104. On Zetkin see Jean H. Quataert, *Reluctant Feminists in German Social Democracy, 1885–1917* (Princeton, 1979), 100–107; and Anna-E. Freier, *Dem Reich der Freiheit sollst Du Kinder gebären: Der Antifeminismus der proletarischen Frauenbewegung im Spiegel der "Gleichheit* (Frankfurt, 1983), 28–32.

20. Lily Braun, "Die Mutterschaftsversicherung," in *Mutterschutz* 2 (1906), 72. On protective legislation Barbara Franzoi, *At the Very Least She Pays the Rent: Women and German Industrialization, 1871–1914* (Westport, Conn., 1985), 60–81; on socialist attitudes see Freier, *Dem Reich der Freiheit*, 99–107 and Quataert, *Reluctant Feminists*, 40–41.

21. On the history of maternity insurance in the German Empire see Alfons Fischer, "Staatliche Mutterschaftsversorgung" in *Die Mutterschaft*, 299–310; Braun, "Die Mutterschaft," *Mutterschutz* 2 (1906): 22–24; Fürth, *Mutterschaftsversicherung*, 4–22; Braun, *Die Frauenfrage: Ihre geschichtliche Entwicklung und wirtschaftliche Seite* (Leipzig, 1901), 545–547; Fürth, *Mutterschaftsversicherung*, 164–167; Braun, "Mutterschaftsversicherung," 75–76.

22. The text of the petition is held in Nachlass Adele Schreiber, vol. 29, and reprinted in John C. Fout and Eleanor Riemer, eds., *European Women: A Documentary History* (New York, 1980), 168; see also Bund deutscher Frauenvereine, "Grundsatze und Fürderungen der Frauenbewegung," 1907; "Schwangeren- und Wöchnerinnenschutz: Resolution der sozialdemokratischen Frauenkonferenz am 22. und 23. September, 1906 in Mannheim," reprinted in *Dokumente der revolutionären deutschen Arbeiterbewegung zur Frauenfrage, 1848–1974* (Leipzig, 1984), 51–52. The text of the insurance law that was passed is in *Reichsversicherungsordnung vom 19 Juli, 1911* (Munich, 1911) #195–200.

23. On decline in infant death rate see Kintner, "Causes of Infant Death," 20–27; Frevert, "The Civilizing Tendency of Hygiene," 338.

24. Key, "Mütterlichkeit," *Neue Generation* 2 (1909): 244. Quataert, "Social Insurance and the Family Work of Oberlausitz Home Weavers in the Late Nineteenth Century," in Fout, ed., *German Women in the Nineteenth Century*, 270–294.

25. Schreiber is quoted in "Kongress für biologische Hygiene," *Hamburger Correspondent*, 14 October 1912; on militarism and suffrage see Amy K. Hackett, "The Politics of Feminism in Wilhelmine Germany, 1890–1918" (Ph.D. diss., Columbia University, 1977), 471; on the development of suffrage organizations see Evans, *The Feminist Movement*, 71–115; Barbara Greven-Aschoff, *Die bürgerliche Frauenbewegung in Deutschland, 1894–1933* (Göttingen, 1981), 132–141; and Bärbel Clemens, *Menschenrechte haben kein Geschlecht! Zum Politikverständnis der Bürgerlichen Frauenbewegung* (Pfaffenweiler, 1988), 35–71.

26. Braun, *Die Frauen und die Politik* (Berlin, 1903), 47; Schreiber's speech on suffrage was reported in *Volkszeitung*, 21 April 1911; Karen M. Offen, "Minotaur or

Mother? The Gendering of the State in Early Third Republic France," unpub. typescript, 1988. I am grateful to the author for allowing me to see this unpublished paper.

27. On the attitudes of American feminists toward *Mutterschutz* see Nancy F. Cott, *The Grounding of Modern Feminism* (New Haven, 1987), 46–50 (quotation 46); and Mary Madeleine Ladd-Taylor, "Mother-Work, Public Policy and the Mothers' Movement, 1890–1930," (Ph.D. diss., Yale University, 1986), 135–225.

28. Alice Salomon, "Das Problem der Mutterschaftsversicherung," *Die Frau* 9 (September, 1902), 729.

Chapter 10. Motherhood as Choice

1. On penalties for abortion see Luc Jochimsen, *218: Dokumente eines Hundert-Jahren-Elends* (Hamburg, 1971), 16; see also Anneliese Bergmann, "Frauen, Männer, Sexualität und Geburtenkontrolle. Die Gebärstreikdebatte der SPD im Jahre 1913," in Karin Hausen, ed., *Frauen suchen ihre Geschichte: Historische Studien zum 19. und 20. Jahrhundert* (Munich, 1983), 85–86; Anna A. Bergmann, "Von der unbefleckten Empfängnis zur Rationalisierung des Geschlechtslebens: Gedanken zur Debatte um den Geburtenrückgang vor dem ersten Weltkrieg," in Johanna Geyer-Kordesch and Annette Kuhn, eds., *Frauenkörper-Medizin-Sexualität: Auf dem Wege zu einem neuen Sexualmoral* (Düsseldorf, 1986), 127–133; James Woycke, *Birth Control in Germany, 1871–1933* (London and New York, 1988), 133–144; and Paul Weindling, *Health, Race and German Politics between National Unification and Nazism, 1870–1945* (Cambridge, 1989), 263–269.

2. S. R. Steinmetz, "Feminismus und Rasse," *Jahrbuch für Sozialwissenschaften* 7 (1904): 752. For more on the antifeminist implications of eugenic theory during this period see Marie-Luise Janssen-Jurreit, "National-Biologie, Sexualreform und Geburtenrückgang: Über den Zusammenhang von Bevölkerungspolitik und Frauenbewegung um die Jahrhundertwende," in Gabriele Dietze, ed., *Die Überwindung der Sprachlosigkeit: Texte aus der neuen Frauenbewegung* (Darmstadt and Neuwied, 1978), 140; Gisela Bock, "Racism and Sexism in Nazi Germany: Motherhood, Compulsory Sterilization and the State," in Renate Bridenthal, Atina Grossmann, and Marion Kaplan, eds., *When Biology Became Destiny: Women in Weimar and Nazi Germany* (New York, 1984); Ann Taylor Allen, "German Radical Feminism and Eugenics, 1900–1918," *German Studies Review* 11 (February 1988): 42–43.

3. Ellen Key, *The Century of the Child* (New York, 1972), 5. On Neo-Malthusianism see Richard Allen Soloway, *Birth Control and the Population Question in England, 1877–1930* (New York, 1976), 133–15.7.

4. Marie Baum, *Rückblick auf mein Leben* (Heidelberg, 1950), 144; C. Hamburger, "Kinderzahl und Kindersterblichkeit in Berliner Arbeiterfamilien," *Die Neue Generation* 5 (1909): 309–314; Rudolf Goldscheid, *Entwicklungswerttheorie, Entwicklungökonomie, Menschenökonomie: Eine Programmschrift* (Leipzig, 1908), 203–217; on Goldscheid see also Weindling, *Health, Race and German Politics*, 139–141.

5. On the organizational history of the Federation of German Women's Organizations leading up to the abortion debate see Richard J. Evans, *The Feminist Movement in Germany, 1894–1933* (London, 1976), 36–71; and Barbara Greven-Aschoff, *Die bürgerliche Frauenbewegung in Deutschland* (Göttingen, 1981), 90–107.

6. "Die achte Generalversammlung des Bundes deutscher Frauenvereine," *Centralblatt des Bundes deutscher Frauenvereine* 10 (1 December 1908): 121–124; quotation 123.

7. "Protokolle (Stenogramme) der 8. Generalversammlung des Bundes deutscher Frauenvereine von 6. bis 9. Okt," Archiv des Bundes Deutscher Frauenvereine, 16/I, Karton 62, Deutsches Zentralinstitut für soziale Fragen, West Berlin, 367–369; quotation 368. For comments on this law see Julie Eichholz, *Frauenförderungen zur Strafrechtsreform: Kritik und Reformvorschläge* (Mannheim, 1908), 28; and Hanns Dorn, *Strafrecht und Sittlichkeit: Zur Reform dies deutschen Rechtsstrafgesetzbuchs* (Munich, 1907), 56–57.

8. "Stenogramm der 8. Generalversammlung," 377, 372. For a discussion of the strategic considerations that led to the decision not to insist on the abolition of 219 see Evans, *The Feminist Movement in Germany*, 134–135. For biographical information of Camilla Jellinek, see *Vorbemerkung*, Nachlass Camilla Jellinek, Bundesarchiv Koblenz.

9. "Stenogramm der 8. Generalversammlung," 416, 418, 440; for background on Pappenheim see Marion Kaplan, *The Jewish Feminist Movement in Germany: The Campaigns of the Jüdischer Frauenbund, 1904–1938* (Westport, Conn., 1979), 69–75. Cf. J. A. and Olive Banks, *Feminism and Family Planning in Victorian England* (Liverpool, 1964); and Linda Gordon, *Woman's Body, Woman's Right: A Social History of Birth Control in America* (New York, 1976), 116–126, 236–245.

10. "Stenogramm der 8. Generalversammlung," 388–399, 422. Bluhm's speech was also reprinted as *Die Strafbarkeit der Vernichtung des keimenden Lebens vom Standpunkt des Mediziners* (Dresden, 1909).

11. "Stenogramm der 8. Generalversammlung," 401, 404.

12. Ibid., 420, 419, 382.

13. Ibid., 459; on Zetkin's views, see Anna-E. Freier, *Dem Reich der Freiheit sollst Du Kinder gebären: Der Antifeminismus der proletarischen Frauenbewegung im Spiegel der "Gleichheit", 1891–1917* (Frankfurt, 1981), 73–80.

14. On the vote and the compromise proposal see "Unsere achte Generalversammlung," *Centralblatt des Bundes deutscher Frauenvereine* 10 (15 December 1908): 23; see also Greven-Aschoff, *Die bürgerliche Frauenbewegung*, 107–118; and Richard J. Evans, "Liberalism and Society: The Feminist Movement and Social Change," in Evans, ed., *Society and Politics in Wilhelmine Germany* (London, 1978), 15–53; on the crisis in the *Bund fur Mutterschutz* see Helene Stöcker, *Krisenmache: Eine Abfertigung* (Berlin, 1810), Box 3, Helene Stöcker Papers, Swarthmore College Peace Collection, Swarthmore College; and Henriette Fürth, "Die Lage der Mütter und die Entwicklung des Mutterschutzes in Deutschland," in Adele Schreiber, ed., *Die Mutterschaft: ein Sammelwerk für die Probleme der Frau als Mutter* (Munich, 1911), 278–298.

15. *Das Furcht vor dem Kinde: ein Mahnruf an das deutsche Volk* (Düsseldorf, 1914), 1; Weindling, *Health, Race and German Politics*, 250–269.

16. Marie Stritt, "Frauenbewegung und Neumalthusianismus," *Die Neue Generation* 6 (1910): 439–446; Stöcker, "Der Kampf gegen den Geburtenrückgang," *Neue Generation* 8 (1912): 597. On socialist women's attitudes see Freier, *Dem Reich der Freiheit sollst Du Kinder gebären*. 86–92.

17. Fürth, "Die Frauen und die Bevölkerungs- und Schutzmittelfrage," reprint from *Archiv für soziale Hygiene und Demographie*, Kleine Kollektion Henriette Fürth, Internationaal Instituut voor sociale Geschiedenis, Amsterdam. This reprint is not dated, but

the speech was probably made in 1915. On birth strike see Bergmann, "Frauen, Männer, Sexualität und Geburtenkontrolle"; and Freier, *Dem Reich der Freiheit*, 80–81.

18. Evans, *The Feminist Movement in Germany*, 169; Heinz Niggemann, *Emanzipation zwischen Sozialismus und Feminismus: Die sozialdemokratische Frauenbewegung im Kaiserreich* (Wuppertal, 1981), 271; Janssen-Jurreit, "National-biologie," 140; Hackett, "Helene Stocker: Left-Wing Intellectual and Sex Reformer," in Bridenthal, Grossmann, and Koonz, eds., *When Biology Became Destiny*, 119; Heide Schlüpmann, "Radikalisierung der Philosophie: Die Nietzsche-Rezeption und die sexualpolitische Publizistik Helene Stöckers," *Feministische Studien* 3 (May 1984): 30; Heide Soltau, "Erotik und Altruismus—Emanzipationsvorstellungen der radikalen Helene Stöcker," in Jutta Dalhoff, Uschi Frey, and Ingrid Scholl, eds., *Frauenmacht in der Geschichte* (Düsseldorf, 1986), 73. For further comments see Allen, "German Radical Feminism and Eugenics."

19. On different interpretations of Darwinism see Schlüpmann, "Radikalisierung," 26; and Allen, "German Radical Feminism and Eugenics."

20. Key, *Century of the Child*, 1; see also Elsbeth Krukenberg, *Die Frau in der Familie* (Leipzig, 1910), 138–140.

21. Fürth, *Staat und Sittlichkeit* (Leipzig, 1912), 16–20; Stocker, "Malthusische Frauenliga," *Mutterschutz* 1 (1905), 125; Grete Meisel-Hess, *Die sexuelle Krise* (Jena, 1909), 309–315.

22. Ruth Bré, "Ruth Bré und der Bund für Mutterschutz," unpub. typescript, n.d., Nachlass Adele Schreiber, vol. 5, Bundesarchiv Koblenz; Alfred Ploetz, "Bund für Mutterschutz." *Archiv fur Rassen- und Gesellschaftsbiologie* 2 (1905): 166; Walther Borgius, "Mutterschutz und Rassehygiene," *Mutterschutz* 1 (1905): 207–212; Evans (*The Feminist Movement in Germany*, 160) contends that the League actually carried out eugenic selection policies in the homes that it sponsored. I have found no evidence of this in the published regulations of these homes (found in Nachlass Adele Schreiber, vols. 30–32). Cf. Allen, "German Radical Feminism and Eugenics."

23. Key, *Century of the Child*, 38–39; Schreiber, "Die Anfänge neuer Sittlichkeitsbegriffe in Hinblick auf die Mutterschaft," in Schreiber, ed., *Mutterschaft*, 163–188; Krukenberg, *Die Frau in der Familie*, 138–140. This question was discussed in many articles in *Mutterschutz* and *Die neue Generation*: among them Max Flesch, "Ehe, Hygiene und sexuelle Moral," *Mutterschutz* 1 (1905): 276–277; and Max von Nissen, "Herr Doktor, darf ich heiraten?" *Mutterschutz* 1 (1905): 341–351. See also Marie Diers, *Die Mütter des Menschen: Gedanken zur Frauenfrage* (Berlin, 1905), 6–7.

24. Texts of petitions and minutes of meetings on the question of compulsory premarital health examinations are held in Reichsgesundheitsamt, 2371 vol. 1: "Gesundheitszeugnisse fur Ehebewerber," Bundesarchiv Koblenz. The committee of the Health Ministry is quoted in *Frankfurter Zeitung*, 26 August 1917. The text of the informational leaflet is given in *Reichsgesetzblatt*, July 6, 1920. The response of German governments to such proposed legislation is discussed in Woycke, *Birth Control*, 118–119.

25. The text of the League's petition, entitled "Einfügung der geschlechtlichen Belehrung in den Schulunterricht," is in Nachlass Adele Schreiber, vol. 29; Henriette Fürth, *Die geschlechtliche Aufklärung in Haus und Schule* (Leipzig, 1903), 23; Wilhelm Schallmayer, *Vererbung und Auslese in ihrer soziologischen und politischen Bedeutung* (Jena, 1910), 367; comments of Henriette Fürth are in Fürth *Die Bekämpfung der*

Geschlechtskrankheiten als bevölkerungspolitisches, soziales, ethisches und gesetzgeberisches Problem (Frankfurt, 1920), 44.

26. Stöcker, "Leitsätze zum Referat von Dr. phil. Helene Stöcker, Hamburg, 1909," unpub. typescript, Nachlass Adele Schreiber, vol. 28; cf. Ploetz, "Ableitung einer Gesellschaftshygiene und ihrer Beziehung zur Ethik," *Archiv für Rassen- und Gesellschafts-Biologie* 2 (1906): 253–259.

27. "Stenogramm der Generalversammlung, 1908", 379, 427, 446; on alcoholism see Elisabeth Meyer-Renschhausen, *Weibliche Kultur und soziale Arbeit: Eine Geschichte der Frauenbewegung am Beispiel Bremens, 1810–1927* (Cologne, 1989), 225–270.

28. Fürth, *Staat und Sittlichkeit* (Leipzig, 1912), 49; Schreiber's program is described in "Die achte Generalversammlung des Bundes deutscher Frauenvereine," 123; see also Maria von Stach, "Mutterschaft und Bevölkerungspolitik," in Schreiber, ed., *Mutterschaft*, 197. Schreiber's position, which was stated in the context of a package of legislation on retarded children is in "Protokoll—Veranstaltungen des Bundes 8. Generalversammlung 1908," Archiv des Bundes deutscher Frauenvereine, 16/I, Karton 62. For a very critical comment on Schreiber's stand on this issue see Evans, *The Feminist Movement in Germany*, 167.

29. Fürth, *Staat und Sittlichkeit*, 49; "Die achte Generalversammlung," 123; see also Fürth, *Die Regelung der Nachkommenschaft als eugenisches Problem* (Stuttgart, 1929), 33–52.

30. Sheila Faith Weiss, *Race, Hygiene and National Efficiency: The Eugenics of Wilhelm Schallmayer* (Berkeley, 1987), 147–158.

31. Evans, *The Feminist Movement in Germany*, 158–170; for another view of individualism and feminist ideology see Karen Offen, "Liberty, Equality and Justice for Women: The Theory and Practice of Feminism in Nineteenth-Century Europe," in Renate Bridenthal, Claudia Koonz, and Susan Stuard, eds., *Becoming Visible: Women in European History* (Boston, 1987), 335–373.

32. Buck v. Bell, 274 U.S. 200 (1926), 207, quoted in Rosalind Pollack Petchesky, *Abortion and Women's Choice: The State, Sexuality and Reproductive Freedom* (Boston, 1984), 88; see also Stephen Jay Gould, "Carrie Buck's Daughter," in *The Flamingo's Smile: Reflections in Natural History* (New York, 1985), 306–318. On the resistance of German public opinion to compulsory sterilization see Schallmayer, *Vererbung*, 402–407. For a very thoughtful comparison of German to American sterilization policies see Gisela Bock, *Zwangssterilisation im Nationalsozialismus: Studien zur Rassenpolitik und Frauenpolitik* (Wiesbaden, 1986), 113–115.

33. Margaret Sanger, *Autobiography* (New York, 1938), 108 ; on eugenic thought in the American birth control movement see Gordon, *Woman's Body, Woman's Right*, 116–135, and Petchesky, *Abortion*, 67–100; on attitudes of British feminist organizations to birth control and abortion issues see Soloway, *Birth Control*, 133–158.

34. Petchesky, *Abortion*, 395; Carol Brown, "Mothers, Fathers and Children: From Private to Public Patriarchy," in Lydia Sargent, ed., *Women and Revolution: A Discussion of the Unhappy Marriage of Marxism and Feminism* (Boston, 1981), 239–300.

Chapter 11. Motherhood and Social Reform

1. See Gertrud Bäumer, *Der Wandel der Frauenideal in der modernen Kultur: Eine Jugendansprache* (Munich, 1911), 19.

2. On the direction of the women's movement after Bäumer's election as president of the BDF, see Richard J. Evans, *The Feminist Movement in Germany, 1894–1933* (London, 1976), 145–176; Barbara Greven-Aschoff, *Die bürgerliche Frauenbewegung in Deutschland, 1894–1933* (Göttingen, 1981), 90–118, and Bärbel Clemens, *Menschenrechte haben kein Geschlecht! Zum Politikverständnis der Bürgerlichen Frauenbewegung* (Pfaffenweiler, 1988), 79–102; on women in social work see Christoph Sachsse, *Mütterlichkeit als Beruf: Sozialarbeit, Sozialreform und Frauenbewegung* (Frankfurt, 1985), 105–125; Susanne Zeller, *Volksmütter: Frauen im Wohlfahrtswesen der zwanziger Jahre* (Düsseldorf, 1987), 36–53, Dietlinde Peters, *Mütterlichkeit im Kaiserreich: Die Bürgerliche Frauenbewegung und der soziale Beruf der Frau* (Bielefeld, 1984), and Ilka Riemann, *Soziale Arbeit als Hausarbeit: Von der Suppendame zur Sozial-pädagogin* (Frankfurt, 1985).

3. Sachsse, *Mütterlichkeit als Beruf*, 147; Zeller, *Volksmütter*, and Peters, *Mütterlichkeit im Kaiserreich*, emphasize class issues; Riemann, *Soziale Arbeit als Hausarbeit*; Marion A. Kaplan, *The Jewish Feminist Movement: The Campaigns of the Jüdischer Frauenbund, 1904–1938* (Westport, Conn., 1979), 69–75, and Elisabeth Meyer-Renschhausen, *Weibliche Kultur und soziale Arbeit: Eine Geschichte der Frauenbewegung am Beispiel Bremens, 1810–1927* (Cologne, 1989), emphasize gender issues.

4. Helene Lange, *Die Frauenbewegung in ihren modernen Problemen* (Berlin, 1914), 144, quoted in Clemens, *Menschenrechte*, 100.

5. Accounts of Salomon's early life are in her autobiography, Alice Salomon, *Charakter ist Schicksal: Lebenserinnerungen*, trans. Rolf Landwehr (Weinheim, 1984), 9–52; see also Sachsse, *Mütterlichkeit*, 138–151; and Zeller, *Volksmütter*, 44–52, and see my comments in chapter 2 on use of autobiographies.

6. Salomon, *Charakter*, 49, 61–67.

7. Ibid., 30, 61; see also Zeller, *Volksmütter*, 46–47.

8. Salomon, *Charakter*, 59, 43, 40; on political implications of social work see Sachsse, *Mütterlichkeit als Beruf*, 116–125, and Riemann, *Soziale Arbeit als Hausarbeit*, 92–99.

9. Sachsse, *Mütterlichkeit*, 125–131; Charlotte Perkins Gilman, *Women and Economics: A Study of the Economic Relations Between Man and Woman as a Factor in Social Evolution* (Boston, 1898), 113–121; Mary A. Hill, *Charlotte Perkins Gilman: The Making of a Radical Feminist, 1860–1896* (Philadelphia, 1980), 259–282; Olive Schreiner, "The Woman Question," in Carol Barash, ed., *An Olive Schreiner Reader* (London, 1987), 63–100.

10. Alice Salomon, "Die Bedeutung der Frauenbewegung fur das soziale Leben," in *Was wir uns und anderen schuldig sind: Ansprachen und Aufsätze für junge Mädchen* (Leipzig and Berlin, 1912), 128–129.

11. Salomon, *Charakter*, 99; on school reform see Lina Hilger, "Die Frauenschule," *Frauenbildung* (1907): 301–315; and "Bestimmungen über die Neuordnung des höheren Mädchenschulwesens," *Frauenbildung* (1909): 392–393; see also James C.

Albisetti, *Schooling German Girls and Women: Secondary and Higher Education in the Nineteenth Century* (Princeton, 1988), 238–273.

12. Salomon, *Soziale Frauenbildung* (Leipzig, 1908), 1–33; quotations pp. 17, 33.

13. Lili Droescher, "Die Kindergärtnerinnenausbildung in der Frauenschule," *Frauenbildung* (1912): 222–225; Ann Taylor Allen, "Spiritual Motherhood: German Feminists and the Kindergarten Movement, 1840–1914," *History of Education Quarterly* 22 (Fall 1982): 319–340; and Albisetti, *Schooling German Girls and Women*, 277.

14. Salomon, *Soziale Frauenbildung*, 94–95; see also Erika Glaenz, *Die geschichtliche Entwicklung der deutschen Frauenschulen für Volkspflege im Rahmen des weiblichen Bildungswesens* (Würzburg, 1937), 10–17, and Sachsse, *Mütterlichkeit*, 138–148. For another view of female professions see Joan Jacobs Brumberg and Nancy Tomes, "Women in the Professions: A Research Agenda for American Historians," *Reviews in American History* (June 1982), 275–296.

15. Salomon, *Die Ausbildung zum sozialen Beruf* (Berlin, 1927), 154.

16. Henriette Goldschmidt, *Was ich von Froebel lernte und lehrte: Versuch einer Kulturgeschichtlichen Begründung der Froebelschen Erziehungslehre* (Leipzig, 1909), 45–130; Johannes Prüfer and Josefine Siebe, *Henriette Goldschmidt: Ihr Leben und ihr Schaffen* (Leipzig, 1922), 148–175.

17. Criticism of *Hochschule* is in Grete Meisel-Hess, *Betrachtungen zur Frauenfrage* (Berlin, 1914), 53–58; Marianne Weber, *Die Teilnahme der Frauen an die Wissenschaft* (Berlin, 1906), 26; see also Albisetti, *Schooling German Girls and Women*, 223–227.

18. Salomon, *Charakter*, 105; see also Daniel Levine, *Jane Addams and the Liberal Tradition* (Madison, Wis., 1971), and Allen F. Davis, *Spearheads for Reform: The Social Settlements and the Progressive Movement, 1890–1914* (New York, 1877); Sachsse, *Mütterlichkeit*, 125–138; and Glaenz, *Geschichtliche Entwicklung*, 7–8.

19. Sachsse, *Mütterlichkeit*, 125–137; Reulecke, "Bürgerliche Sozialreformer," 321; see also Andrew Lees, *Cities Perceived: Urban Society in European and American Thought, 1820–1940* (New York, 1985), 239–256; Salomon, "Soziale Arbeit in Amerika," in *Was wir uns und andern schuldig sind: Ansprachen und Aufsätze für junge Mädchen* (Leipzig, 1912), 40–45; and Adele Schreiber, "Settlements" in Max Taube et al., ed., *Enzyklopädisches Handbuch des Kinderschutzes und der Jugendfürsorge*, 2 vols. (Leipzig, 1911), 2:247–249.

20. On youth programs see Reulecke, "Arbeiterjugend im Kaiserreich"; and Franz Josef Krafeld, *Geschichte der Jugendarbeit: Von den Anfängen bis zur Gegenwart* (Weinheim and Basel, 1984), 21–54; these authors do not mention Gierke or any other women social reformers.

21. Marie Baum, *Anna von Gierke: Ein Lebensbild* (Weinheim, 1954), 32–35; Anna von Gierke, *25 Jahre Verein Jugendheim und 5 Weitere Jahre* (Charlottenburg, 1954), 7–12; see chapter 2 above on use of autobiographies.

22. Baum, *Anna von Gierke*, 25; Gierke, *25 Jahre*, 12.

23. Baum, *Anna von Gierke*, 35; on child labor legislation see Klaus Saul, Jens Flemming, Dirk Stegmann, and Peter-Christian Witt, eds., *Arbeiterfamilien im Kaiserreich: Materialien zur Sozialgeschichte in Deutschland, 1871–1914* (Frankfurt, 1982), 203–213; Hans Scherpner, *Geschichte der Jugendfürsorge* (Göttingen, 1966),

157–169; on school health programs see Paul Weindling, *Health, Race and German Politics Between National Unification and Nazism* (Cambridge, 1989), 209–212.

24. Gierke, *25 Jahre*, 12; on the moralizing purpose of social work see Riemann, *Sozialarbeit als Hausarbeit*, 92–99.

25. Anna von Gierke's essay, "Die organische Theorie in der Erziehung," is published in Baum, *Anna von Gierke*, 46–52; quotation p. 47; Otto von Gierke, *Natural Law and the Theory of Society*, trans. Ernest Barker (Cambridge, 1934); Michael John, *Politics and the Law in Late-Nineteenth Century Germany: The Origins of the Civil Code* (Oxford, 1989), 109–111.

26. Gierke, "Die organische Theorie," quoted in Baum, *Anna von Gierke*, 51; Gierke, *25 Jahre*, 24–25; Reulecke, "Arbeiterjugend im Kaiserreich;" Weindling, *Health, Race and German Politics*, 212–214.

27. On the definition of spouse abuse as a crime, see Linda Gordon, *Heroes of Their Own Lives: The Politics and History of Family Violence: Boston 1880–1960* (New York, 1988), 289–292.

28. Frieda Duensing, *Frieda Duensing: Ein Buch der Erinnerungen, herausgegeben von ihren Freunden*, Mit Beiträgen von Ricarda Huch, Marie Baum, Ludwig Curtius, (Berlin, 1922), 15, 16, 183. This is a collection that contains many of Duensing's speeches and reports, excerpts from letters, diaries and other autobiographical writings, and biographical sketches by friends and colleagues. See also Lina Koepp, *Frieda Duensing als Führerin und Lehrerin: Zwölf Jahre Berliner Jugendfürsorge* (Berlin, 1927). Duensing's life and career are not covered in the main works on women and social work. See my comments in chapter 2 on use of autobiographical material.

29. Duensing, *Ein Buch der Erinnerungen*, 65, 183; see also Gertrud Bäumer, *Gestalt und Wandel: Frauenbildnisse* (Berlin, 1939), 673.

30. Duensing, *Ein Buch der Erinnerungen*, 68, 12.

31. Ibid., 78, 80, 22; for further comments on Duensing's attitude toward socialism see Gertrud Bäumer, *Gestalt und Wandel: Frauenbildnisse* (Berlin, 1939), 674–675.

32. Duensing's trip to London is described by Ludwig Curtius in Duensing, *Ein Buch der Erinnerungen*, 298–299.

33. Duensing, *Ein Buch der Erinnerungen*, 25; Duensing's dissertation is described in Duensing, *Ein Buch der Erinnerungen*, 310; I have not been able to find a copy of it.

34. Duensing, *Ein Buch der Erinnerungen*, 317, 338–340; see also Bäumer, *Gestalt und Wandel*, 668–669; Koepp, *Frieda Duensing*, 7–22, 43–81.

35. Duensing, *Ein Buch der Erinnerungen*, 317.

36. Ibid., 389; on laws on child protection see Sachsse, *Mütterlichkeit*, 72–77, and Detlev J. K. Peukert, *Grenzen der Sozialdiziplinierung: Aufstieg und Krise der deutschen Jugendfürsorge von 1878 bis 1932* (Cologne, 1986), 116–127, statistics, 327. Surprisingly, Peukert does not discuss Duensing's work or ideas. On societies for prevention of cruelty to children see "Misshandlungen von Kindern," in Taube et al., eds., *Enzyklopädisches Handbuch der Jugendfürsorge*, 2:50–51; and Schreiber, "Leiden und Rechte des Kindes," *Die Frau* 5 (1900/01): 243.

37. Duensing, *Ein Buch der Erinnerungen*, 341, 349.

38. Ibid., 359.

39. "Die achte Generalversammlung des Bundes deutscher Frauenvereine,"

Centralblatt des Bundes deutscher Frauenvereine 10 (1 December 1908), 123; petition is published in the *Centralblatt des Bundes deutscher Frauenvereine*, 16 May 1910; the suggested law protecting against alcoholic fathers is in "Protokolle (Stenogramme) der 10. Generalversammlung des Bundes deutscher Frauenvereine vom 2. bis 5. Oktober, 1912 in Gotha," 409, Archiv des Bundes deutscher Frauenvereine, 16/I, Karton 64, Deutsches Zentralinstitut für soziale Fragen, West Berlin. See also Koepp, *Frieda Duensing*, 20–23.

40. Duensing, *Ein Buch der Erinnerungen*, 367. On juvenile court systems see Peukert, *Grenzen der Sozialdiziplinierung*, 68–96, and "Jugendgerichte," in Taube et al., eds., *Enzyklopädisches Handbuch der Jugendfürsorge*, 1:294–298.

41. Peukert, *Grenzen der Sozialdiziplinierung*, 68–96; Gordon, *Heroes of Their Own Lives*, 288–299, and Gordon, "Feminism and Social Control: The Case of Child Abuse and Neglect," in Juliet Mitchell and Ann Oakley, eds., *What Is Feminism? A Re-Examination* (New York, 1986), 63–84.

42. Duensing, *Ein Buch der Erinnnerungen*, 373; Peukert, *Grenzen der Sozialdiziplinierung*, 78–79.

43. Duensing, *Ein Buch der Erinnerungen*, 375,376. On the absence of a defense attorney at juvenile-court proceedings see Peukert, *Grenzen der Sozialdiziplinierung*, 94.

44. Salomon, *Die Ausbildung zum sozialen Beruf*, 154; Duensing, *Ein Buch der Erinnerungen*, 376, 388; Gordon, *Heroes of their Own Lives*, 295.

45. The petition was published in the *Centralblatt des Bundes deutscher Frauenvereine*, 1 April 1910; on similar developments in America see Brumberg and Tomes, "Women in the Professions," 276–295.

45. Gertrud Bäumer, *Die Frau im Volkswirtschaft und Staatsleben der Gegenwart* (Stuttgart and Berlin, 1914), 244.

Conclusion

1. Carol Gilligan, *In a Different Voice: Psychological Theory and Women's Development* (Cambridge, Mass., 1982), 63.

2. Claudia Koonz, *Mothers in the Fatherland: Women, the Family and Nazi Politics* (New York, 1987), xx; Richard J. Evans, *The Feminist Movement in Germany, 1894–1933* (London, 1976), 274–275.

3. Koonz, *Mothers in the Fatherland*, xx, 12.

4. Alice Salomon, *Charakter ist Schicksal: Lebenserinnerungen*, trans. Rolf Landwehr (Weinheim, 1984), 144–167; Adele Schreiber, "Lebenslauf," unpub. typescript, Nachlass Adele Schreiber, vol. 1, Bundesarchiv Koblenz; Maria Juchacz, *Sie Lebten für eine bessere Welt, Lebensbilder Führender Frauen des 19. und 20. Jahrhundert* (Berlin and Hannover, 1955), 94–95; Lina Koepp, *Frieda Duensing als Führerin und Lehrerin: Zwölf Jahre Berliner Jugendfürsorge* (Berlin, 1927), 81–87; Bärbel Clemens, *Menschenrechte haben kein Geschlecht!: Zur Politikverständnis der bürgerlichen Frauenbewegung* (Pfaffenweiler, 1988), 100; see also Christoph Sachsse, *Mütterlichkeit als Beruf: Sozialarbeit, Sozialreform und Frauenbewegung, 1871–1929* (Frankfurt, 1986), 151–173.

5. Helene Stöcker, *Die Frau und die Heiligkeit des Lebens* (Leipzig, 1921), 10; see

also Amy Hackett, "Helene Stöcker: Left-Wing Intellectual and Sex Reformer," in Renate Bridenthal, Atina Grossmann, and Claudia Koonz, eds., *When Biology Became Destiny: Women in Weimar and Nazi Germany* (New York, 1984), 109–130.

6. On role of women in politics see Barbara Greven Aschoff, *Die bürgerliche Frauenbewegung in Deutschland, 1894–1933* (Göttingen, 1981), 168–172; Salomon, *Charakter ist Schicksal*, 173; Juchacz, *Sie lebten für eine bessere Welt*, 95; text of Weimar Constitution is in Herbert Michaelis and Ernst Schraepler, eds., *Ursachen und Folgen des deutschen Zusammenbruchs 1918 und 1945: Eine Urkunden-und Dokumentensammlung zur Zeitgeschichte* (Berlin, 1956), 3:483–485.

7. Sachsse, *Mütterlichkeit als Beruf*, 193–223, 250–286; Susanne Zeller, *Volksmütter: Frauen im Wohlfahrtswesen der zwanziger Jahre* (Düsseldorf, 1987), 53–85.

8. Sachsse, *Mütterlichkeit als Beruf*, 207–223, 286–304; Zeller, *Volksmütter*, 85–180; Atina Grossmann, "Abortion and Economic Crisis: The 1931 Campaign against Paragraph 218," in Bridenthal, Grossman, and Koonz, eds., *When Biology Became Destiny*, 66–86.

9. Greven-Aschoff, *Die Bürgerliche Frauenbewegung*, 180–190; Evans, *The Feminist Movement in Germany*, 181–185.

10. Evans, *The Feminist Movement in Germany*, 237, 239; Koonz, *Mothers in the Fatherland*, 14 (note Koonz's emphasis on women's use of the term "Lebensraum" for domestic space); Salomon, *Charakter ist Schicksal*, 172; Michel Foucault, "Nietzsche, Genealogy, History," in *The Foucault Reader*, edited by Paul Rabinow (New York, 1984), 76.

11. On Nazi measures on maternal and child welfare see Koonz, "The Fascist Solution of the Woman Question in Italy and Germany," in Renate Bridenthal, Claudia Koonz, and Susan Stuard, eds., *Becoming Visible: Women in European History*, 2nd ed. (Boston, 1987), 499–534; Gisela Bock, "Racism and Sexism in Nazi Germany: Motherhood, Compulsory Sterilization and the State," *Signs* 8 (Spring 1983): 400–421; Bock, *Zwangssterilisation im Nationalsozialismus: Studien zur Rassenpolitik und Frauenpolitik* (Wiesbaden, 1986); Jill Stephenson, *Women in Nazi Society* (New York, 1975), 37–74; Evans, *The Feminist Movement in Germany*, 254.

12. Bock, "Racism and Sexism," 413; Bock, *Zwangssterilisation*, 113–115 (comparison between German and American sterilization programs).

13. Koonz, *Mothers in the Fatherland*, 175–220; Koonz, "The Fascist Solution," 522–525; see also Stephenson, *Women in Nazi Society*, 75–185.

14. Koonz, *Mothers in the Fatherland*, 17; Bock, *Zwangssterilisation*, 118–128, 207.

15. Lois Banner, *Women in Modern America: A Brief History* (New York, 1974), 131–168; Nancy Cott, *The Grounding of Modern Feminism* (New Haven, 1987), 51–142; Susan Ware, *Beyond Suffrage: Women in the New Deal* (Cambridge, Mass., 1981); Greven-Aschoff, *Die Bürgerliche Frauenbewegung*, 195.

16. Elaine Showalter "Toward a Feminist Poetics," in Elaine Showalter, ed., *New Feminist Criticism: Essays on Women, Literature, Theory* (New York, 1985), 125–143.

17. Linda S. Alcoff, "Cultural Feminism vs. Post-Structuralism: The Identity Crisis in Feminist Theory," *Signs* 13 (Spring 1988): 405–436.

18. Anna-E. Freier, *Dem Reich der Freiheit sollst Du Kinder gebären; Der Antifeminismus der proletarischen Frauenbewegung im Spiegel der "Gleichheit," 1891–1917*

(Frankfurt, 1981), 53–116; Sachsse, *Mütterlichkeit als Beruf*, 173–186; Zeller, *Volksmütter*, 73–78.

19. Evans, "The Concept of Feminism: Notes for Practicing Historians," in Ruth-Ellen Joeres and Mary Jo Maynes, eds., *German Women in the Eighteenth and Nineteenth Centuries: A Social and Literary History* (Bloomington, Ind., 1986), 255; Greven-Aschoff, *Die Bürgerliche Frauenbewegung*, 195.

20. Rachel Blau du Plessis, "For the Etruscans," in Showalter, ed., *New Feminist Criticism*, 285; Catherine N. Prelinger, *Charity, Challenge and Change: Religious Dimensions of the Mid-Nineteenth-Century Women's Movement in Germany* (New York, 1987), 171.

21. Evans, "Liberalism and Society: The Feminist Movement for Social Change," in Evans, *Rethinking German History: Nineteenth-Century Germany and the Origins of the Third Reich* (London, 1987), 236; Mary Madeleine Ladd-Taylor, "Mother-Work: Ideology, Public Policy and the Mothers' Movement, 1890–1930" (Ph.D. diss., Yale University, 1986); cf. James C. Albisetti, *Schooling German Girls and Women: Secondary and Higher Education in the Nineteenth Century* (Princeton, 1988), 302–304. Koonz (*Mothers in the Fatherland*, 31) defines the dilemma facing female politicians in the Weimar Republic by raising the question, "Were women equal citizens or a special-interest lobby?"

22. Betty Friedan, *The Feminine Mystique* (New York, 1963; reprinted 1977), 271; Shulamith Firestone, *The Dialectic of Sex: The Case for Feminist Revolution* (New York, 1970; reprinted 1972), 91, 206.

23. On historical background of the rise of feminism see Banner, *Women in Modern America*, 228–238.

24. Sylvia Ann Hewlett, *A Lesser Life: The Myth of Women's Liberation in America* (New York, 1986), 149–176; Gilligan, *In a Different Voice*; Nancy Chodorow, *The Reproduction of Mothering: Psychoanalysis and the Sociology of Gender* (Los Angeles and Berkeley, 1978); Sara Ruddick, *Maternal Thinking: Toward a Politics of Peace* (Boston, 1989).

Archival Sources

Bundesarchiv Koblenz
    Nachlass Adele Schreiber
    Nachlass Marie-Elisabeth Lüders
    Nachlass Camilla Jellinek
    Records of the Reichsgesundheitsamt (Bestand R/86):
        2308: Frauenarbeit
        2309: Versicherungswesen
        2369: Bevölkerungspolitik
        2376–77: Bekämpfung der Kindersterblichkeit
        2379: Schwangerschaftsunterbrechung
        2381: Hebammen in Preussen
        2382: Hessen: Zentrale für Mutter- und Säuglingspflege
        3272: Gesundheitszeugnisse für Ehebewerber
    Records of the Reichsversicherungsamt (Bestand R/89):
        404: Mutterschaftsversicherung und Kinderfürsorge
        2122: Akten über Wochenfürsorge

Deutsches Zentralinstitut für soziale Fragen, West Berlin
    Archiv des Bundes deutscher Frauenvereine
        2/III/3: Rechtskommission 1894–1906
        2/III/4: Rechtskommission 1907–1910
        2/IX/5: Kommission für Kinderschutz
        8/1: Sittlichkeitsfragen
        10/1–2: Bildungs- und Erziehungsfragen
        16/1/1: Generalversammlungen 1896–1900
        16/1/2: Generalversammlung 1902
        16/1/5: Generalversammlung 1908
    Nachlass Hedwig Heyl
    Nachlass Anna von Gierke

International Instituut voor Socialgeschiedenis, Amsterdam
    Kleine Kollektion Henriette Fürth

Pestalozzi-Froebel Haus, West Berlin: Archive

Pestalozzi-Froebel Verband, West Berlin: Archive

Niedersächsisches Staatsarchiv, Wolfenbüttel
    Nachlass Karl Schrader

Swarthmore College Peace Collection, Swarthmore, Pennsylvania
    Helene Stöcker Papers

Archival Sources

Staatsarchiv Hamburg
  Politische Polizei S 9000: Verband fortschrittlicher Frauenvereine in Berlin
  Politische Polizei S 20214: Hamburger Ortsgruppe, Deutscher Bund für Mutterschutz
  Politische Polizei S 12843: Deutscher Bund für Mutterschutz
  Medizinalkollegium II, Nr. 22: Bund für Mutterschutz
  Politische Polizei S 7133: Deutscher Fröbel-Verein
  Familienarchive: Nachlass Emilie Wüstenfeld
  Archivalien des Frauenvereins zur Unterstützung der
    Armenpflege von 1849
  Schule des Paulsenstifts

Stadtarchiv Frankfurt Am Main
  Henriette Fürth: Personalakten
  Protokolle des Stadtrats Frankfurt am Main

Zentrales Staatsarchiv der Deutschen Demokratischen Republik, Merseburg
  Ministerium für Volkswohlfahrt, Rep. 191:
    Erziehungsanstalten- und Vereine
    no. 16: Klein-Kinder Anstalt zu Brandenburg
    no. 17: Die Kinder-Bewahranstalten, Berlin
    no. 20: Kleinkinderfürsorge, Berlin
    no. 49: Die Kleinkinder-Bewahranstalten zu Bonn
    no. 64: Pestalozzi-Froebelhaus
    no. 70: Die Klein-Kinder-Schulen zu Breslau
  Ministerium des Innern: Rep. 77
    Tit. 662, no. 122: Bund für Mutterschutz
Zentrales Staatsarchiv der Deutschen Demokratischen Republik, Potsdam
  Auswärtiges Amt, Abt. III, 351:
    35088/1–5: Die Frauen und Kinderarbeit in Deutschland
  Reichsministerium des Innern: Medizinal-Polizei
    9342–9353: Massregeln gegen den Geburtenrückgang
    9421: Menschliche Vererbungslehre und Bevölkerungskunde
    11866–69: Massregeln gegen Geschlechtskrankheiten
    11973–75: Bekämpfung der Säuglingssterblichkeit
    11990: Die deutsche Vereinigung für Säuglingsschutz
    26239: Ehegesundheitszeugnisse
  Reichstag 441, I, 8: Medizinalwesen
    Kommissionsverhnandlungen betr. Bekämpfung von
    Geschlechtskrankheiten
  Reichstag 443, I, 9: Medizinalwesen
    Bevölkerungspolitik))

Index

Abicht, Martha, 216
abortion, 188, 191, 234–235; avoidance of hereditary disease, 200–201; legalization, 191–192, 194, 201; under National Socialism, 236; relationship to infanticide, 192–193; relationship to malnutrition, 201
abuse; child, 221, 223, 225; psychological, 225; sexual, 225; spouse, 223–225
Academy for Women (Lyzeum für Damen), 129
Albisetti, James C., 92, 124
Allgemeiner deutscher Frauenverein (German Women's Association), 97
Althaus, Theodor, 49, 51, 54
Anthony, Katherine, 187
anti-Semitism, 236
Anti-Socialist Laws, 112
Arnim, Bettina von, 82
Association for Home Health Care, 120
Association for the Support of the German Catholics, 52
Association Laws, 186
Association of Female Guardians, 222
Augspurg, Anita, 174; *The Ethical Side of the Women's Movement*, 163; opposition to war, 232
authority: rule setting, 10
authority, maternal, 113; child-rearing, 25
authority, paternal, 43–44, 55, 57, 84, 104, 138–139, 141; breast-feeding, 17, 19; education of children, 20; relationship to maternal love, 71

Baader, Ottilie, 155
Bachofen, Johann Jakob, *Mother-Right*, 160
Barnard, Henry, 109
Baum, Marie, 190
Bäumer, Gertrud, 206, 232, 233
Bebel, August, 160; on economic oppression of women, 166; endorsement of suffrage, 185; socialism, 209; *Woman and Socialism*, 155; *Woman in Past, Present and Future*, 107
Beecher, Catharine, 93

Benas, Henriette. *See* Goldschmidt, Henriette
Berg, Barbara, *The Remembered Gate: Origins of American Feminism*, 56
Berlin Society for the Support of Day-Care Centers, 61
Bernstein, Julius, 196
Bewahranstalten (infant schools), 51
biography, interpretation of, 42–48
birth control, 188, 190–191, 194, 196, 224; avoidance of hereditary disease, 200–201; under National Socialism, 238; relationship to child welfare, 190
birth rate, decline, 177, 189; concern, 173; link to military weakness, 177
"birth strike," 196–197
Bissing-Beerberg, Adolf von, 107
Blackbourn, David, 96
Bluhm, Agnes, 193
Bock, Gisela, 237–238
Boelte, Maria, 109
Bölsche, Wilhelm, 159
bonding. *See* mother-child bond
Book of Good Behavior for Children (Siltenbüchlein für Kinder) (Campe), 20–21
Braun, Lily, 1, 149, 175; advocacy of suffrage, 186; on child labor, 147; endorsement of eugenics, 197; on marriage bans for teachers, 166–167; on maternal control, 162; socialist activities, 156; utopianism, 167–168; woman suffrage, 8
Bré, Ruth: on matriarchy, 180–181; utopianism, 175, 198–199
breast-feeding: financial support, 184; of illegitimate children, 179; laws requiring, 20; link to infant mortality, 177–179; paternal authority, 20; relationship to child support, 179
Breymann, Henriette, 7, 26, 41, 75; career in education, 55, 62–63; communal life, 55; concept of female professionalism, 111; concept of social activism, 111; criticism of government social welfare, 123; on Darwinism, 113; on education prohibitions, 84; founding of girl's school, 89–91; founding

Breymann, Henriette (*continued*)
of Pestalozzi-Froebel House, 115–121, 126–128; involvement in public child-care, 114–115; maternal influence on, 44–45, 68; religious crisis, 48; views on public education, 129
Brown, Carol, 204
Büchner, Luise, *Women and their Vocation*, 92
Bussemer, Herrad-Ulrike, 7, 96, 101

Campe, Joachim Heinrich, *Book of Good Behavior for Children*, 20–21
capitalism, effect on family, 113
career: in child-care, 97–100; effect on family, 92; increased opportunity for women, 172; industrial, 128, 154, 164; influence on feminist theory, 111; and motherhood, 163–171; need for independence, 55; negative effect on motherhood, 158; opportunities for women, 92; relationship to class, 164–165; for single women, 35, 49, 73, 90, 95, 97–100, 119; in social service, 102–103; for women in education, 35, 62–63, 67–72; women's right to, 94
Carpenter, Mary, 86
Cauer, Minna: political activism, 136; radical feminism, 124
celibacy, 166, 170
censorship, effect on feminist movement, 76
Central Agency for Youth Services, 219, 222
Central Association for the Welfare of the Working Classes (Centralverein für das Wohl der arbeitenden Klassen), 65–66, 88
Century of the Child, The (Key), 157, 190
Charlottenburg Youth Center, 215–216
child-care: funding, 242; public, 88, 114–115, 146, 169, 179, 217–218; role of government, 217–218; for working parents, 216
child-rearing: changes in theory, 18–22; class perspectives, 60; effect of kindergarten movement, 59–66; effect on society, 80; as governmental issue, 129; individualism in, 32–33, 47; maternal authority, 25; natural, 21; paternal authority, 17; as public issue, 17, 147; public sphere, 30; reform, 87, 98; religious tolerance in, 52; role of play, 21; secularization, 21, 38; shift to mother-centered, 17; socialist, 170
child welfare, 144; effect of divorce, 75; governmental involvement, 18–22, 127; 217–218; laws regarding, 157; and population growth, 18; regulations, 216; relationship to birth control, 190; socialist activities, 146
Chodorow, Nancy, 244
citizenship, relationship to feminism, 11
Civil Code of German Empire, 135; divorce laws, 141; laws affecting family, 145–148; laws regarding married women, 138; laws regarding single women, 138; opposition by feminists, 136–144; parental rights, 138–139
class: anti-liberalism of working class, 58–59; attitudes toward working class, 56; barriers to communication, 220; conflict, 79–81; female solidarity, 99, 113, 156, 209–210, 228; gender consciousness, 112, 116, 155, 241; growth of middle class, 56; perspectives on child-rearing, 60; reconciliation through kindergartens, 65; relationships, 59; relationship to career, 164–165; relationship to feminism, 12, 62, 112–113; relationship to kindergarten, 60–62, 64–65, 69–70, 86; significance to mother-child bond, 43; social responsibility, 105
Clemens, Bärbel, 6, 232
Committee on Child Protection, 146–147
contextualism, 4
cooperative living, 168–169
Cott, Nancy, 9, 154
court, juvenile, 225–226; role of social worker, 226
Crüsemann, Hedwig. *See* Heyl, Hedwig
culture, relationship to feminism, 4–5, 11
custody, in divorce, 141–143

Darwinism, 113, 158; reform, 159–160
day-care, 61, 222
Dialectic of Sex, The (Firestone), 243
Die Arbeit und die neue Erziehung (Work and New Education) (Marenholtz-Bülow), 86
Die Familie (The Family) (Riehl), 93
Die Frauen und Ihr Beruf (Women and their Vocation) (Büchner), 92
Diesterweg, Adolph, 82; support of kindergarten movement, 67
discourse, public, 2; creation by authority, 10; dominant, 10–11; on family, 2; on reproductive issues, 172; on women and

work, 164; women's role, 67; women's role in shaping, 77
Dittmar, Luise, 75
divorce, 50, 74–75, 161, 224; child custody, 141–143; laws regarding, 75, 103, 138
Dohm, Hedwig: advocacy of suffrage, 109; *The Mothers*, 168; radical feminism, 108; views on condominium living, 167
Douai, Adolf, *Kindergarten and School as Social-Democratic Institutions*, 107
DuBois, Ellen Carol, 77
Duden, Barbara, 28
Duensing, Frieda, 1, 7, 175; child welfare activism, 144; definition of women's cultural role, 219; endorsement of governmental intervention in family, 219, 221; legality of parent-child relationship, 221; opposition to socialism, 221
Dummer, Ethel Sturges, 187

education: access, 4; admission of women to university, 125; adult programs, 120; ban on married female teachers, 143, 152, 166–167, 171; based on maternal discipline, 116; as career for married women, 152; as career for women, 35, 62–63, 67–72, 92, 97–100; college for women, 68; concern with social reform, 60; conventional, 43; day-care, 61; early childhood, 37–38; female-dominated in United States, 72, 131; girls' secondary schools, 87–88, 211; as male-dominated profession, 39, 61–62, 70, 77, 124; methods of Pestalozzi, 22–28; opportunities for women, 73, 242; opposition to women, 158; required for child-care, 98; required for motherhood, 31, 73; role of government, 128; sex, 200; Society for the Education of Women, 67–68; support from socialism, 87; value of play, 61, 88; women's admission to universities, 72, 211; women's right to, 30, 34
Ellis, Havelock, 160, 173; views on birth control, 190
Emile (Rousseau), 20
employment. *See* career
Engels, Friedrich, 160
Enlightenment, French, 27
Epstein, Barbara Leslie, 172
equality: gender, 69, 114–115; gender-neutral, 8

equal rights. *See* rights, equal
Equal Rights Amendment, 239
Erziehung und Unterricht des Weiblichen Geschlechts (Education and Instruction of the Female Sex) (Gleim), 33
Ethical Side of the Women's Movement, The (Die ethische Seite der Frauenbewegung) (Augspurg), 163
eugenics: anti-feminist views, 157–158; association with National Socialism, 197, 202; implications for motherhood, 157–158; mainline, 160; movement, 197–202; social-radical, 160; treatment of the mentally retarded, 201
Evans, Richard J., 5, 96, 188, 195, 197, 203, 231, 241
evolution: endorsement by radical feminists, 156; in feminist theory, 161; theory related to motherhood, 156–163
exploitation, sexual, 98

Fabianism, 164, 221
Faderman, Lillian, 170
family: effect of revolution, 58; child labor, 146–147; child-rearing authority, 17; as community, 140; criticism, 105–106, 147; cultivation of responsibility, 106; defines role of women, 8; divorce, 50, 74–75, 103, 138, 141–143, 161, 224; effect of capitalism, 113; effect of Civil Code, 145–148; effect of industrialization, 69; effect of women's careers, 92; laws affecting, 135, 138–139, 145–148, 208, 242; legal structure, 139; maternal involvement outside home, 51, 56–57, 66; paternal authority, 17, 19–20, 43, 55, 57, 61, 84, 138–139, 141–142; as private sphere, 28–30; in Prussian Legal Code, 18–19; public discourse, 2; as public issue, 23, 96; reform, 58–59, 181; relationship to state, 2, 104–110, 146; role of emancipation, 55; socialist theory, 160; structure, 2; views of J. Fichte, 29; views of G. Hegel, 29
Family, The (Die Familie) (Riehl), 93
Faust (Goethe), 153
Federation of German Women's Organizations, 129, 136; on child support, 144; endorsement of women in juvenile court system, 227; opposition to controversial programs, 206; on parental rights, 141;

Federation of German Women's Organizations (*continued*)
views on birth control, 204; views on maternity coverage, 184; views on reproductive rights, 190–191
Federation of Jewish Women, 191, 193
Federation of Progressive Women's Organizations, 168
Female Association for the Care of the Poor and Sick, 52
Female Teachers' Association, 211
Feminine Mystique, The (Friedan), 243
feminism: abortion viewpoint, 190–195; approach to social problems, 6; biological determinism theories, 114; career opportunities, 35, 95, 97–100; class relations, 62; and class solidarity, 99, 113, 156; comparative, 11–12, 72, 77, 93, 109–110, 130–131, 147, 238–239; conservative, 6; definition, 12; denounced by religious leaders, 108; development of sexuality, 152; division over views on reproduction, 188; domestic, 6; economic independence, 98; endorsement of socialism, 155–156; eugenic theory, 198–202; evolutionary theory, 161; expansion of public role, 145–148; German orientation, 230; ideology based on equal rights, 8; individualist, 72–78; international, 4, 11, 102; maternal, 5, 7, 72–78; moderate, 1, 136; moderate vs. radical, 136, 144; under National Socialism, 235–238; organizations in Germany, 93; organizations in United States, 93; organized, 2, 53, 56–78, 95–110; periodicals, 72–73; propaganda against, 158; public policy approaches, 154; radical, 101, 108, 124, 136, 150–163, 171–172; related to social reform, 60; relational, 11, 136; relationship to citizenship, 11; relationship to class, 12–13, 112–113; relationship to politics, 4–5; right to education, 30; role in development of culture, 4–5, 11, 163; role of government, 147, 182–183; role of religion, 48–49, 51; sexual issues, 136; social, 6; social origin, 41–57; theoretical origin, 17–40; view of paternal authority, 147; woman-centered ideology, 8
Feuerbach, Ludwig, 51, 54
Fichte, Johann Gottlieb, 23; family views, 29
Firestone, Shulamith, *The Dialectic of Sex*, 243

Fliedner, Theodor, 61
foster care system, 146, 179
Foucault, Michel, 9–10, 236
Frauen-Zeitung, 58, 72–73
Frederick (Crown Prince): support for kindergarten, 125
Frederick the Great: biopolitics, 18; reforms, 23
Free Kindergarten Society, 128
free love, 173–174
French Revolution, 27
Frevert, Ute, on infant mortality, 174
Friedan, Betty, *The Feminine Mystique*, 243
Froebel, Carl: on equality for women, 62; role in women's education, 67–69
Froebel, Friedrich, 18; death, 85; development of children's games, 38; on education for child-care, 98; kindergarten movement, 35–40; *Mother and Nursery Songs*, 37; training of women as teachers, 70–71. *See also* motherhood, spiritual
Froebel, Johanna: role in education of women, 67, 69–71; views on divorce, 75
Froebel Seminar, 98
Froebel Society, 97
From Darwin to Nietzsche (Von Darwin bis Nietzsche: Ein Buch Entwicklungsethik) (Tille), 159
Fürth, Henriette, 1, 7, 149, 175, 233; endorsement of eugenics, 197; socialist activities, 156

Galton, Francis, 157–158
Gayette-Georgens, Jeanne-Marie von, 99; on capitalism and motherhood, 113; involvement in public child-care, 115
Gemälde Weiblicher Erziehung (Pictures of Female Education) (Rudolphi), 32
gender: and class, 112, 116; equality, 69, 114–115; injustice based on, 5; relationship to class, 155, 241
General Educational Association, 108
General Educational Union, 39
Gerhard, Adele, 164, 165, 166
German; revolution, 42; unification, 42, 71, 95, 100–104
German Academic Union, 136
German Froebel Society, 105
German Neo-Malthusian Committee, 196

German Woman Suffrage Association, 185
German Women's Association (Allgemeiner deutscher Frauenverein), 97, 100, 102–103, 129; on legal rights of women, 104; on parental rights, 141; views of suffrage, 109
Gierke, Anna von, 1, 7, 233; role in childcare, 215–218
Gilligan, Carol, 3, 229, 244
Gilman, Charlotte Perkins, 161, 166; on public motherhood, 172; *Women and Economics*, 162
Gleim, Betty, 17–18; criticism of Rudolphi, 33–34; *Education and Instruction of the Female Sex*, 33; on motherhood, 30; proposal for careers for women, 35
Goethe, Johann Wolfgang von, *Faust*, 43, 153
Goldscheid, Rudolf, 190
Goldschmidt, Henriette, 7, 41, 95; founding of Academy for Women, 129; founding of German Women's Association, 97, 100; moderate feminism, 136; nationalist views, 101; view of paternal authority, 44; views on public education, 129
Goldschmidt, Johanna, 80; closing of school, 83; founding of Association for the Support of the German Catholics, 52; founding of Hamburg Academy, 66; *Rebekka and Amalie*, 52; reform activities, 67; role in kindergarten movement, 67; *Joys and Sorrows of Motherhood*, 53
Gordon, Linda, 204, 227
"great social household," 79–93, 140
Greven-Aschoff, Barbara, 6, 195, 239, 241
guardianship, 103–104, 139, 145–148, 222; court, 141, 223

Hackett, Amy, 6, 11, 197
Hahn-Hahn, Ida, 46; female emancipation, 50
Hall, G. Stanley, 126
Hamburg Academy for Women, 66–72, 98; closing, 74–75; as educational experiment, 68
Hamburg Froebel Society, 98; training for child-care workers, 99
Hamburg Society for Women's Education, 68
Hammerschlag, Meta, 201
Hamminck-Schepel, Annette, 117–118
Harris, William Torrey, 109
Harrison, Elizabeth, 126

Hartsock, Nancy, 12
Heerwart, Eleonore, 130
Hegel, G.W.F., 130; on family structure, 139; family views, 29–30; public-private dichotomy, 31
Heinz, Bettina, *Ruses of Powerless People*, 6
heredity: effect on child's personality, 157; vs. environment, 199
Heredity and Selection (Vererbung und Auslese) (Schallmayer), 157–158
Heyl, Hedwig, 91, 119; founding of School of Domestic Arts, 115–116; views on female solidarity, 99
Heymann, Lida Gustava, 174; opposition to war, 232
Hippel, Theodor Gottlieb von, 18; *On Improving the Status of Women*, 27; on women's rights, 28
Hirsch, Jenny, 94
Hirschfeld, Magnus, 170
Holst, Amalie, 18; on motherhood, 30; *On the Capacity of Women for Higher Education*, 31; public-private dichotomy, 31
homosexuality, 170–171
Honegger, Claudia, *Ruses of Powerless People*, 6
How Gertrude Teaches her Children (Pestalozzi), 23, 25

illegitimacy, 143, 148, 179; mortality rate, 144, 146
individualism, 24–25; in child-rearing, 32–33, 47; developed in kindergartens, 107; in feminist movement, 182; in public motherhood, 59
industrialization, 42, 79, 111; effect on family, 69; effects on workers' health, 119–120
infanticide, 19, 23; laws, 23, 192; relationship to abortion, 192–193
inflation, effect on children's services, 234
insurance, maternity, 155, 183–185, 244; under National Socialism, 236
International Women's Conference (1904), 166
International Women's League for Peace and Freedom, 233

Jastrow, Hermann, 140–141
Jellinek, Camilla, 192–194, 201

Jessen, Luise, 120–121, 124
Joeres, Ruth-Ellen, 43
Joys and Sorrows of Motherhood, The (Goldschmidt), 53

Kelly, Joan, 13
Kempin, Emilie, 139
Kerber, Linda, 40, 118; "republican motherhood," 56; on women in politics, 77
Kevles, Daniel J., 160
Key, Ellen, 161, 185; *The Century of the Child*, 157, 190; endorsement of suffrage, 161; pacifism, 161; on public motherhood, 172
kindergarten: citizenship objectives, 63–64; class relationships and class conflicts, 60, 64–65; compared to infant schools, 60; criticism by religious leaders, 107; criticism by Sieveking, A., 70; development of individualism, 107; effect on child-rearing, 59–66; governmental approval, 90; governmental prohibition, 83–84; growth, 104–105; incorporation into public schools, 62, 90, 105, 108, 129–131; influence of political developments; international movement, 86, 108; movement by Froebel, 35–40; opens to all classes, 115; programs in United States, 74, 110, 126–127, 130–131; protest against repression, 85–89; public support, 169–170; relationship to class, 61–62, 69–70, 86; relationship to feminism, 97; religious tolerance in, 61, 64; as social organism, 64; support from socialism, 87, 169; survival of movement, 81; teacher-training, 67–72, 90, 97–100; training for women, 67–72; value of play, 38
Kindergarten and School as Social-Democratic Institutions (Kindergarten und Schule als sozialdemokratische Anstalten) (Douai), 107
Kladderadatsch, 84
Koonz, Claudia, *Mothers in the Fatherland*, 7, 230–232
Kraditor, Aileen, 6
Kriege, Matilda, 109
Krukenberg, Elsbeth, 199
Kulturkampf, 105

Lange, Helene, 7, 122; on equality, 1; on female citizenship, 207; as leader of feminist movement, 124–126; on marriage bans for teachers, 167; moderate feminism, 136; on women's nature, 123
laws: abortion, 234–235; affecting single women, 138, 142–144; breast-feeding, 20; child abuse, 223, 225; child labor, 147, 157, 216; child-rearing, 148; child-support, 222; child welfare, 157; divorce, 103, 138, 141–143, 161; educational, 83–84; family, 135, 138–139, 145–148, 242; guardianship, 20, 139, 145–148, 222; illegitimacy, 148; infanticide, 23, 192; marriage, 75, 103, 135, 138–139; parental rights, 138; paternal authority, 19–20; prostitution, 136, 144, 174; single mothers, 19, 173; widows, 20; women's political activities, 206; women's status, 104; working women, 164, 183
Leach, William, 109–110
League for the Protection of Mothers (Bund für Mutterschutz), 173–176, 178, 186, 234; dissolution, 235; endorsement of sex education, 200; views of birth control, 188, 196; views on abortion, 188; views on infant mortality, 184
League of Progressive Women's Organizations (Verband fortschrittlicher Frauenvereine), 136, 168; views on legalization of abortion, 193; views on maternity coverage, 184
League of Protestant Women (Evangelischer Frauenbund), 193
League of Women Voters, 239
Leipzig Association for Female Education, 100–101
Leonard and Gertrude (*Lienhard und Gertrud*) (Pestalozzi), 24–25, 91, 116, 170
Lette, Adolph, 97
Lette Association, 97
Lette-Verein (Lette Association), 97
Levana (Richter, J.), 29, 45
liberation, sexual, 50
Liebknecht, Wilhelm, 107
Lindemann, Mary, 18
Listen der Ohnmacht (Ruses of Powerless People) (Honegger and Heinz), 6
Loeper-Housselle, Marie, 124
Lutheranism, 48
Lütkens, Doris, *Our Children*, 63–64

Malthus, Thomas Robert, 196
Marenholtz-Bülow, Bertha von, 1, 9, 41; on class, 53–54; criticism of maternal role, 44; divorce, 74; influence of utopian socialism, 50; political protest, 85–89; on social motherhood, 49; Society for Popular Education, 88; survival of kindergarten movement, 81; *Work and New Education*, 86
marriage: of convenience, 54–55, 74, 92, 94, 198; egalitarian, 51; eugenic theory, 198; importance of free choice, 74; premarital health examination, 199–200; relationship to women's careers, 75
maternal: discipline, 116; feminism, 7; nurture, 43–44, 48, 71; revolution, 18–22; role and self-esteem, 43
maternity leave, 183–184
Mayer, Josephine, 120
mental retardation, internment, 201–202
Meyer, Bertha, 106
Meyer-Renschhausen, Elisabeth, 6; on women's culture, 10
Meysenbug, Malwida von, 41; career, 54–55; on education prohibitions, 83–84; maternal influence on, 43–44, 68; religious crisis, 48–49; views on women's education, 49, 70
Michelet, Jules, 85
Middendorff, Wilhelm, 62–65
Mill, John Stuart, *The Subjection of Women*, 1, 123
Mind of the Child, The (Die Seele des Kindes) (Preyer), 157
Möbius, Paul, *On the Physiological Feeble-Mindedness of Women*, 158
Monist League, 158
morality, social: source in mother-child bond, 17–18, 24
Morgenstern, Lina, 97, 113
mortality: child, 19, 47; infant, 144, 146, 173–187, 222
Moses, Alfred, 196
Mother and Nursery Songs (Mutter- und Koselieder) (Froebel), 37
mother-child bond, 3, 172, 229; basis of cooperative virtue, 180; in community-building, 35; as origin of altruism, 160; significance of class, 43; source of natural rights, 139; source of social development, 31, 37, 63; source of social morality, 17–18, 24

motherhood: and career, 163–171; choice, 188–205; community-building, 27; educational requirements, 31, 73; effect of career, 158; effect on child's personality, 157; effect on intellect, 158; evolutionary theory, 82, 156–163; as form of creativity, 220; hereditary issues, 157–163; as learned behavior, 114; legal reform, 104; relationship to state, 17; "republican," 40, 56; role in unification, 100–104; social, 12–13, 31, 46, 49, 131, 187; source of ethical authority, 12; source of social development, 34
motherhood, biological, 2, 22, 25–26, 40, 135, 140, 155–163, 165, 180
motherhood, organized: basis for female citizenship, 228
motherhood, private, 1–2, 48–53, 203–205; and policy planning, 2; secularization of child-rearing, 2
motherhood, public, 1–2, 36, 48–53, 145–148, 172, 203–205; charitable work, 51, 56; government intervention, 147; individualism in, 59; maternal ethic, 3; and policy planning, 2; secularization of child-rearing, 2; and social reform, 76
motherhood, single: breast-feeding, 146, 179; child custody, 142–143; morality issues, 180; parental rights, 144–146; in Prussian Legal Code, 19; rights, 182, 198
motherhood, spiritual, 2; autonomy in, 72; basis for female citizenship, 102, 111; class reconciliation, 65; and conservatism, 93; criticism of war, 100–101; force for social change, 80; gender-specific ethic, 116; goal of gender cooperation, 121; introduction to bureaucracies, 112–113; opposed by male teacher groups, 130; public role for women, 36; radical feminist view, 150; relationship to equal rights, 76; social activism, 66; and social reform, 94
Motherhood and Intellectual Work (Mutterschaft and geistige Arbeit) (Simon and Gerhard), 164
Mothers in the Fatherland (Koonz), 7, 230–232
Müller, Paula, 193

Nathusius, Philipp, 108
National American Women Suffrage Association, 187

296 Index

National Housewives' League, 235
National Rural Housewives' League, 235
National Socialism: birth control under, 238; endorsement of eugenics, 197, 202; feminism as a force in, 235–238; maternity insurance, 236; rise of, 4, 7; role of women, 230–231
Naumann, Friedrich, 221
neo-Malthusianism, 190, 194, 196
"Neue Bahnen" (New Avenues), 104
Nietzsche, Friedrich, 159
Niggemann, Heinz, 197

Offen, Karen, 9, 186; on gender cooperation, 121; maternal ideologies, 172; relational feminism, 11
Olberg, Oda, 161, 171
On Improving the Status of Women (Über die bürgerliche Verbesserung der Weiber) (Hippel), 27
On Legislation and Infanticide (Uber Gesezgebung und Kindermord) (Pestalozzi), 23, 173
On the Capacity of Women for Higher Education (Über die Bestimmung des Weibes zur höhern Bildung) (Holst), 31
Otto, Louise: activities in feminist movement, 72–74; advocacy of suffrage, 109; attempt at legal reform, 103; on education prohibitions, 83–84; effect of censorship, 76; on emancipation, 59; equal rights activities, 96; founding of German Women's Association, 97; *New Avenues*, 104; pacifist views, 101; radical feminism, 101; views on emancipation, 75–76
Otto-Peters, Louise. *See* Otto, Louise
Our Children (Lütkens), 63–64

pacifism, 7
Pape, Charlotte, "The Rights of Mothers over their Children," 103–104
Pappenheim, Bertha, 193
Patriotic Women's Association, 103
Paulsen, Charlotte, 41; closing of school, 83; criticism of maternal role, 44; founding of Pestalozzi Society, 51–52; founding of Women's Society for the Support of Poor Relief, 80–81
Peabody, Elizabeth, 108–109
pedagogy. *See* education

Pestalozzi, Johann Heinrich, 9; on child-rearing, 17; educational methods, 22–28; *How Gertrude Teaches her Children*, 23; *Leonard and Gertrude*, 24–25, 91, 116; *On Legislation and Infanticide*, 23; view of women, 23
Pestalozzi-Froebel House, 115–121; involvement in social activism, 126–131; teacher-training, 116
Pestalozzi Society, 51–52
Petchesky, Rosalind Pollack, 205
Peukert, Detlev, 226
philanthropists, 21, 25
Pictures of Female Education (Gemalde weiblicher Erziehung) (Rudolphi), 32
play: role in child-rearing, 21; value in education, 38, 61, 88
Ploetz, Alfred, 157–158, 199
politics: relationship to feminism, 4–5; relation to public motherhood, 76; restriction of women's activities, 79, 94
population quality. *See* eugenics
pornography, 136
power, effect of gender, 10
Prelinger, Catherine N., 6, 51, 53, 65, 68, 242
presentism, 4
Preyer, Wilhelm, *The Mind of the Child*, 157
profession. *See* career
professionalism: conflict with maternalism, 152–153; female, 2, 91, 94, 119; in social services, 112
prostitution: laws regarding, 144; legalization, 174; regulation, 136
Protestant Women's Organization, 235
Prussian General Law (1794): divorce, 141–142
Prussian General Law (1854): divorce, 142
Prussian Law of Association (1850), 84
Prussian Legal Code: rights of single mothers, 19; view of family, 18–19
public-private: dichotomy, 29–31, 56–57, 84, 90, 118; integration, 207; overcoming divisions, 229

Quataert, Jean, 169, 185

"Ragged Schools," 86
rape, 225; marital, 46, 201

Index

Rebekka and Amalie (Goldschmidt, J.), 52
reform: abortion, 191; child-rearing, 98; domestic, 4, 58–59, 93, 135, 161, 181; educational, 87, 124–125, 211; legal, 103–104, 148; political, 125; sexual, 182, 191
reform, social, 2, 56; child welfare regulations, 216; class division, 66; concern with education, 60; and public motherhood, 76; related to feminism, 60; role of government, 207; through spiritual motherhood, 94; women's role, 80, 210
religion: control of education, 83; control of infant schools, 60–61, 105; discrimination, 54; German Catholic, 51, 53, 65; role in feminism, 48–49, 51; tolerance in kindergarten, 61, 64; women's promotion of tolerance, 66–67
Remembered Gate: Origins of American Feminism, The (Berg), 56
Reulecke, Jürgen, 65, 218
Richter, Clara, 116–117
Richter, Jean-Paul, 38; *Levana*, 29, 45
Riehl, W. H., *The Family*, 93
rights: children's, 82, 137, 144; civil, 58; illegitimate children, 137; married teachers, 167; political, 147; relationship to duties, 11; to reproductive choice, 187–205
rights, equal, 4, 27, 234; in education, 30, 34; in feminism, 8, 93; in French Revolution, 27; relationship to spiritual motherhood, 76; theory, 5, 7; views of Froebel, C., 62; Wollstonecraft on, 27
rights, legal: pertaining to mothers, 135–136
rights, parental, 138–139, 221; equal, 140–141; legal, 135–136; married teachers, 167; mothers, 76, 103–104, 135–137, 173; single mothers, 144–146, 182, 198
"Rights of Mothers over their Children, The" (Pape), 103–104
Ronge, Johannes, 51, 74
Rousseau, Jean Jacques, 32; on contracts, 24; *Emile*, 20–21, 23
Ruddick, Sara, 244
Rudolphi, Caroline, 9, 18; on female culture, 32; on motherhood, 30; *Pictures of Female Education*, 32
Ruses of Powerless People (Listen der Ohnmacht) (Honegger and Heinz), 6
Rutgers, Johannes, 190

Sachsse, Christoph, 207, 210
Salomon, Alice, 187; founding of social work as profession, 208; on sexual ethics, 208–209
Salzmann, Christian Gotthilf, 21
Sand, George, 50, 75; on maternal rights, 139
Sanger, Margaret, 204
Schallmayer, Wilhelm: endorsement of sex education, 200; *Heredity and Selection*, 157–158
Schelling, Friedrich, 36
Schirmacher, Käthe, 168, 193
Schmidt, Auguste, 97; founding of Federation of German Women's Organizations, 129; moderate feminism, 136
Schmoller, Gustav, 210
School of Domestic Arts, 115–116
schools, infant, 51, 60, 81, 88; religious control, 60–61, 105, 169
schools, public, 90; incorporation of kindergarten, 62, 105, 108, 129–131; male domination, 70
schools, secondary: entry of girls, 87–88
Schrader, Karl, 120–122, 128
Schrader-Breymann, Henriette. *See* Breymann, Henriette
Schreiber, Adele, 1, 7, 149, 154, 175; advocation of suffrage, 186; endorsement of eugenics, 197; socialism, 233; views on abortion, 194–195
Schreiner, Olive, 161; on public motherhood, 172
Schwarz, C.F.H., 33
Seneca Falls Convention, 77–78
"sex parasitism," 210, 212
sexual: abuse, 46, 201, 225; exploitation, 98; liberation, 7
sexuality: acceptance as positive force, 159; addressed by feminists, 136; development in feminist ideology, 152; free love, 173–174; glorification of heterosexuality, 170; irresponsible male behavior, 143; nonmarital relationships, 50; public discourse, 190; rape, marital, 46; reassessment of women's role, 149
Sheppard-Towner Federal Maternity and Infancy Act (1921), 239
Shorter, Edward, 18
Sieveking, Amalie: criticism of kindergarten, 70; founding of Female Association for the Care of the Poor and Sick, 52

Simon, Helene, 165–166; *Motherhood and Intellectual Work*, 164
Simson, Anna, 137
Smith-Rosenberg, Carroll, 10, 32
Social Democrats, 111–112, 155; endorsement of suffrage, 185; views on maternity coverage, 184
socialism, 209; belief in education, 87; child welfare activities, 146; effect on feminist movement, 149, 155–156; endorsement of protective laws, 183; publications, 127; restrictions against, 112; Saint-Simonian, 50; support of birth control, 196; utopian, 50–51, 56, 68, 83, 169; views on careers for women, 166; women's groups, 127
Social Policy Association, 112
social service: careers for women, 102–103; professionalization, 112; struggle against male domination, 103, 119
social welfare, government sponsored, 122–123
social work: as career for women, 125–126, 209–215; comparative, 214–215; founding by Salomon, A., 208; involvement with single mothers, 143; male domination, 234; role in juvenile court system, 225
society: dependence on child-rearing, 30; Enlightenment model, 27
Society for Family and Popular Education, 115
Society for Popular Education, 88
Society for Prevention of Infant Mortality, 177
Society for Racial Hygiene, 157–158
Society for the Education of Women, 67–68
Soltau, Heide, 197
Stanton, Elizabeth Cady, 148, 168
sterilization, eugenic, 201–204; under National Socialism, 236, 238
Stiehl Regulations (1854), 83
Stöcker, Helene, 1, 149; endorsement of Darwinism, 158–159; family reform, 181; on marriage bans for teachers, 166, 171; "New Ethic," 159; opposition to war, 232–233; professional aspirations, 153–154; reproductive issues, 174–175; sexual liberation, 7; sexual reform, 182; utopianism, 163; views on abortion, 193
Stritt, Marie, 137; on biological motherhood, 140; on illegitimacy rights, 144; on parental rights, 141; views on abortion, 191
Subjection of Women, The (Mill), 123

suffrage, female, 148, 233, 165; advocated by radical feminists, 136; of Braun, L., 8; endorsements, 185–186; history, 6; increased support, 207; lack of German feminist interest, 109; in United States, 77
suffrage, male, 96; based on military service, 102, 186; in Germany, 77
Suttner, Bertha von, 232

Taube, Max, 179; professional guardianship, 146
teaching. *See* education
temperance movement, 172, 199, 224
Thelen, David, 109
Tille, Alexander, *From Darwin to Nietzsche*, 159
training: kindergarten teachers, 67–72, 90, 97–100, 116; for out-of-home work, 99–100
Traun, Bertha, 67; divorce, 74
Treitschke, Heinrich von, 102
Twellman, Margrit, 104

Über die Bestimmung des Weibes zur Höhern Bildung (On the Capacity of Women for Higher Education) (Holst), 31
Uber Gesezgebung und Kindermord (On Legislation and Infanticide) (Pestalozzi), 23
Union of Progressive Women's Organizations, 174
Unsere Kinder (Our Children), 63
utopianism: feminist, 244
Über die bürgerliche Verbesserung der Weiber (On Improving the Status of Women) (Hippel), 27

Varnhagen, Rahel, 50
Varnhagen von Ense, Karl August, 82
Victoria (Crown Princess), support for kindergarten, 115, 125
Von Darwin bis Nietzsche (From Darwin to Nietzsche) (Tille), 159

Webb, Beatrice, 164
Weber, Marianne, 139, 214; on child support, 144
Weigert, Erna, 128
Weindling, Paul, 218
Weiss, Sheila, 202
Wendelstädt, G.F.C., 20

Index

Wentzel-Heckmann, Elise, 121
Westendarp, Amalie, 80
Weyrowitz, Auguste, 97
Wie Gertrude ihre Kinder lehrt (How Gertrude Teaches her Children) (Pestalozzi), 23, 25
Wollstonecraft, Mary, 31; on equal rights, 27
Woman and Socialism (Die Frau und der Sozialismus) (Bebel), 155
Woman in Past, Present and Future (Die Frau in Vergangenheit, Gegenwart und Zukunft) (Bebel), 107
Women and Economics (Gilman), 162
Women's and Girls' Social Work Groups, 208
Women's Association for the Support of Kindergartens of Berlin, 105
Women's School of Social Work, 212
Women's Welfare Association, 136

Wordsworth, William, 29
Work and New Education (Die Arbeit und die neue Erziehung) (Marenholtz-Bülow), 86
Wüstenfeld, Emilie, 41; divorce, 74; on education, 53, 83; on education prohibitions, 83; founding of Hamburg Academy, 66; founding of Society for the Encouragement of Female Employment, 99; maternal influence on, 43; role in kindergarten movement, 67

Zepler, Wally, 166
Zetkin, Clara, 26; on condominium living, 168–169; endorsement of monogamous marriage, 182; opposition to birth control, 196; socialist views, 127, 155; views on abortion, 195